architecture

THE DEFINITIVE VISUAL HISTORY

DK SMITHSONIAN

architecture

THE DEFINITIVE VISUAL HISTORY

EDITORIAL CONSULTANT
DR. BARNABAS CALDER

DK LONDON

Senior Editors Kathryn Hennessy, Angela Wilkes
Senior US Editor Megan Douglass
Senior Designer Mark Cavanagh
Project Art Editor Katie Cavanagh
Designer Judy Caley
Editors Elizabeth Dowsett, Bonnie Macleod, Victoria Pyke,
Alison Sturgeon, Andy Szudek
Picture Researchers Sarah Smithies, Jo Walton
Production Editor Gillian Reid
Producer Rachel Ng
Senior Jackets Designer Surabhi Wadhwa Gandhi
Jacket Design Development Manager Sophia MTT
Managing Editor Gareth Jones
Managing Art Editor Lee Griffiths
Art Director Karen Self
Publisher Liz Wheeler
Publishing Director Jonathan Metcalf

DK DELHI

Senior Editor Anita Kakar
Senior Designer Mahua Sharma
Art Editor Sonakshi Singh
Assistant Art Editor Mitravinda V K
Senior Managing Editor Rohan Sinha
Managing Art Editor Sudakshina Basu
Senior Jackets Coordinator Priyanka Sharma Saddi
Senior DTP Designer Harish Aggarwal
DTP Designers Ashok Kumar, Anita Yadav
Pre-production Manager Balwant Singh
Production Manager Pankaj Sharma
Creative Head Malavika Talukder

First American Edition, 2023
Published in the United States by DK Publishing
1745 Broadway, 20th Floor, New York, NY 10019

A catalog record for this book
is available from the Library of Congress.
ISBN: 978-0-7440-8498-6

DK books are available at special discounts when purchased
in bulk for sales promotions, premiums, fund-raising, or educational use.
For details, contact: DK Publishing Special Markets,
1745 Broadway, 20th Floor, New York, NY 10019
SpecialSales@dk.com

Printed and bound in China

For the curious
www.dk.com

CONTENTS

DIVERSITY

1   BEFORE 300 CE

DEVELOPMENT

2   300–1100

GODS AND RULERS

3   1100–1500

Consultant

Dr. Barnabas Calder is the author of *Architecture: From Prehistory to Climate Emergency*, the first history of the relationship between architecture and energy throughout human history, and *Raw Concrete: The Beauty of Brutalism*. He is a Senior Lecturer in Architecture at the University of Liverpool, UK, and trustee of the Society of Architectural Historians of Great Britain. Twitter/Instagram: @BarnabasCalder

Contributors

Jon Astbury is an architectural historian, curator, editor, and lecturer. He is Assistant Curator in Architecture and Design at the Barbican Centre in London, UK, and has previously held editorial positions at *The Architectural Review* and *Architects' Journal* magazines.

Ian Chilvers is a writer and editor, whose books include *The Oxford Dictionary of Art*, *The Baroque and Neoclassical Age*, and *A Dictionary of Twentieth-Century Art*. He was chief consultant on DK's *Art: The Definitive Visual Guide*.

Dr. Diane Davies is an archaeologist specializing in the Maya, and an honorary research associate of the Institute of Archaeology, University College London. She is the Director of Maya Archaeologist Ltd, which creates educational resources on the Maya, and Chair of the charity Chok Education.

Andrew Humphreys trained as an architect and studied Islamic architecture in Cairo, Egypt, before becoming a journalist and author. He has written for the *Financial Times*, *The Sunday Times*, and *Time Out*, and contributed to *Great Cities*, *The Islam Book*, and *The Architecture Book* for DK.

COLLISION

4 1500–1750

THE RISE OF COAL

5 1730–1900

OIL AND ELECTRICITY

6 1900–1970

Contributors

Dr. Ranald Lawrence is a Senior Lecturer in Architecture at the University of Liverpool, specializing in the history of environmental design and the relationship between buildings and climate. He is a Senior Fellow of the Higher Education Academy, and has worked in architectural practice as a designer and researcher.

Dr. Di Luo is Assistant Professor of Art History and Architectural Studies at Connecticut College, specializing in the evolution of building forms and practices in China and Buddhist Asia. She formerly trained as an architect and worked for architectural firms in Los Angeles and Beijing.

Philip Parker is a historian and former British diplomat and publisher, who studied History at Trinity Hall, Cambridge, UK. He is a critically acclaimed author and award-winning editor, and has been a contributor and consultant for numerous DK titles including *World History* and *Great Cities*.

Catherine Slessor is a writer, critic, and former editor of *The Architectural Review*, and a contributor to *Dezeen*, the *Architects' Journal*, and *The Guardian*. In 2021 she became President of the Twentieth Century Society, dedicated to preserving the UK's modern and contemporary architectural heritage.

Prof. Steven Snape is Honorary Professor of Egyptian Archaeology at the University of Liverpool, UK, and his area of expertise is the interrelationship between the built environment and the natural world in ancient Egypt. He is also the author of *The Complete Cities of Ancient Egypt* and *Ancient Egyptian Tombs: The Culture of Life and Death*.

Dr Doria Tichit is an art historian specializing in South Asian art and architecture. She studied Archaeology and Art at the Sorbonne in Paris, and has a PhD from the Welsh School of Architecture, Cardiff University, UK. She lectures on South Asian art for the School of Oriental and African Studies, the V&A, Sotheby's Institute of Art, and Birkbeck College, in London.

CRISIS
AND HOPE

7 1970 ONWARD

Iain Zaczek is a writer, researcher, and art historian. He studied at Wadham College, Oxford, UK, and at the Courtauld Institute of Art in London, where he specialized in architecture. He has authored more than 30 books and contributed to many others, including *The Art Book* and *Design: The Definitive Visual Guide* for DK.

INTRODUCTION

Architecture shapes our lives. Many people now spend a large part of their time indoors, and more than half of the human population today live in cities, surrounded by buildings. Most of the world's cities are growing rapidly, swallowing up farmland and wilderness and establishing patterns of buildings, roads, and open spaces that may last for centuries, just as traces of the layouts of ancient and medieval cities are still visible in modern Rome and Istanbul.

Good architecture can make us happier and healthier, improving our relationships with nature and with other people. It can give us the spaces we need for socializing, fostering relationships between neighbors, and encouraging us to get out and about without being dependent on cars and the destructive roads that they require. Well-designed and cleverly constructed buildings can also give us daily moments of pleasure, comfort, and relaxation in our homes and places of study or work.

Grand public architectural projects can represent the defining statements of the priorities and capacities of an entire society. When a new cathedral was built in the wealthy medieval trading city of Florence, for example, its designers left an opening for an enormous dome—138 ft (42 m) across—despite the fact that no one had ever built a dome of this size so high above the ground before. If the builders failed to find a solution, they would be lumbered with a very public failure towering over their city. What clearer statement of confidence could a city make in the technical capabilities of its architects, engineers, and builders than to set them such a giant and public challenge?

Architecture can form the defining image of a city or a whole nation—the Sydney Opera House, the Taj Mahal, and the Eiffel Tower are all used as symbols of the countries in which they are found (Australia, India, and France, respectively). Similarly, Japanese houses of wood and paper, floored with tatami mats, Georgian country houses in Britain, New York brownstones, and adobe villages in Mexico each carry powerful associations, which are frequently exploited in the movies.

PAST, PRESENT, AND FUTURE

This book introduces the finest examples of architecture, taking you on a beautiful and fascinating journey through thousands of years of human ingenuity, artistry, and skill. It also throws down a challenge to us in the 21st century: the world of architecture is facing its biggest and most urgent threat to date—the climate emergency. Constructing and running buildings produces nearly 40 percent of all humanity's climate-changing emissions. We need to adapt—urgently and radically—what we choose to build and how we choose to build it. We also need to make fundamental improvements to many of our existing buildings, to help reduce their demand for fossil-fuel energy.

As we come to terms with this immense challenge, it turns out that some powerful solutions lie in the past. This book features thousands of years' worth of what we need now—sustainable, beautiful architecture, constructed from local materials and suitably adapted to the climate. Embracing the history of architecture has never before been so critically important to the present and future of life on Earth.

Barnabas Calder

Barnabas Calder

◀ **View of the Duomo** in Florence, Italy, from "Giotto's Bell Tower"

1

DIVERSITY

BEFORE 300 CE

SHELTER

Humans started constructing dwellings at least 400,000 years ago. Hunter-gatherers and early farming societies used locally sourced materials to make homes that protected them from severe weather.

Shelter is one of humanity's basic needs, and evolving strategies to meet it shaped the first forms of building. Very early hominins (human ancestral species) lived in caves, rock shelters, or in tree-nests, much as modern apes do, although evidence of organized stones at Olduvai Gorge in Kenya suggest that nomadic hunters may have been creating structures 1.8 million years ago. Such shelters may have been temporary, perhaps just brush-wood lean-tos needing no or minimal foundations.

The first clear evidence of house-building comes from Terra Amata, near Nice in France. Post-holes in the ground (into which wooden pillars would have slotted), stone foundations, and the remains of cooking hearths indicate some kind of building 400,000 years ago.

THE MESOLITHIC PERIOD

As populations grew after the last Ice Age, around 12,000 years ago, groups expanded into new areas, adapting their lives and their homes to a dazzling range of environments. Houses built from wood appeared, and in

> "Göbekli changes everything. It's elaborate, it's complex, and it's pre-agricultural."
>
> Ian Hodder, Director, Archaeology Center, Stanford University

regions with more extremes of temperature, like West Asia, mud-brick houses kept the internal temperature more constant.

THE NEOLITHIC PERIOD

Many earlier structures and whole settlements may have left no trace, but from 9000 BCE there is growing evidence of larger settlements—sometimes related to increasing levels of dependence on domesticated crops, which encouraged people to spend more of the year in the same place. This evidence includes the honeycomb-like clusters of mud houses in settlements such as Çatal Höyük in Turkey, dating from around 7500 BCE. In other areas, simple wooden huts gave way to elaborate longhouses around 5500 BCE. Although stone had been used for houses, as at Skara Brae in Orkney, it was now also used for the first truly monumental structures, such as the dolmens of late Neolithic Korea, the megaliths of northwestern Europe, and imposing stone temples in Malta. Raising rocks of several tons required teamwork and a clear plan. In a sense, the first architects had arrived.

MAMMOTH STRUCTURES

Many early shelters were variations of pit houses: sunken dug-outs with wood or branches above. However, in parts of modern-day Ukraine, the Czech Republic, and Poland, people 25,000 years ago also used mammoth tusks and bones to build frames, which they then covered with animal hides.

Mammoth hut reconstruction in Mezhyrich, Ukraine, made from bones and tusks

JŌMON PIT HOUSE

JAPAN, C. 10,000 BCE

The Jōmon people who settled in Japan were hunter-gatherers known for making some of the world's earliest pottery. From around 10,000 BCE, they built pit houses like this reconstruction. Dug into the ground, the houses had chestnut log frames and internal hearths for warmth. By 6,500 BCE, villages of several hundred dwellings had begun to appear.

SUNKEN STRUCTURES

The remains of pit houses have been found across the Northern Hemisphere and in South America. Many cultures excavated hollows for dwellings and other buildings. Posts secured in the ground supported the roof, and the earthen floor was beaten hard or paved with flagstones.

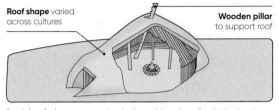

Roof shape varied across cultures

Wooden pillar to support roof

Earth insulation was warming in the cold and cooling in the heat.

▲ **Complex wooden frame**
The Jōmon were skilled woodworkers, able to fashion sophisticated joints in both their buildings and day-to-day objects. Rafters helped support the weight of pit-house roofs, along with the main vertical pillars.

▲ **Kaya-thatch roof**
Made with dried-out kaya grass, Jōmon thatch created a secure, waterproof roof surface, which helped water drain down into surrounding ditches. Highly durable, kaya-thatch roofs can last for 70 years.

Hole in roof apex allowed smoke to escape

Thatch laid with kaya grass

Rafters made from chestnut wood

Central section supported by internal pillar

Steep pitch to the ground assisted with drainage

KEY **ELEMENTS**

Early homes were built according to the materials available and best suited to the local climate. When no longer needed, the houses disappeared back into the landscape.

BUILDING WITH WOOD

In areas of higher rainfall, such as northern and central Europe and northeastern North America, where timber was abundant in forests, wood was the primary building material. Versatile and easily repaired, timber could make a cozy home for sitting out the bitter northern winters.

▲ **Wattle and daub**
The space between vertical wooden stakes is woven with thin branches, reeds, or vines to create panels (wattle). These are then coated with clay or mud, often mixed with animal dung or straw (daub), which sets to form a protective exterior wall.

BUILDING WITH MUD

In warmer areas, Neolithic builders used locally abundant mud or clay, either as plaster or in the form of sun-dried bricks. Buildings stayed cool but needed frequent rebuilding as the mud decayed.

◄ **Mud houses**
At Çatalhöyük in modern-day Turkey, around 6,000 people lived in mud houses packed so tightly together that walkways were on top of the buildings. Access was via a hole in the roof, as in this reconstruction.

▼ **Dense housing**
Excavations at Çatalhöyük reveal the honeycomb structure of the houses from around 7500 BCE. Mud was plastered on the exterior for strength, but when a house decayed, its inhabitants simply built a new house on top.

BUILDING WITH STONE

Stone's hardness and strength makes for resilient buildings, but it is harder to shape than timber or mud brick, and heavier, so traditional homes were built from irregular stones found nearby. Carved or very large stones were used for prestigious buildings.

▲ **Sandstone housing**
The cluster of red-sandstone houses in the Scottish Neolithic village of Skara Brae on Orkney were occupied between 3200 and 2200 BCE. The dwellings were set into an old midden (garbage mound) which provided insulation, and they had "built-in" stone furniture such as beds and cupboards.

▲ **Monumental dolmens**
Korea has the highest concentration and variety of dolmens—megalithic monuments that often marked tombs. Many are characterized by a capstone resting on two or more stone uprights. There are around 30,000 dolmens in Korea (40 percent of the world's total), erected between 3000 and 1000 BCE.

▲ **Limestone temples**
Mnajdra is one of several megalithic temple complexes built on Malta around 3000 BCE. Huge limestone slabs weighing up to 22 tons form the walls, internal monumental passageways, and courtyards. The stone has been carved with spiral animal and vegetable motifs.

OTHER **ANCIENT STRUCTURES**

The Neolithic period brought many changes to architecture and society as new farming technologies and the social systems they supported spread and mingled.

1. Stonehenge
Salisbury Plain, UK, 2500 BCE

The stone circles at Stonehenge were begun around 2500 BCE. They use bluestones weighing 2½–5½ tons, which were transported from Wales, and massive 22-ton sarsen stones. The visible stones were part of a very large ceremonial center where important seasonal rituals and festivals were celebrated.

2. Sopot houses
Vinkovci, Croatia, 5000 BCE

The Sopot culture of the northern Balkans created rectangular wooden houses around 5000 BCE using interlaced layers of sticks and timbers, with thatched roofs and multiple internal rooms. The settlements were mainly set along river banks. Reconstructions have been built at the Sopot Archaeological Park.

3. Khirokitia
Larnaka, Cyprus, 7000–4000 BCE

The Neolithic village of Khirokitia in southern Cyprus was set on a steep hill surrounded by a stone wall. Each house consisted of several cylindrical stone- and mud-built structures grouped around a courtyard. Layers were added to the walls over time, so that the room inside came to be only half the diameter of the whole building.

"Those huge, rude masses of stone, set on end and piled each on other, turn the mind on the immense force necessary for such a work."

Edmund Burke, Anglo-Irish statesman and philosopher, describing Stonehenge in *A Philosophical Inquiry into the Origin of Our Ideas of the Sublime and Beautiful*, 1757

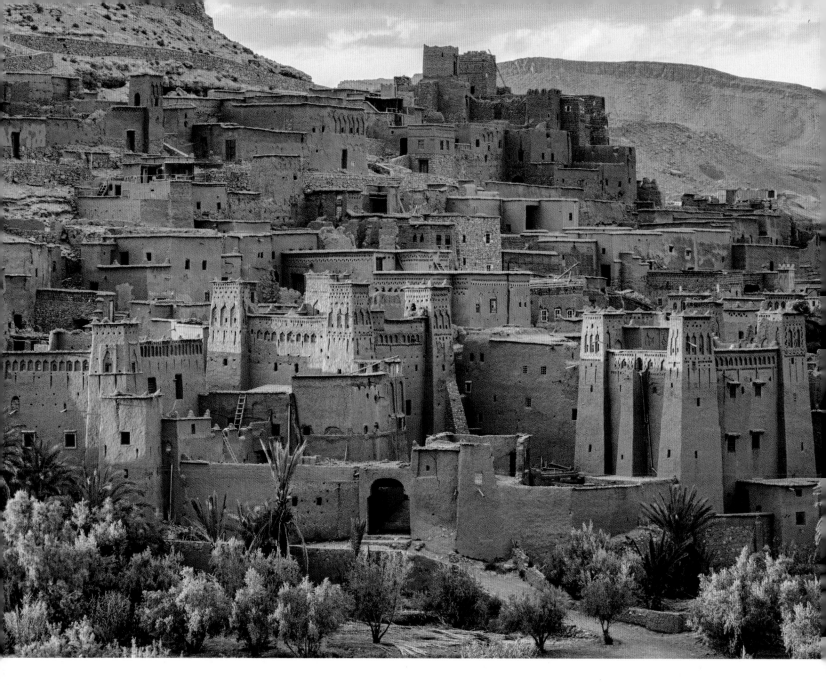

▲ **Robust fortifications**
Aït Benhaddou is an imposing *ksar* (fortified village) on a caravan route through Morocco's Atlas Mountains. Its dwellings, defensive walls, and towers, constructed with adobe bricks and rammed earth, date in their present form from the 17th century.

▲ **Skyscraper city**
Shibam is nicknamed "the Manhattan of Yemen" for its soaring mud-brick houses, which stand up to 10 stories high. Since the 16th century, the town's hillside location, dense layout, and adobe walls have provided protection for a large population.

"If a nation has a tradition of building with mud then that's a part of their culture. If this is lost, then we will have also lost ourselves."

Architect Diébédo Francis Kéré, 2013

MUD

Buildings made of mud are one of the most ancient forms of architecture. Robust, cheap, and flexible, mud as a material dates back more than 10,000 years and has enjoyed a recent revival.

Earth mixed with water and left to dry is a wonderful building material. Mud is abundant and adaptable, and does not require quarrying, expensive tools, or fuel to prepare it. Buildings made from mud need protection from water, and can require periodic repair, but at the end of their useful life they return harmlessly to the soil they rose from. Mud also has a high thermal load, meaning that heat penetrates the walls slowly and is then released gradually, providing a constant internal temperature. This makes it particularly valuable in climates with hot days and cooler nights.

EARLY MUD-BUILDING
Mud constructions are most widespread in hot, dry regions due to the thermal properties of mud and its vulnerability to water. For millennia, it was the primary construction material in parts of the Sahel in Africa, in southwest North America, and in the Middle East. Mud buildings appeared in Jericho in Palestine as early as 9000 BCE and in Mehrgarh in the Indus Valley

around 7000 BCE. As long ago as the 13th century BCE, mud was used for vast structures such as the Ramesseum—the necropolis of the Egyptian pharaoh Ramses II.

A VERSATILE MATERIAL
The simplest construction with mud involves laying mud and leaving it to dry before adding the next layer. Mixing it with additives like sand and straw forms cob—a stronger bonding material that can become as strong as concrete—and pre-shaping mud into bricks provides even greater strength and flexibility. Earth can also be stabilized by adding chalk, lime, and gravel— a technique used in parts of the Great Wall of China. Adding clay-based mortars, which expand or shrink at the same rate as mud, helps prevent cracking.

With its very low environmental impact and fire resistance, mud is becoming a popular choice of sustainable material—though in some cases, the amount of cement added to stabilize it casts doubt on its green credentials.

▲ **Modern interpretation**
The HIKMA complex in western Niger combines religious and secular spaces. Completed in 2018, it is a contemporary expression of traditional mud-built architecture with compressed earth bricks made from locally excavated soil.

▲ **Beehive houses**
The beehive-shaped mud houses in Harran, Turkey, have a funnel-shaped dome that allows smoke to escape and air to circulate. The weight-distributing structure is also resistant to earthquakes. Houses like these have been built since at least 1000 BCE.

ANCIENT BRICK PRODUCTION
Leveling mud in wooden molds created adobes, even-shaped mud bricks. These were left to dry for several weeks, creating strong blocks for building larger structures, without having to wait for each layer to dry. Mud bricks were in common use in Egypt by 2500 BCE.

Egyptian figures make mud bricks in a fresco in the Tomb of Rekhmire in the ancient city of Thebes.

▲ **Entrance to Babylon**
One of the inner city gates of Babylon, the Ishtar Gate was commissioned by King Nebuchadnezzar II (r.605–562 BCE). It is covered with blue-glazed bricks and tiles, as well as reliefs of lions, bulls, and dragons.

ANCIENT NEAR EAST

The ancient Near East covered what is now modern Iraq, southwestern Iran, and northeastern Syria. The fertile plains bordering the Euphrates and Tigris rivers saw the construction of the world's first cities.

The peoples of the ancient Near East—a region later named Mesopotamia (between the rivers) by the Greeks—are credited with numerous inventions, including the written word, the 24-hour day, and the ceramic plate. They were also the first people to plan and build cities, such as Uruk, which was founded in the 4th millennium BCE. Archaeological evidence suggests that Uruk may have housed 40,000 citizens at its height, and was probably the largest city in the world in its day. The city was fed by intensive grain farming, fertilized by the rich mud brought to the fields by the seasonal flooding of the Tigris and Euphrates.

MONUMENTAL BUILDINGS

Because there was little stone in the region, Uruk was built out of clay, which was shaped in molds and dried in the sun to form mud bricks. The city was enclosed by a wall, and its public buildings were built on a massive scale. The largest of these was a ziggurat (a stepped tower) dedicated to the sky god, Anu.

Standing on an artificial hill, and rising 40 ft (12 m) above the plain of Uruk, the ziggurat had a long, steep processional stairway, which led up to a tall, white temple.

Even more imposing was the ziggurat built in the city of Ur some 2,000 years later. This had a succession of steep-sided platforms, each of which was smaller than the one below it, so that the building rose in a series of square terraces. These tiers probably expressed the metaphorical distance between the human world and the realm of the gods. Only priests and rulers could visit the topmost shrine.

For some of the most important buildings, patrons spent extra for a surface more durable than mud brick. At Uruk, one temple was clad in colorful stone cones pushed into the mud, while the builders of later palaces and temples sometimes invested in burning large amounts of dried plant matter to fire bricks until they became hard and waterproof.

An outer layer of fired bricks covers a core of mud bricks

EARLY WRITING

The earliest known writing was produced in Mesopotamia around 3000 BCE. It was composed of pictograms (symbols rather than letters), which were drawn on damp clay tablets using a pointed tool. These early writings contained numbers, and they were probably made by temple officials to record things such as how much grain and beer they had in their stores.

Pictograms recording the allocation of beer, c. 3100–3000 BCE

Base consisting of more than 720,000 stacked mud bricks

ZIGGURAT OF UR

NASRIYAH, IRAQ, c. 2100 BCE

The imposing Ziggurat of Ur overlooked what was once a great walled city. It originally had a wall all around it and stood at the heart of a religious complex. Like all ziggurats, it had no interior chambers, but had a single temple on top of it. In this case, it was a temple dedicated to Nanna, the moon god.

▲ Weep holes
To prevent water damage, the ziggurat's walls were built at a slant. Drainage channels carried rainwater away, and "weep holes" enabled moisture to escape from the core.

▲ Ceremonial staircase
The ziggurat had three flights of stairs, each with 100 steps—a central ceremonial flight and two ascending from the corners either side. The stairs met at a broad gateway on the top.

RECONSTRUCTION

Originally built by King Ur-Nammu and his successors in the 21st century BCE, this three-tiered ziggurat was made of mud bricks, with each layer bonded with bitumen. It was heavily restored in the 6th century BCE, and then partly rebuilt on the orders of Saddam Hussein in the late 20th century.

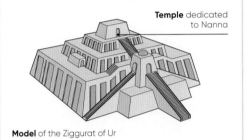

Temple dedicated to Nanna

Model of the Ziggurat of Ur

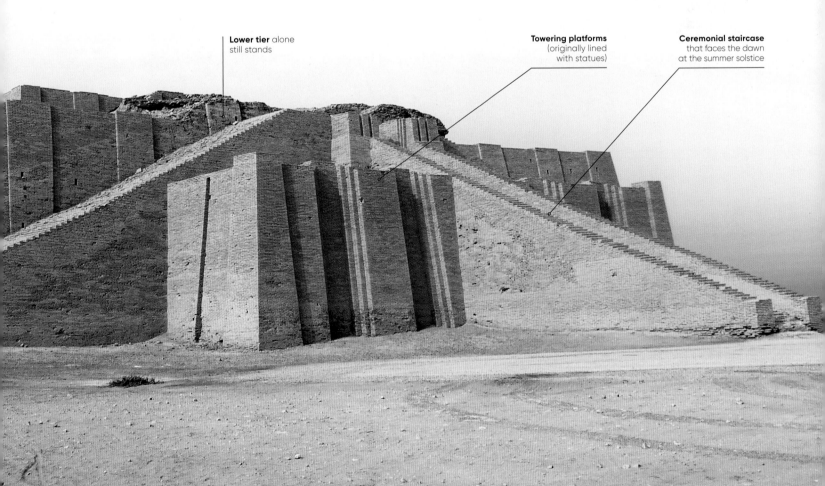

Lower tier alone still stands

Towering platforms (originally lined with statues)

Ceremonial staircase that faces the dawn at the summer solstice

KEY **ELEMENTS**

Bricks made of river mud and clay were the key building materials
in the ancient Near East. They were mostly dried by the sun, but
for special projects bricks could be baked to make them stronger.

DRAINAGE AND IRRIGATION SYSTEMS

Some of the most complex canal systems in the ancient world were built in the Near East,
where virtually all agriculture depended on irrigation. The success of these systems
enabled large cities with dense populations to thrive for more than 6,000 years.

◄ **Ancient aqueducts**
This clay tablet illustrates
how the gardens at Nineveh,
an ancient Mesopotamian
city on the River Tigris, were
irrigated by an immense
network of canals. These
canals brought water from
the mountains via channels
and aqueducts.

THE FIRST CITIES

Archaeological evidence suggests that the first
cities were built in the Near East, some 6,000
years ago. Including Eridu, Uruk, and Ur, they
arose in places where the land was fertile enough
for people to settle into communities that then
developed centralized governments. Similar
cities later grew up along the Nile River in Egypt,
the Indus River Valley on the Indian subcontinent,
and along the Yellow (Huang) River in China.

Reconstruction of Eridu, overlooking the Persian Gulf

ANIMAL CARVINGS

Ancient Near Eastern buildings were decorated
with images of all kinds of animals. These included
creatures that evoked divinity, kingship, and the
fertility of the natural world.

▲ **Lamassu**
The mythological lamassu was a creature that offered
protection. This carving of one guarded the throne
room of King Sargon II of Assyria (r. 722–705 BCE).

◄ **Mushhushshu**
Prestigious structures
such as the Ishtar Gate
in Babylon used bricks
that were coated in
colorful minerals, then
fired to make a durable,
decorative surface. This
dragonlike creature is a
mushhushshu—a hybrid
of a lion and an eagle,
with a horned head and
a snake's tongue.

◄ **Marble seal**
Many animals, including
dogs, sheep, donkeys,
pigs, and cats, were first
domesticated in the
Near East. Craftspeople
immortalized their
shapes—the handle of
this seal is in the shape
of a reclining ram.

1

ANCIENT NEAR EASTERN BUILDINGS

Stone and tile friezes, sumptuously carved capitals, and rock-cut tombs all testify
to the splendors of ancient Near Eastern architecture, but only a few buildings have
survived intact from this glorious era.

3

1. Chogha Zanbil Ziggurat
Susa, Iran, c. 1250 BCE

The Chogha Zanbil Ziggurat was built
at the center of a complex of temples,
palaces, and royal tombs, which was
protected by three concentric walls.
Originally, it had five stepped levels.

2. Nimrud
Mosul, Iraq, c. 1350–610 BCE

The city of Nimrud was the second
capital of the Assyrian Empire, one
of the greatest civilizations of its age.
Its ruins include a palace built by
Ashurnasirpal II (r. 883–859 BCE).

3. Tabira Gate
Ashur, Iraq, c. 3000–2001 BCE

Little remains of Ashur, the first capital of
the Assyrian Empire. Its most complete
structure is a monumental, triple-arched
gate, which is thought to have been
part of a processional route to a ziggurat.

2

"The birth,
rise, and fall
of ancient
Mesopotamia
occupies fully
half of all history."

Paul Kriwaczek, *Babylon: Mesopotamia
and the Birth of Civilization*, 2010

▲ Stone carving

Baroque architecture features some of the most elaborate stone decoration ever conceived. This carving on the Wall Pavilion of the Zwinger Palace, Dresden, is one of the peaks of the style. Dating to 1709–1712, it was restored after being severely damaged in World War II.

▲ Dry-stone masonry

The Great Enclosure, in southeastern Zimbabwe, is one of the most impressive examples of a mortarless building complex. This medieval city of the Shona people may have housed 18,000 residents at its peak.

> "One might regard architecture as history arrested in stone."

A. L. Rowse, *The Use of History*, 1946

STONE

Varied in color and texture, and requiring skill and time to work, stone is prized for its strength, durability, and widespread availability, and is often beautiful in appearance.

Stone is one of the oldest known building materials. Neolithic stone structures have been found in several locations, including at Skara Brae (c. 3100–2480 BCE) in Scotland, and at Ggantija (c. 3600–2500 BCE) in Malta. Much larger buildings, such as the Egyptian pyramids, also date from the 3rd millennium BCE. Stone can be a humble and cheap material, using mortarless construction to fit together stones in their natural state. At the opposite end of the spectrum, using very large stones—weighing thousands of tons on occasion in ancient Egypt and the Roman Empire—is a display of awe-inspiring power, and highly refined carving shows off wealth and sophistication.

VARIETIES OF STONE
Stone varies greatly in quality and in its suitability for building. Hard stones, such as granite, wear very well but are difficult to cut or carve without modern tools. Softer stones, such as sandstones and limestones, are far easier to quarry and work. Stones can also be found in

a beautiful range of colors. White stone is particularly arresting, and has always been highly prized—two famous examples are Portland limestone from the UK, and Carrara marble from Italy.

BUILDING WITH STONE
Many techniques have been developed for building lasting stone structures. These include the Inca practice of shaping stones to interlock like jigsaw pieces, shaping stones into cuboids that stack in a very stable manner, as seen in the Pyramids of Giza in Egypt, and bonding stones together with lime mortar, as seen in the Roman and later European tradition.

Stone buildings can last an enormously long time with relatively little maintenance, and stand up well to weather. Perhaps the greatest threat to them has been the usefulness of their materials: time and again the stones from disused buildings have been carefully removed and reused in new buildings, for practical reasons and sometimes also symbolic ones.

▲ Megalithic masonry
A single slab of marble weighing hundreds of tons makes up this intricately carved path up the axial line of the Forbidden City in Beijing, China. The stone was transported by sleigh along an ice path in a display of technological sophistication and immense power.

▲ Polychrome masonry
Columns made of different kinds of marble flank the doorways of St. Mark's Basilica, in Venice, Italy. Different colors indicate different places of origin, and were a way of showing off the ability to source and transport exotic stones.

TYPES OF MORTARED MASONRY
Using loose stones in their natural irregular shapes saves the effort of quarrying, but requires more skill from the builders, as well as more mortar to fill the gaps. Quarrying cuboid stones saves on mortar and allows less skilled builders to produce reliably robust walls.

Irregular gaps between blocks are filled with mortar

Fine joints require only a small amount of mortar

Rubble masonry, made of uneven stone courses

Ashlar masonry, made of neat stone blocks

ANCIENT EGYPT

The colossal stone structures of the ancient Egyptians represent only a small proportion of their building, but their longevity over the millennia has led them to dominate our view of Egyptian architecture.

Two classes of building were of particular importance to powerful ancient Egyptians: temples and tombs. Temples were revered as homes for the gods, while tombs were homes for the dead. Unlike vernacular architecture, these two types of building needed to last forever, and so were made from the most durable materials available. From the beginning of the Old Kingdom, c. 2700 BCE, stone became the preferred material for royal tombs—chiefly pyramids—and as succeeding pyramids became larger, so did the stone blocks used in their construction. It was only later that temples were constructed entirely from stone, but by the beginning of the New Kingdom, c. 1550 BCE, temples commissioned by the king had become massive stone structures that dominated cityscapes.

STONE FOR CONSTRUCTION

The availability of stone for building was key to these developments. In the north of Egypt, limestone quarries (although of variable quality) were to be found close to major construction sites, so that the interiors of major pyramids, for example, could be filled with stone that only needed to be transported a short distance. In the south of Egypt, sandstone was the most readily available stone for building, and quarries that provided stone of a good, regular quality made it possible to construct the best-surviving temples of the New Kingdom and Greco-Roman periods, especially at Thebes.

The presence of a natural transportation route in the form of the Nile River allowed the long-distance movement of harder and more decorative stones from quarries many hundreds of miles from the buildings they embellished—granite from Aswan on Egypt's southern border, basalt from the Western Desert, quartzite from near Cairo, and calcite (Egyptian alabaster) from Middle Egypt.

A LASTING ACHIEVEMENT

People rightly marvel at the longevity of these enormous structures, although there is nothing intrinsically mysterious about them. Very fertile farmland meant that the pharaohs had a huge population at their disposal to summon for works. Good surveying and administration were crucial, but the level of technology involved in construction was fairly simple.

HOUSES FOR THE GODS

Egyptian temples were seen as, quite literally, houses for the gods. The innermost part of the temple was the sanctuary, where the image of the god was kept (usually in the form of a statue) and the daily ritual of washing, dressing, and feeding the god was carried out. Gods did not require congregational worship, but rather private service carried out in the sanctuary by priests called "servants of the god."

Ramses II applies makeup to a statue of the god Osiris in his cenotaph temple at Abydos.

▶ **Carved from a cliff**
An important variant in temple-building, especially in the New Kingdom, was the temple cut directly from the living rock (in situ). The most famous example is the Temple of Ramses II at Abu Simbel in Nubia.

"It is built of fine sandstone, worked with gold."

Amenhotep III on the stela at his temple for Amen-Ra, W.M.F. Petrie, *Six Temples at Thebes*, 1897

THE GREAT PYRAMID OF KHUFU

GIZA, EGYPT, C. 2570 BCE

Pyramids are often regarded today as archetypal of ancient Egyptian architecture, although their narrow geographical location in northern Egypt meant that most Egyptians would never have seen one. Used as royal tombs from the 3rd to 13th Dynasties (c. 2700–1650 BCE), the largest and most complex examples date from early in the 4th Dynasty. The form of the pyramid itself was probably a compromise between height (in order to be seen from a distance) and broad-based stability.

Khufu's pyramid, rising from the Giza Plateau

STEP PYRAMID OF DJOSER

The pyramid built for King Djoser around 2700 BCE at Saqqara is the oldest monumental stone building in the world. The building technology was inspired by even older monumental mud-brick buildings, but its innovation was the creation of a stepped structure—the centerpiece of a complex of buildings forming the royal tomb. The stepped form was superseded by straight-sided pyramids, but both Djoser and his architect, Imhotep, were revered by later Egyptians as both innovators and demigods.

Six steps may represent a "stairway to heaven" for the dead king

At 226 ft (69 m), the pyramid is the tallest in the Saqqara necropolis

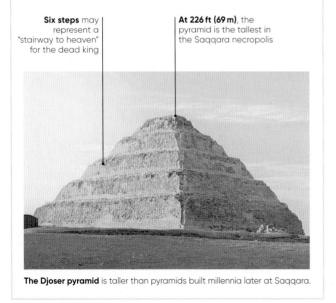

The Djoser pyramid is taller than pyramids built millennia later at Saqqara.

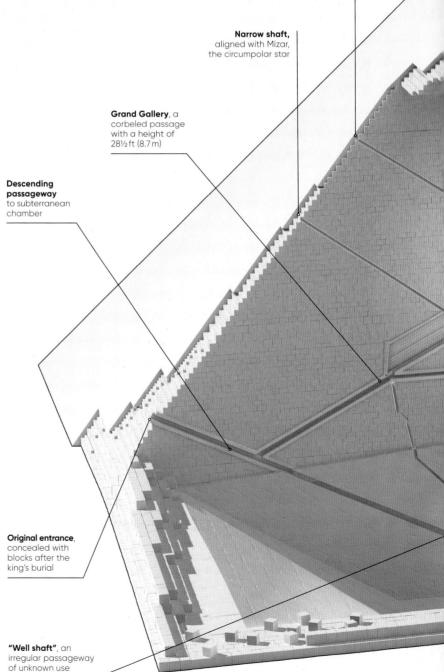

Narrow shaft, aligned with Alpha Draco, the polar star

Narrow shaft, aligned with Mizar, the circumpolar star

Grand Gallery, a corbeled passage with a height of 28½ ft (8.7 m)

Descending passageway to subterranean chamber

Original entrance, concealed with blocks after the king's burial

"Well shaft", an irregular passageway of unknown use

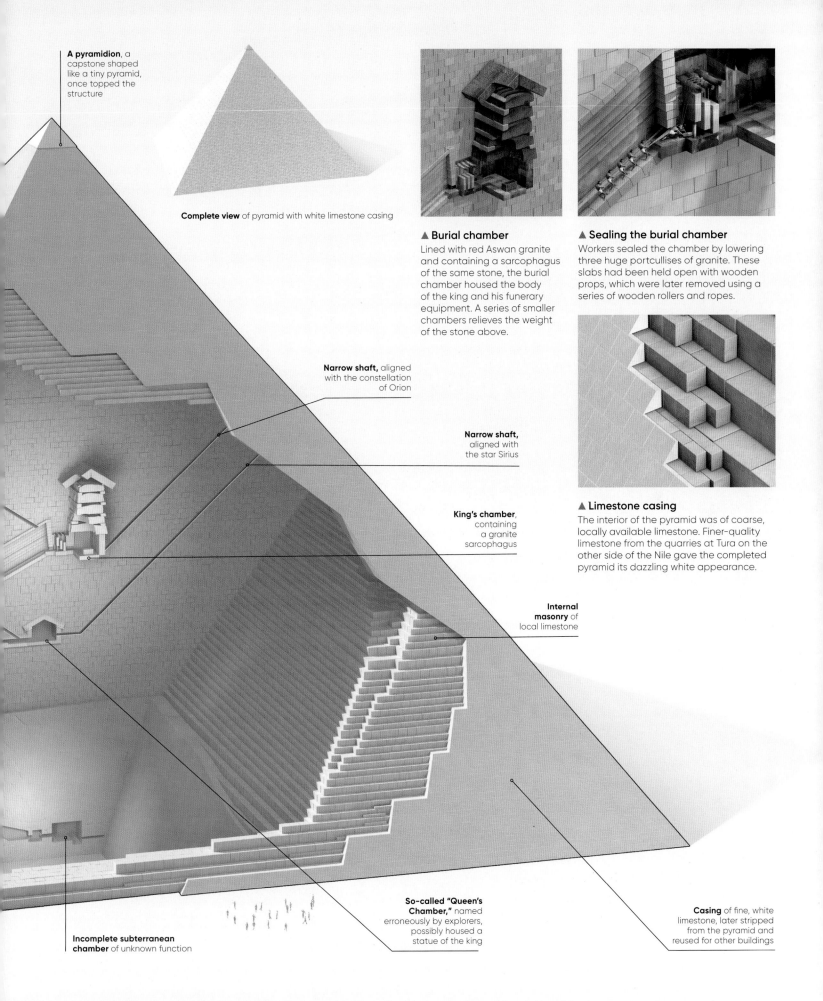

A pyramidion, a capstone shaped like a tiny pyramid, once topped the structure

Complete view of pyramid with white limestone casing

▲ Burial chamber
Lined with red Aswan granite and containing a sarcophagus of the same stone, the burial chamber housed the body of the king and his funerary equipment. A series of smaller chambers relieves the weight of the stone above.

▲ Sealing the burial chamber
Workers sealed the chamber by lowering three huge portcullises of granite. These slabs had been held open with wooden props, which were later removed using a series of wooden rollers and ropes.

▲ Limestone casing
The interior of the pyramid was of coarse, locally available limestone. Finer-quality limestone from the quarries at Tura on the other side of the Nile gave the completed pyramid its dazzling white appearance.

Narrow shaft, aligned with the constellation of Orion

Narrow shaft, aligned with the star Sirius

King's chamber, containing a granite sarcophagus

Internal masonry of local limestone

Incomplete subterranean chamber of unknown function

So-called "Queen's Chamber," named erroneously by explorers, possibly housed a statue of the king

Casing of fine, white limestone, later stripped from the pyramid and reused for other buildings

KEY **ELEMENTS**

Much of the individual character of ancient Egyptian architecture comes from both the use of available raw materials, and also specific decorative elements, which were used to emphasize the nature and function of particular buildings, especially those of temples and royal tombs.

MUD BRICK

Mud brick was a cheap and easily produced building material, available to all. It was made from the mud of the banks of the Nile or local canals, molded using simple wooden molds, and left to dry in the sun. Mud-brick structures ranged from small domestic houses to royal palaces and the interiors of some Middle Kingdom pyramids.

PYLON ENTRANCES

One of the most obvious defining features of many temples, especially of the New Kingdom and Greco-Roman Period, was the pylon entrance: two huge, symmetrical towers that flanked the central doorway. Their purpose was to give a suitably imposing entrance to the temple, and they also provided a large surface on which to depict the king with the gods or destroying his enemies.

▲ **Multi-layered, mud-brick walls**
The Egyptian state used mud brick to its full potential in military architecture, creating huge, complex structures, such as the Middle Kingdom fortress-town of Buhen.

▲ **Gateway to the gods**
Built by Ramses III, this small temple to the god Khonsu at Karnak has one of the best-preserved examples of a pylon gateway. Grooves on the exterior housed flagpoles taller than the pylon itself.

COLOSSAL STATUES

Creating colossal statues in their own image was one of the ways that kings could demonstrate their authority and semidivine status. These superhuman depictions required substantial resources to quarry the stone and transport it to the site, typically a temple, where the statue was erected. Usually made from a vast block of one of the hardest building stones (granite or quartzite), many such statues were made during the New Kingdom.

▶ **Superhuman stature**
Ramses II created a series of colossal statues of himself to be placed in temples and worshipped as gods. This example at Luxor is inscribed "Ra of the Rulers."

INFLUENCE OF EARLY ARCHITECTURE

The influence of mud-brick Egyptian architecture on stone architecture is clear, with stone blocks initially used in much the same way as mud bricks. Another, more surprising, influence was the ephemeral architecture of simple structures made from reeds and matting. Decorative motifs derived from this "primitive" architecture may have invoked the distant past in buildings connected with the gods.

Dummy chapels at Saqqara are stone-filled replicas of primitive reed and matting structures.

COLUMN CAPITALS

In the columned halls of ancient Egyptian buildings, columns had several decorative elements, from the shafts, which were covered in texts and figures of gods and kings, to the elaborate capitals that topped them. These capitals often invoked the landscape of the natural world and its mythological connection to the gods.

◄ "Floral" capital
The most popular type of capital was floral in design. Some of the earliest of these imitated palm trees and lotus and papyrus plants, while later examples, such as these from Khnum Temple in Esna, were elaborate combinations of different plants.

► Hathor capital
Column capitals showing Hathor, the sky goddess, usually appeared in buildings associated with her, such as the Hathor shrine in Queen Hatshepsut's mortuary temple at Deir el-Bahri. The face could be shown on two or four sides of the capital.

RELIEFS AND WALL PAINTINGS

The internal, and often external, walls of Egyptian buildings were often covered with relief carving or paintings that reflected the building's purpose. Deep, sunken relief was most suitable for external, sunlit parts of buildings, while interiors could feature the more time-consuming and expensive raised relief.

◄ Raised tomb relief
This delicate raised and painted relief depicts Merenptah, a king of the 19th Dynasty, greeting the sun god Ra in the afterlife. It exemplifies the best of the relief decoration found in royal tombs and temples in the New Kingdom.

◄ Tomb painting
The workers who decorated the royal tombs of the New Kingdom, in the Valley of the Kings, created some of the liveliest tomb paintings of ancient Egypt for their own tombs. The workers depicted themselves enjoying a pleasant afterlife, as in this example from the tomb of Sennedjem at Deir el-Medina.

ANCIENT EGYPTIAN BUILDINGS

While ancient Egypt's monumental architecture appeared to remain very conservative during its more than 3,000-year history, architects and artists often made subtle innovations that affected the appearance of individual buildings or the style of entire periods. Major developments were the abandonment of the royal pyramid-tomb and the creation of the "Valley of the Kings" at the start of the New Kingdom.

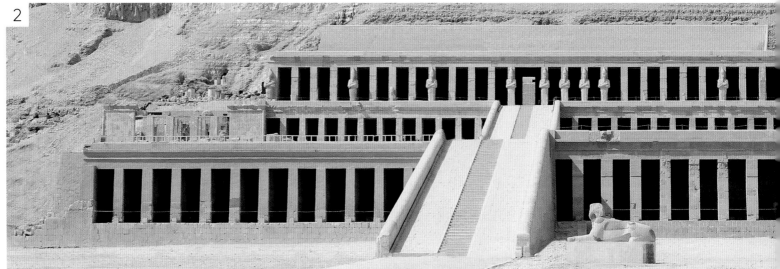

1. Temple of Ramses III
Medinet Habu, Thebes, c. 1187–1156 BCE

As apparent in this aerial view, the temple, built to serve the cult of the dead king Ramses III, was part of a complex of buildings, including offices and storerooms, within a tall mud-brick enclosure wall.

2. Deir el-Bahri
Thebes, c. 1970 BCE

One of the most unusual temples built in ancient Egypt, the mortuary temple of Hatshepsut rises in a series of terraces with decorated colonnades, all joined by central ramps.

3. Luxor Temple
Luxor, c. 1279–1213 BCE

Ramses II presided over the work on the front of Luxor Temple, built as a subsidiary temple to Karnak, with its standard pylon entrance fronted by matched pairs of colossal statues and obelisks.

4. Temple of Hathor
Dendera, 54 BCE

Taking their basic architectural forms from New Kingdom buildings, temples of Egypt's Greco-Roman Period placed a heavy emphasis on reliefs depicting the mythology of the temple's gods.

5. Tomb of Ramses III
Valley of the Kings, completed 1153 BCE

Less immediately impressive than pyramids of the Old and Middle Kingdoms, the New Kingdom's royal tombs had underground corridors and chambers, with painted reliefs of the king's journey to meet the gods.

5

6 7

6. Bent Pyramid
Dahshur, c. 2600 BCE

Not all ancient Egyptian buildings look perfect. The so-called Bent Pyramid—one of three attributed to King Sneferu—may look bent due to a change in plan after the original angle of the sides was considered too steep.

7. Valley Building, Pyramid of Khafre
Giza, c. 2570 BCE

Few buildings better demonstrate the Egyptian use of huge, single blocks of hard, heavy stone than the granite pillars and architraves of the Valley Building, a part of the pyramid-complex of King Khafre.

AMEN-RA TEMPLE

KARNAK, LUXOR, EGYPT, c. 1500–380 BCE

The Karnak temple complex is one of the largest series of religious structures in the world. It was added to and changed over a period of 2,000 years, but its central and most important building was the temple built for Amen-Ra.

1

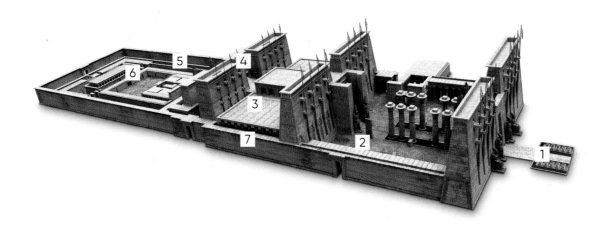

1. Processional entrance
The temple was oriented east–west, toward the Nile and the rising sun, and approached along a processional avenue lined with sphinxes. The entrance to the temple was through a standard pylon gateway, which gave access to a huge open courtyard.

2. Colossal statue of Ramses II
The first courtyard was filled with a series of minor monuments, including chapels built for Ramses III and Seti II, a colonnade of the Nubian king Taharqa, and a colossal statue of Ramses II, 49 ft (15 m) tall.

3. Great Hypostyle Hall
One of the most impressive features of this temple is the Great Hypostyle Hall—largely built for Seti I and Ramses II. The hall covers a total of 59,202 sq ft (5,500 sq m) and contains 134 columns, the tallest in the central "nave" rising to 69 ft (21 m) in height.

4. Central avenue
Like most temples, Karnak was designed to be symmetrical, so the procession of the god could pass through the center of the various halls, courts, and pylons, and between the pairs of statues and obelisks that flanked the central axis.

5. The Red Chapel, the central sanctuary
Toward the rear of the temple was the sanctuary, the functional heart of the building, where the image of the god was kept and offerings were made in a daily ritual. Although it was later demolished, the red quartzite sanctuary built by Hatshepsut has been reconstructed.

6. Tent-pole columns
The unusual "tent-pole" shape of these columns in the Akh-Menu building at the rear of the Amen-Ra temple may have reminded Thutmose III, who commissioned them, of his many military campaigns in the Near East and Nubia to establish Egypt's New Kingdom empire.

7. Temple complex
Viewed from the east, most of the key features of the Amen-Ra Temple can still be seen by visitors today. In the distance is the Theban mountain containing the tombs of New Kingdom rulers in the Valley of the Kings.

2

4

3

5 6

7

▲ Subterranean structures

The 6th-century Basilica Cistern in Istanbul is a reservoir built for conserving drinking water for the city above. Large stone columns were removed from Roman temples and other grand buildings and repurposed into supports for the vast underground structure.

▶ Ornamental columns

Columns are often used as decorative features to flank doorways. At the 17th-century Church of the Assumption in Cabra, Spain, two were given a baroque twist and are only strong enough to support the ornamental masonry above.

"Consider the momentous event in architecture when the wall parted and the column became."

Louis Kahn, Estonian-American architect, 1901–1974

COLUMNS AND PIERS

Designed to support arches, vaults, roofs, and floors, columns and piers offer great scope for decoration and enable architects to create forestlike vistas both inside and outside buildings.

One of the great challenges for architectural designers has always been how to build large indoor spaces. A roof can be as wide as a tree trunk is high, but making it span further is very difficult. Before the 19th century, the common solution was to space columns or piers out across the interior of a building for the roof timbers or masonry vaults to rest on. These supports could be timber, as in much of East Asia, or stone, as often seen around the Mediterranean. Ancient Egyptian halls were built with such substantial columns that many are still standing more than 3,000 years later.

INNOVATION AND EVOLUTION

The ancient Greeks produced column designs, which the Romans later adapted and spread across their empire. These designs went on to influence Mediterranean, European, and European-inspired architecture around the world in an ongoing process of copying, adapting, and blending existing ideas with new rules, styles, and associations.

Roman architects liked to use single stones for the column shaft. This meant transporting giant, 50-ft (15-m) blocks of granite thousands of miles around the Mediterranean coast from Aswan in Egypt to Rome.

Later, Romanesque and Gothic architects thickened their columns into broad piers—a supporting mass of masonry that is usually either rectangular or square in cross-section. These would often be decorated with complex clusters of smaller columns.

MODERN BUILDINGS

With the rise of coal in the 19th century, iron and steel became cheap enough to use for building on an industrial scale. The strength of these metals enabled much thinner columns and wider spacing between them.

Such technological innovations prompted designers to respond with fresh styles of architecture. By the early 20th century, thanks to reinforced concrete, it was possible for a whole building to sit atop slender columns.

▲ Piers and colonnettes

In order to support tall vaults that exert a sideways pressure on columns, Gothic architects used sturdy piers, often surrounded with mini columns (colonnettes) to look like delicate clusters, as found in the chapter house of Wells Cathedral in the UK.

▲ Iron columns

Pairs of iron columns hold up the train shed roof at Liverpool Street Station, London. Raised in the late 19th century, these slender columns are strong enough to support a huge glass-and-iron roof, which shelters numerous platforms below.

SETTING A MOOD

Columns are often among the most prominent elements of a building. They can be used to create impact and communicate a particular character or ambience, from solemn to elegant to light-hearted.

Strength
Wooden Minoan columns taper downward, producing a sense of strength and power.

Beauty
A key element of highly decorated Thai temples is the quantity and quality of soaring columns.

Humor
Some modern columns are charming, like these shaped like gas pumps by Farrells in London.

ANCIENT GREECE

The ancient Greeks developed one of the most widely imitated styles of architecture in western civilization. Some 2,500 years after their heyday, their buildings are still famous all over the world.

Between 900 and 323 BCE, a distinctive culture of independent city-states flourished in Greece and its adjoining islands. These cities were dependent on the labor of enslaved people, working on farms that grew grain, grapes, and olives. Neighboring cities developed subtly different religious architecture. Superficially similar and simple, Greek temples were full of subtle detail, designed to delight the privileged minority of male citizens who commissioned and enjoyed them.

ATHENS AND BEYOND

Greek builders drew on a plentiful supply of good building stone (especially smooth, white marble) as well as clay for making roof tiles and ornaments. Many temple details are probably derived from lost older wooden temples, in a widespread pattern of religious architecture looking backward to an idealized past. The best Greek stonework was of remarkably high quality: masons cut blocks precisely, laid them with very thin joints, and devised hidden metal clamps to affix them together, minimizing the use

of mortar. The result was a very smooth surface that proved to be an excellent background for carvings or a base for brightly colored decoration. This kind of architecture reached its peak in Athens, the most prosperous Greek city-state—widely regarded as the birthplace of democracy and the progenitor of numerous Greek colonies around the Mediterranean.

Like other Greek cities, Athens had a range of civic buildings, such as a bouleuterion (council chamber), open-air theaters, and stadiums. However, the most important and enduring of these ancient buildings were the temples, each of which was dedicated to a deity. Set on prominent sites, often on rocky outcrops, Greek temples, with their rows of columns and distinctive decoration and sculpture, had a huge influence not only on Greek architecture, but also on Roman and later Renaissance and Neoclassical building styles. Key elements that were much copied were their three styles of column, known as "orders" (see p.40), and the entablatures they supported. These orders provided a set of guidelines that dictated the proportions and details of the most visible parts of Greek buildings. They were so widely used that they became symbolic of the artistic and cultural achievement of ancient Greek civilization.

MINOAN ARCHITECTURE

A predecessor of Greek civilization was the Minoan culture of ancient Crete. The Minoans used wooden beams and columns (which tapered at the base) in the construction of their palaces. These features probably influenced Greek architecture, although the Greeks had a different approach to proportion.

The restored north entrance of the Minoan Palace of Knossos, Crete

▶ **Porch of the Caryatids**
Many writers have argued that Greek columns, with their capitals (heads) and bases (feet), were based on the human form. A suggestion of this can be seen in the Erechtheion, a temple in Athens, which has statues of women, known as "caryatids," instead of columns.

"Greek architecture is the flowering of geometry."
Ralph Waldo Emerson, American essayist (1803–1882)

THE PARTHENON

ATHENS, GREECE, 447–438 BCE

One of the most complete surviving Greek temples, the Parthenon was dedicated to Athena, the patron goddess of Athens. Built on the Acropolis, a rock standing high above the city, it was surrounded by other buildings and statues. Built with 24,000 tons of marble from Mount Pentelikon, it was adorned with friezes showing a ceremonial procession, together with carved reliefs of battles from Greek mythology.

The Parthenon, rear view

▶ **Brightly colored**
Traces of pigment on surviving statues indicate that the Parthenon's walls and sculptures were originally painted. Blues and reds (reconstructed here) highlighted costume details and enhanced the building's ornamentation.

Antefix ornament covers tile joints

Opisthodomos (small inner room) serves as city's main treasury

Metope (square panel) contains carved reliefs

Columns of blocks of rough stone; fluting added later to avoid chipping

Doric columns taper and lean slightly inward

Platform rises three steps above the ground

▲ **Entablature details**
The metopes, with their carved reliefs around the entablature, were separated by vertical bands known as "triglyphs." These, and the little peg-like shapes below them, probably represent older wooden temple beam-ends.

▲ **Optical illusion**
All of the Parthenon's columns lean inward slightly; continued upward, they would meet about 7,200 ft (2,200 m) above the center of the roof. This and other subtle distortions were to make the building yet more beautiful.

> "Earth proudly wears the Parthenon, As the best gem upon her zone"
>
> Ralph Walso Emerson, "The Problem", *American Poetry: The Nineteenth Century, Vol. I*, 1993

Complete view of the Parthenon

STATUE OF ATHENA

The 38-ft- (11.5-m-) high statue of Athena, goddess of wisdom, warfare, and crafts, sat on a cedar-wood throne, and was covered in ivory and gold to represent the goddess's skin and clothes. Athena holds a spear and a shield in one hand and a statue of Nike, the goddess of victory, in the other. The figure was made by a team of craft workers supervised by the sculptor Phidias.

A replica of the original statue of Athena

Statue of Nike

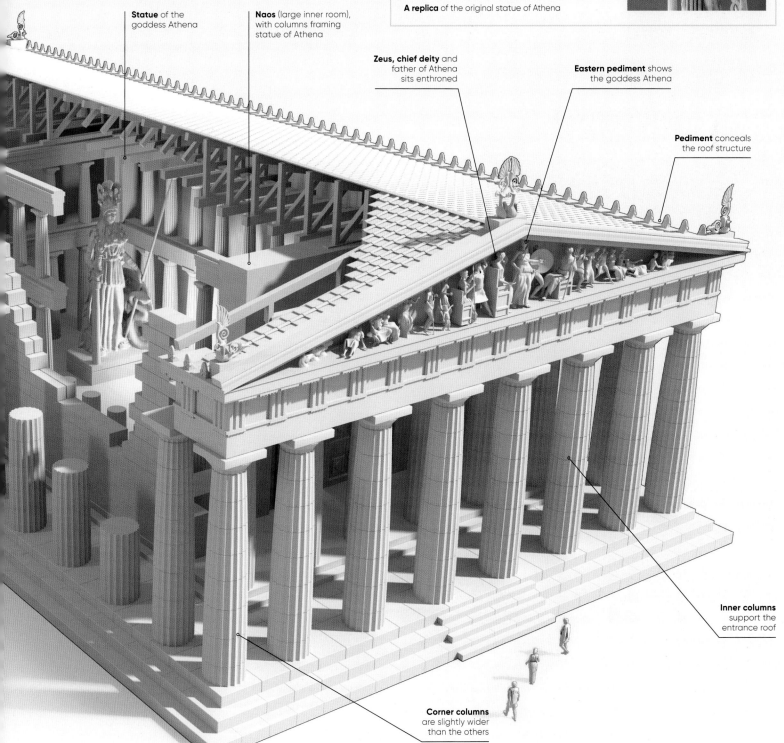

Statue of the goddess Athena

Naos (large inner room), with columns framing statue of Athena

Zeus, chief deity and father of Athena sits enthroned

Eastern pediment shows the goddess Athena

Pediment conceals the roof structure

Inner columns support the entrance roof

Corner columns are slightly wider than the others

KEY **ELEMENTS**

Greek architects excelled at fine detail and knew exactly which adjustments had to be made to give a building the correct proportions. However, they were also masters of town planning, and had a keen eye for placing buildings at the very best locations.

PROPORTIONS

The Greeks developed standard proportions for many aspects of their architecture. For example, the height of an Ionic column was usually about 9 times its diameter at the base, and it usually had 24 flutes. An entrance front usually had an even number of columns, so its doorway had a column on either side.

◀ **Corinthian proportions**
The Corinthian order is clear to see at the temple of Zeus at Olympia. Its columns are slender and rise to a height of almost ten times their diameter. Their carved capitals support what remains of the building's entablature.

ACROPOLIS

Greek cities often had an acropolis (high city). This was an area on top of a hill or rock that was developed during the settlement's early years as a fortified stronghold. Although fortifications survive on some of these acropolises, they were largely removed to make way for temples and public buildings.

▲ **Religious center**
The Athenian acropolis became the site not only of the Parthenon, but also of the Erechtheion and the temple of Athena Nike. The height of the site enabled Athenians to see the sanctuary of Athena from anywhere in the city.

THREE TYPES OF COLUMN

The guidelines, or orders, that the ancient Greeks produced to standardize their architecture described three main types of column. The Doric column was the simplest: it had no base and had a very plain top. The Ionic column was slimmer, and had a capital featuring large spiral scrolls. The Corinthian column had the most elaborate capitals, featuring the carved leaves of the acanthus plant.

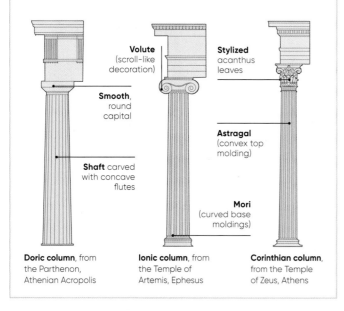

Volute (scroll-like decoration)

Stylized acanthus leaves

Smooth, round capital

Astragal (convex top molding)

Shaft carved with concave flutes

Mori (curved base moldings)

Doric column, from the Parthenon, Athenian Acropolis

Ionic column, from the Temple of Artemis, Ephesus

Corinthian column, from the Temple of Zeus, Athens

AGORA

Cities were at the heart of Greek culture, and each had a special area set aside for political, commercial, and social activities. This area, known as the agora (gathering place), was home to council buildings, markets, gymnasiums, and colonnaded spaces known as stoas (covered walkways).

◀ Meeting place

A stoa was a multipurpose building in which everything from public meetings to art exhibitions took place. The agora of Athens had several stoas, one of which, the stoa of Attalos, was rebuilt in the 20th century.

▼ Planned space

Agoras had plenty of space for market stalls and gatherings. This 19th-century engraving of the agora at Athens shows a stoa, a temple, various statues, and a "tholos" (round colonnaded structure; see p.42).

SCULPTURE

The Greeks produced some of the finest sculpture of the ancient world, predominantly in the form of friezes and pediments. Athens had several marble workshops, in which renowned sculptors, such as Phidias, produced extraordinarily lifelike carvings.

▶ Honoring the gods

Phidias' meticulously carved north frieze of the Parthenon (controversially housed at the British Museum in London) shows a lively procession that took place as part of the annual Panathenaic Festival.

▲ Frontal view

Figures are usually shown from the side in Greek temple sculpture. This head-on view of a chariot, from a temple in Selinunte, Sicily, is a rare glimpse from a different perspective.

◀ Zeus and Hera

This part of the Parthenon frieze shows Zeus and Hera, king and queen of the gods, sitting on their thrones. Around them, people bear offerings to the goddess Athena.

ANCIENT GREEK BUILDINGS

The best-preserved buildings of ancient Greece are generally temples. However, a number of other grand structures also bear witness to the Greeks' architectural genius. These include the oldest surviving open-air theaters and stadiums.

1

3

2

4

1. Stadium of Delphi

Delphi, Greece, 4th century BCE

With its raked stone seating, which held up to 6,500 people, this is one of the best-preserved stadiums of ancient Greece. The Pythian Games were held here in honor of the god Apollo, whose sanctuary stands nearby.

2. Tholos of Delphi

Delphi, Greece, c. 375 BCE

This circular temple was part of a sanctuary dedicated to the goddess Athena. It had a ring of 20 Doric columns, which supported a dome. The dome itself was an unusual feature, and bore a series of innovative reliefs.

3. Propylaea

Athens, Greece, 437–432 BCE

Standing at the top of a long flight of steps, the Propylaea was the monumental gateway to the Acropolis. It provided a ceremonial entrance for religious processions, and had two side rooms, one of which was a picture gallery.

4. Tower of the Winds

Athens, Greece, 2nd century BCE

The octagonal Tower of the Winds has friezes that depict the eight deities of the winds. Originally, it was adorned with sundials and housed a clepsydra (water clock). It also had a weather vane on its roof.

5. Second Temple of Hera

Paestum, Italy, c. 450 BCE

The city of Paestum, in southern Italy, was an important Greek colony. It had several Doric temples, including two dedicated to the goddess Hera. The limestone columns of the Second Temple taper dramatically.

5

6 7

6. Ancient Theater of Epidaurus
Epidaurus, Greece, 4th century BCE

This building has all the key features of an ancient Greek theater: almost circular rows of banked seats, a circular area for dancers, and a rectangular stage beyond. The theater could seat up to 16,000 people.

7. House of the Masks
Delos, Greece, 150–100 BCE

This elaborate house, which was built around a courtyard, has mosaic floors and stonework painted to look like marble. It is believed to have been where traveling actors stayed when they were performing at the theater in Delos.

ACHAEMENID EMPIRE

In the mid 6th century BCE, the Achaemenid Empire emerged from what is now Iran. Craftspeople from across the empire shaped a new architecture, different from anything that had gone before.

▲ Behistun Inscription
A large Achaemenid-era rock relief on a cliff near the city of Kermanshah in Iran depicts Darius I, attended by two servants, addressing various conquered peoples. The inscriptions describe battles waged by the king in three languages: Elamite, Old Persian, and Babylonian.

The Achaemenid (First Persian) Empire is traditionally believed to have been founded by Cyrus II, also known as Cyrus the Great (r. 559–530 BCE). During his 30-year rule, he laid the foundations for the largest empire the ancient world had seen. Stretching east and west into what is now southeast Europe, northern India, and Egypt, the empire reached its greatest extent under Cyrus's successors, Cambyses II, Darius I, and Xerxes I. Cyrus and Cambyses were responsible for the greater military conquests, but it was Darius (r. 522–486 BCE) who stabilized the empire and initiated a number of major Persian building projects.

Cyrus's original capital was at Pasargadae, in present-day southwestern Iran, where little beyond the king's own mausoleum remains today. Darius built a new capital, Persepolis, farther south, and the rich trove of architectural treasures within this palace complex reveals much about the Achaemenids. It is clear that the empire embraced many cultures. Historians have identified building and decorative styles employed at Persepolis that have their roots across the empire, fusing Babylonian and Assyrian styles with Greek and Egyptian ones. This eclectic mix of imported elements and traditions incorporated in a seamless collage became a quintessential feature of the new Persian architecture.

MULTINATIONAL PROJECTS

The integration and subjugation of nations is made explicit in reliefs that adorn the staircases leading to the Apadana (audience hall) at Persepolis. These depict a procession of representatives of 23 distinct peoples in their native attire, headdresses, and hair styles, all presenting tribute to the great Achaemenid king.

Darius built another large palace at Susa, in what is now western Iran. Like Persepolis, this was constructed on an artificially raised platform, and included a residential palace, an audience hall, and a monumental gate. The apadana takes the form of a hypostyle hall, a vast interior space with a ceiling supported by a field of columns. Only the foundations of the palace at Susa survive, but a large clay tablet discovered by archaeologists describes the materials used in the construction and lists the different countries and peoples involved. Cedar wood came from Lebanon, precious stones from Sogdiana (modern-day Central Asia), ivory from Ethiopia and Sind (Pakistan), and baked bricks from Babylon.

Elaborate capitals top columns

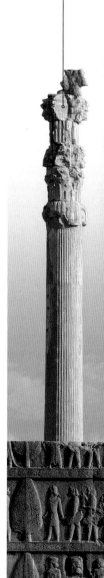

FALL OF THE ACHAEMENIDS

In 334 BCE, Alexander the Great invaded Persia. He defeated the army of Darius III at the Battle of Issus and captured Persepolis and Susa. On Alexander's death, his empire was divided among his generals. Persia was given to the Macedonian-born Seleucus I Nicator, and became a center of Hellenistic culture during what is known as the Seleucid Empire. Native Iranian rule would be restored by the Parthians in the 3rd century BCE.

Detail from a Pompeii mosaic depicting the Battle of Issus

PERSEPOLIS

SHIRAZ, IRAN, c. 518 BCE

Nestled into the base of Kuh-e Rahmat (Mountain of Mercy) in southwest Iran, Persepolis is the greatest surviving monument of Achaemenid architecture. Begun by Darius I, the palace complex was enlarged by successive rulers before being razed by Alexander the Great in 330 BCE.

▶ **Huge doorways**
The second-largest room at Persepolis after the Apadana was the Throne Hall, also known as the Hundred-Column Hall. Built from stone and mud brick during the reign of Xerxes, it was accessed by eight great stone doorways.

▶ **Apadana reliefs**
The two monumental stone staircases leading up to the platform are lined with exquisite friezes showing processions of subjects, as well as soldiers, horses, and chariots. The detail of the hair and clothing of the carved figures, and the gifts they carry for the king, is extraordinary.

◀ **Bull's head**
The foreparts of bulls, lions, and mythical creatures adorn many of the porticoes and columns at Persepolis. In a style developed by the Achaemenids, double-headed stone capitals were used to support the wooden beams of the ceiling.

Columns are tall, slender, and fluted

Columns supported the roofs of the main halls

Sculpted friezes depict wild animals

A leveled stone platform houses the palace complex

A staircase with wide, shallow steps leads up to the platform

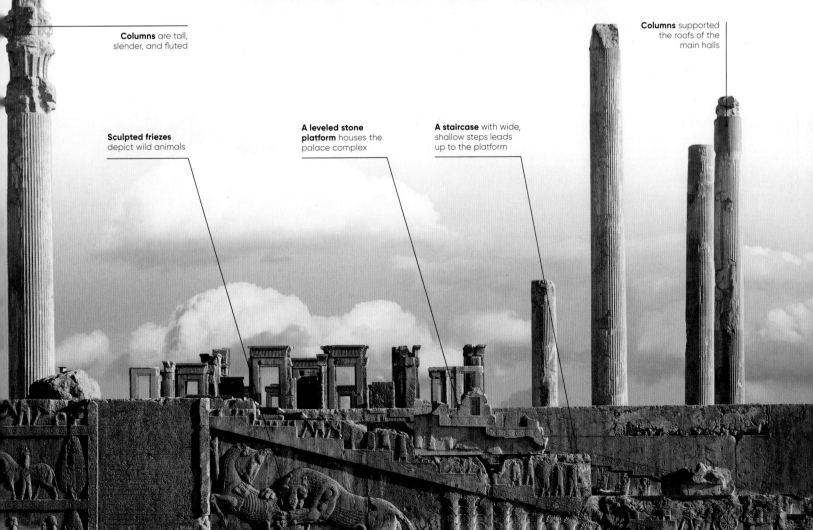

KEY **ELEMENTS**

The most important Achaemenid buildings were raised on platforms built of large stone blocks. Ornamental lavish staircases led up to these platforms, on which were set multiple columned halls.

COLUMNED HALLS

The Achaemenids constructed great halls with ceilings supported by multiple rows of columns, like the hypostyle halls found in ancient Egypt. These buildings would have been colorfully painted, with intricate stone carving and decorative capitals topping some of the columns.

► White stone columns
Cyrus the Great built several columned halls at his capital, Pasargadae. The residential palace was smaller than the main audience hall, but had more columns, and both were surrounded by porticoes. The halls looked out over a formal garden, irrigated by water in stone channels.

▲ Fluted column
By the reign of Darius I, the design of columns had evolved from the simple tiered designs used at Pasargadae to elongated columns with a bell-shaped base and fluted shaft. This example is at the Palace of Darius at Susa.

TILED FRIEZES

As well as developing new techniques for carving stone friezes, as seen at Persepolis, the Achaemenids adopted a range of other styles from the peoples they conquered, including the Babylonian tradition of using tiled friezes to adorn important buildings.

▲ Common motifs
Little remains of Darius's palace at Susa, but friezes probably lined its staircases, walls, and doorways. One of several recurring designs, the winged bull was a common motif in ancient Assyria, a pre-Achaemenid civilization in the Near East. These bulls were often given a human head, and were called lamassu.

▲ Colorful glaze
Unlike the carved friezes that adorn the walls of Persepolis, the friezes from the Palace of Darius at Susa are composed of separate molded bricks covered in brown, yellow, white, green, and black glazes. Firing and glazing these bricks was very expensive, making them an impressive feature.

▲ Telling a tale
Another panel from the walls of Darius's palace at Susa shows bearded Persian archers with their bows and quivers, wearing richly decorated robes and gold bracelets, and carrying spears. This is part of a larger frieze thought to represent the Immortals, who formed the king's personal bodyguard.

ACHAEMENID BUILDINGS

Stone and tile friezes, sumptuously carved column capitals, and rock-cut tombs all testify to the splendors of Achaemenid architecture, but no more than one or two entirely intact buildings survive from this glorious era.

1. Tomb of Darius
Naqsh-e Rostam, Iran, c. 490 BCE

Darius I is buried at Naqsh-e Rostam, along with three other Achaemenid kings. The tombs are carved high up into a cliff face. They take the form of a cross with a central entrance, above which are large panels with figures of the king and smaller attendant figures.

2. Tomb of Cyrus the Great
Pasargadae, Iran, 6th century BCE

As well as being the first dynastic capital of the Achaemenid Empire, Pasargadae was the final resting place of Cyrus the Great. His tomb is a modest stone kiosk on top of a stepped platform. Its only decoration is a single carved rosette on the entrance facade.

3. Cube of Zoroaster
Naqsh-e Rostam, Iran, 5th century BCE

The function of this simple stone kiosk remains unknown. It has minimal decoration and a staircase leading to a small interior chamber. Raised on a stone platform, the building sits before a rectangular depression at the foot of the cliffs and their carved tombs.

"The people of Babylon blessed my kingship, and I settled all the lands in peaceful abodes."

Cyrus II, *The Cyrus Cylinder*, 539 BCE

PARTHIAN AND SASANIAN ARCHITECTURE

Two ancient dynasties—the Parthians and the Sasanians—ruled what is now Iran for almost 900 years. Their building style shaped architecture from Asia Minor to northern India.

For around 900 years, the Parthians and then the Sasanians were the dominant political force in the Middle East, trading and warring with the Romans, the Byzantines, and Asian powers as far east as China. While their architecture drew on older Persian traditions, and on ideas and techniques learned from Rome and other neighbors, the Parthians and Sasanians also made remarkable innovations.

VAULTS AND ARCHES

In a landscape lacking in stone and timber, Parthian and Sasanian designers made extensive use of brick, as had their ancient predecessors in Mesopotamia. Unlike the structurally simple, solid ziggurats of earlier millennia, however, Parthian and Sasanian architects built great bridges and vaulted spaces, able to compete with the most ambitious structures of Rome.

A key difference was that, where Roman architects used the geometrically satisfying circle to set out their vaults and domes, Parthian designers found that the best shape for a freestanding arch or vault is a U-like form—the inversion of the curve formed by a hanging chain (see box below). This enabled Parthians to build some of the largest column-free spans before modern times.

One of the notable room types of their palace architecture was the *iwan*—a vaulted room enclosed on three sides but open on the fourth side, providing shade and fresh breezes in the hot summer sun and plenty of indirect light by which to conduct royal business.

The Taq-i Kisra is one of the largest iwans of its day. Unlike Roman vaults, which required a temporary wooden structure to support them during construction, the Taq-i Kisra was built using the large, flat end wall as a support for the arch, saving on wood—a scarce resource on the Mesopotamian plains.

THE SQUINCH

The Sasanians solved the problem of placing a dome on a square building by inventing the squinch. This is a type of arch placed at each corner of the square, together converting the square into an octagon, on which it is easy to place a dome. A dome chamber in the palace built at Firuzabad by Ardashir, founder of the Sasanian Empire, is believed to be the earliest known example of a squinch.

After the Arab Muslim conquest of Persia, which took place between 633 and 654 CE, the Arabs adopted elements of Sasanian architecture and absorbed them into the expanding vocabulary of Islamic architecture.

◀ **Parthian power**

The caravan city of Hatra, Iraq, lies on what was once the border between the Roman and Parthian empires. Its ruins, which include the towering south gate, reveal the extent to which it was fortified against invaders.

THE CATENARY ARCH

A catenary curve is the shape that a chain forms when it hangs from its ends. The forces of tension (coming from the hooks holding the chain) and the force of gravity (pulling it downward) exactly balance. When it is inverted, the forces of tension become forces of compression, and the curve becomes the most stable shape that an arch can have. The Parthians used this principle to build the Arch of Ctesiphon, which stands freely under its own weight.

A catenary arch, based on the physics of the catenary curve

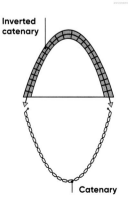

TAQ-I KISRA

SALMAN PAK, IRAQ, 3RD–6TH CENTURIES CE

This partial facade and arch are all that remain of a Sasanian-era palace complex and city. For more than 800 years the city served as the capital of the Persian Empire under the Parthians and the Sasanians. Its vaulted space is a classic example of an iwan.

▲ Wall decoration
The Sasanians decorated their buildings with elaborate stucco reliefs. This design of alternating palmettes and flowers was found on masonry unearthed in the Taq-i Kisra area.

Catenary arch over 110 ft (30 m) in height

Walls made of fired brick

Iwan walled on three sides and open on the fourth

PARTHIAN AND SASANIAN BUILDINGS

▲ Fortresses of Nisa, Turkmenistan, c. 250 BCE
Nisa was a capital of the Parthian Empire, in what is now Central Asia. What remains of it today are two large artificial hills covering the ancient ruins of what were once a fortress with multiple towers, a royal palace, and some Zoroastrian temples.

▲ Palace of Ardashir, Iran, c. 224 CE
This palace, constructed by the first of the Sasanian kings, is notable for its three great domes and imposing iwan. It was built beside a pool that was fed by a natural spring, perhaps in honor of the Persian goddess of water, Anahita.

"The whole of Islamic architecture borrowed from this tradition, once Islam had conquered Persia."

Robert Byron, *The Road to Oxiana,* 1937

▲ Multiple arches

The Romans built aqueducts, such as the Pont du Gard in France, to carry water across valleys. For all their beauty, they were infrastructure rather than art, and the projecting stones used to support the wood used in construction were never chiseled flat as they were in more aesthetically minded projects.

▶ Horseshoe arches

The horseshoe or keyhole arch is a common feature of Islamic architecture. It is particularly striking when used in a series, as in this portico in the Mosque-Cathedral of Córdoba, in Spain.

"An arch consists of two weaknesses which, leaning one against the other, make a strength."

Leonardo da Vinci, Italian architect (1452–1519)

THE ARCH

Designed to span areas and bear weight, arches have for thousands of years been increasing the technical capacity of architecture, and enhancing its beauty.

Stone and mud brick are strong when they are squashed, but weak when twisted or pulled. This makes them good for building walls, but less useful for spanning rooms or large wall openings—for wide spans, the lintel stone that bridges the gap became prohibitively thick and heavy.

As early as the 2nd millennium BCE, clever builders came up with the arch as a solution: the bricks or stones were small enough to work with, and each one was being compressed, rather than twisted like a lintel. Building an arch required a wooden scaffold called a centering, on which to assemble the individual blocks, known as voussoirs. Once the keystone had been secured at the top of the arch, and the mortar given time to set, the centering could be removed and reused elsewhere.

THE TRIUMPHING ARCH

It was ancient Roman designers who scaled up the quantity and size of arches they built, and distributed them around the Mediterranean with their growing empire. Roman engineers figured out that large rooms could be covered by a continuous arch—a vault. They also used arches for infrastructure, particularly to carry artificial streams across valleys in order to supply their town centers with clean drinking water from the mountains.

Roman arches and vaults tended to be thick and heavy, with huge outer walls resisting the sideways thrust that their shape produces (see below). Through the medieval period, Byzantine, Islamic, and Gothic architects developed an increasingly refined understanding of the most structurally efficient shapes for arches, and where they needed additional lateral support. This allowed builders to construct much lighter, higher, and more transparent buildings.

With their leaping rhythm of curves, arches are often the most memorable feature of a building. Adding to this appeal, designers through history have frequently singled them out for special treatment, like adding carvings, as found on many Islamic and Gothic arches.

▲ **Pointed arches**
Pointed arches, which produce less sideways thrust than semicircular ones, allowed more flexibility of design. Masons emphasized continuous vertical elements in buildings such as Cologne Cathedral in Germany, whose arches seem to surge up to heaven.

▲ **Catenary arches**
The attic of Casa Milà, a house built by Antoni Gaudí in Barcelona, Spain, is spanned by catenary arches, which support the roof. The physics of catenary arches means that they do not require buttresses to resist sideways thrust (see p.48).

ARCH STRUCTURE

Arches are held together by compression. Their weight, and the weight of the masonry above them, bears down on each voussoir and is transferred to the base, or springing, of the arch. An arch also creates an outward force, known as thrust, which would push the arch apart if it were not supported on either side by strong walls, piers, or buttresses.

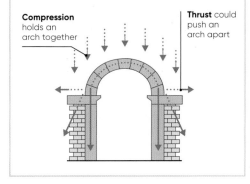

Compression holds an arch together

Thrust could push an arch apart

ANCIENT ROME

The Romans amassed the largest empire of their time, and wherever they conquered they transformed the local architecture with their own, imperial style.

From their base in Italy, the Romans built up their vast empire between the 3rd century BCE and the 3rd century CE. For much of that time, they ruled most of Europe, Turkey, Mesopotamia, the eastern Mediterranean, and part of North Africa. Their conquests brought not only the demand for new buildings, roads, and towns, but also the need for resources—an enormous labor force and a rich, varied source of materials, from clay to marble, with which to build on a massive scale.

ENGINEERING GENIUS

The Romans drew on the architectural legacy of their neighbors, the Greeks, adopting their orders of columns and other traditions. However, thanks partly to the skills required by their enormous army, the Romans were ground-breaking engineers. They developed the arch, the vault, and the dome, and devised ways of using materials such as concrete that enabled them to build new kinds of structure. Arches and vaults had existed before, but they had never been used on the scale that the Romans

achieved. Standardizing the sizes of bricks and tiles and developing large-scale production methods also enabled them to build bigger and faster. They built imposing palaces, multistory apartment buildings, and impressive aqueducts that provided a clean water supply. They also erected other structures, such as theaters, amphitheaters, and race tracks, to entertain and pacify the peoples that they conquered, who might otherwise grow rebellious. These and other grand buildings, such as imperial palaces and triumphal arches (which were adorned with sculptures and inscriptions commemorating military victories), demonstrated the sheer power of the empire.

The Romans also used building materials to show off their imperial power and to inspire awe in conquered peoples. Massive concrete walls gave the strength needed to support heavy vaulted and domed structures. The walls of major buildings were often clad in exotic marbles imported from distant parts of the empire to provide a range of opulent colors. Likewise, porticoes were supported by marble columns, sometimes consisting of a single shaft that had been carried a great distance to the building site. Most of these buildings are now in ruins, but enough of them still stand to illustrate the magnificence of Roman architecture.

THE ROMAN FORUM

At the heart of Rome was the Forum, an area where political speeches and other public events took place. With its temples, triumphal arches, government buildings, markets, and statues commemorating great emperors and generals, it brilliantly combined the need for a public space with a display of imperial power and magnificence.

Rome's Forum, with the portico of the Temple of Saturn in the foreground

▶ **Arch of Trajan**
The arch dedicated to Emperor Trajan (98–117 CE) bears relief carvings showing his triumphal procession after conquering Dacia (Romania).

"I found Rome a city of mud brick and left it a city of marble."

Caesar Augustus, quoted by Suetonius, *Divus Augustus*, 121 CE

THE COLOSSEUM

ROME, ITALY, 71–80 CE

Begun by the emperor Vespasian, this enormous amphitheater was completed about eight years later under Titus. It was built to stage gladiatorial contests and other spectacles. Raked seating accommodated an audience that may have been as large as 80,000. There were separate entrances for the gladiators, and beneath the arena were the cells where they waited to fight and animal cages.

The Colosseum as it looks today

ROMAN CONCRETE

The huge buildings of the Roman Empire would have been impossible without the large-scale use of concrete, which could be made without the specialized skill of the stone mason or bricklayer. Unskilled workers made concrete by combining aggregate (usually large pieces of stone) with a binding mortar consisting of lime mixed with volcanic ash. Skilled Roman builders then faced the concrete core with a thin layer of brickwork. This took far less time than building with masonry.

A concrete wall with brick facing at Ostia Antica

▲ Awning
Roman writers speak of a canvas awning that could be pulled across the Colosseum to shade the audience. Although it is not known exactly how it was held in position, upright posts around the perimeter of the building helped to secure it in place.

▲ Passageways
All around the interior of the Colosseum, beneath the tiers of seats, run tunnel-like passages. Staircases off these tunnels lead up to the different levels of seating. The layout was designed to make it easy for spectators to reach their seats.

▲ Under the arena
A labyrinth of rooms and access corridors lay beneath the arena. Lifts and ramps brought combatants, the wild animals they often fought, and scenery up to the stage.

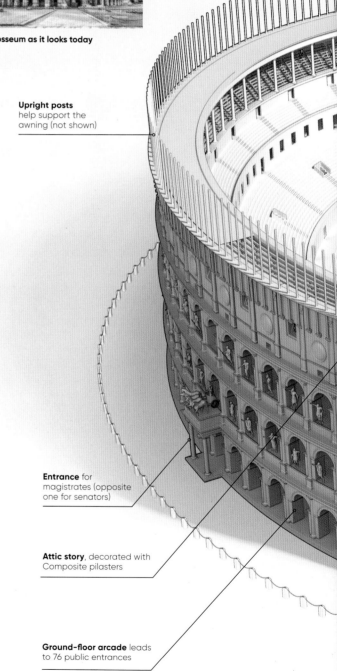

Upright posts help support the awning (not shown)

Entrance for magistrates (opposite one for senators)

Attic story, decorated with Composite pilasters

Ground-floor arcade leads to 76 public entrances

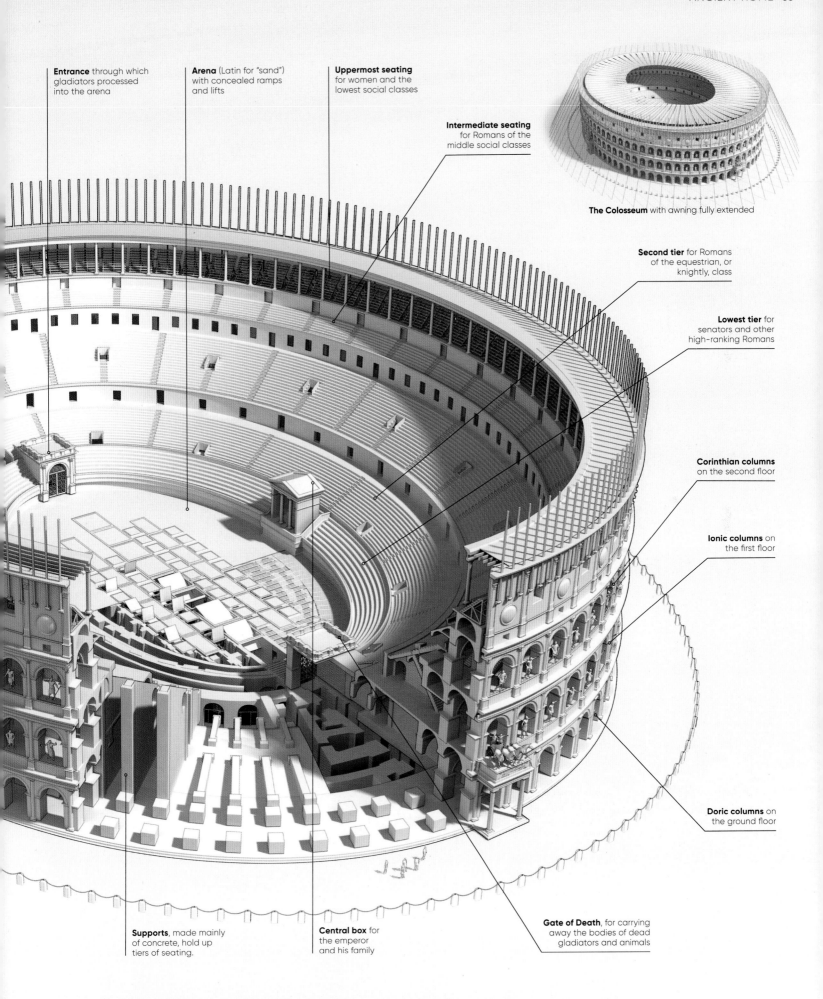

Entrance through which gladiators processed into the arena

Arena (Latin for "sand") with concealed ramps and lifts

Uppermost seating for women and the lowest social classes

Intermediate seating for Romans of the middle social classes

The Colosseum with awning fully extended

Second tier for Romans of the equestrian, or knightly, class

Lowest tier for senators and other high-ranking Romans

Corinthian columns on the second floor

Ionic columns on the first floor

Doric columns on the ground floor

Supports, made mainly of concrete, hold up tiers of seating.

Central box for the emperor and his family

Gate of Death, for carrying away the bodies of dead gladiators and animals

KEY ELEMENTS

Many of the distinctive features of Roman architecture, such as arches, domes, and vaults, relied on the Romans' ability to produce concrete and bricks. Their enormous workforce used these materials to build large, spacious structures.

VAULTS

The Romans built vaults to create tall, impressive interiors without wooden roof trusses. The most common design was the half-cylinder or barrel vault. If two of these intersected at right-angles, they formed a cross vault. Roman vaults were usually made of concrete, which the builders laid using a temporary wooden framework to support the concrete while it was setting.

MONUMENTAL COLUMNS

Columns commemorated the deeds of Rome's emperors and military leaders. They formed landmarks in city centers, and their height indicated the importance of the people they honored. The Romans developed a form of carved relief that depicted military victories and spiraled around each column.

▲ Barrel vault and semidome
The caldarium (hot bath) of Rome's Forum bath complex is topped by a barrel vault and terminates in a rounded apse roofed by a semidome. Both the vault and the dome were built using concrete.

▲ Imperial triumphs
The column of Marcus Aurelius (161–180 CE) in Rome commemorates the emperor's victories against various peoples. The relief teems with action, and spirals up to a statue of Marcus Aurelius on top.

WALL CONSTRUCTION

The Romans were using concrete by the 3rd century BCE, and they soon discovered that it was so strong that it did not need to be faced with large stones. Instead, they dressed it with small stones laid randomly or in rough courses, creating a system known as *opus incertum*. Later, they used square facings laid in diamond patterns (*opus reticulatum*), or simply faced concrete walls with courses of standard bricks (*opus testaceum*).

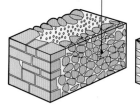

Small stones were used irregularly, with larger ones for door and window openings

Regular patterns of stones resembled a net

Standardized bricks formed a simple facing

Opus incertum

Opus reticulatum

Opus testaceum

DOMES

The Romans created larger domes than any previous builders, producing some of the most stunning interiors of the ancient world. Concrete made it possible for them to make the required curved shape without having to cut blocks of masonry to size. It was also the perfect material for building massive supporting walls.

◄ **Concrete mixes**
For the dome of the Pantheon, the builders used different mixes of concrete—a heavier brick and tufa aggregate at the bottom, and a lighter pumice stone aggregate farther up.

ARCHES

Semicircular arches enabled the Romans to span much wider spaces than the flat stone lintels used by the Greeks. These arches spanned openings for doors and windows and supported roofs in large buildings such as basilicas or baths. They were built of either concrete or bricks, both of which were easy to produce in large quantities.

▲ **Triumphal arch**
After military victories, emperors processed into Rome with their troops, often passing through a triumphal arch, such the Arch of Constantine (312).

◄ **Arcades**
Trajan's market in Rome, one of the first shopping malls, has rows of arched openings. They are made of concrete faced with narrow bricks.

TOWN PLANNING

The Romans' conquests gave them the chance to build whole new towns from scratch. These were arranged in grid patterns, with the main paved streets meeting at a Forum. City blocks known as *insulae* (islands), contained shops with multistory apartments above. Larger houses, built around courtyards, were built for the upper classes. Towns such as Pompeii, Herculaneum, and Ostia Antica are good examples of this kind of town planning.

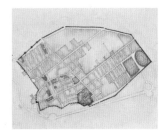

Pompeii's street plan shows the Forum on the left, the amphitheater on the right, and a grid of streets in between.

ANCIENT ROMAN BUILDINGS

The Romans built on a large scale all over their empire, from Spain to the eastern Mediterranean. They constructed temples, houses, and libraries, erecting entire cities and networks of roads.

1

4

2

3

1. Maison Carrée
Nîmes, France, c. 7 BCE
Roughly twice as long as it is wide, the Maison Carrée (Square House) has the typical proportions of a Classical temple. One of the best-preserved Roman temples, it was dedicated during the reign of Caesar Augustus.

2. Insula house
Herculaneum, Italy, 6th–7th centuries BCE
Buried, like Pompeii, under volcanic ash after the eruption of Mount Vesuvius, Herculaneum has well-preserved insula blocks. Some have shops on the ground floor and apartments above, while others are just residential.

3. Baths of Caracalla
Rome, Italy, 211 BCE
This vast complex of baths, which included changing rooms and gymnasiums, could accommodate 1,600 people. It was heated by hot air that rose from a furnace through ducts running under the floors.

4. Palace of Diocletian
Split, Croatia, early 4th century CE
Built as the retirement home of the emperor Diocletian, this building is part palace and part fortress. The complex measures 705 x 575ft (215 x 175m), and included granite columns that were imported from Egypt.

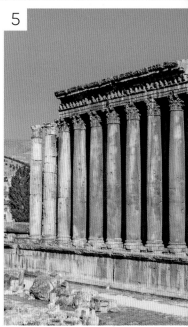

5

5. Temple of Bacchus
Baalbek, Lebanon, 2nd century CE
The Romans built several temples at Baalbek that showed their skill with large blocks of stone. The Temple of Bacchus, one of the best preserved, was originally ornately carved.

6. Library of Celcus
Ephesus, Turkey, 1st or 2nd century CE
One of the largest Roman libraries, the Library of Celcus has niches in its walls that originally contained shelves for thousands of papyrus scrolls. It was built as a memorial for a former proconsul of Asia.

7. Alcántara Bridge
Alcántara, Spain, 104–106 CE
Roads and bridges were vital for connecting the Roman Empire. Large, arched structures such as the Alcántara Bridge, over the Tagus River, were extremely expensive to build; this one was paid for by local towns.

THE PANTHEON

ROME, ITALY, 113–125 CE

Built under emperors Trajan and Hadrian on the site of an earlier temple, the Pantheon is dedicated to all Roman gods. Its outstanding feature is its dome, which—with a diameter of 142 ft (43 m)—was the largest dome in the ancient world.

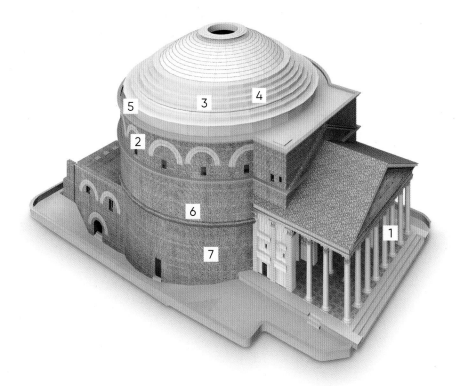

1. Portico
The portico's 16 columns are each made of a single piece of granite approximately 40 ft (12 m) tall, brought all the way from Egypt. At the top of each column is a Corinthian capital carved in contrasting white marble from Greece.

2. Outer walls
Several large relieving arches on the exterior walls of the temple help the structure bear the weight of the massive dome above. The arches and the surrounding masonry are made of brick and Roman concrete.

3. Coffered ceiling
Five concentric rings of indentations called coffers line the interior of the dome. Since the masonry of the central sections is thinner, these reduce the weight of the structure. They also make its shape more legible from ground level.

4. Dome
Measured from the floor, the height of the huge unreinforced concrete dome is equal to its diameter, giving the interior perfect proportions. In the middle of the dome is a 30-ft- (9-m-) wide circular opening called an oculus which lets in light and makes the building seem less massive.

5. Semidome
A semicircular apsidal recess is set opposite the entrance. When the temple became a Christian church in the 7th century, this space housed the altar. Later, a mosaic with a pattern of crosses and foliage was added to the semidome above.

6. Capitals
A set of niches lines the interior walls, supported by tall Corinthian columns that echo those of the portico. Their capitals are richly carved with acanthus leaves. The many different colors and patterns of stone on display demonstrated the emperor's power to bring luxurious, heavy building materials from all over the vast empire.

7. Exterior
The Pantheon's magnificence speaks of the amount of labor and skilled craftsmanship the emperors could command, but even they made economies: the columns of the portico were originally meant to be 25 percent taller, but their size was reduced to save costs.

5

4 6

7

EARLY BUDDHIST ARCHITECTURE

Buddhist architecture blossomed from the 3rd century BCE onward, with the construction of monuments along trade routes as well as pilgrimage sites to commemorate the teachings of the Buddha.

Although the founder of Buddhism, Siddhartha Gautama (most commonly referred to as the Buddha, meaning "enlightened one") died in the 5th century BCE, the earliest surviving Buddhist structures date from the 3rd century BCE. The Buddhist monument par excellence is the stupa, a solid hemispherical domed brick or stone structure. It first appeared as a non-Buddhist burial mound containing the relics of prestigious people, but later came to symbolize *parinirvana* (release from the endless cycle of rebirths). A stupa is therefore the focus of devotion, be it in the form of a reliquary or a memorial marking the location of an event in the Buddha's life. Some stupas are sheltered in a chaitya (prayer hall). Monasteries, or vihara, were often found near chaityas. They were usually square in plan and surrounded by small square cells to accommodate the monks.

DEVELOPMENT

Mauryan emperor Ashoka (r. c. 268–c. 232 BCE) played a key role in the spread of Buddhism, and is said to have erected 84,000 stupas to distribute Buddhist relics across India. While no original structures have been found intact, it is thought that many were encased in later buildings. Stupas were soon richly decorated with sculptural reliefs, marking their importance to Buddhist worship. Three pilgrimage sites stand out from this early phase: Bharhut, in Madhya Pradesh, whose stupa (3rd–2nd centuries BCE) is known for its dark red sandstone gateway and railings; Sanchi, Madhya Pradesh (see opposite); and Amaravati, Andhra Pradesh, whose now-lost impressive dome was covered with elaborate narrative sculpture (3rd century BCE–1st century CE).

People also began to carve structures out of solid rock in the 3rd century BCE, and numerous Buddhist caves were excavated, notably in India's Western Ghats between the 2nd century BCE and the 2nd century CE. Cave construction was revived in the 5th century CE, as seen at Ajanta and Ellora, Maharashtra.

The relief carvings on the gateways, railings, and facades of these early edifices, depicting rural dwellings, urban settlements, and defensive structures, offer a glimpse into the wooden architecture of the period. Formidable catalogs of architectural forms, they also reveal how collections of aedicules or pavilions come together to form larger buildings, and the shapes that would be formalized in later Indian temple architecture.

◀ **Sacred gate**

The crossbars and shafts of the toranas, or monumental gateways (1st century BCE–1st century CE), of Sanchi's Great Stupa are finely carved with narratives depicting the Buddha's life and previous lives. He is represented by symbols such as empty thrones, footprints, trees, and wheels.

WHEEL OF LAW

After his enlightenment at Bodh Gaya, the Buddha went to the Deer Park at Sarnath, Bihar, to give his First Sermon, in which he expounded the fundamental principles of Buddhism: the Four Noble Truths and the Noble Eightfold Path. The event is said to have set in motion the Wheel of Law. In this relief, worshippers surround a wheel placed on a pillar reminiscent of Ashoka's pillars—a series of monolithic columns built across the Indian subcontinent in the 3rd century BCE.

Carvings on the west pillar of the Great Stupa's south torana (gateway), Sanchi

GREAT STUPA

SANCHI, INDIA, 3RD CENTURY BCE–1ST CENTURY CE

Situated on a major trade route, Sanchi is home to India's best-preserved group of Buddhist monuments. The core of the Great Stupa probably dates to the 3rd century BCE, but the structure was often enlarged. By the 1st century CE, encased in brick and stone and plastered over, it had reached 120 ft (36.6 m) in diameter.

STUPA STRUCTURE

A stupa is composed of distinctive parts. The *anda* (dome) represents the seed of life, from which rises the *yasti*, a single pillar that echoes the *axis mundis*, the pivot of the universe. Three parasols top the structure, auspicious symbols marking the sanctity of the place. The four *toranas* (gateways) indicate the cardinal points, while the *vedika* (outer railing) symbolically separates the sacred from the profane.

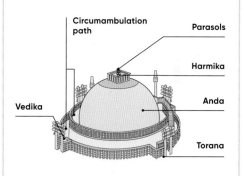

The key structural elements of the Great Stupa

▲ Buildings within buildings

The eastern torana (gateway) features an urban setting, with a crenellated loggia, barrel-roofed buildings, and balconies, whose different parts are treated like small units, or aedicules.

▲ Ritual walk

For visiting pilgrims to perform the circumambulation ritual (walking around the stupa), two paths were laid out, one reached via a double staircase. Their stone balustrades imitate post and rail construction.

▲ Spirit guardian

This bracket relief represents a *yakshi*, a female nature-spirit guardian, holding the branch of a flowering tree. Images of fertility, auspicious motifs to ward off evil, these entities guard the space.

A yasti (pillar) represents the axis that the world spins on

Parasols at the apex of the dome symbolize royalty and protection

Torana (gateway) at each cardinal point

The vedika (outer railing) denotes sacred space

Anda (solid dome) faced with bricks

KEY **ELEMENTS**

Early Buddhist architecture required the work of several groups of skilled workers, including stonemasons and sculptors. Excavated from the top down into steep hillsides, caves showcase a range of architectural forms.

PETRIFIED CARPENTRY

In many early Buddhist structures, both freestanding and rock-cut, timber architecture seems to have been transposed into stone. Craft workers retained the ornamental attributes of wooden structural elements and even imitated the texture and grain of timber.

▲ **Rock-cut palace**
At Bhaja, Maharashtra, Cave 12 (2nd century BCE) has a facade resembling a multistory palace, with balconies supported by brackets and decorative screens on either side of a large horseshoe window that reveals a rib cage of hooped beams.

▲ **Pillared prayer hall**
The 2nd-century BCE Great Chaitya at Karla, Maharashtra, is the largest rock-cut chaitya in India. Its barrel-roofed vault is adorned with wooden ribs that have no supporting role. Octagonal pillars separate the nave from the aisles.

DECORATION

Early Buddhist monuments are adorned with exquisite stone carvings, many showing scenes from the Buddha's life and *jatakas* (previous lives). They remind devotees of the various rituals they must carry out to achieve enlightenment.

▲ **Horseshoe motif**
Small, decorative, blind low-relief replicas of the large horseshoe window rhythmically punctuate the facade of Cave 7 at Bedsa (1st century BCE). Reinforcing the idea of connection between interior and exterior spaces, the horseshoe motif is also dominant in later Indian temple architecture.

▲ **Murals**
The cave complex of Ajanta contains the earliest surviving example of mural paintings in India. Created using the tempera technique, they cover the walls and ceiling. In Cave 1, dating back to the 5th century CE, attendants are depicted pouring water over a prince within a palatial building.

▲ **Human form**
By the 5th century CE, the Buddha appears with anthropomorphic features on the cave facades of Ajanta, in Maharashtra. In the chaitya of Cave 19, shown here, he is even caught emerging from the inner stupa, dispelling fear and imparting reassurance with his right hand.

EARLY BUDDHIST BUILDINGS

In the 5th century CE, Buddhism was thriving in India, and the styles and architectural forms that developed at this time spread beyond the Indian subcontinent.

1. Ajanta caves
Maharashtra, India, 2nd–1st centuries BCE and 5th–6th centuries CE

Nestled into a horseshoe-shaped escarpment, the 30 rock-cut caves of Ajanta are an astonishing architectural achievement. The first caves were excavated between the 2nd and 1st centuries BCE, while the later ones were excavated during the Vakataka dynasty in the 5th to 6th centuries CE.

2. Dhamekh Stupa, Sarnath
Uttar Pradesh, India, 6th century CE

This impressive stupa is a cylindrical structure made of bricks and stone. Though its core probably dates from the 3rd century BCE, the stupa has been enlarged many times, and is now 92 ft (28 m) in diameter. It commemorates the First Sermon and the formation of the Sangha, the Buddhist community.

3. Chaitya no 19, Ajanta
Maharashtra, India, 5th century CE

The facade of this chaitya demonstrates Buddhist architectural refinement at its peak. The horseshoe window, for instance, has a flowery crown and ears, dormers are repetitively placed on the eaves, and chains of barrel-roofed pavilions appear over the doorways and across the top of the facade.

▲ **Painted bas-relief**
The platforms and plazas that make up the Huaca de la Luna (Pyramid of the Moon) feature murals, such as this larger-than-life-size depiction of nude prisoners, destined for sacrifice.

EARLY SOUTH AMERICA

Early cultures in Andean South America were able to thrive across the region's highly varied environments, creating monumental constructions, sculpture, and art.

Andean South America stretches from southern Colombia through Ecuador, Peru, the western half of Bolivia, northwestern Argentina, and Chile. This area has five major environmental zones: coastal desert; highland valleys; lowland and highland tropical forests; and the Altiplano (high plain)—grassland over 13,120–16,400 ft (4,000–5,000 m) above sea level. Long before the Inca (see pp.156–159) dominated the region, ancient Andean cultures adapted to these habitats and created impressive architecture.

Caral, in the Norte Chico region of Peru is the oldest city in the New World, c. 2600 BCE. It had rectangular, terraced pyramids, once reaching 85 ft (26 m), and large circular ceremonial structures. Platforms were built with *shicra* (rock-filled, plant-fiber bags). The civilization arose without the development of ceramics, a hallmark of other complex societies worldwide.

Another important ancient Andean center is Chavín de Huántar (1100–500 BCE), one of the most impressive ceremonial sites in the Andean highlands, near the modern city of Huaraz, Peru. At its center was a complex of rectangular, stone masonry platforms. The New Temple platform was composed of three superimposed levels of interlocking galleries and rooms, which were covered by flat slabs and separated by adobe and stone walls. The interior walls of these passageways were sometimes painted, and a network of shafts provided ventilation.

The exterior of the platform was faced with dressed granite, which was once adorned with sculpted human and animal heads. Carvings include figures that combine the natural features of people, snakes, jaguars, caimans, and birds, all interwoven with intricate geometric and curvilinear designs. The Chavín art style went on to influence the art of other areas and cultures long after the site had been abandoned.

CEREMONIAL CENTER

The Moche culture, thriving in 100–700 CE, had its center near Trujillo, along the north coast of Peru. Here it constructed the giant Huaca del Sol (Pyramid of the Sun) and Huaca de la Luna (Pyramid of the Moon), the largest adobe mounds in the Americas. The pyramids were built in segments, in similar, discrete rectangular units using millions of stacked adobe bricks of molded, smoothed and sun-dried mud.

Huaca de la Luna is a 100-ft- (30-m-) high complex of platforms, walls, and courtyards. Intricate and monumental murals were found on the structures at the top. Elite tombs discovered buried in the platforms as well as the plazas, contained the remains of human sacrifices, confirming its ceremonial function.

RAIMONDI STONE

A stele from Chavín de Huántar depicts the Staff God, who is seen throughout Andean South America as a supreme deity. He holds two staffs and wears an elaborate headdress. This stele is a good example of "contour rivalry," a feature particular to Chavín art, whereby the elements of the design can be rotated 180 degrees and still be visually meaningful, or acquire additional meaning by revealing further imagery.

This illustration of carvings on the standing stone shows the focus on symmetry and interconnection in Chavín design.

CHAVÍN DE HUÁNTAR TEMPLE COMPLEX
ANCASH PROVINCE, PERU, 1100-500 BCE

A major ceremonial center in the north-central highlands of Peru, this site consists of an old and new temple, galleries, a U-shaped platform, and a circular sunken court. Sculptures include tenoned stone heads embedded in the upper portions of walls.

The New Temple rises about 45 ft (13 m) above the surrounding terrace

▲ **Corridor**
Passageways are around a meter wide and some of the galleries appear to be offering rooms—one filled with seashells and another containing over 800 ceramic vessels of food offerings.

The central core of the site included a complex of rectangular, stone masonry platforms

Sunken plaza in front of the New Temple

EARLY SOUTH AMERICAN BUILDINGS

▲ **Cerro Sechin,** Casma Valley, northern Peru, 1500 BCE
This site has several buildings of clay and stone, but the bas-reliefs (seen in this detail on the perimeter wall) are the most striking element. Images of warriors are interspersed with mutilated bodies and body parts, such as heads or intestines.

▲ **Chankillo,** south of Casma Valley, Peru, 400-50 BCE
The main feature of the remote site of Chankillo is a fortified temple with massive walls, restricted gates, and parapets. There is also an astronomical observatory consisting of 13 towers with staircases. These may have been used as solar horizon markers.

▲ **Huaca del Sol,** Trujillo, Peru, c. 100–800 CE
This pyramid rose over 130 ft (40 m) high and measured 1,100 ft by 525 ft (340 by 160 m). It contained over 130 million adobe bricks, many with symbols on them, perhaps identifying their makers. Structures and artifacts at the site suggest both secular and domestic activities of a political elite.

EARLY MESOAMERICA

Without metal tools, the wheel, or beasts of burden, Mesoamerican cultures built impressive structures, as seen at Teotihuacan, Mexico, one of the ancient word's most dramatic preindustrial cities.

The term "Mesoamerica" refers to the southern part of North America, extending to most of Central America, and is defined by the presence of common cultural traits. The ancient cultures living in Mesoamerica included inhabitants of the great city of Teotihuacan, the Zapotecs, Mixtecs, Toltecs, Olmecs, Maya, and Aztecs.

Teotihuacan ("the place of the gods" in Nahuatl, the Aztec and Toltec language) is in the valley just north of today's Mexico city. It emerged around 150 BCE and was inhabited until 700 CE. The city covered more than 7.8 sq miles (20 sq km) and was dominated by pyramids, ceremonial causeways, and elite residential complexes. At its peak, the population was between 125,000 and 200,000. Little is known of those who ruled, and evidence of royal tombs has yet to be found.

The city was fully urbanized and laid out in a grid that took its orientation from the north–south ceremonial avenue that is called the Street of the Dead. In this grid, there are at least 2,200 rectangular apartment compounds. These residences were generally arranged around a central courtyard and built with stone and volcanic rock, and then coated with a layer of clay and stucco. The most important buildings contained magnificent mural paintings.

Teotihuacan was divided into approximately 22 neighborhoods or *barrios*. There is evidence that people from other areas of Mesoamerica also lived here, including the Maya and Zapotecs. Each *barrio* maintained its own distinct identity in its style of buildings, burials, and craft goods.

CONTEMPORARY CULTURES

The Zapotec's capital was at Monte Alban, Oaxaca, Mexico. Here there is a concentration of architecture erected on an artificially flattened summit of a hill, with a defensive wall surrounding it. The majority of the population lived on the hillsides in residential terraces that were held in place by stone retaining walls. The complexes contained several rectangular rooms surrounding a patio. In the main plaza, several stelae were discovered, each of which depicted an emissary from Teotihuacan meeting a Zapotec official. This imagery confirms that there was an alliance between the two cultures.

A PLANNED CITY

The ceremonial center of Teotihuacan contained monumental architecture, such as the Pyramids of the Sun and Moon, and a *cuidadela*, which may have been the bureaucratic center of the city and included the Feathered Serpent Pyramid. The 1½-mile- (2.4-km-) long Street of the Dead runs from north to south, connecting at the *cuidadela* with an east to west avenue.

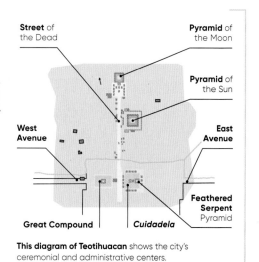

Street of the Dead

Pyramid of the Moon

Pyramid of the Sun

West Avenue

East Avenue

Feathered Serpent Pyramid

Great Compound

Cuidadela

This diagram of Teotihuacan shows the city's ceremonial and administrative centers.

PYRAMID OF THE SUN

TEOTIHUACAN, MEXICO, 0–150 CE

Standing at close to 230 ft (70 m) high, this pyramid was the oldest construction at Teotihuacan. Later, the pyramid was enhanced with a platform and the sides finished in the style of *talud-tablero* (see box below). A 337 ft (103 m) tunnel was constructed beneath the pyramid with chambers that may have contained a royal tomb.

▲ Main stairway

The 248 stairs on the pyramid are of varying sizes. The pyramid was built using a unit of length called a *vara* (32 in/0.83 m). The base is 260 *varas*, the number of days in the sacred calendar in ancient Mesoamerica.

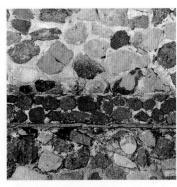

▲ Stonework detail

The main body of the pyramid was built in a single construction phase with clay, rocks, adobe bricks, and sand. The cut-stone exteriors of the pyramid are thought to have been faced with plaster and painted.

TALUD-TABLERO

One of the main characteristics of Teotihuacan architecture is the *talud-tablero*. *Tablero* (recessed rectangular panels) are separated by *talud* (sloping aprons). This architectural style is seen in many areas of Mesoamerica. Whether the presence of this architectural style indicates migration or colonization by Teotihuacanos or merely the exchange of ideas and styles with the city's neighbors is subject to debate.

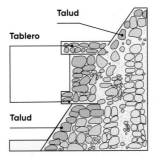

Talud

Tablero

Talud

Cross-section showing the *talud-tablero* style used at Teotihuacan

Thick, white lime plaster once covered the surface and was painted red

Step pyramid structure of concentric platforms or terraces

A temple, possibly made of wood and thatch, was probably located at the top

Stairway on the west side of the pyramid

KEY **ELEMENTS**

Mesoamerican pyramids were generally built in successive layers over time. Several superimposed structures are found in the Pyramid of the Moon, as well as in the Feathered Serpent Pyramid.

STEPPED PYRAMIDS AND PLATFORMS

A hallmark of Mesoamerican architecture is the presence of stepped pyramids, often with a temple on top that contained ritual items. These were built on stone platforms.

▼ Pyramid of the Moon

An example of a stepped pyramid with a platform in front of it, this 147 ft (45 m) pyramid, built in 150–200 CE, contained over 13 sacrificial victims, as well as sacrificial animals, including eagles, jaguars, pumas, wolves, and rattlesnakes.

LOAD BEARING

With the absence of pack animals in Mesoamerica, materials were carried by the people themselves using tumplines. A tumpline was a strap, probably woven from maguey (agave plant) fiber, which was placed across the forehead to support a sling on the back. All the stone used in the construction of Mesoamerican monumental architecture was carried in this way.

Mesoamerican merchants used the tumpline to carry goods.

DECORATIVE DETAILS

Stone carving is a feature at Teotihuacan and other early Mesoamerican sites, and the feathered serpent deity (Quetzalcoatl) is a common motif. Murals, especially in some of the Teotihuacan residences, also depict ancient deities.

▲ Engraved stelae

This is one of around 300 carved stone slabs that form a huge gallery at the hilltop site of Monte Alban, Oaxaca, Mexico. The slabs are referred to as the *danzantes* (dancers), but they probably represent prisoners of war, with blood running from their wounds.

▲ Intricate murals

A mural in the Tepantitla compound, Teotihuacan, shows butterflies and a water goddess with symbols relating to agricultural fertility. Dancing figures hold branches and speech scrolls (curling markings that indicate words or sounds) extend from their mouths.

▲ Frieze

A detail from the frieze on the *tablero* of the Pyramid of the Plumed Serpents, Xochicalco, Mexico, shows seated figures wearing quetzal headdresses followed by plumed serpents, creatures with a rattlesnake body and feathers of the quetzal bird.

EARLY MESOAMERICAN BUILDINGS

Stepped structures are a common feature of early Mesoamerican sites, such as Teotihuacan and Cholula, which were laid out in a grid pattern. Monte Alban is an exception, being built on a hilltop without a grid layout.

1. Feathered Serpent Pyramid
Teotihuacan, Mexico, 150–300 CE

This pyramid was constructed in three stages over the course of 150 years. It consisted of a rubble-filled interior with stone masonry and a sculpted facade. More than 200 individuals, mostly male warriors, were sacrificed and buried at the pyramid along with rich offerings.

2. North Platform at Monte Alban
Oaxaca, Mexico, c. 300 BCE–100 CE

This platform, which was located in the capital of the Zapotec culture (500 BCE–800 CE) has a wide stairway leading to a colonnaded hall. This overlooks a huge sunken patio, which is enclosed by high pyramidal platforms.

3. Great Pyramid of Cholula
Puebla, Mexico, 200 BCE–600 CE

The Great Pyramid was first constructed in 200 BCE with adobe bricks, which were painted red and black. In 280 CE it was extended with adobe and stone in the *talud-tablero* style.

2

DEVELOPMENT

300–1100

MAYA ARCHITECTURE

From 2000 BCE to 1697 CE, the ancient Maya built spectacular cities and monumental buildings supported by sustainable urban agriculture beneath the rainforest canopy of Mesoamerica.

▲ **Sculptured facade**
A detail from the facade of the Nunnery Quadrangle at the ancient Maya town of Uxmal, Yucatán, Mexico, shows a sculpture with a mosaic weave pattern and a snake—most likely a feathered serpent.

The Maya originated in what is now Central America and Mexico, centered in the countries of Belize, Guatemala (home to many of their modern descendants), the western portions of Honduras and El Salvador, the Yucatán Peninsula, and the Mexican states of Chiapas and Tabasco. Long before European invasions began in 1493, the Maya built extensive cities, including enormous temple-pyramids, standing stones (stelae), and ball courts, all without the use of metal tools, the wheel, or pack animals.

Maya cities generally contained a ceremonial center where their limestone temple-pyramids, palaces, and ball courts were located. Pyramids were stepped, with a central staircase and a small temple on top. These pyramids were built in layers; each generation would build a larger shell over the previous structure. Ball courts were used for their ball game (*pok-ta-pok* or *pitz*), a game using a rubber ball, and many centers had causeways (roadways) called *sacbe*.

Most buildings were supported by platforms built of rubble and earth. Architects took advantage of local limestone outcroppings for construction material, and limestone was also burned to make lime for plaster—either for floors or roads, or to coat the surfaces of masonry buildings. Structures were generally painted red, but traces of other pigments, such as yellow, blue, and black, still adhere to many Maya monuments.

ASTRONOMICAL ARCHITECTURE

E-Groups are typical Maya architectural complexes. These usually consist of a large stepped pyramid to the east of the complex, and three smaller structures to the west. Together, the buildings may have functioned as astronomical observatories. The Maya also made elaborate and accurate calendars, which were used in astronomical calculations and to record important events, such as conquests. The text sculpted into many Maya buildings, and written in codices (paper books), describes the calendar and the life histories of rulers, and is testament to another Maya achievement: they developed the most complex writing system of any pre-Columbian American culture.

HIEROGLYPHIC WRITING

The city of Copán in Honduras is famous for its Hieroglyphic Stairway. Each block of stone is carved with a hieroglyph making a total of 2,200 glyphs—the longest text in the Maya world. The glyphs name the city's rulers: the founder of Copán was K'inich Yax K'uk' Mo' (Great Sun First Quetzal Macaw), who took the throne in 426 CE.

The Hieroglyphic Stairway at Copán, Honduras, has 63 steps.

Nine levels, matching the Maya underworld, make up the pyramid

TEMPLE OF INSCRIPTIONS

PALENQUE, MEXICO, c. 690

This stepped funerary pyramid is named for the three panels of glyphic inscriptions inside the temple. These include a history of one of the greatest Maya rulers, K'inich Janaab' Pakal, who became king in 615 CE. His tomb is in the base of the structure.

TOMB FOR A KING

The king's tomb was accessed via a staircase beneath a trap door in the rear chamber of the upper temple. In addition to the staircase, a narrow, stone-lined tube ran from the temple floor down into the burial chamber. Too narrow to accommodate a person, it was perhaps for speaking to the spirit of the king. A roof comb once topped the temple but is now missing.

Pakal's tomb was built before the stairs, pyramid, and temple.

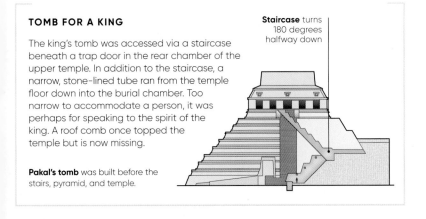

Staircase turns 180 degrees halfway down

▲ **Reliefs on the temple**
The piers (wide columns) outside the temple bear hieroglyphic text and once had colorfully painted stucco reliefs, including standing figures that relate to the royal dynasty.

▲ **Tomb**
The limestone sarcophagus in the tomb was richly carved, bearing portraits of Pakal's ancestors. Inside, Pakal's remains were found, resplendent in jade jewelry and with a mosaic jade death mask.

◄ **Pakal's sarcophagus lid**
Sculpted on the solid limestone lid is a depiction of the reclining king being resurrected from the Earth, or perhaps descending into the underworld only to rise up to the heavens to be reborn as a god.

Upper temple has a frontal gallery and rear chamber

One of six piers covered in stucco reliefs

A flight of 69 stairs ascends the front of the pyramid

KEY ELEMENTS

The Maya have found harmonious ways to live within an impressive diversity of ecosystems across a very large area, and their ancient architecture reflects that range.

PYRAMID-TEMPLES AND PLATFORMS

Maya "pyramids" were not strictly pyramidal: their four faces did not meet at a common point like Egyptian pyramids. Accessed by stairs, they were used mainly for ceremonies carried out at the top and watched from below.

◀ **Pyramid-temple**
Temple 1 at Tikal is a good example of a stepped funerary pyramid. The huge roof comb was once decorated with a giant sculpture of the king Jasaw Chan K'awiil, entombed there in 734 CE.

▲ **Platform**
Used for rites and ceremonies, platforms were a common feature of Maya architecture. The Platform of the Cones (Venus platform) at Chichén Itzá, Mexico, was constructed in the *talud-tablero* style with feathered serpent heads.

STELAE

Made out of limestone, stelae were standing stones with portraits of the rulers in high relief on one side and texts detailing their exploits on the other sides. These carved upright stones are found at many Maya cities.

▲ **Portrait of a king**
As was typical, this stela from Copán, Honduras (erected 711–736 CE), shows the image of a Maya ruler: Waxaclajuun Ub'aah K'awiil. In the detailed carving, the king holds a double-headed bar, an instrument of royalty, to his chest.

CORBELED ARCHES

The corbeled arch was a distinctive feature of Maya construction, used to support the superstructure of a roof. These were constructed from horizontal layers (courses) of stone, with each layer projecting a little beyond the layer below.

▶ **Successive arches**
This example of the corbeled arches at the Palace of Palenque, the ruler's residence, shows how the lower layers of the arch rely on the upper layers to stabilize the structure, which would otherwise fall in on itself.

DECORATIVE ELEMENTS

Both plaster and stone were used to decorate Maya temple-pyramids. Stucco was hand modeled and painted, while stone-carved features were coated first with plaster then painted. Early stucco reliefs later gave way to massive decorations set on roof combs.

▲ **Stucco mask**
This stucco head of a deity on a stairway at Cerros, Belize, is shown with chin strap and earflares (ornaments with sacred significance), framed by a double-headed serpent motif.

▲ **Roof combs**
Crowning the top of Maya temples, as on the Temple of the Sun, Palenque, roof combs were modeled in either stucco or stone mosaics crafted over tenoned (interlocking) stone.

MAYA BUILDINGS

Around 900 CE the Maya world went through a transitional period in terms of the location of their cities and style of their art and architecture. The influence of ideas from central Mexico is quite clear from this time.

> "... the laying and polishing of the stones are as perfect as [...] the best modern masonry."
>
> **John Lloyd Stephens**, *Incidents of Travel in Yucatan, Vol I & II*, 1843

1. Structure 19 (The Labyrinth)
Yaxchilan, Mexico, 700–800 CE
This temple is composed of nine vaulted chambers located on three levels and connected by stairways. The southeast facade has four doors with three door-sized niches in between them, creating the impression of seven functional doorways.

2. Copán ball court
Honduras, 738 CE
The Maya ball court was laid out in an I-shape and divided into two halves by a line perpendicular to its long axis. Opposing teams faced each other across this dividing line. The ball, a rubber sphere, could be hit with the elbows, hips, and knees, but never the head, hands, or feet.

3. El Castillo (Temple of Kukulcán),
Chichén Itzá, Yucatán Peninsula, 1000 CE
This pyramid has nine terraces and a flat-topped temple with four doorways and two feathered serpent columns. The four staircases have 91 stairs each, which, together with the top platform, gives a collective total of 365 steps—the number of days in the solar year.

ANCESTRAL PUEBLO

Villages in the form of towering, multistory apartment buildings were a hallmark of the architecture of the Ancestral Pueblo, an ancient Indigenous culture from the southwest United States.

The term pueblo (Spanish for village), was used by Spanish colonists to refer to the communal buildings of the Ancestral Pueblo (formerly Anasazi), whose culture reached its peak between 750 and 1350 in the southwest US. Villages were usually made up of complexes, sometimes five stories high, built from adobe bricks, stone blocks, and other local materials. They also often had kivas—circular, underground rooms (see box below).

Chaco Canyon, in northwest New Mexico, was a major center of Ancestral Pueblo culture between 850 and 1150 and is known for its monumental public and ceremonial buildings consisting of multistory residential complexes and kivas. Here, the Ancestral Pueblo built at least nine large towns or "Great Houses" and many small villages. The layout of Pueblo Bonito is typical of the region's planned communities. A huge, D-shaped complex with more than 700 rooms, it was like a four-story apartment building. There was limited access to the inner rooms, which were used for storage, and the outer rooms, which had T-shaped

windows, were used as living areas. The walls were core and veneer—a rubble infill bonded with mud was covered with finely cut sandstone and faced with adobe plaster. The rooms were around central courtyards, and the most important rooms, such as the kivas, were at the back of the complex. Kivas were round ritual rooms. They could be small or very large, such as the Great Kiva at Pueblo Bonito, which was 65 ft (20 m) in diameter.

At least 200,000 wooden beams were brought to the canyon from distances more than 50 miles (80 km) away. Lengths of timber called *viga* were used to support the ceilings and different stories. The dry climate has preserved the wood, so archaeologists have been able to use dendrochronology (the study of tree rings) to date the buildings there.

CLIFF DWELLINGS

Later, many pueblos were built into cliff faces in positions that were easy to defend, such as those at Mesa Verde in southwest Colorado. As elsewhere, the ground floors of these buildings were used as granaries. They did not have doors and had to be accessed from the roof. People used ladders to reach the upper floors.

By late 1200, the Ancestral Pueblo had moved south, away from drought and perhaps wars. One of the places they settled in was Taos, New Mexico, the site of Taos Pueblo—a building that has been lived in for centuries.

◀ **Aligned doorways**
This view inside Pueblo Bonito shows how the doorways in the towering sandstone walls were often built in line with one another.

KIVAS

A kiva was a circular, underground room used for domestic, ritual, and social functions. It had a roof made of beams and a wide masonry bench all around it. On the floor was a central hearth with a deflector, vent outlets, and a *sipapu*. This was a small hollow in the floor that symbolized the "navel of the earth," where the Ancestral Pueblos' ancestors were said to have first emerged into the world.

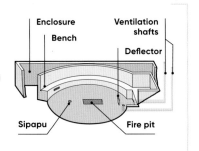

Enclosure   Ventilation shafts
Bench   Deflector
Sipapu   Fire pit

This cross-section of a kiva shows the key parts of the ritual structure.

PUEBLO BONITO

CHACO CANYON, NEW MEXICO, 850–1150

Built in stages over the centuries, Pueblo Bonito is one of several Great Houses in the area with the characteristic D-shaped layout, internal storage rooms, exterior high-ceilinged residential rooms several stories tall, and kivas.

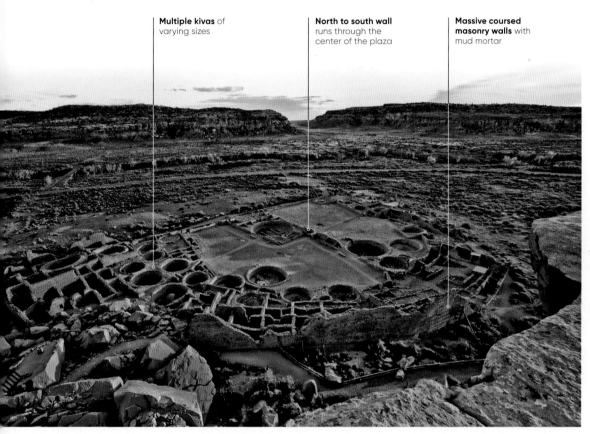

Multiple kivas of varying sizes

North to south wall runs through the center of the plaza

Massive coursed masonry walls with mud mortar

▲ T-shaped doorway

The outer rooms have T-shaped doorways and windows. They face the courtyard and served as living quarters. The courses of stone (all the same height) were carefully laid.

▲ Protruding beams

The wooden beams or *viga* used for horizontal support usually protrude from the walls. The wood has been preserved by the dry climate at Chaco Canyon.

PUEBLOS

▲ Casa Rinconada, Chaco Canyon, c. 11th century
This Great House has many kivas, including this Great Kiva. A ceremonial meeting place, it once had a roof made of pine beams and access was by a ladder. It is 63 ft (19.2 m) across and the walls were originally at least 11 ft (3.4 m) tall.

▲ Cliff Palace, Mesa Verde, 1190–1280
One of the larger cliffside villages at Mesa Verde, this has 150 rooms and 23 kivas and was probably a center for the surrounding community. It was built from sandstone blocks and wooden beams bound together with mortar made from soil, ash, and water.

▲ Taos Pueblo, New Mexico, 1000–1450
This adobe complex, which has been occupied for centuries and is still lived in today, shows how each floor is set back from the one below in Pueblo buildings, like a stepped pyramid. The roofs on one floor form terraces for the floor above them.

▲ **Patterns in stone**
The granite slabs of Great Zimbabwe were often laid in geometrical patterns. This herringbone motif appears occasionally, as do others featuring chevrons and squares.

AFRICAN FORTIFICATIONS

The massive encircling stone wall and interior enclosures of Great Zimbabwe are the most striking architectural achievement of ancient Africa south of the Sahara.

As kingdoms developed in ancient and medieval Africa, fortifications became a feature of the landscape. The pharaonic fort of Buhen, in southern Egypt, was a complex arrangement of battlements and buttresses that covered 140,000 sq ft (13,000 sq m). Likewise, the earthwork walls of Benin ran not only the 9-mile (15-km) circuit of the city itself, but extended over 9,320 miles (15,000 km) into the surrounding area. Most impressive of all was Great Zimbabwe, in the southeast of modern Zimbabwe, which formed the focal point of a medieval kingdom of the Shona people. Its massive dry-stone walls are not only the largest by far of the area's *dzimbabwe* (large houses of stone) fortifications—they are unparalleled anywhere in Africa.

MATERIALS AND TECHNIQUES
Granite hills provided the basic material with which Great Zimbabwe was built. The stone naturally fractured from the hill face, producing regular, cuboid pieces that lent themselves to

"Among the gold mines of the plains ... there is a fortress built of stones of marvelous size."

Vicente Pegado, Portuguese official from Sofala (in Mozambique), 1531

being laid in successive courses and being shaped by dolerite hammerstones. The resulting walls and enclosures covered over 1,800 acres (730 hectares), the centerpiece being the Great Enclosure, the walls of which were up to 20 ft (6 m) wide and 36 ft (11 m) tall.

The walls of Great Zimbabwe were laid without foundations or mortar, their close-fitting granite blocks and wide bases ensuring their stability. They were raised to their optimal height and then extended on either side without scaffolding. They had no wall-top walkways, which limited their defensive use during a siege, but their enormous height would have deterred all but the most determined attackers. Within the walls there is evidence of a number of buildings (possibly dwellings) and ceremonial platforms, made mostly of *daga*—a locally abundant red clay soil that was also daubed onto the exterior of the walls to create a uniform appearance. These remains are a reminder that the Great Zimbabwe complex was both a fortification and a living capital.

ZIMBABWE'S BIRD
The most unusual archaeological finds at Great Zimbabwe were eight soapstone birds, which were originally attached to walls and monoliths across the site. Although they are not naturalistic—their legs are unnaturally plump and their wings lack plumage—they possibly represent the bateleur eagle, which was sacred to the Shona people. The bird has since become the national emblem of Zimbabwe, and features on banknotes and coins.

A soapstone bird, perched on a column in Great Zimbabwe

GREAT ENCLOSURE

GREAT ZIMBABWE, 12TH–15TH CENTURIES

Also known as the Elliptical Building, the Great Enclosure has a circumference of 820 ft (250 m) and contains more stones than the rest of the ruins combined. It has Great Zimbabwe's finest quality stonework, and includes several earlier enclosures as well as *daga* platforms and dwellings.

Rectangular entranceway

Stone structures predating the Great Enclosure

Thick outer walls replaced an earlier wall

▲ **Narrow passage**
On the east side, most of an old wall was retained as a new wall was built, creating a narrow passage between the two.

▲ **Conical tower**
This tower may have been a granary, used to store important grain crops in a safe and dry environment.

AFRICAN FORTIFICATIONS

▲ **Hill complex,** Great Zimbabwe, 900
Set on a narrow granite ridge above a sheer cliff, the Hill Complex of Great Zimbabwe consists of a series of walled enclosures separated by narrow curved passages. The oldest part of Great Zimbabwe, it has 16-ft- (5-m-) deep *daga* (earthen and mud brick) deposits that date to around 900 CE.

▲ **Khami,** Zimbabwe, 1450
Capital of the Rozwi state, which replaced Great Zimbabwe at around 1450, Khami, west of Bulawayo, is dotted with terraces and platforms. It was built from laminar granite and dolerite (harder stones than were used at Great Zimbabwe), and features retaining walls and foundations.

▲ **Naletale,** Zimbabwe, 17th century
The capital of the Rozwi kingdom after it moved from Khami, Naletale consists of an elliptical stone enclosure of dry-stone granite walls, which feature herringbone and chevron patterning with inserts of red-brown ironstone. Small towers on the outer wall may have belonged to subsidiary chieftains.

▲ **Colorful decoration**

Unique among the Lalibela rock-hewn churches, Biete Mariam's carved interior is adorned with a series of vividly colored biblical scenes and geometric ornamentation.

ETHIOPIAN ROCK CHURCHES

Painstakingly carved out of the ground or cliff faces, the extraordinary rock churches of Ethiopia are one of the earliest surviving examples of buildings for Christian worship, and many are still in use today.

The empire of the ancient Aksum civilization, which encompassed parts of modern-day Ethiopia, Eritrea, and Sudan, was an early home to Christianity. The region formally adopted the religion in the 4th century—one of the first parts of the world to do so—but the presence of Christianity there can be dated back to the 1st century. The area has a remarkable collection of around 200 rock-hewn Christian churches, of which the most significant 11 are in Lalibela, in the northern Amhara region of Ethiopia. These were commissioned by King Gebre Mesqel Lalibela of the Zagwe dynasty, who ruled between 1181 and 1221. In the Middle Ages, when Christianity was on the rise in Europe, the Ethiopian Orthodox Church was isolated and literally driven underground.

LABORIOUS EXCAVATION

Legend states that King Gebre Mesqel Lalibela carved the churches at Lalibela himself with the help of angels, but in reality their construction took teams of builders and

"The entire edifice had been shaped the way a sculptor frees a figure from a raw block of stone."

Nicholas Clapp, *Sheba*, 2001

craftsmen around 24 years to complete. The churches were created by slowly digging down and removing material, using handheld axes, hammers, and chisels. Once excavated, the resulting blocks of stone were further carved out to form rooms inside, with doors, windows, floors, and stairs. The region's characteristic "tuff" stone—a type of solidified volcanic ash—is soft, which means that it is relatively easy to cut and shape.

Externally, the churches are austere, with most modeling confined to the windows and doors, which often feature Aksumite motifs or Islamic-style ogee curves. Interiors are usually plain, but some have richly colored murals.

Four of Lalibela's churches are freestanding, while the others are partially attached to existing sections of rock. A network of trenches and tunnels links them together, providing access for church officials, pilgrims, and visitors. As well as being a UNESCO World Heritage Site, Lalibela remains an important focus of Christian pilgrimage.

A NEW JERUSALEM

Located in the Simien Mountains in the Ethiopian Highlands, the complex of churches at Lalibela was seen as representing Jerusalem at a time when Muslim conquest of the Holy Land made pilgrimage to the real Jerusalem very difficult. The development of these places of worship, laboriously carved into cliffs or excavated out of the ground in inhospitable mountainous terrain, was driven by a quest for spiritual isolation as well as the need for a concealed and enduring form of architecture.

The Simien Mountains provided a remote and rugged rocky landscape.

Carved stone string courses break up the imposing mass

Blind windows in the Aksumite style feature on the lowest story

The door faces west as the church sits on an east-west axis in the Christian convention

BETE GIYORGIS

LALIBELA, ETHIOPIA, 12TH–13TH CENTURIES

With a cruciform shape and robustly modeled facades, Bete Giyorgis (The Church of St. George) is one of Lalibela's most notable churches. Constructed from the top downward, the freestanding monolith stands more than 43 ft (13 m) below ground.

◀ **Cruciform plan**
The distinctive form of Bete Giyorgis was created by outlining a Greek cross on the rock face and then digging down to create a cruciform-shaped block.

◀ **Ogee window**
A feature of Islamic and Gothic architecture, the double curved ogee arch shapes a window that is supported by Aksumite "monkey head" corbels. It is decorated with carvings of vine tendrils.

ROCK CHURCHES

▲ **Biete Abba Libanos,** Lalibela, Ethiopia, 12th–13th centuries
Semi-monolithic, "The House of Abbot Libanos" is attached to the rock face above. It was carved from front to back rather than from the top down. Like all the Lalibela churches, it is still used by the Ethiopian Orthodox Church.

▲ **Biete Medhane Alem,** Lalibela, Ethiopia, 12th–13th centuries
Carved with cruciform and round arched openings, the freestanding, monolithic structure of Biete Medhane Alem (the House of the Redeemer of the World) is the largest of the Lalibela churches. It is also home to the revered 12th-century Lalibela Cross.

▲ **Abuna Gebre Mikael,** Tigray, Ethiopia, c. 14th century
The domed interior of Abuna Gebre Mikael is beautifully decorated with colorful frescoes. Carved into a sandstone cliff in the Gheralta Mountains, the church stands in Ethiopia's far northern Tigray region.

EARLY CHRISTIAN AND BYZANTINE ARCHITECTURE

The first Christians and their successors in the Byzantine Empire developed new buildings in which to worship—churches and baptisteries. The most spectacular were covered in bright mosaics.

From the 1st century CE onward, Christianity spread from Palestine to other parts of the Mediterranean, notably the coasts of Asia Minor, Greece, and Rome. From these centers, Christian missionaries and travelers took the faith around the Roman Empire, but they were often persecuted, so they worshipped discreetly, in private houses and other suitable buildings.

In the 4th century, the Roman emperor Constantine I gave Christianity official recognition, and Christians were able to build dedicated churches. At first, they modeled these on the usual Roman building for public assembly, the basilica. There was no standard form of Christian basilica, but these buildings usually had a long main section, the nave, for the congregation, and a smaller separate space at the east end, where the clergy celebrated mass. Such churches varied widely in size and sometimes formed part of a group, with other structures, such as a baptistery, the tombs of prominent figures, and perhaps a bell tower built nearby.

CROSSES AND DOMES

Constantinople (now Istanbul), capital of the eastern Roman Empire, became a major Christian center. As well as building basilicas, the Byzantines developed a new kind of church, with a cross-shaped plan, a dome at the center, and sometimes other domes in the roof, too. The most outstanding of these was the great church of Hagia Sophia (the divine wisdom), which was so large and awe-inspiring that it influenced the builders of many smaller churches.

The structures of these domed churches and basilicas, and the techniques used to decorate them, were learned from the Romans, but these new buildings were very different. Built at a time of worsening climate, shrinking populations, and plague, Byzantine churches and cathedrals reused cladding stones, column shafts, and anything else they could from disused pagan Roman buildings. These buildings began a trend in which Christian churches and cathedrals became the largest, most elaborate, and most prestigious buildings in Europe for nearly 1,000 years.

BAPTISTERIES

Baptism is a purification rite that marks a person's formal entry into the Christian church. Originally, it took place either in a room within a church or in a baptistery building. Early Christian baptisteries, such as the Lateran Baptistery in Rome, were usually small buildings, square or octagonal in shape, with a font containing holy water in the middle.

The Lateran Baptistery, founded by Pope Sixtus III in 440

HAGIA SOPHIA

ISTANBUL, TURKEY, 532–537

Architects Isidorus of Miletus and Anthemius of Tralles were experts in geometry, which helped them design the dome of Hagia Sophia. The size of the building and its beautiful mosaics made Hagia Sophia the most famous church in the Byzantine Empire.

▲ Crowning glory
The central dome is 107 ft (33 m) in diameter, making it the second-largest dome of the ancient world after the Pantheon in Rome. The mosaics, made of stones and glass, glitter in the light from the many surrounding windows.

▲ Grand entrance
The narthex is a corridor that acts as a porch and gathering space for people as they enter the church. Its roof is made of a series of cross vaults, and its walls are clad in sumptuous colored marbles.

CENTRALIZED PLAN

The dome covers the center of the church, which has a cross-shaped plan. Beyond the eastern semidome is the semicircular apse, where the main altar once stood. Upper galleries to the sides and rear of the church accommodated further worshippers. The entrance courtyard, or atrium, was added later.

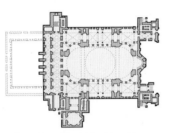

Floor plan of Hagia Sophia, with its vaulting shown in broken lines

Central dome, atop four supporting piers

Dome supports counter the outward thrust of the structure

Windows pierce the drum beneath the dome

Minarets, added from the 15th century, when the church became a mosque

Rows of windows, separated by masses of supporting masonry

Semidome (eastern)

Apse (eastern focus of the building)

Outer wall of thick masonry

KEY ELEMENTS

Byzantine builders were highly skilled at developing cross-plan churches and basilicas. They excelled at decorative detail, combining purely ornamental carvings with a variety of images that honored patrons and church leaders, and illustrated Christian teachings.

BASILICAS

Byzantine basilicas varied greatly in size, ranging from small, simple buildings to the vast churches of Rome and Ravenna. The basic layout could be enlarged by adding aisles on either side, which made room for a larger congregation and for priests to process through the building. The focus of the interior was the sanctuary. This was the most sacred space in the building, where the finest mosaics were usually located.

▲ **Aisled basilica**
Built c.549, Sant' Apollinare in Classe, Italy, was designed to be as spacious as possible. Light streams in from its side windows, and from a clerestory—a row of windows above the arches.

BELL TOWERS

Although church bells were introduced in the 4th century, bell towers were uncommon before the later Byzantine period. They were built as close to the church as possible, on sites that could bear their enormous weight. Over the years, these towers became valued landmarks for travelers.

▲ **Round tower**
The tower of Sant' Apollinare in Classe, Italy, has large upper openings that enable the sound of the bells to carry. Built before the coast silted up, it was a helpful landmark for sailors.

CARVED DETAILS

Byzantine sculptors used both abstract and figurative elements in their designs, and produced capitals in several different styles. They adopted the Romans' most popular design of carved scrolls and acanthus leaves, but also experimented with new styles, combining abstract shapes with images of animals that represented Christian themes. The lamb (symbolizing Christ) and the dove (the Holy Spirit) were common motifs. Working with great precision, sculptors gave the empire's most important churches extraordinarily detailed capitals.

Corinthian design, based on a Roman model, in St. Demetrius, Thessaloniki

Basket-weave pattern, combined with dove motifs, in Hagia Sophia, Istanbul

Intricate carved roundels, with lambs and crosses, at San Vitale, Ravenna

DOMES

From Italy to Constantinople, domes became a common feature of churches built in the cross-plan style. Smaller churches usually had a single, central dome—larger ones, when they could be afforded, had additional domes over the sanctuary, the nave, and the transepts.

▲ Dome interiors
The stone ribs that supported a dome divided it into segments. These were often filled with glittering mosaics of biblical figures, such as the portraits of saints in the dome at St. Savior in Chora, Istanbul.

▲ Dome exteriors
Byzantine domes were often relatively tall and topped with cupolas shaped like miniature domes, which made them even taller. This extra height meant that churches such as San Marco in Venice towered over their surroundings.

MOSAICS

Byzantine artists applied the Roman technique of mosaic-making to Christian subjects. They used tesserae of colored stone or glass, sometimes combined with gold leaf, and occasionally angled the pieces to catch the light from different directions.

◄ Line and pattern
Early Christian mosaics, such as the portrait of St. Theodorus in Saints Cosmas and Damian in Rome, show how artists used simple lines to delineate facial features. These were often combined with intricate patterns on fabrics.

▲ Image of power
A 6th-century mosaic in San Vitale, Ravenna, shows Byzantine emperor Justinian I standing among members of the clergy. Bearing a crown and a halo (and holding a bowl to be used in the mass), he embodies both secular and spiritual power.

▲ Light and shade
By the 13th century, Byzantine artists were using different shades of color to produce mosaics of great subtlety. The larger-than-life Deesis in Hagia Sophia, Istanbul, features carefully graded skin tones and a variety of blues in Christ's robe.

BYZANTINE BUILDINGS

Byzantine architecture spread west from Istanbul as far as Italy, as well as eastward in Turkey and beyond. The eastern style was more flamboyant, featuring elaborate curved domes.

1. Church of Panagia Kapnikerea
Athens, Greece, c. 1050

Built on the site of a pre-Christian temple, Kapnikerea is one of the oldest churches in Athens. It consists of a main cross-shaped, domed church, a smaller chapel, and a large entrance narthex with multiple doorways.

2. Cathedral of St. Sophia
Novgorod, Russia, 1045–1050

The onion-shaped domes of St. Sophia are typical of 11th-century Russian architecture. Built on tall drums, they are elongated at the top, which gives them extra height, and helps to throw off heavy snow.

3. The Chora Church
Istanbul, Turkey, 11th century

The Chora Church has many of the key features of Byzantine architecture—domes set above generous windows, an apse, and walls with blind arcades that mirror the shapes of the windows. The minaret is a later addition.

4. Mausoleum of Galla Placidia
Ravenna, Italy, c. 450

The Mausoleum of Galla Placidia was built by a Christian empress, perhaps in thanks for surviving a shipwreck. It contains mosaics that depict scenes from the life of a saint (possibly St. Vincent) who drowned at sea.

1

2

4

3

5

6

7

5. St. Mark's Basilica
Venice, Italy, 11th century onward

St. Mark's evolved over several centuries to become one of the most elaborate Byzantine churches. It has a highly ornate exterior, complete with colored stonework and dazzling mosaics.

6. St. Sophia Cathedral
Kyiv, Ukraine, 11th century

Boasting 13 domes, St. Sophia contains the tombs of Kyiv's rulers from the time of its construction until the Mongol invasion of 1240. Damaged in the 13th-century conflict, the cathedral was restored in the 16th century.

7. Basilica of San Vitale
Ravenna, Italy, 6th century

Built in one of the capitals of the late Roman Empire, San Vitale, like many Byzantine churches, has a plain, brick exterior but a highly ornate interior. It has an octagonal central space.

▲ Domes and semi-domes
The Sultan Ahmed Mosque, also known as the Blue Mosque, in Istanbul, is a 17th-century Ottoman building roofed with a combination of domes and semi-domes. Its ceilings are covered with thousands of ceramic tiles.

▲ Corbeled dome
The cells of an ancient monastery on the island of Skellig Michael, off Ireland, are what are known as corbeled domes. Each stone layer is offset from the one below it, producing sloping walls that meet at the top like a dome.

"An angelic, not a human, design."

Michelangelo, describing the Pantheon in Rome, Italy, early 1500s

DOMES

Designed to be imposing, domes both dominate landscapes and open up interiors. Expensive because of the engineering challenges they pose, large domes tend to adorn only the grandest of buildings.

Small, domed structures made of branches and thatch were constructed in prehistoric times. Larger, mud-brick domes date back to at least the 2nd millennium BCE, when they were built in Mesopotamia. Similar brick structures were also erected in the 1st millennium BCE in Europe and China, but large domes made of durable material such as stone only became widespread during the Roman period. Societies influenced by Rome continued to build domes for centuries, like those constructed in Europe during the Renaissance period and in Turkey under Ottoman rule.

BUILDING A DOME

Domes are made in many shapes and sizes. They can have circular, elliptical, or polygonal bases, and in profile can be semicircular, shallow, pointed, or even onion-shaped. To build one, all but the smallest domes pose huge engineering challenges, including how to secure this dramatic feature to the top of a square or rectangular building. Builders of the ancient world solved this problem by inventing ingenious structures, such as squinches and pendentives (see box), which helped transfer the weight of the dome to the walls beneath it.

Domes are also made of many different materials. The first large-scale domes were generally made of brick or stone, but these required a great deal of support from the walls and piers beneath them. Architects then devised ways of making domes lighter (by using lighter stone or giving them thinner shells) or by strengthening them with concealed vaults. By the 19th century, cheap fossil fuels enabled the construction of strong, comparatively light iron frameworks to underpin new domes.

Today, geodesic domes made of interlocking steel struts enclose the largest volumes of space using the smallest possible amount of building material. There is an appealing drama to the curve of a dome—ancient or modern—rising above a roofscape composed largely of straight lines.

▲ Elliptical dome
Resting directly on the building's elliptical walls, the huge dome of London's Royal Albert Hall is an iron frame filled with glass. In spite of its relative lightness, it still weighs more than 545 tons.

▲ Geodesic dome
Made of hundreds of struts braced together to form hexagons or triangles, geodesic domes, such as the Biosphere in Montreal, are very light in weight, but can enclose extremely large spaces.

SQUINCHES AND PENDENTIVES

To get from four piers to a circular dome requires clever engineering. Sasanian builders bridged diagonally from pier to pier with squinches, creating a robust octagon on which to stand the dome. Byzantine engineers invented the pendentive: a larger dome rising from the piers, cut into by arches and cut off at the top, leaving a circle on which to stand the new dome.

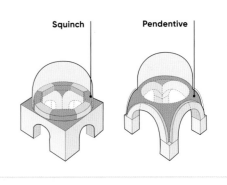

Squinch   Pendentive

EARLY ISLAMIC ARCHITECTURE

The religion that emerged from the deserts of the Arabian Peninsula in the
7th century inspired new forms of architecture, which spread rapidly around
the eastern Mediterranean, North Africa, and up into Europe.

"Islamic architecture" is a catch-all phrase for buildings that were constructed by a diverse array of peoples spread across a vast geographical region over several centuries. The factors that shaped this architecture often owed more to topography, climate, the materials that were available, and existing cultural traditions than they did to religion, but a distinctive architectural style was already evident in the early Islamic era, the prime example of which was the mosque.

The earliest Arabian mosques were simple, mud-walled, courtyard gathering places. As Islam spread, and political power became centered on Damascus (under first the Umayyad dynasty: 661–750) and then Baghdad (under the Abbasid dynasty: 750–1258), the mosque developed its own distinct architectural

vocabulary. Initially, this was influenced by other, pre-Islamic artistic traditions. Two of the earliest surviving Islamic monuments— the Umayyad-era Dome of the Rock (692) and the Umayyad Mosque (see pp.94–95)—

THE ORIGINS OF ISLAM

In 570 CE, Muhammad ibn Abdallah was born in Mecca. According to Islamic belief, he was visited by the angel Jibrail (Gabriel), who revealed to him what would become the Qur'an. Although he was driven out of Mecca, he returned to the city and conquered it—and the following year, a Muslim army set out to convert the Arabian tribes to Islam.

The Kaaba in Mecca became the most sacred site in Islam

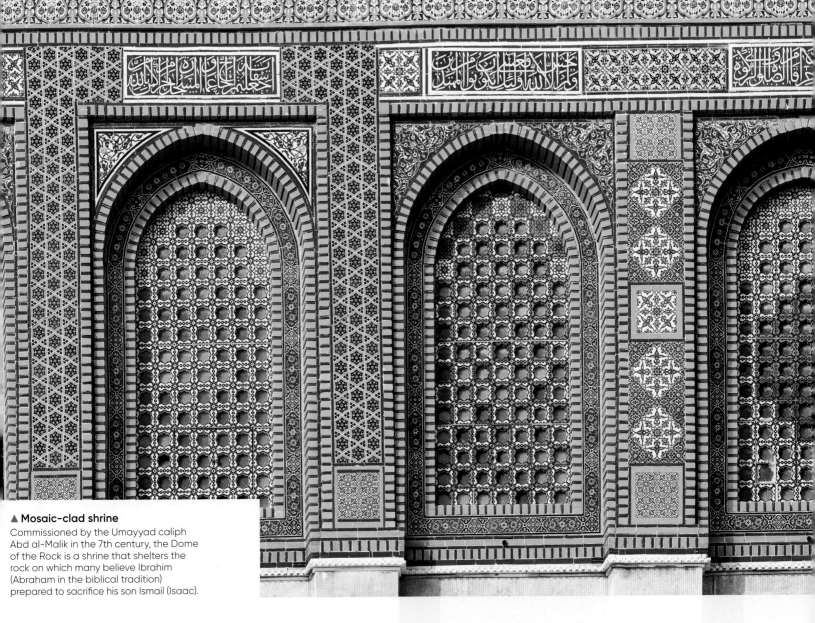

▲ Mosaic-clad shrine
Commissioned by the Umayyad caliph Abd al-Malik in the 7th century, the Dome of the Rock is a shrine that shelters the rock on which many believe Ibrahim (Abraham in the biblical tradition) prepared to sacrifice his son Ismail (Isaac).

are both covered in dazzling mosaics crafted by artisans who were steeped in the Byzantine tradition. The Umayyads also took from Greek and Roman architecture, often quite literally, incorporating elements such as columns and capitals into their own buildings. Likewise, the Abbasids built in the Mesopotamian tradition, using fired bricks rather than mud brick—the fire fuel to bake these bricks made them much more expensive, but also much more durable.

DEVELOPING STYLES
As Muslim armies marched across North Africa, new dynasties emerged that continued to take local building traditions and adapt them to Islam. In 711, Muslims from North Africa (the Moors) invaded Spain, which at the time was divided between warring Christian states.

The conquerors called this new territory "Al-Andalus," and they turned it into one of the world's leading cultural and economic centers.

Moorish architecture borrowed from earlier Spanish Visigothic traditions, adding elements originating from Syria. Another dynasty, known as the Fatimids (969–1171), arose in Tunisia. The Fatimids seized Cairo and made it their capital,

which remained the regional center until its rulers were vanquished by the Ottomans more than 500 years later. During this time, the city's artisans refined key elements of Islamic architecture. These included new kinds of domes and arches, and decorative carvings that featured intricate arabesques, Arabic script, and geometrical patterns.

"He sought to build a mosque that would be a wonder to the world ..."
Historian al-Maqdisī, on al-Walīd, architect of the Great Mosque of Damascus, 10th century

UMAYYAD MOSQUE

DAMASCUS, SYRIA, 705–715

Also known as the Great Mosque of Damascus, the Umayyad Mosque is the world's oldest surviving stone mosque. Occupying the site of a former Roman-era temple, and later a Christian church, it set down a marker proclaiming the legitimacy of Umayyad rule. Although the Dome of the Treasury and the Minaret of the Bride were added during the Abbasid period (750–1258), and the building has since been restored several times, the Umayyad Mosque retains its original design.

The Umayyad Mosque seen from above

▶ Minarets

The Great Mosque has three minarets: the Minaret of the Bride, which dates back to the Abbasid era in the 9th century; the Minaret of Isa, which dates to the mid 13th century; and the Minaret of Qaitbay (right), which dates to the late 15th century.

FLOOR PLAN

Early mosques featured a courtyard for outdoor prayers, including a covered hall that sheltered the faithful from the midday sun. The Great Mosque embellished this basic design, adding a basilica-style prayer hall with three parallel aisles and a perpendicular nave leading from the mosque's entrance to the mihrab (prayer niche).

Plan of the Grand Mosque

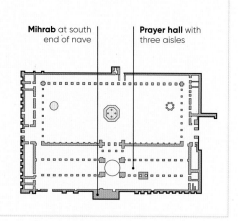

Mihrab at south end of nave

Prayer hall with three aisles

"The value of a prayer in ... Damascus [is] thirty thousand prayers."

Sufyan al-Thauri, 8th century

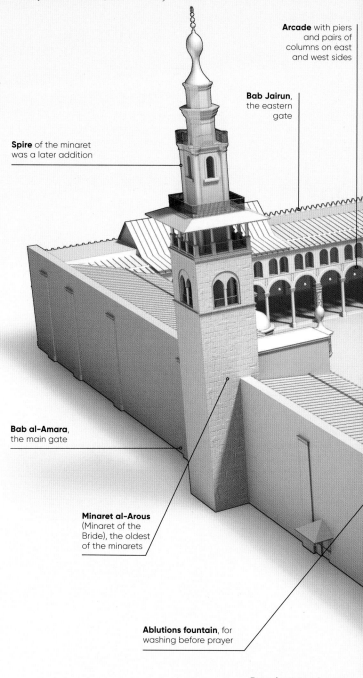

Arcade with piers and pairs of columns on east and west sides

Bab Jairun, the eastern gate

Spire of the minaret was a later addition

Bab al-Amara, the main gate

Minaret al-Arous (Minaret of the Bride), the oldest of the minarets

Ablutions fountain, for washing before prayer

Formal courtyard, surrounded by arcades on all sides

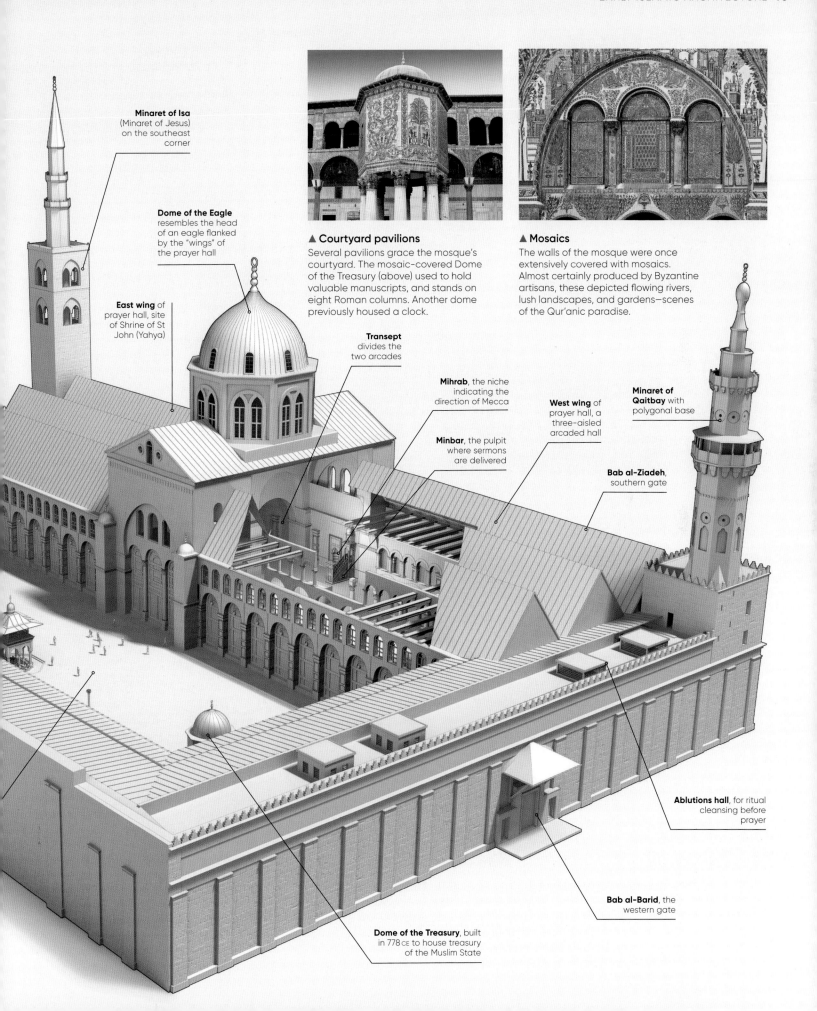

Minaret of Isa
(Minaret of Jesus)
on the southeast
corner

Dome of the Eagle
resembles the head
of an eagle flanked
by the "wings" of
the prayer hall

East wing of
prayer hall, site
of Shrine of St
John (Yahya)

▲ Courtyard pavilions

Several pavilions grace the mosque's
courtyard. The mosaic-covered Dome
of the Treasury (above) used to hold
valuable manuscripts, and stands on
eight Roman columns. Another dome
previously housed a clock.

▲ Mosaics

The walls of the mosque were once
extensively covered with mosaics.
Almost certainly produced by Byzantine
artisans, these depicted flowing rivers,
lush landscapes, and gardens—scenes
of the Qur'anic paradise.

Transept
divides the
two arcades

Mihrab, the niche
indicating the
direction of Mecca

Minbar, the pulpit
where sermons
are delivered

West wing of
prayer hall, a
three-aisled
arcaded hall

**Minaret of
Qaitbay** with
polygonal base

Bab al-Ziadeh,
southern gate

Ablutions hall, for ritual
cleansing before
prayer

Bab al-Barid, the
western gate

Dome of the Treasury, built
in 778 CE to house treasury
of the Muslim State

KEY ELEMENTS

The basic vocabulary of Islamic architecture was set early, during the Umayyad era. Later dynasties—notably the Fatimids of North Africa, the Mamluks of Cairo, the Ottomans of Turkey, the Timurids of Central Asia, the Safavids of Iran, and the Mughals of northern India—all added innovations of their own.

MINARETS

The minaret was designed to provide a platform high above the surrounding neighborhood from which the muezzin could proclaim the call to prayer. The call was issued five times per day: at dawn, noon, mid-afternoon, sunset, and nightfall.

▲ **Square minaret**
Aleppo's main mosque is just a few years younger than the Great Mosque of Damascus. Its five-story, square minaret, crowned with a roofed veranda, is clearly related to Christian church architecture.

◀ **Conical minaret**
The gigantic Abbasid-era minaret at Samarra, in what is now Iraq, has a unique ascending-spiral, conical design. Its shape is likely to have been inspired by the ziggurats of ancient Mesopotamia.

DOMES

The Byzantine tradition of dome-building was embraced by Islamic architects, who saw the dome as a representation of the vault of heaven. In early mosques, a small dome was usually placed above the mihrab—the niche indicating the direction of Mecca. Later, as domes became bigger, they were given a more central position above the prayer hall.

▶ **Domed cube**
The small mausoleum in Bukhara, Samarkand, was built in the 10th century. It features four of the oldest-known squinches—structures that support a dome on a square platform.

▶ **Golden dome**
The earliest surviving Islamic dome, the Dome of the Rock, belongs to this unique shrine in Jerusalem, completed in 692. The dome is constructed of wood covered with metal sheeting. It has been rebuilt numerous times. The current roof is finished with gold plating.

ARCHES

Early examples of Islamic architecture feature rounded arches similar to those found in Roman and Byzantine buildings, but Muslim architects soon developed the arch and produced pointed, horseshoe, and multifoil variants. The liberal use of such arches is a widespread feature of Islamic architecture.

◄ Horseshoe arch
The horseshoe arch is designed so that the half-circle of the arch starts to turn in on itself before it meets the top of its supporting columns.

▲ Pointed arch
As early as 884, Muslim builders were using the pointed arch, which later became a key feature of European Gothic architecture.

ORNATE PATTERNS

Islamic artisans decorated their buildings with geometrical patterns, rather than pictures of living creatures. These patterns, which symbolize the transcendent oneness of God, were designed to draw the viewer's attention away from anything earthly or temporal.

◄ Muqarnas
Stone carving was often applied to the interior decoration of a dome to create breathtaking patterns. The Abbasid Zumurrud Khatun Mosque, in Baghdad, boasts stalactite-like vaulting known as muqarnas.

▲ Stone carving
From the early period of Islam, the Umayyad Mshatta Palace, in Jordan, featured carved-stone depictions of animals. Such images soon became taboo, however, and were replaced by geometrical designs.

◄ Tiling
Brightly colored glazed tiles displayed clever geometric design and beautiful calligraphy. They were also proof of the vast trade network needed to obtain the rare minerals used for their colors. The heat required to make them was also expensive.

EARLY ISLAMIC
BUILDINGS

The large empires ruled by successive Islamic dynasties required buildings for ruling and commerce, as well as for worship. Among these were houses, palaces, fortresses, and commercial premises.

1

3

2

1. Fortress of al-Ukhaidir
Near Karbala, Iraq, 775

Built during the Abbasid era to protect trade routes, this desert fortress has several architectural innovations. These include a great hall with a pointed barrel-vault, and transverse arches that run from side to side across the vaults.

2. Al-Aqsa Mosque
Jerusalem, Palestine, 7th–8th centuries

The third most holy site in the Islamic world is the Al-Aqsa complex, which includes the Al-Aqsa Mosque and the Dome of the Rock. The mosque was largely rebuilt in the 11th century after being damaged during an earthquake.

3. Bab al-Futuh
Cairo, Egypt, 1087

When they captured Egypt in 969, the Fatimids built a new city and called it al-Qahira (Cairo). The builders protected it with high defensive walls, including the Bab al-Futuh gate.

4. Great Mosque of Mahdiya
Mahdiya, Tunisia, 10th century

The monumental entrance is the only part of the original Great Mosque of Mahdiya. Its design derives from the triumphal arches that the Romans built in the region, but with horseshoe rather than semicircular arches.

4

5. Sultan Han
Sultanhanı, Turkey, 13th century

A han, also known as a "khan" or "caravanserai," was a fortified merchants' lodge. The Sultan Han was built by the Seljuk Turks during the reign of Sultan Kayqubad I.

5

6 7

6. Great Mosque of Córdoba
Córdoba, Spain, 8th century

The Great Mosque (or Mosque–Cathedral) of Córdoba was built when Córdoba was the capital of Muslim Al-Andalus. It was the first major monument of Moorish architecture to be built on the Iberian Peninsula.

7. Kharraqan Towers
Kharraqan, Iran, 1067–1093

The two tower-mausoleums of Kharraqan date from the Seljuk period of medieval Persia. Built of brick, they are carved with geometrical patterns, an early example of such ornamentation in Islamic architecture.

ROMANESQUE

As Christianity spread across central and western Europe, churches, especially larger ones that were the seat of a bishop or abbot, evolved into the most impressive buildings of the time.

The prevailing style of architecture between the 10th and 12th centuries featured semicircular arches, massive walls, small windows, and often elaborate ornament. Builders drew on Roman ways of constructing walls, arches, and vaults: walls, for example, consisted of a thick rubble core with smooth masonry facing. As a result, this style later became known as Romanesque, despite its builders adapting Roman methods, devising, for instance, more sophisticated, and less massive, ways of constructing stone vaults.

Few houses of this period have survived, so most of the Romanesque buildings standing today are churches and cathedrals. Many of these are variations on the Roman basilica design, with a long nave for the laity (non-clergy) plus a shorter sanctuary for the priests. However, they often have numerous extra spaces: two or more side aisles; transepts or cross-arms; and several small side chapels, each containing its own altar. This makes large Romanesque churches complex buildings, in which different spaces of varying height and size open up as the visitor walks around them. Outside, there is usually at least one tower.

> "Romanesque ... extending the structural daring with minimal visual elaboration."
>
> **Harry Seidler**, architect, 1923–2006

Churches were by far the tallest buildings in medieval towns, and some Romanesque cathedrals still dominate Europe's cities.

DETAIL AND DECORATION

Many Romanesque churches are strikingly plain, lacking the marble cladding or mosaics of Roman or Byzantine buildings. Instead, their impact comes from their massive masonry. Yet in some parts of Europe, such as Italy, England, and Burgundy in France, masons were given the scope to decorate their buildings, inside and out. They enlivened expanses of blank wall with rows of blind arches, and highlighted entrances by surrounding doorways not with one arch, but with several recessed arches, known as orders. To these, sculptors added intricately carved capitals and reliefs in the tympanum, the semicircular panel at the top of the arch. A lot of this carving was focused around the main doorways into the church, usually at the west end. The west front of Romanesque churches therefore became the most carefully designed part of their exterior, forming a composition of doorways, windows, gables, and often towers, to impressive effect.

SCULPTORS AND TRAVELERS

The large tympanum over the west doorway at Autun Cathedral in France depicts the souls of the dead being separated into the saved and the damned. Among the saved are two pilgrims. Pilgrimage gave artists and patrons the chance to see the latest styles in the churches they visited, and Romanesque sculpture methods may have spread along these routes.

Tympanum showing the Last Judgment, in which the souls of the dead are sorted

MAINZ CATHEDRAL

MAINZ, GERMANY, 975–1037

The towering sandstone cathedral of St. Martin in Mainz was built between 975 and 1037, with further work on the east end around 1100. Its apses, multiple towers, small windows, and blind arcading are typical of the larger German cathedrals of this period, as is the steep pitch of its roofs.

TWIN-APSE PLAN

Like several German Romanesque cathedrals, Mainz has apses at both the east and west ends of the building. This makes it possible to have two main altars, and from the outside, the curved apse walls indicate where the most sacred areas of the building lie. Double aisles make the cathedral especially wide, although the massive internal piers (load-bearing pillars) reduce the sense of space.

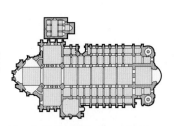

Plan showing twin apses and double-width aisles at Mainz Cathedral

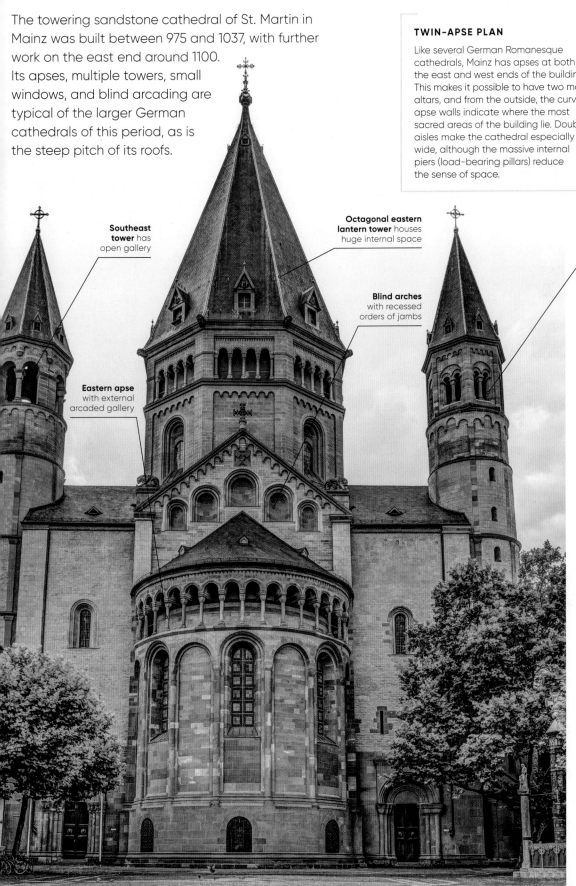

Southeast tower has open gallery

Eastern apse with external arcaded gallery

Octagonal eastern lantern tower houses huge internal space

Blind arches with recessed orders of jambs

Southwest tower has pairs of openings under single arch

▲ **Symbolic sculpture**
Mainz Cathedral features some vivid sculpture. This lion, high on the building's exterior, is trampling on a basilisk, a mythical reptile said to have a deadly stare. The lion may represent Christ overcoming evil.

▲ **Bulky pillars**
The heavy stone vaults require strong support from below, provided by the massive rectangular piers of the nave arches. These, like many Romanesque examples, are plain—a simple, straight molding marks the transition between pier and arch.

KEY **ELEMENTS**

Builders found ways to reduce the oppressive effect of massive masonry, by using carved ornamentation or dividing large structures such as piers into smaller or more slender elements.

ARCADING

Rows of arches run around the outer walls of many Romanesque buildings. Some shelter open galleries or walkways; others are completely blind, with stretches of stonework behind. These arcades make otherwise blank walls more pleasing to look at and break up the mass of thick, solid masonry.

Slender shaft of white marble topped by carved capital

Arches of open arcades with galleries behind on upper tiers

Lozenge motif, made using marble of different colors, decorates blind arcading

◀ **Open and closed**
The west front of Pisa Cathedral in Italy has blind arcading along the ground floor and rows of open arcades above. Ancient Roman stonework continued to be reused as cladding to Romanesque churches.

DOORWAYS

To signal that the visitor is entering a sacred place, Romanesque doorways are given prominence, with features such as carved arches and tympana. Doorways are often wide, to allow processions to pass through.

▲ **Making an entrance**
Bad roads meant that transporting stone was very expensive, so medieval churches tended to be built in local stone. Special stones from farther away could be used for key details, like the gray column shafts around the main doorway of St. Paul in Nîmes, France.

APSES

The east end of a Romanesque church often ends in a semicircular apse, which houses the high altar. If there are several apses, they form intimate chapels, each with its own altar dedicated to a different saint.

▲ **Fit for an altar**
The apse of Lund Cathedral in Sweden has typically Romanesque blind arcading. Several round-arched windows direct light onto the altar within. The altar is on a raised floor, so the lower parts of the apse's wall have no windows.

VAULTING STYLES

Romanesque masons used barrel vaults for some buildings, but as this type of arched roof created too strong an outward thrust to use in large buildings, they adopted cross vaults. They also introduced the stronger but lighter ribbed vault, which spreads the load laterally and diagonally across the vault in narrow ribs and arches, and produces less outward thrust.

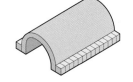

A Roman-style barrel vault uses a lot of heavy stone so is unsuitable for wide spans.

A cross vault is still heavy, but handles the structural forces better.

A ribbed vault is more structurally efficient and requires less stone.

PIERS AND COLUMNS

The piers supporting arches and vaults varied widely in design, from simple rectangular masses to uprights surrounded by clusters of slender columns. With the varying patterns of light coming from the windows, the more complex piers produced a constantly changing interplay of light and shadow.

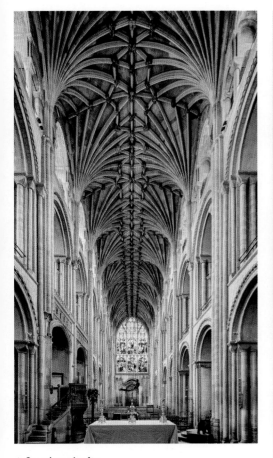

▲ Soaring shafts
At Norwich Cathedral in the UK, the arches of the nave have piers surrounded by a multitude of slim, vertical shafts. Some of these shafts rise all the way from the floor to the springing of the ceiling vault (a later Gothic addition) far above, emphasizing the building's impressive height.

▲ Combined effect
In the nave of Durham Cathedral in the UK, the stone vaulted ceiling is supported by two types of pier. Simple cylindrical columns, incised with bold geometric designs, alternate with groups of shafts.

ORNAMENTATION

Romanesque architecture is known for its abundant decoration, which masons carved on arches, capitals, corbels, and elsewhere. Basic motifs often take the form of repeating patterns, such as zigzags, ovals, squares, and ropelike forms, but there is also much figurative carving.

▶ Recurring design
Every other stone column in the nave of Durham Cathedral is decorated with a repeating geometric pattern. These were all brightly colored when new.

▲ Carved corbels
Stone brackets supporting part of a roof or wall, corbels were often carved, usually with Christian symbols, like these at Puente Arenas, Spain, which seem to be the symbols of the four Evangelists.

ROMANESQUE
BUILDINGS

As well as its range of surface decoration, Romanesque architecture is notable for the height of its buildings, many endowed with towers, domes, turrets, and spires.

1

3

2

1. "Jew's House"
Lincoln, England, c. 1170

This rare surviving house from the Norman period in England retains a semicircular-headed doorway and upper windows in the Romanesque style, although the ground floor has been much altered. Similar houses made with a timber frame would have been common in the 12th century.

2. Baptistery
Parma, Italy, 1196–1216

Built of a pink-tinged Verona marble, the octagonal baptistery at Parma features the deeply recessed doorways, carved tympana, and multilevel galleries typical of Romanesque architecture. The pointed arches at the top give a hint of the Gothic style that was soon to follow.

3. Pisa Cathedral
Pisa, Italy, 1063–1092

Faced in multicolored marble and encased from top to bottom in arcading, the exterior of this exceptional Romanesque building combines a range of stylistic influences, including decorative patterns from Armenia and bronze doors that recall those in Constantinople (modern-day Istanbul).

4. Durham Cathedral
Durham, England, 1093–1133

Built to house the relics of the revered Saint Cuthbert, Durham Cathedral retains much of its Romanesque fabric. From the outside, the two western towers are the outstanding 12th-century features. Much of the outer masonry is also original, including the upper windows and the blind arcading at ground level.

4

5. Abbey Church of Sainte Foy
Conques, France, 11th century

Saint Foy, an early Christian martyr, had a shrine in this place of pilgrimage from the 8th century, but the church was later rebuilt in the Romanesque style. A series of small chapels extend from the large eastern apse, visible as mini-apses radiating around the church's east end—a popular arrangement in this period.

5

6

7

6. Church of St. Michael and All Angels
Earls Barton, England, 10th-century tower

In England, before the 1066 Norman conquest, some church towers rose in a series of levels decorated with patterns of narrow stone bands called pilaster strips. The tower at Earls Barton is a well-preserved example, and its patterning may recall the framework of timber-framed buildings that no longer exist.

7. Abbey church
Maria Laach, Germany, 11th–12th centuries

By the 12th century, Maria Laach was a prominent center of monasticism and scholarship. It had an impressive church to match its importance, with multiple towers, an apse at each end, and an unusual western porch sheltered by an arcade running all the way along the west front.

EARLY IMPERIAL CHINA

Despite political upheaval and external influences, wood remained the material of choice for early imperial Chinese architects, loved for its pliability, resilience, tensile strength, and natural texture.

The First Emperor of a unified China, Qin Shi Huang (r. 221–210 BCE), was a visionary of state-building. He consolidated his power through infrastructure, opening roads, digging canals, and building palaces and the Great Wall. While the luxury of his Efang Palace is known only through literature, Qin's mausoleum, with its 8,000 terra-cotta soldiers, offers a glimpse into the unprecedented scale and magnificence of Chinese architecture under early imperial rule.

Han (202 BCE–220 CE) emperors inherited the Qin legacy. The imperial residence in Chang'an (modern-day Xi'an) featured palaces, shrines, temples, and parks. With the development of theories including yin-yang (about opposite yet interrelated universal forces), the Five Elements (wood, fire, earth, metal, and water), and the trinity between heaven, earth, and man (or emperor), Chinese architecture became a human-scaled representation of the cosmos.

The official opening of the Silk Road in the 2nd century BCE introduced Buddhism and new architectural forms, such as the stupa, to China's heartlands. In the period of disunity following the collapse of the Han dynasty, Buddhism exerted a lasting impact on Chinese architecture, as rival imperial patrons built rock-cut temples and stone pagodas alongside wooden structures. The trade routes also brought new materials and scientific knowledge to China. These external influences both enriched and challenged the long-revered post-and-lintel construction system—in which timber-framed structures were pieced together like a jigsaw puzzle—without destabilizing its predominance in Chinese architecture.

COMING OF AGE

The mixing of architectural styles culminated with the reunification of China under the Tang (618–907), whose capital Chang'an may have reached a population of 3 million—the greatest city of the time—served by markets, temples, and an imperial palace and park. The Tang oversaw a sophisticated wooden building style, with broad overhanging eaves, robust beams and columns, and a clever bracketing system. This style was emulated by later dynasties.

CHINA'S GOLDEN AGE

The flourishing of wooden architecture under the Tang dynasty stimulated artistic depictions of grand palaces, pagodas, and watchtowers. This gave birth to a new genre in Chinese painting—*jiehua* (ruled-line paintings), which aimed to capture the accurate geometry and proportion of built forms and the aesthetic principles they embodied. Wooden halls and pavilions can be seen in this wall painting from the Mogao Caves, a treasure trove of Buddhist art.

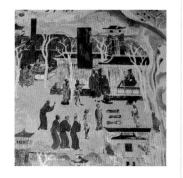

Detail of a mural from the Mogao Caves, Gansu Province

"Like a pheasant on flying wings; Is the [hall] ..."

Book of Songs, Western Zhou dynasty, c. 1046–771 BCE

Chattra (finial) at top mounted on double lotus pedestal

SONGYUE PAGODA
HENAN PROVINCE, CHINA, 523

Built on the Central Mountain of China's Five Sacred Mountains, the unusual brick-built Songyue Pagoda is the country's oldest surviving pagoda. It embodies the "axis mundi," a celestial axis passing through Earth and connecting it to the heavens above.

INDIAN STUPAS

The spread of Buddhism from India was accompanied by distinctive designs for religious buildings. Early Indian stupas were large, hemispherical, earthen mounds built to house Buddhist relics and commemorate the founder and first teachers of the religion. Unlike the Indian prototype, however, Chinese pagodas have a more elongated and slender body that emphasizes the verticality of the structure.

Sanchi Stupa, Madhya Pradesh, India, 3rd century BCE

▲ **Decorative niches**
Eight carved stupa-shaped niches with Indian-style pointed arches surround the pagoda's lower section. They are placed on lion seats, and separated by columns with lotus-flower capitals and pedestals.

Eaves densely stacked in 15 layers

Body of pagoda made entirely of bricks

Double-height door, one of four entrances on the cardinal points

▲ **Dodecagonal shape**
This pagoda's 12-sided shape may have been adapted from the design of Indian hemispherical stupas. The brick corbeling (stepped brackets) of the pagoda body creates a smooth, gently tapered outline.

KEY ELEMENTS

The Yellow and Yangtze river valleys yielded abundant timber for wooden construction, while earth and clay for building walls and ramparts and for fired ceramic roof tiles came from the nearby loess plateau.

THE RIGHT SITE

Feng shui is the ancient Chinese wisdom of observing topographical features and following the "veins" and *qi*-energy flows of the terrain. *Feng shui* masters identify the most favorable orientation and location before building begins.

▲ Urban planning
This reconstruction of Chang'an's Daming Palace shows its grid plan, which originated from ancient land administration and taxation practices but later assumed calendrical and metaphysical meanings.

◄ Symmetry
Constructed in the *louge* (pavilion) style, the two side pagodas at the Chongsheng Temple in Yunnan Province accentuate the centrality of the Tang-dynasty pagoda in the middle, with its curved silhouette and 16 tiers. Symmetry is a desirable quality in *feng shui*.

COLOR

The five primary colors in Chinese architecture—red, green/blue, yellow, white, and dark blue/black—are each matched with one of the Five Elements, and a particular season and direction. They represent a link between microcosm (architecture) and macrocosm (heaven and earth), a theory established by the Han dynasty.

◄ Yellow
As seen on the walls of Xichan Temple, Fujian Province, yellow speaks of royalty and brilliance, and calls to mind the warmth and light of the sun and the luster of gold. Often used for the roof tiles of palaces and monasteries, it signifies the center of the world and the element earth.

▲ Red
The vermilion red of the Jinci Shrines in Shanxi Province is thought to bring happiness and good fortune. Both the color of the cardinal direction south and the symbol of fire, red is used on walls and columns to ward off evil spirits.

◄ Blue and green
Ancestral shrines, including Saint Mother's Hall at the Jinci Shrines, and altars to heavenly deities often have blue and green roof tiles. Associated with the east and the element of wood, blue-green is the color of dragons and evokes the idea of immortality.

EARLY IMPERIAL CHINESE BUILDINGS

Over the first millennium of imperial China, the versatile timber frame and bracketing system, combined with stone arches and vaults, gave birth to architectural and engineering wonders.

1. Guanyin Pavilion
Dule Temple, Tianjin, 984

Famous for its wide overhanging eaves suspended on huge multi-stepped brackets, this pavilion is also remarkable for the floor-to-ceiling atrium within. Wooden stairs lead to the middle and upper floors, creating a spiraling route around the central statue.

2. Foguang Temple
Shanxi Province, 857

One of the earliest known wooden structures in China, the Foguang Temple is a classical example of Tang architecture. The overhanging eaves were compared to the wings of birds in the ancient Chinese anthology *Book of Songs*.

3. Zhaozhou Bridge
Hebei Province, 6th–7th centuries

Spanning more than 120 ft (37 m) with a single arch, this original design by Li Chun is an unusually early example of China's mastery of stonemasonry. The open shoulder arches reduce the bridge's weight and improve the passage of water in times of flood.

4. Great Wild Goose Pagoda
Ci'en Temple, Xi'an, Shanxi Province, c.650

Unlike the Songyue Pagoda (see p.107), this brick pagoda adopts a simpler square plan, enabling it to reach a height of 210 ft (64 m). Each of its seven stories is accessible through interior wooden staircases. The structure's stout, robust appearance is characteristic of Tang-dynasty architecture.

EARLY KOREA

The stone tombs and pagodas of Korea are early examples of East Asian building forms, while the wooden structures document the spread of Buddhist material culture from China.

Traditional Korean architecture, though best known for its wooden construction techniques, also displays astonishing craftsmanship in stone. Stone burial mounds and chamber tombs in Korea evolved from megalithic dolmens (huge prehistoric monuments), which still dot the landscape. Goguryeo kingdom (37–668 CE) tombs featured domed or lantern ceilings, with corbeling bracket technology similar to that of North and Central Asia. The gold crowns, gold belts, and jade pendants from these early tombs bear images of trees and antlers that suggest early kingship in Korea had shamanistic roots.

Buddhism entered Korea from China in 372 CE. The kingdom of Paekche (18 BCE–660 CE) was instrumental in forming links with South China and transmitting the new religion and its architectural forms to Japan. Yet indigenous vaulting and corbeling methods continued to characterize Korean Buddhist architecture—notably at the 8th-century Seokguram Grotto (part of the Bulguksa temple complex), whose interlocking stone blocks and domed sanctuary evoke both Chinese Buddhist rock-cut temples and Goguryeo burial chambers. Korean pagodas also took their own form, adopting a more angular, straight-lined body shape than the curved Chinese prototype, with unique proportions and geometric layouts. The pair of stone pagodas at the Bulguksa temple represent the earliest forms of Buddhist monument based on a square or octagonal plan.

WOODEN ARCHITECTURE

Far fewer wooden structures have survived from early Korea, but older forms have been reproduced in later buildings. The oldest wooden building in Korea, the main hall of the Bongjeongsa temple, was rebuilt in the 13th century, but is believed to reflect the style of the Unified Silla period (668–935). The use of round lower rafters and square upper rafters under the eaves maximizes the span of the roof, and makes for a heavy roof structure relative to the lightness of the columns. The Goryeo period (918–1392) saw further developments in wooden architecture under the influence of China's Song dynasty, and Korea's wooden structures became increasingly technically complex and lavishly ornamented.

◀ **Elaborate roof**
The Geungnakjeon Hall at the Bongjeongsa Temple is a three-bay structure of modest size with a gabled roof supported on *chusimp'o* (column-head bracket sets). The linked blue-green floral and geometric patterns of the roof contrast with the plain wall beneath.

KEEPING WARM

Ondol, a traditional Korean underfloor heating system, emerged no later than the 4th century BCE in the north of the Korean peninsula. It is derived from prehistoric pit houses, where the hearth ensured the survival of the family in freezing winters. Heated air is channeled from the kitchen stove via flues to other rooms and escapes through holes in the exterior walls.

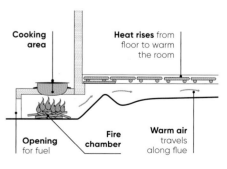

***Ondol* underfloor heating** system, showing the flow of heated air from kitchen to sitting room

BULGUKSA TEMPLE
GYEONGJU, SOUTH KOREA, 8TH CENTURY

Located to the southeast of Gyeongju at the foot of the mountains, with the sea to the east, the Bulguksa temple compound is a quintessential example of Unified Silla architecture. The Daeungjeon Hall (shown below) is at the center of the north-south axis, as is customary in Buddhist temple layouts.

Curved roof covered with concave and convex clay tiles

Raised platform

Latticed doors

Tap'o style column-head and intercolumnar bracket sets

▲ **Fire extinguisher**
Brackets supporting the beams and roof above are vividly painted and lavishly carved—here into a dragon head. These aquatic animals are benevolent guardians thought to suppress fire.

EARLY KOREAN BUILDINGS

▲ **Buseoksa Temple,** Yeongju City, South Korea, 676
This three-by-two-bay wooden pavilion is notable for its simple structure, stout appearance, and openness to the surrounding views. It serves as a gate to the temple's main hall, a prelude to the Buddhist "Land of Bliss."

▲ **Tomb of King Kongmin,** Kaesong, North Korea, 1372
The twin burial mounds of King Kongmin (r. 1351–1374) and his queen follow the imperial Chinese model, with their stone statues of animals, civil officials, and generals. The construction, however, honors the Korean tradition of stone-chamber tombs.

▲ **Octagonal Nine-Story Stone Pagoda,** Pyeongchang, South Korea, 7th century
This pagoda at the Woljeongsa Temple rises on a lotus pedestal and is topped with an elaborate *chattra* (finial). Its densely packed upturned eaves mimic a wooden pagoda, and its tapering body is reminiscent of the Songyue Pagoda in China.

EARLY JAPAN

Japan's long-established ties with China and Korea brought a mature system of wooden construction to the country. Blended into the native cultural fabric, this produced unique architectural styles.

▲ **Towering Todaiji**
The Great Buddha Hall (Daibutsuden) of the Todaiji Temple is one of the world's largest wooden structures at 170 ft (52 m). It features a Chinese-style double-eave roof suspended on multitiered brackets, while the curved gable is typically Japanese.

The Shinto shrines at Ise and Izumo exemplify Japan's earliest wooden building forms. The original structures were modified Yayoi-period (c. 300 BCE–300 CE) granaries, made from simple columns embedded into the ground and a thatched roof adorned with *chigi* (criss-cross finials) and *katsuogi* (billets). These structures share the post-and-lintel, mortise-and-tenon construction method typical in China and Korea. The temple at Ise is rebuilt every 20 years to carefully replicated designs, making it both one of Japan's oldest and newest buildings, and allowing its sustainable local materials to age gracefully but never deteriorate.

IDEOLOGICAL INSPIRATION

The arrival of Buddhism from Korea in the 6th century CE brought profound changes to early Japan's architectural landscape, including refinements such as upturned eaves, ceramic roof tiles, intricate bracketing, and the elevation of buildings above a stone platform. Shintoism had no iconographic representation, whereas Mahayana (Greater Vehicle) Buddhism offered an established cosmology. Reinforcing the ideal of divine kingship, the Asuka (552–645 CE), Hakuhō (645–710), and Nara (710–794) periods saw the construction of magnificent Buddhist halls and pagodas, including Horyuji, founded by Prince Shotoku, an early patron of Buddhism. Centuries of building and rebuilding of wooden temples ensued, whereby Chinese archetypes and Japanese traditions clashed and mingled and produced a range of styles in the process.

Chinese belief systems and political ideologies spurred the planning of imperial capitals, first in Fujiwara in the 7th century, and later in Nara and Kyoto—all emulating the symbolic grid plan of the Tang Chinese capital, Chang'an. These cities became early centers of Buddhist practices. In contrast, 8th-century Buddhist architecture emphasized asceticism and sought isolation from urban tumult. The mountain monasteries of Enryakuji and Muroji abandoned Horyuji's symmetrical layout, instead adopting a free plan following the uneven topography. The modest facade of their wooden halls gave off an archaic aura. Amid this architectural synthesis of mountain worship and monastic practice, a new religion, Shugendo, emerged.

SPREAD OF BUDDHISM VIA KOREA

According to the *Nihon shoki* (Chronicle of Japan), in 552, the king of Paekche in Korea presented a golden statue of the Buddha to the Japanese emperor Kinmei (r. 539–571). An architect from Paekche later helped with the construction of Horyuji, transmitting the timber-frame technique learned from South China. After the fall of Paekche in 660, Japanese pilgrim monks carried Chinese ideas back from Chang'an.

Stone pagoda of Mireuksa, a Paekche Buddhist temple

Tiled roof replaces thatched roof of early Shinto shrines

Columns and brackets originally painted red

GOLDEN HALL

HORYUJI TEMPLE, IKARUGA, JAPAN, 607

The tripartite structure of the Golden Hall (*kondo*)—the hip-and-gable roof (*irimoya*), the columns and brackets on a grid plan, and the stone platform with stairs pointing to the four cardinal directions—demonstrates the conscious adoption of Chinese models.

◀ Interior grid
The stout columns and latticed ceiling of the interior form a rhythmic spatial framework for the central Buddhist statues. The curved brackets and subtly swelling columns balance the rectilinearity of the grid.

▲ Hip-and-gable roof
The triangular gables at the end of the hipped roof are combined with the skirting eaves beneath to form a highly distinctive roofline. The projecting eaves rest on flying rafters and stepped brackets.

Railings with frog-leg struts and lattice panels

PLAN OF COMPLEX

The east-west parallel positioning of the Golden Hall and the Five-Storied Pagoda at Horyuji is a rare case in East Asian Buddhist architecture. This unconventional design grants equal visual importance to the two key structures, the former serving as a worship hall and the latter enshrining the Buddha's relics. Later Buddhist temples follow a more standardized form, with the main buildings positioned along the north-south axis.

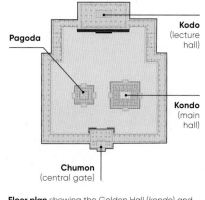

Pagoda

Kodo (lecture hall)

Kondo (main hall)

Chumon (central gate)

Floor plan showing the Golden Hall (*kondo*) and pagoda positioned side by side

Cloud-shaped bracket set (*kumo tokyo*) rests on each wooden column

Coiling dragons intricately carved on corner columns

KEY ELEMENTS

The veneration for nature embedded in Japanese belief systems led to distinctive design approaches that rejected artifice and sought to express the innate "spirit," or natural qualities, of organic materials.

NATURAL COLORS AND TEXTURES

Contrary to the Chinese custom of painting columns red, the Japanese preferred to keep the original wood color. The wooden structural pieces are connected with mortise-and-tenon joints, without any nails, ensuring the stability of the structure through earthquakes and tsunamis.

▲ Panoramic platform
The main hall of the Kiyomizu-dera is suspended from a steep hillside and raised on a gigantic "hanging" timber frame. The deep compound roof covers a broad, open, multi-pillared hall and veranda, which enable pilgrims to enjoy a panoramic view of the natural landscape.

◄ Unpainted columns
The pristine wooden columns of the Zaodo befit the serene atmosphere of the Yoshino mountains, where the Kinpusenji Temple was founded in the 7th century. The complex has since become a Shugendo pilgrimage site.

TORII GATES

A torii consists of two inwardly inclined pillars joined by a tie beam, with a horizontal lintel on top. It epitomizes the Shinto aesthetic of understated refinement and natural beauty, and is the spiritual threshold between the profane and the divine.

▲ Entrance to another world
Set before a wooden bridge, the *shinmei* torii at the Ise Grand Shrine marks the entrance to the sacred realm of the Naiku (inner shrines). Unlike the Buddhist emphasis on the central axis, the route to this Shinto shrine takes several turns, each indicated by a torii.

▲ Spiritual passage
The Senbon Torii of the Fushimi Inari Grand Shrines, developed from earlier torii types, each have a lintel with a gently curved ridge and a central post between the lintel and tie beam. The 1,000 torii gates create a unique spiritual path to the inner shrine.

ASUKA ART

Buddhism reached Japan during the Asuka period, and the differences between Buddhist and Shinto aesthetics and ritual practices led to distinctive building styles, inside and out. The interiors of Asuka Buddhist temples were filled with golden statues and brightly colored paintings. One significant pictorial motif was the Amida Buddha seated in his Pure Land, a Buddhist paradise and heaven where virtuous souls were reborn in the Lotus Pond.

Wall painting from Horyuji showing the Amida Buddha in his Buddhist paradise

EARLY JAPANESE BUILDINGS

The archaic look of Wayo (Japanese style) Buddhist temples built in the 6th to 8th centuries under the influence of Paekche Korea and Tang China contrasts with that of later Tenjikuyo (Indian style) structures.

1. Shitennoji Temple
Osaka, Japan, 7th century CE

The layout of the Shitennoji complex emphasizes the north-south axis, placing the main gate, pagoda, Golden Hall, and Lecture Hall along this line and encircling the compound with a corridor. Like Horyuji, the Wayo temple buildings have a tiled hip-and-gable roof and cloud brackets.

2. Matsunoo Taisha Shrine
Kyoto, Japan, 701

The worship hall (*haiden*) stands in the center of the courtyard and serves as a stage for Shinto rituals. This open structure features a wooden floor raised on short posts, a veranda, and a cedar-bark-covered roof that faces the audience on a gabled end—distinguishing it from China-inspired Buddhist halls.

3. Nandaimon Gate, Todaiji
Kyoto, Japan, 8th century (rebuilt 1203)

This gate is remarkable for its huge pillars (some reaching a height of 65 ft/20 m), rainbow beams, stacked struts and bearing blocks, and multi-stepped bracket sets, all serving to create a soaring but elegant structure. It is a rare example of the Tenjikuyo style

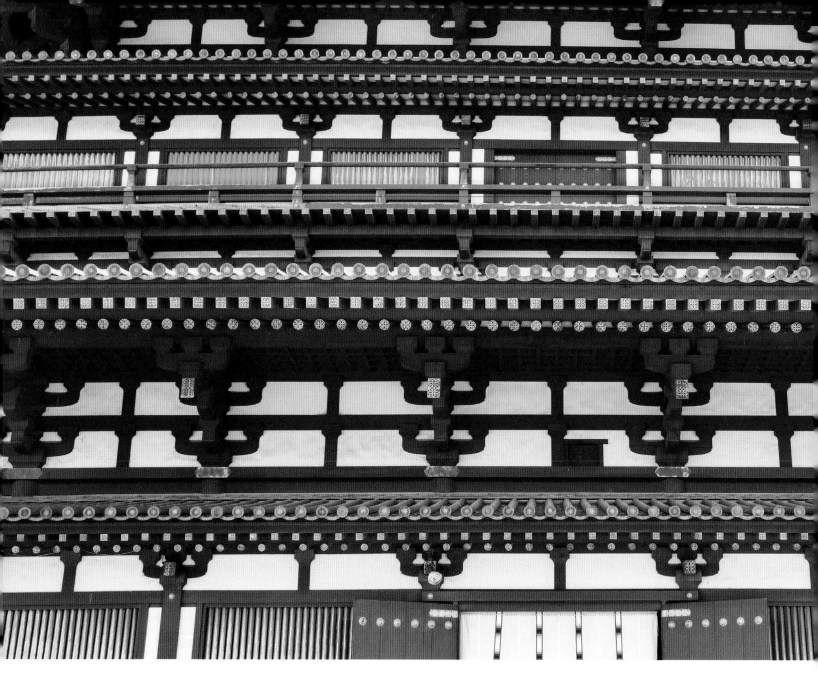

▲ Pagoda
This five-story pagoda, which dates from the 1640s, is part of the Buddhist temple complex of Tō-ji, in Kyoto, Japan. Viewed from below, the structure of its four-part wooden roof is clearly visible.

▲ Longhouse
Viking longhouses, like this reconstruction in Trelleborg, Denmark, usually had wooden frames. Their main supports were upright posts set into the ground, and their walls were made of either wood or wattle and daub.

> "Wood is universally beautiful to man. It is the most humanly intimate of all materials."
>
> **Frank Lloyd Wright,** American architect (1867–1959)

TIMBER

Trees have provided humans with construction materials for millennia, for everything from simple farm buildings to grand temples. Timber's importance is rising again today in the face of the climate emergency.

Timber has been used as a building material all over the world because it can span across floors relatively inexpensively and efficiently. In places where forest is particularly abundant, or where other good building materials are scarce, wood has been used to construct entire buildings. These range from the rapidly erected seasonal shelters of some hunter-gatherer groups to elaborately carved religious buildings that can last for many centuries.

In countries such as Finland, where cold was a massive challenge and timber was plentiful, houses were conventionally built out of whole logs. By contrast, where denser populations threatened the timber supply, in places such as China and much of northern Europe, timber detailing reduced the number of large trunks needed through the use of smaller timbers cleverly joined to build robust walls and roofs.

For most of human history, timber has been assembled using sophisticated joints rather than iron nails or screws, because the amount of scarce firewood required to shape metal connectors made them more expensive than cultivating the skills of low-paid carpenters. The design of these joints became a high art in many cultures, such as Japan, where it is associated with prestige and exquisite taste.

A MATERIAL FOR THE FORWARD-LOOKING

Scarce in some places, timber is always slow-growing, and trees take up a lot of land. Wood cultivation in densely occupied areas therefore required planning—growing enough to sustain the needs of future generations. People had to plant and tend trees that they knew would only grow to become good timber many years later.

Today, timber is widely expected to play an important role in helping to reduce architecture's huge contribution to climate-changing emissions. Trees take carbon dioxide out of the atmosphere and store it harmlessly in timber. Yet the way in which timber is grown often damages the soil and reduces biodiversity. The solution must involve building less as well as switching from concrete and steel to timber.

▲ Timber-framed houses
Houses with timber frames, such as these in Bernkastel-Kues, Germany, were common throughout much of medieval Europe. Most have box frames, braced with diagonal and cross timbers to add strength and reduce the effects of warping.

▲ Wooden church
Part of a monastery founded in the 16th century at Krekhiv, near Lviv, this is one of Ukraine's many wooden churches. Its walls are made of logs that are laid horizontally and meet at overlapping joints at the corners. Its roof is covered with shingles.

JOINTS

The weakest points in a timber structure are usually the places where the pieces of wood meet. Carpenters in many cultures have made an art out of designing a plethora of different joints—such as mortise and tenon joints and lap joints—that allow a building to move and distort a little over time without falling apart. Notching and carving each timber into a snugly fitting jigsaw requires great skill, but avoids the need for nails, screws, or glues.

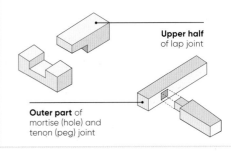

Upper half of lap joint

Outer part of mortise (hole) and tenon (peg) joint

BUDDHIST ARCHITECTURE

As Buddhism continued to spread across Asia, helped by the patronage of powerful dynasties such as Tang China and Pala India, distinct architectural forms emerged and evolved.

By the 6th century CE, Buddhism had spread from India to Central, East, and Southeast Asia, reaching as far as Japan and Indonesia, and branching into different sects and schools as it went. Mahayana (Greater Vehicle) Buddhism developed a strong foothold in East Asia, while the more conservative Theravada Buddhism proved popular in the south. Two unique architectural trends—one of wooden construction and the other masonry—came to dominate the northern and southern "halves" of Buddhist Asia respectively.

There were clashes, but on the whole, the tolerant attitude of Buddhists toward other religions, as well as a conscious absorption of preexisting belief systems and their literary and artistic traditions, helped Buddhism thrive. To some extent, this resulted in religious coalescence, but political turmoil in places also led to the persecution of Buddhist monks and nuns and temples being burned down.

By the end of the 8th century, Buddhism had largely declined in the Indian subcontinent, except in Pala-dynasty India and Sri Lanka. Nonetheless, it left its mark on Central Java, where the Shailendra dynasty constructed masterpieces such as the Borobudur Great Stupa. The emergence of Vajrayana (Diamond Vehicle) and Tantrayana Buddhism at this time highlights the pressure felt by the religious community to rejuvenate. Islamic forces had already advanced into the Hindu Kush and turned many revered Buddhist monasteries into ruins. Attacks on Buddhist icons continued under the steppe kingdoms and the Mongol rule of Genghis Khan, and well past the 14th century. Of those that survived this onslaught, many have since met their demise, including the colossal standing Buddhas at Bamiyan in Afghanistan, destroyed by the Taliban in 2001.

DIVERGING STYLES

The Buddhist structures that still stand display a conscious adoption of Indian archetypes as well as a response to local cultures. The stupa became the elongated, rectilinear pagoda in East Asia, with an accessible multilevel interior derived from wooden watchtowers. In the trans-Indus area, it developed into a terraced, cruciform megastructure. At its latest stage of development, Buddhist architecture assumed a complete cosmic dimension: the mandala became the ideal blueprint for temple design, as demonstrated by King Yeshe-Ö's Tholing Monastery in western Tibet, where Buddhism finally found a safe haven.

◀ **Tower of Buddhas**
The famous pagoda of the 6th-century Tran Quoc Temple in Hanoi, Vietnam, is an 11-story hexagonal structure rising in the middle of a small island. The elongated building hosts many small Buddhas.

BUDDHIST ICONOGRAPHY

As Buddhist art evolved from aniconic (nonhuman or animal) to figurative representations, Buddhist iconography also expanded from the depiction of Siddhartha Gautama, the historical founder of the religion to that of a holy assembly including the Buddha's past and future incarnations, various *bodhisattvas* (enlightened beings), and the Four Heavenly Kings (Buddhist demigods).

Tibetan painting showing an assembly of the Buddha

BOROBUDUR GREAT STUPA

CENTRAL JAVA, INDONESIA, 9TH CENTURY

Built on top of a natural hill using volcanic rock, the spectacular Borobudur Great Stupa measures 370 ft (113 m) on each side and is 138 ft (42 m) tall. The multi-terraced structure is a manifestation of the three realms of the Buddhist universe.

◄Open stupa

Small stupas encircle the central stupa, and each one contains a seated Buddha. The unique latticed form of the stupas lets in light to illuminate the Buddhas within. It also makes it possible for worshippers to peer inside the stupas.

◄Stories in stone

The winding galleries between terraces are carved with narrative scenes depicting the Buddha's life stories. Scenes of torture on the ground terrace warn worshippers of the dangers of material and worldly pleasures.

MANDALA

The design of Borobudur is based on the mandala, a cosmological diagram with distinctive geometric features and religious symbolism. Early Buddhist stupas share some architectural traits with the mandala: they have a sacred enclosure with four cardinal gates, transition from the square to the circle, and worshippers follow a clockwise path from the outside in toward the center.

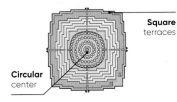

Square terraces

Circular center

Symbolic, geometric form of Borobudur

Latticed stupas holding seated Buddhas

Parapets made of miniature stupas and niches

The central stupa is 26 ft (8 m) tall

Three circular terraces represent *Arupadhatu* (Realm of formlessness)

Ground terrace represents *Kamadhatu* (Realm of desire)

Five indented square terraces represent *Rupadhatu* (Realm of forms)

KEY ELEMENTS

As Buddhism spread, the stupa, still the mainstay of Buddhist architecture, evolved into a more complex building with worship halls, assembly spaces, and monks' living quarters.

STUPA SHAPES

A range of geometric forms and architectural styles developed, built with varying materials and adapted to specific topographies, but these new forms still adhered to the basic structure and symbolism of the earliest hemispherical stupa.

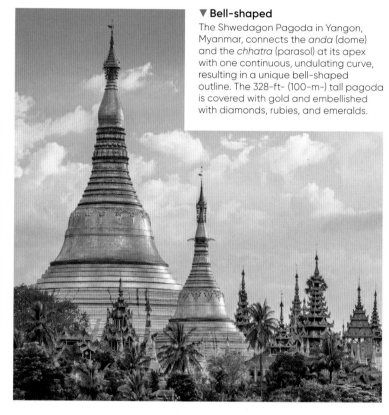

▼ Bell-shaped

The Shwedagon Pagoda in Yangon, Myanmar, connects the *anda* (dome) and the *chhatra* (parasol) at its apex with one continuous, undulating curve, resulting in a unique bell-shaped outline. The 328-ft- (100-m-) tall pagoda is covered with gold and embellished with diamonds, rubies, and emeralds.

▲ Ellipsoid

The Jetavana Dagoba in Anuradhapura, Sri Lanka, has an ellipsoid dome, like the classical Great Stupa at Sanchi, India. Rising 404 ft (123 m) above ground, it expresses its creators' ambition to build on a grander, cosmic scale.

CROSS-SHAPED

By the 8th century, in Mahayana Buddhism, the indented cruciform had become an important architectural form—typified by a cross-shaped terrace, upon which is a stupa with four chapels attached to the central core, the four cardinal directions recalling the *torana* gates of Sanchi's Great Stupa. The indented cruciform (seen here at Paharpur) is a hybrid of stupa and temple, as the chapels, courtyard, and 200 cells along the square enclosure form a proper *mahavihara* (great monastery) for the Buddhist community.

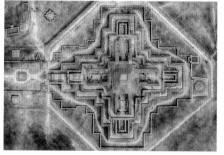

Aerial view of the Mahavihara at Paharpur, Bangladesh

▲ Tiered pagoda

Multistory pagodas like the Seigantoji Temple of Japan's Wakayama Prefecture deviated from the Indian prototype, instead adopting the rectilinear construction style of wooden towers and pavilions.

▲ Stepped pyramidal

The triple terraces of Kathmandu's Boudhanath stupa can be traced back to Central Asian prototypes with starlike pedestals. The eyes painted on the cubic base of the *chhatra* are distinctive of Nepalese stupas.

BUDDHIST BUILDINGS

From Korea to Indonesia, the pervading Mahayana iconography and cosmology created atmospheric sacred landscapes dominated by colossal Buddhas and forests of stupas and temples.

1. Bagan
Myanmar, 9th century

More than 2,000 Buddhist temples and stupas stand on the wide river plains of Bagan, the capital of the eponymous Buddhist kingdom founded in 849. Often built around a central core, with four entrances and a proliferation of spires, these towering structures evoke the cosmological vision of the mandala.

2. Chandi Sewu
Java, Indonesia, 8th century

Shaped from volcanic rock at the foothills of Mount Merapi, 250 chapels surround the main temple of Chandi Sewu. They are arranged in a series of nested squares that echo the layout of the Borobudur Great Stupa. Fierce, kneeling *dvarapalas* (doorkeepers) guard the entrances to a sacred realm.

3. Seokguram Grotto
Gyeongju, South Korea, 8th century

The Korean technique of using dressed stone to build an authentic dome under an artificial mound gives this grotto a unique aura, while its position in the mountains speaks of the Buddhist ideal of asceticism. The granite Buddha is surrounded by a pantheon of guardian kings and enlightened beings.

> "All is one; one is all."

Mahayana Buddhist view of the myriad universes and their ultimate unity in the Cosmic Buddha

INDIAN TEMPLES

The 10th to 13th centuries in India were characterized by a cultural effervescence. More and more temples were built, on an increasingly grand scale, and distinct architectural traditions emerged in the north and south of the country.

The focus of spiritual life, as well as social, educational, and economic centers, temples have dominated the landscape of India for centuries and are still being built today. Geometry, architecture, cosmic symbolism, and sculpture come together in temples to create a place dedicated to meeting the divine.

The earliest surviving temple complexes in India date from the 4th century CE, and evolved from earlier timber buildings, as revealed by early Buddhist stone structures (see pp.62–65). By the 7th century, two architectural traditions had emerged—the Nagara in the north and the Dravida in the south. These interpreted their architectural legacy in different ways, both in the selection of components and how the elements were put together. New idioms emerged and regional trends developed.

From the 10th to the 13th centuries, temple building intensified. In the 11th century, several colossal complexes were constructed, such as the Brihadishvara at Thanjavur, Tamil Nadu; the Lingaraja at Bhubaneshwar, Odisha; and the Shiva Temple at Bhojpur, Madhya Pradesh.

Indian architecture is conceived in terms of aedicules: miniature reproductions of buildings are combined, embedded in or projected from one another to form a full-scale building. The way in which these components are arranged defines the type of building, and also creates a sense of movement, giving the impression that both the temple and the divine unfold in front of the eyes of the worshippers.

NAGARA TRADITION

In 7th-century northern India, the three general types of shrine were the barrel-roofed Valabhi; the pyramid-shaped Phamsana, which had multiple eaves; and the Latina, which had a curved spire. By the 9th century, the Valabhi and the Phamsana shrines had fallen out of fashion, but their general forms survived—to be used as aedicules of full-scale temples. Valabhi pediments, for example, became a common component, and Phamsana halls were incorporated into larger structures.

Latina temples, by contrast, went on to dominate the landscape of northern India until the 10th century. Their curved spires were adorned with horseshoe-arch motifs and topped with a ribbed cushion-like structure. The Shekhari and the Bhumija types were composite types that evolved from the Latina. A Shekhari shrine, such as the Kandariya Mahadeva Temple (see opposite), has multiple half-Latina spires cascading down the cardinal axes, with a cluster of pillar-like elements between them. Bhumija temples developed in a different way. These have vertical chains of "pillars" flowing from the top of the tower to its base, between the spines facing north, south, east, and west.

MEETING THE DIVINE

A Hindu temple is the temporary abode of a deity, who resides within the cult object placed in the sanctum, once it has been honored by a priest through *puja* (ritual acts). Worshippers enter the temple for *darshana*—to see their revered deity and be seen by him or her in return. While the deities Vishnu, Devi, and Surya may be revered in a humanlike cult object, Shiva inhabits a pillar-like symbol called a linga.

Monumental linga of the Shiva Temple at Bhojpur, Madhya Pradesh

KANDARIYA MAHADEVA TEMPLE
KHAJURAHO, MADHYA PRADESH, INDIA, 11TH CENTURY

Dedicated to the god Shiva during the reign of the Chandela king Vidhyadhara (r. c.1003–1035), the Kandariya Mahadeva Temple is the grandest temple at the site of Khajuraho. This yellow sandstone structure is an exquisite example of Shekhari architecture, and has four half-Latina spires projecting from each side of the main shrine.

STEPPED DIAMOND

The Kandariya Mahadeva Temple is an example of the late Shekhari type, which adopted a stepped-diamond floor plan and quarter spires. The resulting multiplication of wall facets provided more surfaces for carving. Inside, the sanctum is surrounded by an ambulatory (walking passage), making it seem as though an inner temple is enshrined within a bigger one.

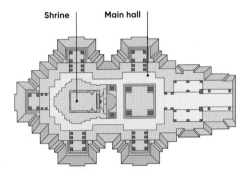

Shrine　Main hall

Floor plan of the Kandariya Mahadeva Temple

▲ Divine pantheon
More than 800 deities and attendants are carved on the exterior of the temple, arranged according to a hierarchy that radiates from the linga within. This vision of the divine unfolding offers worshippers a path to understanding divine reality.

▲ Inner sanctuary
A dark square chamber, known as the *garbhagrha* (womb chamber), at the core of the sanctum houses the linga, which symbolizes creation and the transcendental dimension of Shiva.

Each spire is topped with a ribbed crowning

Half-embedded Latina spires cascade down cardinal axes of the main shrine

Main hall

Entrance to the temple

KEY **ELEMENTS**

Indian temple architecture is continually in renewal, but the 10th to 13th centuries saw temple forms proliferate. The combination of different regional features in one edifice also became common.

TYPES OF SHRINE

Once the various types of shrine had been established, they were used as aedicules that were then pieced together to form full-scale buildings. These compositional elements were put together in different ways, making each temple unique in appearance.

▶ **Latina type**
Typical of late Latina temples, the 11th-century Vamana Temple at Khajuraho in Madhya Pradesh has a 21-story shrine adorned with spines decorated with a mesh pattern. It also has extremely compressed corner pavilions.

▲ **Bhumija variation**
The 11th-century sandstone Udayeshvara Temple at Udayapur in Madhya Pradesh is a fine example of Bhumija architecture. It is composed of a seven-story shrine built on a 28-point star plan. Chains of pillar-like components cascade down the spire.

DECORATION

Over time, some structural elements were turned into decorative motifs—so much so that their primary function and origins are unrecognizable. Complex geometric designs govern how these motifs are combined to form new patterns.

▲ **Backbone**
The Udayeshvara Temple has lattice spines that are characteristic of late northern Indian architecture. Made of flattened out and interwoven horseshoe arches, these spines are framed by pillar-like parts, each of which is crowned with a miniature Bhumija spire that incorporates southern Indian elements.

▲ **Horseshoe pediments**
Known as *gavakshas*, horseshoe arch forms appear everywhere in Indian architecture. Derived from dormers in wooden buildings, cascading and overlapping *gavakshas* form the pediments of the niches sheltering the deities on the external walls of the 12th-century Shiva Temple at Kiradu in Rajasthan.

▲ **Radiating rings**
Miniature lotus domes and petals unfurl in the concentric rings of the corbeled ceiling (built using overlapping pieces of stone) of the Sun Temple at Modhera in Gujarat, which dates from the 11th century. A pendant bursts out of the matrix at the heart of this radiating pattern.

INDIAN TEMPLES

Two main temple traditions emerged in southern India, one in Karnataka and the other in Tamil Nadu. In both regions, temples generally have the profile of a pyramid, but the floor plans and their crowning details vary, as well as the range of pavilion types used.

1. Chennakeshava Temple
Somnathpur, Karnataka, 13th century

Raised on a high platform, this richly adorned temple is composed of a large hall decorated with pierced screens, along with three star-shaped shrines made up of pavilions that seem to burst apart. This type of plan was particularly popular in southern Karnataka in the 11th century.

2. Kashivishveshara Temple
Lakkundi, Karnataka, 11th century

This temple, made of chloritic schist, a stone that is good for intricate carvings, has characteristics of several architectural traditions. Although most of its features are typical of southern Indian architecture, it also contains elements of northern Indian buildings, such as images of Shekhari and Bhumija shrines.

3. Bridhadeshvara Temple
Thanjavur, Tamil Nadu, 11th century

The Bridhadeshvara Temple stands in a vast enclosure, entered via a monumental *gopura* (barrel-roofed gateway), a feature typical of later southern temple complexes. Its 216-ft- (66-m-) tall pyramidal shrine is made up of square-domed, barrel-roofed, and arch-dormer, gable-roofed pavilions.

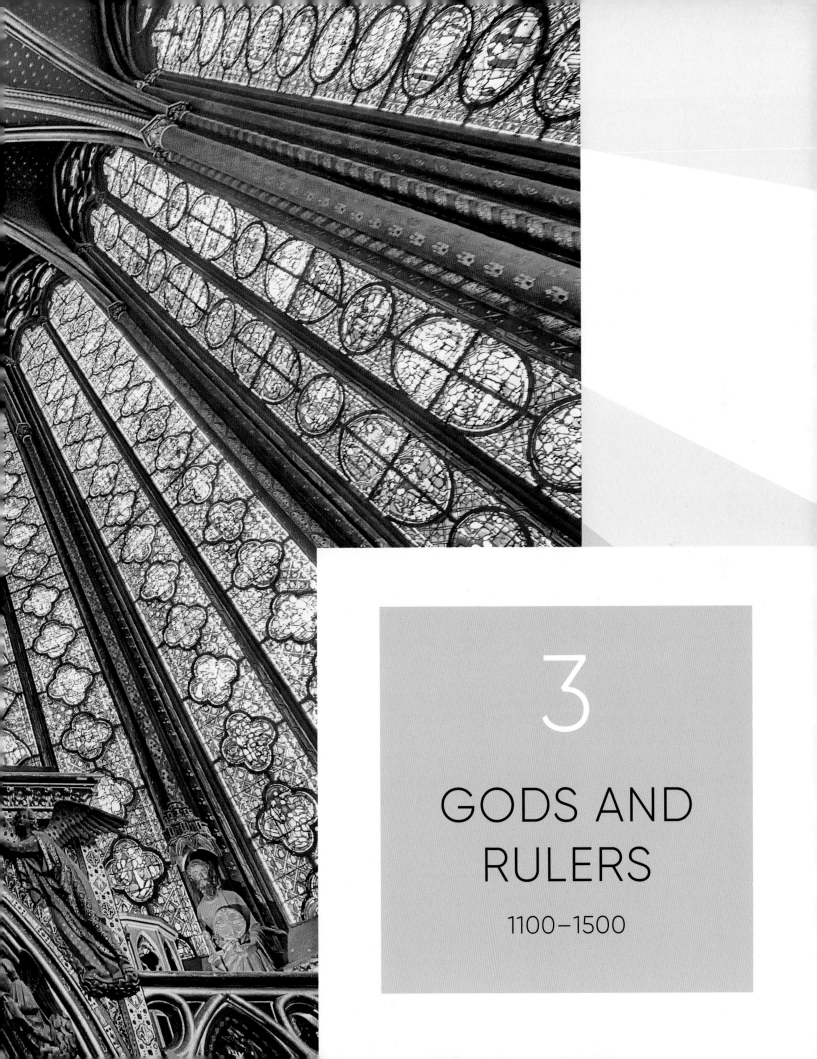

3

GODS AND RULERS

1100–1500

THE KHMER DYNASTY

Reflected in an expressive and sophisticated culture of temple building, the architecture of the Khmer dynasty showed a mastery of form and materials in bringing heaven to earth.

Extending across Southeast Asia from the 9th to the 15th centuries, the powerful Khmer Empire was centered on the magnificent city of Angkor in modern Cambodia. Expressed through art, buildings, sculpture, and engineering, Khmer culture was extraordinarily rich and sophisticated, and its legacy of temple architecture survives to this day. At its height from the 11th to the 13th centuries, Angkor was one of the largest settlements in the preindustrial world, occupied by 750,000 people. As well as constructing the city's majestic temples, Khmer architects and engineers devised a vast network of reservoirs and canals to sustain rice cultivation. Now designated a UNESCO World Heritage Site, Angkor Wat and its surrounding temples embody a superlative mastery of stonemasonry and carving, both figurative and decorative, as well as formal planning and landscaping.

EMBRACING HINDU COSMOLOGY

In celebrating the divine authority of Khmer kings, Khmer architecture reflected Hindu belief systems and cosmology. Hinduism spread across Southeast Asia through the activities of Indian merchants, and Hindu architecture became cross-fertilized with various local traditions. Khmer temples were conceived as monumental recreations of Mount Meru, the sacred temple-mountain and divine abode of Hindu gods. The mountain's five peaks were

> "It is grander than anything left to us by Greece or Rome."
>
> **Henri Mouhot**, French naturalist and explorer, on the temple of Angkor Wat, 1860

abstracted in the form of "prangs" (stepped pyramidal towers), surrounded by ponds and moats symbolizing the cosmic ocean.

THE ACHIEVEMENT OF ANGKOR WAT

Early Khmer temples consisted of a tower sanctuary, home to the primary deity, typically Shiva or Vishnu. Enclosed within a concentric series of walls, these early buildings showed the influence of Indian rock-cut temples. Over time, however, Khmer architecture became more distinct from that of the Indian subcontinent. Begun around 1120, under the aegis of King Suryavarman II, Angkor Wat elaborated on the basic organization of stepped pyramids within a walled compound to add multiple towers, culminating in a supreme expressive unity of architecture and art. Today, Angkor Wat is the best preserved of all the Angkor temples.

◄ **Hidden gem**
This elaborately carved wall at the temple of Preah Khan (meaning Royal Sword), built in the 12th century by King Jayavarman VII to honor his father, is now partly engulfed by nature on the Angkor site.

HINDU SYMBOLISM

The symmetrical layout of walls and courts are approached on a long axial causeway. Historically, moats and pools would have completely encircled the temple, representing the cosmic ocean. Originally dedicated to the Hindu god Vishnu, Angkor Wat was long ago converted into a Buddhist shrine and focus for Buddhist pilgrims.

Aerial view of the huge Angkor Wat temple complex, now surrounded by jungle

ANGKOR WAT

SIEM REAP, CAMBODIA, 1150

As the supreme architectural achievement of the Khmer dynasty, Angkor Wat was the principal state temple. Designed as a symbolic representation of Mount Meru, sacred domain of the Hindu gods, it features three galleried enclosures crowned by five stepped towers.

▲ Bas-relief
This detail from the "Churning of the Ocean of Milk" gallery depicts the eternal struggle between good and evil that churns the *amrita*, the elixir of everlasting life, from the primordial ocean.

▲ Corbel arch
Intricate stepped corbel arches constructed from blocks of sandstone have a limited span, so there are no large internal spaces in the temple. Once laid, the stone was embellished by craftsmen.

▲ Inner terraces
Three rectangular stepped galleried enclosures, one on top of the next, represent the physical and spiritual ascent to the abode of the gods to reach the shrine of the deity.

LAYOUT OF ANGKOR WAT

Central to the temple's layout and structuring of space was the experience of worshippers. Nested sets of galleries focus on the main shrine with its five towers (or "quincunx"). Access to the upper parts of the temple was reserved for priests and royalty, with ordinary people being admitted only to the lowest level.

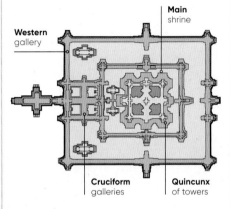

Western gallery

Main shrine

Cruciform galleries

Quincunx of towers

Angkor Wat faces west, unlike most Khmer temples.

Moat around the complex represents the ocean around the world

Central shrine below central tower

Central tower symbolizing Mount Meru

Five towers represent five peaks

Covered galleries run along the length of the temple

KEY ELEMENTS

As religious buildings were constructed in stone, many of the Khmer temples survive. Their distinctive stepped towers and intricate decoration have their roots in Hindu architecture.

PRANGS

Usually richly carved, prang towers or spires are stepped structures. The form has its origins in the *shikhara* (meaning mountain peak) towers characteristic of Indian temple architecture, which, like many other elements, were adapted by the Khmer Empire.

◄ **Early prang**
Bakong temple's single central prang is an early example (c. 9th century) of Khmer temple mountain architecture. Originally it would have been decorated with sculptures and carvings.

COLONNETTES

Small, slender, decorative columns called colonnettes are used to support, frame, or embellish doorways or walls. In Khmer architecture the subtle differences in their elaborately carved forms, which evolved over time, can be used to date buildings from particular eras.

▲ **Attractive infill**
A row of voluptuously carved colonnettes decorate a blind window in the temple of Banteay Srei at Angkor, known for the lavishness and complexity of its sandstone ornamentation.

CARVINGS AND RELIEFS

The surfaces of Khmer temples are always exuberantly decorated with a vivid cavalcade of deities, dancers, and mythological beasts. The softness of the local sandstone made carving relatively easy, enabling craftsmen to display their skills.

▲ **Detailed figures**
This 82-ft- (25-m-) long structure known as the Terrace of the Leper King, which may have been a cremation platform, is covered in finely sculpted figures, featuring armed guardians, celestial beings, and Garudas (mythological bird mounts of Vishnu).

▲ **Stone faces**
The famous "face towers" of the 12th-century Bayon temple support a number of gigantic, serenely smiling faces. Some have speculated that the model was King Jayavarman VII, others that it is the four-headed Hindu god Brahma.

▲ **Symbolic icon**
This exquisite devata, or demigoddess, is sculpted into the walls of Banteay Srei, a 10th-century temple dedicated to Shiva, the third god in the Hindu triumvirate. The temple's red sandstone is easy to carve and lends itself to lavish decoration.

KHMER BUILDINGS

Beyond Angkor Wat, the vast Angkor site contains numerous other temple complexes—some now almost buried by jungle—which span the centuries and give a sense of the richness of Khmer architecture.

1. Preah Khan
Siem Reap, Cambodia, 12th century

Structured around four concentric walls that embrace a labyrinth of shrines, courts, halls, and pavilions, Preah Khan is jointly dedicated to Buddhism and Hinduism, and features spectacular sculptures. It is now partly overgrown by the surrounding vegetation.

2. Bayon
Siem Reap, Cambodia, 12th century

Dominated by the enigmatic "face towers," featuring 216 smiling faces, the Bayon temple lies at the very center of Angkor Thom. This city was established by King Jayavarman VII on the Angkor site, based on the plan of a mandala (a Hindu representation of the universe).

3. Banteay Srei
Siem Reap, Cambodia, 10th century

Smaller in scale than most Khmer temples, the jewel-like Banteay Srei is also unusual in that it was commissioned by two courtiers rather than a monarch. Dedicated to Shiva, its red sandstone carvings are especially beautiful, many featuring celestial figures.

"Here in the middle of the Cambodian jungles one caught a glimpse of the myths and legends of medieval India."

Tariq Ali, *Street Fighting Years*, 2018

IMPERIAL CHINA

Under Mongol rule, imperial China became truly multiethnic. Traditional wooden architectural forms evolved and new hybrid styles emerged that embraced a wide range of cultural identities.

The legacy of 10th-century Tang architecture continued into the subsequent Liao, Song, and Jin dynasties. Wooden construction became standardized and codified, its principles and ethical values explained by court architect Li Jie in the first building manual, *Yingzao Fashi*, in 1103. The Mongol conquest of China in the 13th century, however, presented new challenges and stimulated innovations. Mongol khans substituted their yurts for wooden palaces, decked sumptuously with gold and silver.

CULTURAL COMMINGLING

Buddhists, Confucians, and Daoists mixed with Muslims, Christians, and Zoroastrians, among others, in China's cities. This diverse population advocated for a similar "multilingualism" in architecture: mosques, churches, and synagogues were built, testing the tenacity and adaptability of China's age-old wooden construction methods. Marble minarets and brick domes stood among wooden pagodas and halls, inspiring new hybrid forms. Although the timber frame retained the ritual functions and religious and regal symbolism acquired under Tang rule, imperial patrons began to

> "A sunny pleasure-dome with caves of ice!"

Samuel Taylor Coleridge envisaging the Mongol ruler's palace in the poem "Kubla Khan," 1816

seek alternative ways to express their vision of a heavenly empire. Wealth and power were still conveyed through size, but with added ornament—meticulous carving, painting, and gilding of beams, brackets, walls, and ceilings.

The Mongol Yuan dynasty (1271–1368) made Beijing their new imperial capital, constructing a walled, square city centered on the imperial palace, its remaining blocks laid out on a grid plan and arranged symmetrically along the north-south axis. Ming (1368–1644) and Qing (1644–1911) emperors added the Temple of Heaven in the southeast of the city and a vast system of parks and lakes in the northwest, turning the city into the ultimate symbol of political legitimacy and cultural supremacy.

State patronage of Buddhism continued, as seen in the bottle-shaped stupas, diamond-throne pagodas, and terraced Lamaist temples that were built in Beijing. Jesuit missionaries brought templates of European palaces to the imperial court, and added novelty to park designs, as at Yuanmingyuan. Besides these influences, imperial Chinese style at its peak also embraced "naturalness" (*ziran*), as seen in the idyllic gardens and retreats of South China.

CHANGING TIMES

China fluctuated between periods of unity and fragmentation. Unity during the Yuan, Ming, and Qing dynasties brought economic and population growth, territorial expansion, and advances in science, engineering, and the arts, which in turn led to the development of new architectural forms, structures, and styles.

Multiple tiers of brackets support broad eaves

THE HALL OF PRAYER
TEMPLE OF HEAVEN, BEIJING, CHINA, 1420 (REBUILT 1890)

Located at the northern end of the 1,312-ft- (400-m-) long path that runs through the Temple of Heaven complex, the Hall of Prayer is the crowning glory of the carefully configured spatial sequence, where the emperor offered annual sacrifice and prayed for a good harvest.

Golden bulbous finial
on conical roof

Three layers of eaves represent tripartite universe (heaven, Earth, humanity)

ROUND HEAVEN, SQUARE EARTH

The layout of the Temple of Heaven conforms to the ancient Chinese cosmological view that "Heaven is round as a stretched canopy and Earth is square as a chessboard." The sacred composition of the circle and the square is translated here into a circular structure surrounded by a square enclosure of walls and subsidiary buildings. This layout can be traced back to that of the Han-dynasty *mingtang* (hall of light).

The circular Temple of Heaven is positioned in a square enclosure.

Lintels painted with golden imperial insignia

▲ **Blue hue**
The deep saturated blue of these glazed roof tiles evokes heaven in Chinese beliefs and is the color of the cardinal direction east, which is associated with dragons—seen here carved on the end tiles.

▲ **Symbolic pillars**
Inside the Hall of Prayer, four inner and 12 outer columns stand for the four seasons, the 12 months of the year, and the 12 hours of the day. This design demonstrates the importance of time to a farming society.

KEY ELEMENTS

Wood and earth still dominated, but cast iron, glazed ceramics, and porcelain expanded the repertoire of building materials and styles. Free-form gardens broke the rigid symmetry of Chinese mansions.

DEFENSIVE WALLS

Walls define boundaries. Chinese walls not only fortify and protect, but also separate spaces and social groups. City walls were typically built using rammed earth reinforced by timbers, their construction announcing the birth of a city and the consolidation of political power.

▲ **Social divide**
Chang'an (now Xi'an), the ancient capital of the Tang dynasty, retained its political importance under the Ming and Qing. Its walls served as a reminder of the social hierarchy prescribed in Confucian ritual.

◄ **Deterring invaders**
Construction of the Great Wall started in the 4th century BCE to curb the incursions of the northern nomads, but expansion and repair work continued into the 16th century. The wall runs from northeast China across Mongolia to the Taklamakan Desert.

TIMBER JOINTING SYSTEMS

The post-and-lintel, mortise-and-tenon construction of the Chinese timber frame makes it resilient to earthquakes and strong winds. The number and size of brackets, the stand-out feature of this structural system, indicate the overall scale and cost of the building, and the social rank of its owner.

▲ **Branch of brackets**
Wooden bracket arms (*gong*) and bearing blocks (*dou*) form different combinations of *dougong* brackets to support beams and transfer the weight of a roof onto its columns. Foguang Temple's stacked *dougong* are like a flowering tree.

▲ **Triangular truss**
The *wujia* (Chinese truss) supports the purlins, resulting in a gently curved roofline. In the vernacular architecture of the south, shown here, the use of the truss creates an open-ended roof that maximizes natural lighting and ventilation.

METALWORK

A few rare pagodas made of cast iron demonstrated the smelting technology and metalworking of the Song dynasty (960–1279), made possible by the growing use of coal rather than wood charcoal. Other metal structures also appeared around this time, such as bronze halls and pavilions.

Slender body made possible by the use of iron

▶ **Cast to perfection**
The Danyang Iron Pagoda at the Yuquan Temple, Hubei Province was cast in 1061. Nearly 60 ft (18 m) high, the 13 levels of this weighty masterwork were cast separately to emulate a wooden pagoda with flying eaves.

IMPERIAL GARDENS

Rooted in the ideals of nature, picturesque scenery, and creation, Chinese gardens emulated miniature mountain peaks and river valleys. They served as urban retreats, offering scholar-officials a rural, peaceful, and elegant life away from mundane obligations.

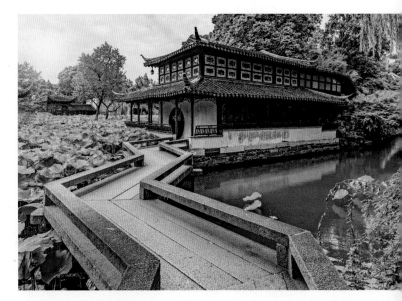

▲ **Different perspectives**
The zigzagging stone bridge of the Humble Administrator's Garden in Suzhou, Jiangsu Province, leads to a wooden pavilion in the center of the garden, next to a lotus pond, creating a journey that invites visitors to slow down and savor the views.

ANIMAL SCULPTURES

Zoomorphic design in China emerged as early as 4000 BCE. Dragons, phoenixes, *qilin* (Chinese unicorns), lions, and other animals are often seen as intermediaries between humans and heaven, and emblematic of nobility, longevity, morality, benevolence, and good fortune.

▲ **High-ranking roof**
The procession on this Forbidden City roof ridge is headed by a celestial figure riding an animal and leading other magical beasts and birds. There are 10 in total—a number that indicates the highest rank of Chinese architecture.

▲ **Dazzling dragon**
In the middle of the Nine Dragon Screen–wall in the Forbidden City is a yellow dragon depicted head-on against a background of blue sky and turbulent turquoise sea. The use of glazed ceramic tiles creates a glossy surface and brings out the vivid colors.

▲ **Mythical landscape**
Seventeen semicircular arches give this stone bridge at the Summer Palace a rhythmic appearance. Inspired by private gardens in South China, the giant lake and islands recall the fabled islands of the immortals in Chinese mythology.

IMPERIAL CHINESE BUILDINGS

A timeless architectural style emerged from the Tang legacy, seen in palace buildings, temples, tombs, and parks. Nonetheless, external cultural elements continued to exert their influence.

1

3

2

1. Stela Pavilion, Ming mausoleums
Beijing, 1435

The double-eave hip-and-gable roof gives this imperial mausoleum pavilion an aura of solemnity. It enshrines an enormous stone stela recording the emperor's achievements and opens onto a "spirit path" leading to the burial chamber.

2. Shakyamuni Pagoda
Yingxian, Shanxi Province, 1056

At 220 ft (67 m), this pagoda is the tallest wooden structure in East Asia. Its ingenious double-core design, along with four mezzanines that act as cushions between the five stories, has ensured structural stability through multiple earthquakes.

3. Huayan Temple
Datong, Shanxi Province, 1062

The hipped roof and "owl-tail" roof ornaments of this structure speak of imperial patronage. Liao-dynasty architecture was closely aligned to Tang styles, and the Huayan Temple demonstrates a robustness akin to earlier examples.

4

4. Yuanmingyuan
Beijing, 18th century

Jesuit missionaries at court helped design the vast parks of the Yuanmingyuan, which boast Baroque-style marble columns and balustrades (shown here), and fountains and labyrinths, all combined with Chinese eaves and plant motifs.

5

6 7

5. Yonghe Palace–temple
Beijing, 1694
With its "flying galleries" and wing towers, the multistory Wanfu Pavilion evokes the image of a heavenly palace. Housing a statue of the Maitreya Buddha, this Lamaist temple is a blend of early imperial Buddhist pavilion designs.

6. Huajuexiang Mosque
Xi'an, 8th century (rebuilt 14th century)
Unlike the north-south axis of Chinese temples, this mosque has an east-west sequence that starts with a wooden entrance hall and ends with a columned hall, where the mihrab (prayer niche) is on the west wall, pointing to Mecca.

7. Zhenjue Temple Diamond Throne Pagoda
Beijing, 1473
Seated on a vast base is a group of five "dense-eave" stone pagodas, arranged in a quincunx layout (like the five on a die). They represent the Five Buddhas of a Tibetan mandala, with the main deity in the center of the geometric shape.

▲ **Fluid spaces**
Shakkei (borrowed view)
is a landscape-design
technique that creates
a multilayered view by
incorporating a distant
object into the foreground.
Here, a pair of open sliding
doors form a picture frame
of the trees in the garden
of Kyoto's Nijo Palace.

MEDIEVAL JAPAN

The rise of the military class, led by shoguns, in the 12th century saw arts and culture flourish in Japan. Castles, teahouses, villas, and Zen Buddhist temples were built as the country's architecture was rejuvenated.

Symmetry and formality characterized Heian-period (794–1185) architecture. Aristocratic residences were built in the *shinden* (sleeping hall) style, with subsidiary structures laid out around a central building. By the 14th century, however, a less formal style started to gain favor among the military class, inspired by the abbot's chamber in a Buddhist monastery. The refined *shoin* (study) style—which later evolved into the more distinctive form of *sukiya* (teahouse)—had an asymmetrical layout, and came with its own elaborate design vocabulary, especially for the interior space.

DIFFERENT WAYS TO IMPRESS

Although *shinden* and *shoin* represent two contradicting aesthetic principles, Japanese residences in both styles shared common features. They used tatami mats as a modular unit of space, emphasizing a largely seated lifestyle, while sliding doors (*fusuma*) enabled the flexible partitioning of rooms, as well as breaking the boundary between the building's interior and exterior.

Fit for a scholar, a typical *shoin* room featured an alcove with staggered shelves (*chigaidana*) and a built-in desk (*tsukeshoin*). Nijo Palace, built in 1603 for shogun Tokugawa Ieyasu, combines the style with polychrome paintings of animals and seasonal scenes, featuring, for example, the cypress tree, which symbolizes longevity and strength. The palace's sliding doors and paneled walls, coated in gold and silver, create an atmosphere of wealth and illumination. By contrast, aligned more to the *sukiya* aesthetic, 17th-century imperial villas such as the Katsura are unadorned. Their style instead evokes a sense of intimacy, nostalgia, and rurality through the integration of tea rooms; gardens; ink landscape paintings; and a warm, earthy color palette.

Nearly 100 castles were built in the 16th and 17th centuries, many commissioned by Japan's three unifiers, Oda Nobunaga, Toyotomi Hideyoshi, and Tokugawa Ieyasu. Serving as military headquarters and administrative bases, these towering wooden structures were inspired by multistory Buddhist pagodas.

Broad veranda
provides viewing
platform

THE TEA CEREMONY

The ritual of tea drinking is said to have been refined by tea master Sen no Rikyū (1522–1591). Tea drinking was valued by aristocrats and Buddhist monks alike for its medicinal benefits, the bitter taste helping to enhance mental clarity during meditation. The design of tea utensils, teahouses, and tea gardens embodied the Zen philosophy about the imperfection and impermanence of creation.

Ihoan teahouse, Kōdai-ji Temple, Kyoto

Natural rocks
border lake

GOLDEN PAVILION

KYOTO, JAPAN, 1397 (LATER REBUILT)

Originally built as a centerpiece for shogun Ashikaga Yoshimitsu's personal villa and converted to a Buddhist temple after his death, the Golden Pavilion perches on a corner of an artificial pond in a spacious garden. Inspired by Chinese examples, the garden and pavilion also inherited elements from Heian *shinden* residences.

REFLECTING NATURE

Water is an essential element in Japanese garden design. The reflection of the pavilion in the lake maximizes the perceived vertical depth of the natural landscape, the rippling effect of water providing an ever-changing, unpredictable view. This conveys the Zen teaching about the empty, impermanent nature of all things, an illusion that can be dispelled only by achieving enlightenment.

Woodblock print by Hiroshi Yoshida, 1933

▶ Island in the sea
A porch stretches out into the water from the pavilion, drawing the eye toward a pile of rocks that represent the islands of immortals. It mimics the fishing stations (*tsuridono*) of Heian houses.

▲ Architecture and time
Snow, rain, and the changing appearance of plants are incorporated into Japanese building and garden design and associated with seasonal rituals and festivities.

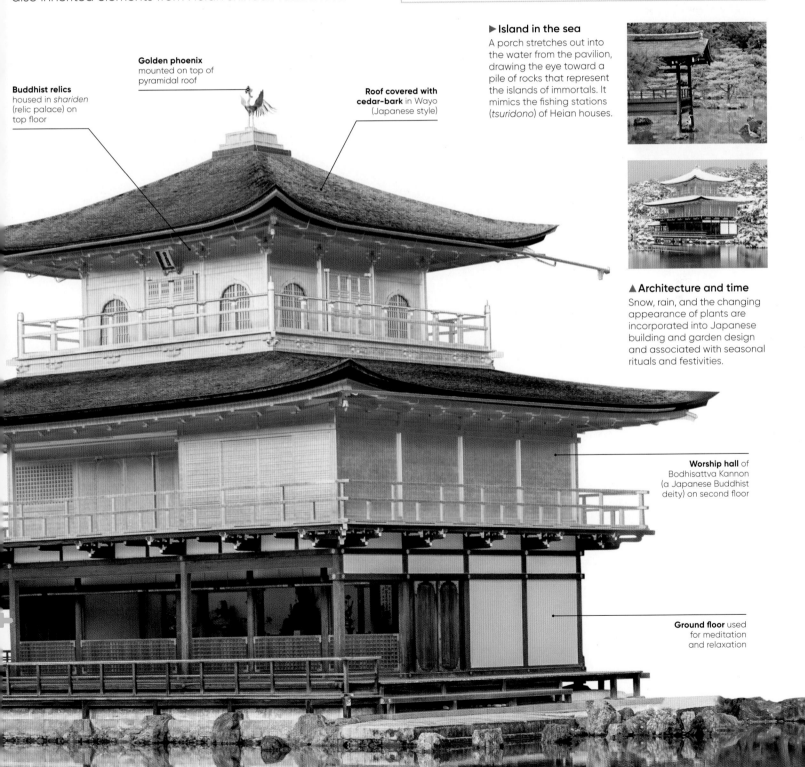

Buddhist relics
housed in *shariden* (relic palace) on top floor

Golden phoenix
mounted on top of pyramidal roof

Roof covered with cedar-bark in Wayo (Japanese style)

Worship hall of Bodhisattva Kannon (a Japanese Buddhist deity) on second floor

Ground floor used for meditation and relaxation

KEY **ELEMENTS**

The towering castles and dazzling shrines and temples of 12th- to 17th-century Japan were balanced by the subdued elegance and understated beauty of tearooms and villas.

CURVED GABLES

The undulating bargeboard (*karahafu*), though also called "Chinese gable," is found only in Japan. Often ornamented with metallic fittings or woodcarvings, the raised curve line signals an important architectural feature, such as the entrance to a building complex.

▲ **Elaborate entrance**
Built in the *Zenshuyo*, or "Zen style," the Karamon Gate at the Kencho-ji temple emphasizes symmetry and formality. Its exuberant floral and cloud patterns are Chinese-inspired, but the wooden shingles of the roof are typically Japanese.

▲ **Curves and corners**
At Himeji Castle, Chinese-style triangular gables alternate with Japanese curved gables, generating a rhythmic, compound roofline. The seven-story tower is built around a central heart pillar made of a single trunk of silver fir.

SLIDING DOORS

Made of paper mounted on wooden frames, *fusuma* (sliding doors) often bear paintings themed to fit the room. The doors can be shut for privacy, and different combinations of open and closed doors make for a versatile interior space, with natural ventilation and lighting.

TEAHOUSES

The *sukiya* teahouse is not only an architectural style but an embodiment of the Zen philosophy of *wabi sabi*—imperfection and silence. It is often attached to a larger structure or built as a stand-alone "hut" approached by a path of stepping stones.

◀ **Natural space**
The flexible partitioning at Katsura Imperial Villa makes it possible to adjust the size and configuration of the room according to climate, audience size, and occasion. Paper creates an ephemeral feel; its yellowed, undecorated surface matches the tatami floor mats and wooden ceiling.

◀ **Tea room**
The small, intimate *chasitsu* (tea room) at the Golden Pavilion features an irregular timber bordering one side of the central alcove (*tokonoma*). A single hanging scroll serves as an object of contemplation or a conversation-starter between tea master and guests.

MEDIEVAL JAPANESE BUILDINGS

Beneath the surface differences of medieval Japanese buildings lies a common philosophy of integrating wooden structures with gardens and the natural landscape to create an immersive spiritual experience.

1. Phoenix Hall, Byodoin temple
Uji, Kyoto Prefecture, 1043

The pair of golden phoenixes on both ends of this hall's ridgepole is echoed by the U-shaped structure, whose two side wings resemble a bird in flight. Modeled on a Chinese palace gate, the Phoenix Hall is an architectural incarnation of Amida Buddha's Pure Land.

2. Yomeimon Gate, Nikko Toshogu
Nikko, Tochigi Prefecture, c. 1600–1650

The impressive gate to this shrine is inspired by the Buddhist *chumon* which, unlike minimalist torii gates, assumes a royal magnificence suitable for the first shogun of the Tokugawa Shogunate. The blue roof, gilt polychrome brackets and lintels, and carved dragons lure the visitor up the staircase to the space within.

3. Ryoanji rock garden
Kyoto, c. 1500

A quintessential example of the Japanese "dry landscape" (*karesansui*), this rock garden uses no water yet conjures up images of peaks in the clouds and islands in the sea through carefully arranged rock piles and raked gravel. This miniaturized, abstract picture of nature calls for contemplation.

> *"Ichi-go ichi-e (one time, one meeting)"*
>
> **Japanese saying attributed to tea master Sen no Rikyū**, accentuating the idea of transience embedded in the design of teahouses and tea rooms, 16th century

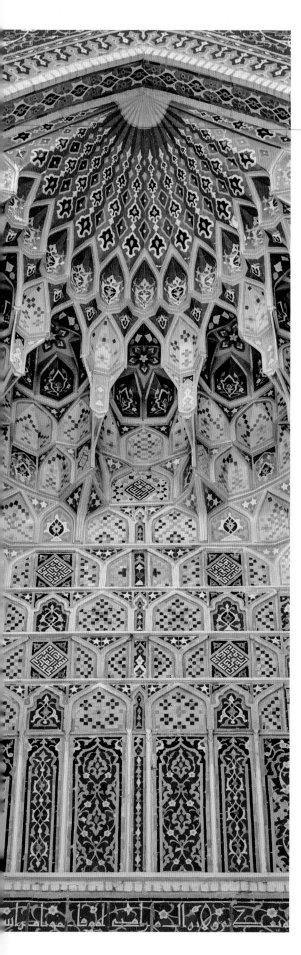

THE TIMURID DYNASTY

In the late 14th century, a new dynasty arose in Central Asia and tore through the Islamic world in a frenzy of destruction. In its wake, it left a dazzling architectural legacy.

The Timurids, named for their leader Timur (1336–1405), were a Turko-Mongol tribe who came from the Central Asian steppe. Timur's armies toppled rival Islamic dynasties and conquered territory in Central Asia and across what is now Iran, Iraq, southern Russia, and northern India. Like other formidable rulers, Timur deployed fear as a military tactic to secure his conquests. After one rebellion, he cemented prisoners alive into the city walls.

As their empire grew, the Timurids developed beautiful cities with a rich urban culture. Nowhere was this displayed to greater effect than in Timur's capital of Samarkand, in present-day Uzbekistan.

SAMARKAND

Bringing craftsmen from the lands that he had conquered to Samarkand, Timur initiated one of the most brilliant periods in Islamic architecture, building on the traditions of the Seljuks—a Turko-Persian empire from 1037 to 1194. The Seljuks had ruled from various capitals in Iran and Central Asia, where they created brick buildings decorated with tiles and carved stucco. The earliest Timurid building is believed to be the Mausoleum of Khawaja Ahmed Yasawi (1389) in present-day southern Kazakhstan. Its innovative use of space, along with its vaults, domes, and decoration set the style for subsequent Timurid buildings.

In Samarkand, his favorite city, Timur promoted monumental architecture, using new forms of engineering and the finest materials available. Timurid buildings were typically designed on a symmetrical axis, with multiple minarets and large, often ribbed, double domes (in which an internal dome supports an outer, more bulbous dome shell).

These buildings combined colossal scale with the finest of detailing. Soaring iwans were entirely covered in glazed tiles patterned with arabesques and floral designs, while domes were tiled in brilliant blues—in these dry lands, blue was a reference to both water and the heavens. The culmination of Timurid style is the Gur-i Amir (Tomb of the King), a 1404 complex in Samarkand that contains the tombs of Timur, his sons, and his grandsons. After Timur's death, the oasis city Herat, in modern Afghanistan, became the new Timurid capital and an important center of intellectual and artistic life in the Muslim world.

LASTING LEGACY

Although the Timurid Empire lasted for fewer than 150 years, its architecture represents a pinnacle of Islamic arts. The buildings that Timur and his descendants created went on to have great influence on Iran during the Safavid dynasty and also gave rise to the Mughal school of architecture in India.

◀ **Vibrant tiling**
Gur-i Amir, the burial place of Timur, boasts impressive decoration, including an entrance portal elaborately tiled with muqarnas—ornamental, stalactite-like moldings from the Islamic period.

TIMUR

The son of a minor nobleman, Timur was born in present-day Uzbekistan in 1336. In his youth, he was a bandit, and was shot by two arrows. One hit his right leg and made him lame, leading to his European names, Timur the Lame or Tamerlane. He became a military leader, picking up followers and winning sufficient victories to proclaim himself sovereign in Balkh, in modern Afghanistan, in 1370.

A modern statue of Timur surveys his lands in Samarkand, not far from his final resting place at Gur-i Amir Mausoleum.

MOSQUE OF BIBI KHANUM

SAMARKAND, UZBEKISTAN, 1404

A masterpiece of Timurid architecture, the Mosque of Bibi Khanum was dedicated to Timur's Chinese wife. At the time it was built, it was one of the largest and most magnificent buildings in the Islamic world.

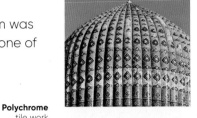

◄ Colorful domes
Two ribbed domes top the side iwans, while the largest iwan has a smoother 130-ft (40-m) cupola. The Timurids built the inner and outer domes different shapes, with a space between them, so that the interior looked different from the exterior.

A minaret stands at each corner of the site

Monumental portal arch

Polychrome tile work

The largest of four iwans around the central courtyard

Bulbous, ribbed dome

TIMURID BUILDINGS

▲ Ak-Saray Palace, Shakhrisabz, Uzbekistan, 1380–1404
Ruined piers that lost their arch long ago are all that remain of the original majestic entrance of the Ak-Saray Palace. Timur ordered that it be built in the city of his birth to celebrate victory in battle.

▲ Shah-i Zinda, Samarkand, Uzbekistan, 11th, 15th, and 19th centuries
Although it was founded in the 11th century, this mausoleum complex dates mainly from the Timurid era. Its ten small mausoleums feature some of the most ornate Timurid tile work.

▲ Ulugh Beg Madrasa, Samarkand, Uzbekistan, 1417–1421
Another of Samarkand's marvels is the Registan—three madrasas (Islamic schools) on three sides of a square. This madrasa was built by Timur's grandson, Ulugh Beg; the others were built later in Timurid style.

ARCHITECTURE OF THE ISLAMIC WEST

In a pattern seen worldwide, the Islamic architecture of the western Mediterranean from the 8th century was at once international and local, adopting and adapting motifs to suit regional conditions.

Early Islam spread rapidly along the coastline of the Mediterranean by conquest, conversion, and trade. By the early 8th century, Muslim armies had conquered the western end of North Africa and the Iberian Peninsula (modern-day Spain and Portugal). United by easy sea transportation, these new western Islamic territories maintained strong political and cultural ties right up to the conquest of Granada by the Christian-ruled kingdoms of Aragon and Castile in 1492.

The Islamic rulers of Al-Andalus, which took up much of the Iberian Peninsula, graced their new kingdom with beautiful buildings such as the Great Mosque of Córdoba (see p.99). Córdoba remained the seat of Muslim power in the region until the ruling Umayyad dynasty (711–1031), weakened by a series of civil wars and revolts, was overthrown in the 11th century. After this, Al-Andalus was divided into a patchwork of rival principalities known as *taifas*.

Grand palaces were built to house the rulers of the *taifas*, including the Aljafería Palace in Zaragoza, the Alcazaba of Málaga, and the Alcázar of Seville—a city that the Almohad dynasty (1130–1269) developed as their capital. These palaces were impressive in scale and order, well-fortified, and decorated with lavish and skillful craftwork. True to Islamic tradition, their ornamentation usually featured geometric rather than figurative motifs. The use of thick stone walls, gardens, and ornamental pools ensured comfortable conditions for the elite inhabitants in the heat of summer.

In 1238, work began on one of the wonders of world architecture, the Alhambra (see pp.148–149). Built by Muhammad I, first emir of the Nasrid dynasty (1230–1492), on a hill overlooking Granada, this palace-fortress was continuously extended and adapted by later Nasrid rulers.

NORTH AFRICA

Across the Mediterranean, in North Africa, the Almoravid dynasty (1062–1147) founded Marrakech in Morocco as their capital. In the late 11th century, they helped defend the Iberian Islamic territories against Christian armies, reuniting the *taifas* of Al-Andalus in the process. Their successors, the Almohads, ruled swathes of North Africa and Al-Andalus. Under the rule of a single dynasty, the two territories developed a shared architectural style.

When Spain finally fell to the Christian armies in 1492, the architectural heritage of Al-Andalus was kept alive in North Africa by the Marinids (1276–1554) and the dynasties that followed. In the imperial cities of Fès, Meknes, Marrakech, and Salé, many great mosques, madrasas, and palaces were built, featuring stuccowork and mosaic tiling, and showing the experimentation with different arch types that is characteristic of the region's Islamic architecture.

◀ **Bou Inania Madrasa**
This combination of religious college and mosque in central Fès was completed in 1350, during the Marinid period. One of the high points of Moroccan architecture, it has exquisite interior decoration.

A BEACON OF MULTICULTURALISM

In the 11th and 12th centuries, Muslims, Christians, and Jews lived together in harmony in Spain, to the benefit of all. As science and scholarship flourished, this western outpost of Islam made great contributions to the development of thought and the humanities, including commentaries on Jewish law by Maimonides and on philosophy by Ibn Rushd, better known in the west as Averroes.

Statue of Averroes in Córdoba, Andalusia

KOUTOUBIA MOSQUE

MARRAKECH, MOROCCO, 1158

The Koutoubia takes its name, which means "Mosque of the Booksellers," from the merchants who once filled the surrounding streets and specialized in holy texts. Its minaret contains a ramp that is broad and tall enough for the muezzin to ride a horse up to the top.

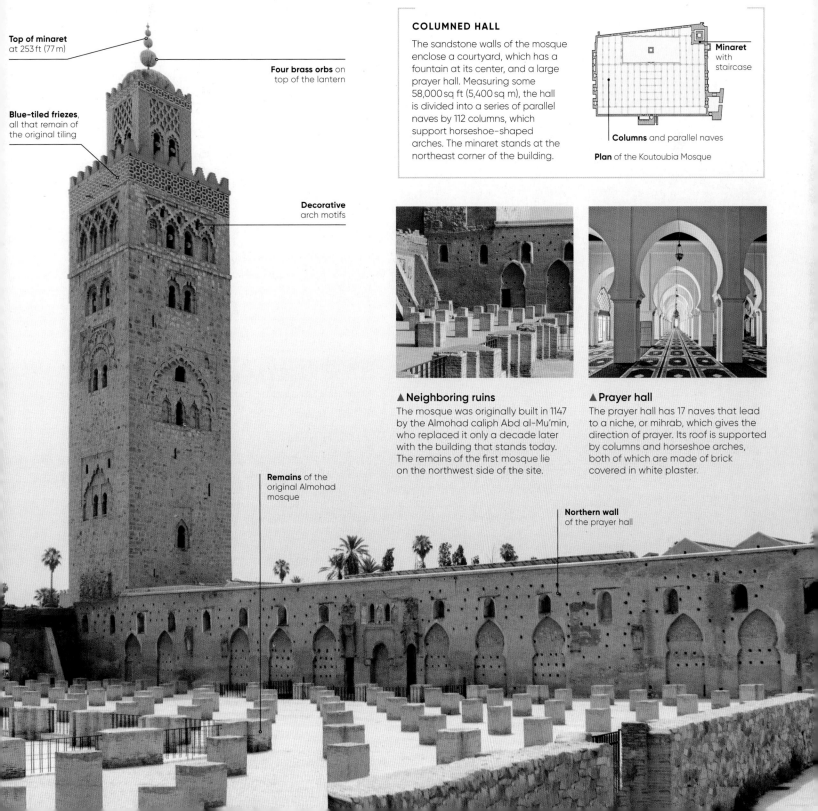

Top of minaret at 253 ft (77 m)

Four brass orbs on top of the lantern

Blue-tiled friezes, all that remain of the original tiling

Decorative arch motifs

Remains of the original Almohad mosque

Northern wall of the prayer hall

COLUMNED HALL

The sandstone walls of the mosque enclose a courtyard, which has a fountain at its center, and a large prayer hall. Measuring some 58,000 sq ft (5,400 sq m), the hall is divided into a series of parallel naves by 112 columns, which support horseshoe-shaped arches. The minaret stands at the northeast corner of the building.

Minaret with staircase

Columns and parallel naves

Plan of the Koutoubia Mosque

▲ Neighboring ruins

The mosque was originally built in 1147 by the Almohad caliph Abd al-Mu'min, who replaced it only a decade later with the building that stands today. The remains of the first mosque lie on the northwest side of the site.

▲ Prayer hall

The prayer hall has 17 naves that lead to a niche, or mihrab, which gives the direction of prayer. Its roof is supported by columns and horseshoe arches, both of which are made of brick covered in white plaster.

KEY **ELEMENTS**

The architecture of the Islamic West melded Syrian Umayyad elements with North African Berber and Spanish Visigothic influences to produce a distinctive and sophisticated style.

STUCCO

In Islamic architecture, the art of chiseling or molding fine designs into plaster that was still damp appeared during the Umayyad period in the area now known as Syria and Jordan, but it reached its finest expression in Muslim Al-Andalus and North Africa.

▲ **Plant motifs**
Some of the finest stucco decoration in Morocco, as in the Ben Youssef Madrasa in Marrakech above, was created during the reign of the Saadian sultans (1510–1659).

▶ **Filigree decoration**
In Spain, the best stuccowork dates from the Nasrid era (1230–1492). In the Alhambra, multifoil arches are lavishly decorated with filigree calligraphy and arabesques.

GARDENS

The Islamic gardens of Al-Andalus and Morocco are geometric in layout and combine water features, secluded walkways, and fragrant and colorful plants. They were designed to give visitors a foretaste of the Paradise gardens described in the Qur'an.

TILING

The Islamic architectural tradition of tiling was carried into North Africa and Spain, where its color palette widened under the influence of the Berbers of the Atlas Mountains.

▲ **Topiary**
Islamic gardens were carefully planned so that tall trees provided shade, smaller trees produced fruit, and flowerbeds released all kinds of fragrance. The 14th-century garden of the Alcázar de los Reyes Cristianos in Andalusia also has statuesque topiary.

▲ **Water features**
As Islam first emerged in the deserts of Arabia, it was natural that water became a symbol of Allah's mercy. It is therefore one of the three key elements of Islamic gardens. The Alcázar de los Reyes Cristianos was built by Christian monarchs, but is typically Islamic in style, with a long pool and many fountains.

▲ **Zelije tiling**
The distinctive Moorish style of tiling, as displayed in the Alcázar, Seville (see right), is known as zelije. Large pieces of tiles are cut to size and then hand-carved before being left to dry, kiln-fired, and glazed. In accordance with Islamic tradition, their designs are geometric and nonfigurative.

ISLAMIC WEST BUILDINGS

The architecture of the Islamic West is found in southern Spain, particularly in Andalusia. The same style is also common across Morocco, Algeria, and Tunisia.

1. The Giralda
Seville, Spain, 1198

The great bell tower of Seville is actually the minaret of a mosque that once stood on the site but was demolished (bar the minaret) to make way for the neighboring Christian cathedral. The minaret was completed in 1198, but the belfry is a later Christian addition.

2. The Alcázar
Seville, Spain, 13th century

Originally a Muslim palace and fortress, the Alcázar was built in the 10th century and then greatly expanded in the 12th century. It was largely destroyed after the Christian conquest of Seville in 1248, but was rebuilt in the Mudéjar style, which combined Moorish, Romanesque, Gothic, and Renaissance elements.

3. The Almoravid Koubba
Marrakech, Morocco, 12th century

This simple kiosk is all that has survived in Marrakech from the era of the Almoravids, the founders of the city. It dates back to the reign of the Berber emir Ali Ben Youssef (1107–1143), and was probably part of the complex in the mosque where ablutions took place.

1

3

2

ALHAMBRA

GRANADA, SPAIN, 1232–1390

Built by southern Spain's Muslim rulers, the sultans of the Nasrid dynasty, the fortified palace of the Alhambra (Red fortress) is one of the wonders of Islamic architecture.

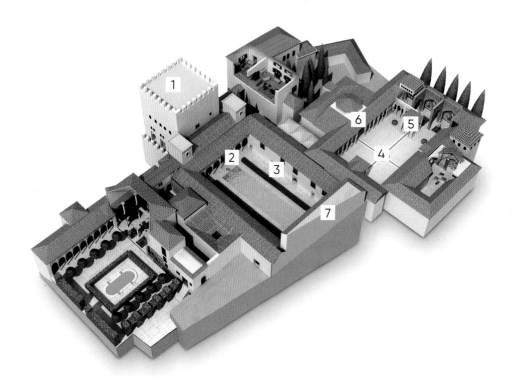

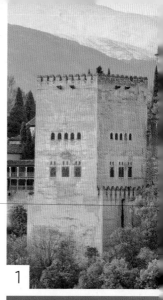

1. Comares Tower

At 148 ft (45 m) in height, the Comares Tower contains some of the most important rooms of the palace. The tower's thick stone walls made it strong and secure, and its height ensured that it was a good vantage point.

2. Court of Myrtles

This long courtyard is built around a large rectangular pool that is fed by two fountains. The water reflects the symmetrical arcades at either end, which feature slender columns, tall arches, and elaborately carved upper walls.

3. Wall decoration

Many of the Alhambra's rooms have a tiled skirting with strong, colorful patterns that contrast effectively with the monochrome carvings on the walls above. These were designed and executed by highly skilled artists and craftsmen.

4. Court of Lions

The courtyard's arcade consists of multifoil arches, a typical Islamic form, in which each side of the arch is split into a series of small curves. Clusters of slender columns support the arches.

5. Daxara's Mirador

A small room that acts as a gazebo, this *mirador* (lookout) is an indoor space from which people can enjoy looking at the courtyard garden beyond, creating a link between the interior and exterior.

6. Hall of the Two Sisters

The walls are covered in fine plaster decorations, yet the most striking feature of the room is the dome. A series of small windows illuminate the *mocárabes* (intricate plaster forms that hang like stalactites), also known as muqarnas, to create patterns of light and shade.

7. The red fortress

Seen from a distance, the massive crenellated towers rising above the red brick and stone walls that gave the palace its name, make the Alhambra look forbidding. It is arranged, however, around several courtyards and gardens. These arched courtyards provide shaded areas with pools and fountains where people could go and relax.

SUDANO-SAHELIAN ARCHITECTURE

The traditional structures of West Africa, south of the Sahara, were built with an abundant local material, resulting in some astonishing buildings that achieve comfort without air conditioning.

The Sudano-Sahelian zone is a narrow geographic band stretching across Africa, coast to coast, from below the Sahara to above the Equator. It includes parts of Mauritania, Mali, Niger, Chad, and Sudan, among other countries. Historically, the region has buildings made of mud brick (adobe) and mud plaster that blend into the landscape, with earthen elements used to emphasize shadow and texture. In many cases, whole communities collaborate in the construction and maintenance of buildings. Made from locally available materials of earth, water, straw, and timber, mud-brick buildings are well ventilated and insulated, making them comfortable in the heat of the day.

LOCAL VARIATION
Although the architecture across this region has shared characteristics, there is a variety of styles. A major center of one style of earthen architecture is Djenné in present-day Mali, once an important stop on the trans-Saharan trade route and a historic center of Islamic scholarship. Most of the buildings, including the remarkable Great Mosque, are made of sun-baked, earthen bricks coated with plaster. The traditional flat-roofed houses are built around small central courtyards—an arrangement that is common across North Africa. Conical projections decorate the tops of walls, and entrances are often framed by pilaster-like buttresses and topped with pinnacles.

The architecture of the Hausa people of northern Nigeria is a variation on this style. The houses can be much more generous in size and include a wide range of architectural features, such as multiple stories, vaulting, and domes, all made with rammed earth, mud bricks, and timber. Facades are sometimes intricately decorated with designs sculpted into the mud surfaces. A notable example of monumental Hausa architecture is the 19th-century Great Mosque of Zaria, which has parabolic arches created from palm wood plastered in mud, and a roof of shallow domes.

REGULAR REGENERATION
Mud-brick structures need constant maintenance to repair erosion from rain and cracks caused by changes in temperature and humidity. Older buildings are sometimes completely rebuilt. Entire communities often take part: at Djenné, repairing the mosque has given rise to an annual festival that includes a race to see who is first to deliver the mud plaster to the mosque.

Annual repairs to the Great Mosque are carried out by hand.

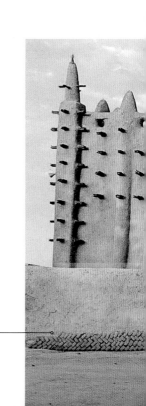

Raised platform to protect the mosque from floodwater

GREAT MOSQUE OF DJENNÉ

MALI, 13TH–14TH CENTURIES (REBUILT 1906–1907)

The Great Mosque that stands today is its third reconstruction, completed in 1907 during French colonial rule. The world's largest mud-brick building, it has towering, fortresslike walls strengthened by riblike buttresses, and three minarets. The earthen roof is supported by a forest of huge mud-brick pillars.

▲ Ostrich egg
The conical spires of all three of the mosque's towering minarets are topped with ostrich eggs. The largest of all birds' eggs, these are a symbol of fertility and purity in Mali.

▲ Platform
The entire mosque rests on a platform that is 10 ft (3 m) above the marketplace. This platform protects the mosque from the occasional floods of the nearby Bani River.

▲ Interior
The only locally available wood for roof construction is from palm trees. Palm wood beams cannot cover a wide span, so a lot of internal supports are required, resulting in a relatively narrow interior space.

Central tower, around 29½ ft (16 m) in height

Cone-shaped spires or pinnacles on each minaret are topped with an ostrich egg

Sun-baked ferey (earth bricks) and mortar of sand and earth, coated with a mud plaster

Bundles of *toron* (rodier palm sticks) project from the facade, acting as permanent scaffolding

KEY ELEMENTS

The key defining feature of Sudano-Sahelian architecture is that the earth itself is the primary building material. This is compacted to form walls, baked as bricks, or used as plaster on the exteriors of buildings.

◀ **Mud minaret**
At 89 ft (27 m), this mosque in central Niger boasts the highest tower constructed of mud brick. It serves as a minaret to the mosque and was also used as a watchtower at times in the past.

CONICAL EARTHEN TOWERS

Although it looks like a minaret, the earthen pillar in Sudano-Sahelian architecture embodies older, sacred aspects of traditional local belief systems, including the veneration of ancestors.

◀ **Hive-like tower**
The small, earthen towers attached to some mosques, such as here at Larabanga, are very similar in their hive-like shape to the tombs of marabouts (saints and holy men) that are found across Saharan Africa.

MUD BRICK (ADOBE)

Mud bricks are typically made using a wooden mold packed with a mixture of wet earth and chopped straw. Brickwork is then usually covered with a smooth, protective layer of mud plaster.

PROTRUDING TIMBERS

The facades are decorated with *toron*, stakes of wood that project from the walls like spines on a cactus. These are partially decorative or symbolic, but also serve a practical purpose as ready-made scaffolding.

▲ **Earthen walls**
This detail of a Hausa wall in Niger shows a pile of loosely stacked adobe bricks between two plastered adobe walls. Plaster may consist of a mixture of earth and rice husks. Every year a new layer of plaster has to be applied after the rains to protect buildings.

▲ **Decorative toron**
Buildings such as the Tomb of Askia, in Gao, Mali, suggest that the *toron*'s purpose is not always practical, because this 15th-century pyramidal burial mound is too small to need scaffolding. The stakes are also too slender and placed too close together to support much weight.

▲ **Supporting structures**
A detail of the Sankore Mosque in Timbuktu shows how pairs of rods have been embedded in the walls. Bundles of palm rods are sometimes added, as can be seen on the Djenné Mosque, where they provide a surface wide enough for a person to sit astride while carrying out repairs.

SUDANO-SAHELIAN BUILDINGS

Whether whitewashed or left with natural, mud-plaster facades, the organic forms of traditional Sudano-Sahelian buildings blend into the surrounding landscape and are connected to their communities, who have to maintain them regularly.

1. Larabanga Mosque
Ghana, c. early 1400s

This small mosque was probably first constructed in the early 15th century, making it one of the oldest in West Africa. It has been partially rebuilt many times in its long history.

2. Sankore Mosque
Timbuktu, Mali, 1300s

Originally built in the 14th century (and rebuilt and continuously restored since), this is one of three historic mosques in Timbuktu, Mali. All are exceptional examples of earthen architecture, and together they form part of the city's Islamic University.

3. Yaama Mosque
Yaama, Niger, 1962

Built in traditional style, the mosque was renovated in 1975. A central dome and four corner towers were added, each of them built to a unique design. The tops of the walls are crenellated. The mosque has undergone regular repair over time.

AZTEC ARCHITECTURE

Although they inherited a long architectural tradition in Mesoamerica, Aztec builders were also innovative, and built twin-stair pyramids in their capital, Tenochtitlan, in Mexico.

The Aztec Empire flourished in Mexico for two centuries after the founding of Tenochtitlan (now Mexico City) in 1325. In architecture, the Aztecs followed the style of their forebears: the circular buildings seen in early Mesoamerican buildings are also present at most Aztec sites. The Aztecs' most notable innovation was the twin-stair pyramid, with temples located at the top, erected at the heart of their settlements.

Aztec cities were built around a rectangular public plaza, a ceremonial center where all the most important religious and administrative buildings were. These included temples, palaces, platforms, and ball courts. Residential areas were built beyond the ceremonial center.

ARCHITECTURAL FEATURES
The Aztecs built primarily with adobe, wood, stone, and lime plaster. Proportion and geometrical uniformity were key features, as was religious symbolism. Eagles, serpents, conch shells, and sea creatures were recurrent motifs.

"With such wonderful sights to gaze on we did not know what to say, or if this was real that we saw before our eyes."

Bernal Díaz de Castillo on entering Tenochtitlan with Cortés in 1519, *The Conquest of New Spain*, c.1550

THE VENICE OF THE AMERICAS
At the Aztec capital, two islands—Tlatelolco and Tenochtitlan—made up the city itself, which was connected to the mainland by three human-made causeways. Two aqueducts brought fresh water into the city, and the Aztecs built a huge dyke 10 miles (16 km) long, with sluice gates, so they could control flooding from the lake. Because canals and waterways formed the main transportation links within the city, Tenochtitlan has been described as the Venice of the Americas.

At the center of the city was the sacred precinct. Here stood the twin-stair pyramid Templo Mayor (Great Temple), which was 196 ft (60 m) tall and had views right across the city.

When the Spanish invaded in 1519, they set up base in the Basin of Mexico at Tenochtitlan. By this time, the population of the city was nearing 200,000 and the Aztec Empire covered more than 500 city-states, but by 1521, the Spanish had destroyed the empire.

CHINAMPAS
Rectangular plant beds, *chinampas* had water on three sides. The beds were cut into the bottom of a lake and filled with layers of mud and vegetation. Narrow canals were left between them so canoes could reach each one. *Chinampas* were extremely productive because they were not dependent on rain. Some still exist today, in Xochimilco and Chalco, Mexico.

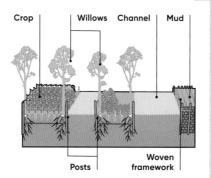

Crop | Willows | Channel | Mud

Posts | Woven framework

The fertile soil of *chinampas* was used to grow crops such as corn, beans, and squash.

TENAYUCA TWIN-STAIR PYRAMID
MEXICO CITY, MEXICO, c. 1200

Most Aztec cities were destroyed in the Spanish conquest or buried under more recent buildings, but this excellent example of the innovative architectural style of the Aztecs has survived at Tenayuca, on the outskirts of Mexico City.

Shrines to two deities would once have topped the stairs

Double pyramid, a major Aztec innovation

Slabs coated with cement made of sand, lime, and crushed *tezontle* (volcanic rock)

Temple base surrounded by a low platform with rows of serpents on three sides

Twin stairs rise from a single platform

▲ Serpent wall
The pyramid is surrounded on three sides by a serpent wall (*coatepantli*) of nearly 150 carved stone serpents of the deity Huitzilopochtli.

▲ Tenoned serpents
Large, carved serpent heads are fastened onto the walls and around the base of the pyramid.

AZTEC BUILDINGS

▲ Temple Calixtlahuaca, Hidalgo, c. 1100–1520
This circular pyramid was dedicated to the wind god Ehecatl. It was built in four stages and several high-status burials were made in front of the stairs. A stone sculpture and a sacrificial stone have been excavated near the pyramid.

▲ Templo Mayor, Tenochtitlan, 1325
The base of Templo Mayor has this imposing stone effigy of a serpent along one side. Little now remains of the great temple itself, but it was dedicated to two deities, Tlaloc (god of rain) and Huitzilopochtli (god of warfare, sun, and sacrifice).

▲ House of the Eagles, Malinalco, 1500s
Built as a sanctuary for the elite Eagle and Jaguar warriors, this temple is partly cut into the rock. The entrance resembles the open jaws of a serpent, and inside is a semicircular bench sculpted with eagles and a jaguar. Another eagle is carved into the floor.

INCA ARCHITECTURE

The Inca in South America built extensively when expanding their empire. They built administrative centers, storage facilities, and royal retreats, such as Machu Picchu.

By 1500, the Inca Empire was the largest in the Americas. It ruled over ten million people and its territory stretched more than 2,500 miles (4,000 km) across present-day Ecuador, Peru, Bolivia, and Chile. From 1400, the Inca had been undertaking huge construction programs as they expanded their dominion. As well as housing, administrative centers, storage facilities, and royal palaces, they also built extensive agricultural terraces, irrigation systems, and road networks. Paved roads extended for thousands of miles, with rope suspension bridges and hundreds of *tambos* (rest houses and food stores) along the way for *chasquis* (runners carrying messages).

URBAN PLANNING

The Inca established their capital of Cusco in the southern highlands, and laid it out in the shape of a puma—an Inca symbol of strength and life on Earth.

A hallmark of Inca architecture is the *kancha*— a grouping of residential single-story buildings around a courtyard. In many cases, they were enclosed by walls with a single entry. This model was used for all homes, from simple dwellings to royal palaces, such as Coricancha in the center of Cusco. Coricancha means "golden enclosure" and was so named because gold plates once clad its walls, but these were melted down by the Spanish after they captured the city in 1533.

CONSTRUCTION TECHNIQUES

Buildings were made from a clay called adobe or from stone—blocks of which could weigh more than 110 tons. Blocks that were too heavy to be carried by one person or a beast of burden, such as a llama, may have been moved with wood rollers and poles. Some stones still have marks where ropes or levers were attached. Evidence of polish on their bases suggests blocks may also have been dragged.

The finest Inca architecture was built during the reign of Pachacuti (1438–1471). The ruler carried out great construction works at Cusco and above the city, at the fortress of Sacsahuamán. This was also the era of the estate of Ollantaytambo and the great royal retreat of Machu Picchu. The remains of all these sites can still be seen today.

BLENDING WITH THE LANDSCAPE

The Inca were good at building settlements adapted to the local topography. Machu Picchu blends into the mountain ridge on which it was built, surrounded by massive peaks. The Inca used rocks that they found locally for building, but they also transported materials there. They carried large stones over long distances and difficult terrain, which was a significant achievement given that they did not have iron tools or vehicles with wheels.

The royal estate of Machu Picchu seems to form part of the mountainous landscape.

Main city gate is the entrance to the citadel

Land terraced for agricultural use

MACHU PICCHU

SOUTHERN PERU, 1450

The 15th-century royal retreat or religious site of Machu Picchu stands at an elevation of 8,000 ft (2,400 m) on an Andean mountain ridge. In 1912, American explorer Hiram Bingham led the excavation of the site, bringing international attention to the Inca Empire.

> "... the stones are [...] so carefully fitted together one on top of the other without mortar, that the joins are hardly visible."
>
> Father Bernabé Cobo, *History of the New World*, 1653

▲ Temple of the Sun

The Torreón (Tall Tower) or Sun Temple has a rounded, D-shaped wall and a stepped, diagonal entrance. Its set of niches alternate with windows, one of which is oriented toward the rising sun on the summer solstice.

▲ Intihuatana

On the citadel's highest point sits a sacred stone pillar and platform. Its use is unknown, but it could be astronomical—on the equinoxes, the pillar casts no shadow. There is also a Intihuatana stone at a site in Pisac.

▲ Temple of the Three Windows

Near the main plaza is a temple wall with three large trapezoidal windows looking out across the site. The walls are assembled with stones cut to fit together precisely without mortar. They would once have had a roof over them.

▲ Elite residence

Machu Picchu contained elaborate dwellings with the finest stone carving to house the ruler and his court. From 300 to 1,000 people would have lived on site; most of them commoners who worked the land.

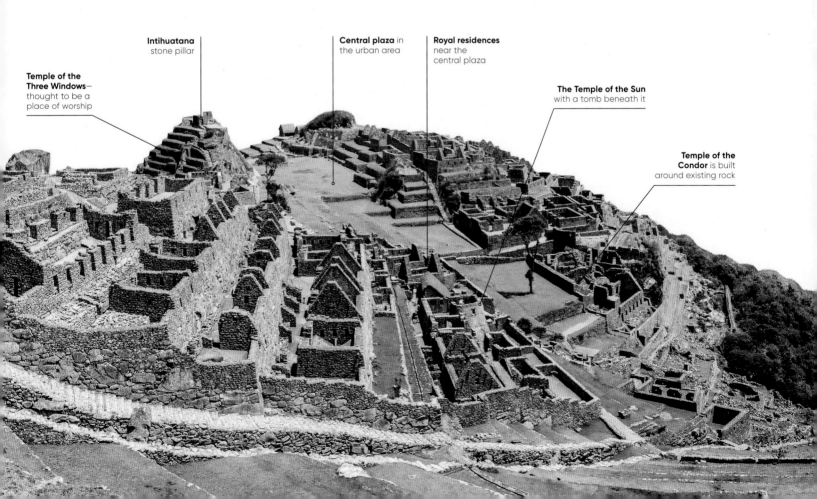

Intihuatana stone pillar

Central plaza in the urban area

Royal residences near the central plaza

Temple of the Three Windows— thought to be a place of worship

The Temple of the Sun with a tomb beneath it

Temple of the Condor is built around existing rock

KEY ELEMENTS

Inca architecture involved artisanal skill, but also mastery of their challenging environment. The Inca understood how to build to withstand earthquakes and maximize agriculture.

MORTARLESS STONEWORK

Cut (or "dressed") stone was intricately shaped to fit together snugly without mortar. This method helped buildings resist earthquakes, as did sitting them on beds of smaller mortarless stones. Such foundations could shift slightly without compromising the structure of the building above.

◀ **Twelve-angled stone**
Once part of an Inca palace, this stone is a famous example of how Inca stonemasons would painstakingly shape rocks to fit those around them. Cut from green diorite, the 12-sided stone is now set in the wall of the Archbishop's Palace in Cusco.

HILLSIDE TERRACING

The Inca transformed their steep, inhospitable landscape into fertile, productive land for feeding a vast empire. Around 3,860 square miles (1 million hectares) of terraces grew corn, potatoes, and other crops.

◀ **Stepped fields**
By building retaining walls of fieldstone and mud mortar, the Inca created level ground for planting. They scooped out the soil from each bed, laid stones at the bottom for water drainage, then loosely replaced the earth, providing very productive growing conditions for food crops.

▶ **Environmental harmony**
The terraces reduced soil erosion, retained heat from the sun, and conserved water. Crops were fed by a complex network of irrigation channels; some even bringing glacial run-off from the mountains. Terraces were so effective that many are still in use today.

TRAPEZOIDAL FORMS

The trapezium—with two parallel and two angled sides—is common in Inca architecture, especially for doors, windows, and niches. The slanted shape provides more structural stability than a rectangle. Walls themselves also often slant, which makes them more stable.

▲ **Trapezoidal doorway**
Wide at the bottom and tapering upward, this trapezium-shaped door stands in the royal sector of Machu Picchu. It has a single frame (or "jamb"), but double jambs, which create a framed effect, were also common.

▲ **Trapezoidal niches**
Niches are recesses in walls, either carved or built with slanted (or "battered") stones. According to Spanish accounts, the niches on the terraces at Ollantaytambo in southern Peru were once covered in bright flowers.

INCORPORATING LIVING ROCK

One of the hallmarks of Inca architecture was the use of "living rock"—rock in its natural position. The Inca carved it in situ and added extra stone on and around it, for example beneath the Temple of the Sun and in the Temple of the Condor, both at Machu Picchu.

◀ **Old and new**
At Machu Picchu, a naturally formed cave sits under the Sun Temple and was used as a Royal Tomb. Its existing bare rock has been engraved and integrated with worked stone brought in from elsewhere.

INCA BUILDINGS

The Inca left no written records, but the many archaeological sites of their architecture reveal spiritual, administrative, agricultural, and domestic details about their lives and sophisticated civilization.

1. Ollantaytambo
Sacred Valley, southern Peru, 1400s

At Ollantaytambo are the remains of an extensive settlement with palaces, religious and defensive structures, and *kancha* compounds (up to six one-room buildings facing onto an open patio). Highlights include a fountain carved from stone, the Temple of the Sun made with six monoliths, and a grand set of terraces that cascade down a steep hill.

2. Sacsahuamán
Cusco, Peru, 1400s

Sacsahuamán, situated at 12,200 ft (3,700 m) on a hill above the Inca capital of Cusco, was an imposing fortress and ceremonial complex with great masonry walls built without mortar. The site has three tiers of massive, zigzagging walls facing an open plaza—a great architectural feat.

3. Tambo Colorado
Coastal southern Peru, 1470

Tambo Colorado (also known as Puka Tampu) was a residence for Inca nobility and military troops. It has a mix of Inca elements and those reminiscent of the earlier Chimu culture's capital at Chan Chan, Peru. The adobe-built architecture flanks a large trapezoidal plaza, with adjoining *kanchas*. Paint traces remain on the walls, some in bold bands of red, yellow, black, and white.

LONGHOUSES

Up to 328 ft (100 m) in length, wooden longhouses housing many families were the centerpieces of the villages of Indigenous peoples on both the east and west coast of North America.

Long, thin dwelling houses for multiple families have appeared among several cultures, such as the Indigenous peoples of Borneo and the Vikings of Scandinavia, but they reached a peak of sophistication in the 19th century among Indigenous peoples of North America. Timber-built and semipermanent, longhouses provided an ideal solution for secure, communal living in areas where resources were sufficiently abundant to provide both the wood for construction (which might require hundreds of trees) and a stable food supply, which meant that the community could stay in one place.

EAST COAST LONGHOUSES

The richly forested terrain around the Great Lakes of northeast North America led the Haudenosaunee (often called the Iroquois) to develop a tradition of longhouse construction—their name means "People of the Longhouse." Generally around 82 ft (25 m) long, 20 ft (6 m) high, and 20 ft (6 m) wide, the outer frame for a building was made from timber poles stripped of bark. The Haudenosaunee bent younger, more flexible saplings to create curved rafters for the roof and reinforced them internally with horizontal poles. They then used the stripped bark to create wall and roof coverings, sewn together with bark strips. The openings at each end were covered with hides to allow access and to let smoke escape (it also vented through

openings in the roof). Haudenosaunee longhouses were home to up to 20 families from an individual clan. They slept on raised platforms sectioned-off, and several families would share a firepit in the central aisle and store their possessions in sacks and cupboards.

WEST COAST LONGHOUSES

Indigenous peoples of the salmon-rich coastal regions of the Pacific Northwest, such as the Tlingit and Haida, also built longhouses. Up to 492 ft (150 m) long, these were constructed on a split-log frame, which was in turn covered with log planks made from easily worked, locally abundant red cedar. They usually had a single entrance facing the sea. The front of the building was often intricately carved with the spirit animal of the clan that lived in the longhouse, while standalone carved totem poles were set up outside. Divided internally into booths for individual families, the walls were not bonded together, so that if the community moved, the longhouse could simply be dismantled and rebuilt elsewhere.

◄ **Animal carvings**
Carved with animals such as ravens, beavers, and wolves, the 25 poles in the Saxman Totem Park are replicas of those left in villages abandoned by Indigenous Alaskan peoples.

TOTEM POLES

Indigenous peoples of the Pacific Northwest carve totem poles to commemorate ancestors and important events, or as shame posts to ridicule wrongdoers. Up to 59 ft (18 m) high and generally made of cedar wood, they reached the peak of their production in the late 19th century. They often portray animals sacred to a clan such as beavers, thunderbirds, bears, eagles, or ravens.

Totem pole from the Saxman Totem Park, Alaska

TLINGIT LONGHOUSE

TOTEM BIGHT STATE PARK, ALASKA, 1941 (REPLICA)

This replica of a chieftain's longhouse has a typical single, low, oval entrance, but the stylized raven painted on its front is unusual, as is the carved story totem, which was added at a later date. The Totem Bight site also contains 13 carved totem poles from the local Tlingit and Haida peoples.

▲ **Totem pole**
This pole at the front of the longhouse tells the story of the raven who brought light into the world by stealing it from the house of a rich chieftain (the figure shown here at the base of the pole).

▲ **Interior**
The carved house-posts at the east end of the longhouse support the rafters that hold up the roof. They are positioned in front of the central firepit, which kept the inhabitants warm.

Raven shown stealing box containing sunlight

Natsilane, hero of the Tlingit creation story

A guardian figure with a spruce root hat warns of intruders

Entrance painting stylized as ravens' heads

Roof made of strong elm planks

LONGHOUSES

▲ **Beaver Clan House,** Saxman Village, Alaska, 1894 (reconstruction)
Both the painted decoration and the entrance totem poles to either side of the longhouse depict beavers, an animal that symbolized determination and wealth.

▲ **Eagle House,** 'Ksan Village, British Columbia Canada, 1970 (reconstruction)
The 'Ksan Native Historical Village contains replicas of longhouses and totem poles from the region's Gitxsan Nation, including this one topped with an eagle figure.

▲ **Haida Village,** Museum of Anthropology (MOA), Canada, 1958-1962 (reconstruction)
The totem poles, created between 1958 and 1962, at the Haida Village in Vancouver were mostly carved by the renowned Haida artist Bill Reid, using old original poles as his models.

GOTHIC

From the mid 12th century, a new style of architecture, now known as Gothic, spread across Europe. Used especially for church buildings, it featured pointed arches, ribbed vaults, and stained-glass windows.

Gothic architecture evolved over several centuries, partly in response to the Catholic Church's demand for churches that were taller and better lit than those built in the Romanesque style. However, building on a large scale was hindered by the fact that large, round arches require thick masses of stone to support them, which reduces the size of the windows and the height of the overall structure. In response, medieval masons incorporated pointed arches, which they combined with thinner walls, slender piers, and external flying buttresses. By supporting the structure with stonework outside the building, the buttresses made it possible to have both higher walls and larger windows.

LIGHT AND SPACE

One of the very first Gothic building projects was the mid-12th-century east end of the Abbey of St. Denis, north of Paris, where Abbot Suger wanted an interior that was filled with light. By the 13th century, complete new Gothic cathedrals were being built across France and much of Europe as masons traveled from one building site to another, taking the new style with them. As they became more confident, the masons built higher and higher, and adorned their churches with increasingly lavish carvings.

Masons in different countries also developed local versions of Gothic, ranging from the French Flamboyant Gothic of the 15th century to the inventive vaulting patterns of central and eastern Europe in the 15th and 16th centuries. Meanwhile, as towns and cities became more prosperous through trade, they adapted Gothic to build ornate town halls, markets, and houses—the great cloth halls of Flanders are among the most outstanding of these secular buildings.

BUILT TO LAST

Gothic proved to be very successful, with masons discovering that they could use flying buttresses and arches to create buildings with almost no walls at all. Sometimes there was a disaster, such as when Beauvais Cathedral in France partly collapsed. However, many Gothic churches still stand, their height, elegance, and dazzling design evidence of the engineering and artistic brilliance of their masons.

STONE MASONRY

Stonemasons were responsible for every aspect of Gothic design. A master mason planned the building and provided working masons with templates for details such as vaulting ribs or window mullions. These workers were not only skilled with their tools, they also had to know everything about stone, from its strength to its suitability for fine carving.

In Sherborne Abbey, in the UK, even the vaulting ribs are meticulously carved.

▶ **Chapter house**
This octagonal room in Salisbury Cathedral, in the UK, is held up by a stone skeleton of piers, vaulting ribs, external buttresses, and a slender central column.

"The heart of the sanctuary glows in splendor ... and the magnificent work shines, inundated with a new light."

Abbot Suger of St. Denis, France, on the new Gothic choir of his abbey

AMIENS CATHEDRAL

AMIENS, FRANCE, 1220–1270

The largest, and one of the most impressive, of the great French Gothic cathedrals, Amiens was built in only 50 years. Such a brief construction period was rare for a Gothic cathedral, and it accounts for Amiens' remarkably consistent style. Its soaring interior, with a vault 140 ft (43 m) high, and its striking west front with portals surrounded by stone statues, are two of its outstanding features.

The west front of Amiens Cathedral

▲ Rose window

Rose (circular) windows are common in Gothic cathedrals. They gave masons the freedom to design intricate decorative tracery (stone bars dividing the circle). They also gave glaziers the opportunity to fill the spaces with color.

▲ Portal sculptures

Statues of apostles, saints, and bishops surround the cathedral doorways, while the spaces above the doors are filled with relief carvings. These carvings illustrate key biblical events, such as the Annunciation and the birth of Jesus.

Steeply pitched roof supported by a wooden framework

North transept, lit by a large, stained-glass window above the cathedral's north portal

Polygonal turret, carrying a staircase to the upper levels

Flying buttresses support the internal vault

Lower parts of the flying buttresses bear the weight of the masonry above

GOTHIC STRUCTURE

A cross-section of Amiens Cathedral shows how its vault is supported by two kinds of arch—those inside the building and two wings of external flying buttresses. These flying buttresses transfer the weight of the vault laterally and downward to the masonry below. This definitive Gothic invention enabled masons to build cathedrals that were taller, more spacious, and brighter than ever before.

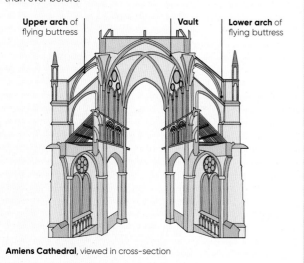

Upper arch of flying buttress

Vault

Lower arch of flying buttress

Amiens Cathedral, viewed in cross-section

> "... Gothic architecture remains the very soul of the Middle Ages."
>
> **Arthur Symons**, British poet and critic, *The Symbolist Movement in Literature*, 1899

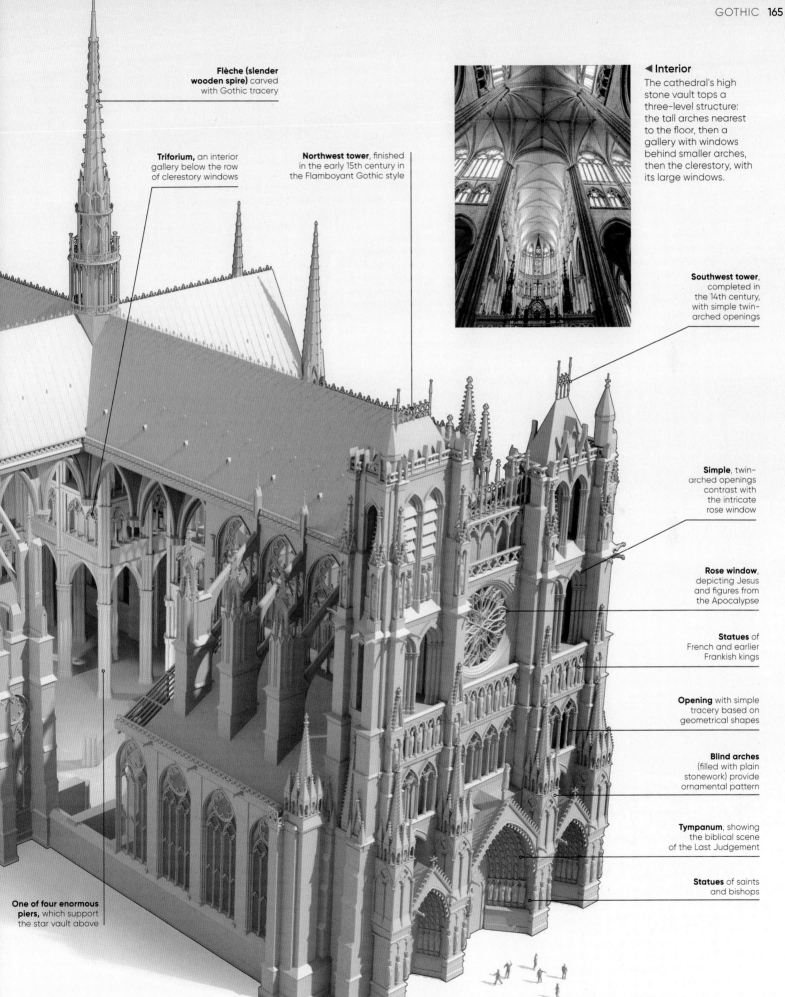

Flèche (slender wooden spire) carved with Gothic tracery

Triforium, an interior gallery below the row of clerestory windows

Northwest tower, finished in the early 15th century in the Flamboyant Gothic style

◀ **Interior**

The cathedral's high stone vault tops a three-level structure: the tall arches nearest to the floor, then a gallery with windows behind smaller arches, then the clerestory, with its large windows.

Southwest tower, completed in the 14th century, with simple twin-arched openings

Simple, twin-arched openings contrast with the intricate rose window

Rose window, depicting Jesus and figures from the Apocalypse

Statues of French and earlier Frankish kings

Opening with simple tracery based on geometrical shapes

Blind arches (filled with plain stonework) provide ornamental pattern

Tympanum, showing the biblical scene of the Last Judgement

Statues of saints and bishops

One of four enormous piers, which support the star vault above

KEY ELEMENTS

Gothic architecture required the work of several groups of skilled craft workers, including stonemasons, woodworkers, and glaziers. Among the most important features of the style are vaulting, window tracery, stone- and woodcarvings, and stained-glass windows.

VAULTED CEILINGS

The pointed arch enabled masons to build beautiful stone-vaulted ceilings, which act as visual climaxes to Gothic interiors, encouraging the worshipper to look upward to the heavens. The protruding ribs form patterns in the ceiling, and these became more and more complex as vault design developed during the Middle Ages. Large stones known as "bosses" were set at the points where the ribs intersect, and the masons carved these with human heads, foliage designs, and biblical motifs.

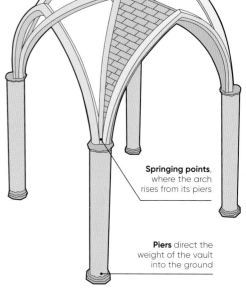

Diagonal ribs connect the center of the vault with the springing points of the arch

Pointed arches direct their weight toward the piers

Springing points, where the arch rises from its piers

Piers direct the weight of the vault into the ground

▲ **How rib vaulting works**

A characteristic feature of Gothic architecture is the pointed arch, which is less inclined to press outward than the round arch. Pointed arches are used in rib vaults, which, although partly supported by external buttresses, are held up by vertical piers.

◀ **Late-medieval vaulting**

The ornate vaulted ceiling of the Divinity School at Oxford University in the UK displays the complex patterns of ribs that were achieved in the 15th century.

WINDOW TRACERY

Medieval masons devised an array of different designs for tracery (the stonework that divides the upper part of the windows into sections). Early Gothic windows were simple lancets—tall, narrow, pointed shapes with no tracery at all. Later, these lancets were grouped together and given increasingly complex tracery. By the 14th century, dazzlingly ornate designs had become popular.

Quatrefoil, a four-lobed design, here topping a two-light window

Intersecting tracery, a pattern of criss-crossing stone bars

Reticulated tracery, a netlike pattern of repeating motifs

Geometrical tracery, a combination of circles and other shapes

Flamboyant tracery, a complex web of curvilinear designs

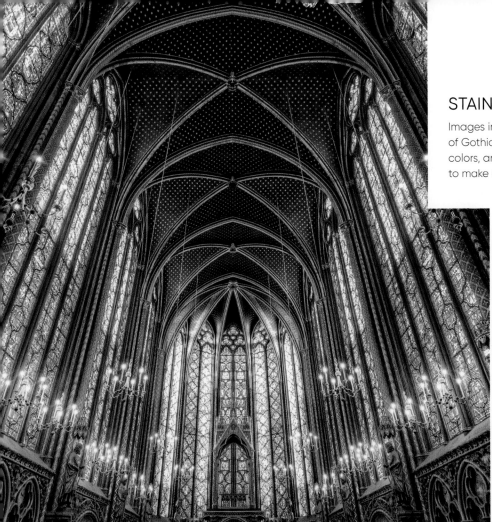

STAINED-GLASS WINDOWS

Images in glowing sun-lit stained glass filled the windows of Gothic churches. Glaziers used additives to achieve vivid colors, and the large amounts of costly firewood required to make and work the glass made it a supreme luxury.

◄ **The full effect**
In the Sainte-Chapelle in Paris, masons and glaziers worked together to create an interior suffused with colored light and images.

▲ **Color palette**
The stained glass in Chartres Cathedral in France has colors that were derived from wood ash and copper.

CARVINGS

Three-dimensional and relief carvings in stone or wood added to the store of saintly and biblical imagery in Gothic churches. They also enriched the buildings with ornamental flourishes of leaves, fruit, and abstract patterns.

◄ **Carvings in wood**
The wooden choir screen in Winchester Cathedral, in the UK, separates the nave from the chancel. Such screens are often topped by architectural canopies with pinnacles and other ornaments similar to those on the outside of the building. This screen is partly medieval and partly Victorian reconstruction.

▲ **Grotesques**
Masons often carved monsters on the exteriors of churches, such as this gargoyle at York Minster, in the UK. Although there is debate about what they signify, they are possibly symbols of the sinful world that the faithful leave behind on entering a church.

◄ **Figure sculptures**
The stone figures that line the western portals of Strasbourg Cathedral in France represent Old Testament prophets. They were used to help explain Christianity to congregations who mostly could not read or write.

GOTHIC CHURCHES

Gothic architecture developed more and more regional variants as masons worked independently across Europe. Their buildings began to reflect their own design preferences, or those of the churchmen and families who employed them.

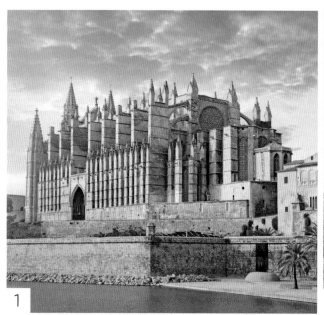

1

2

3

4

1. Palma Cathedral
Mallorca, Spain, 13th–17th centuries

Like many churches in Mediterranean Spain, Palma Cathedral has large, heavy buttresses, and huge interior spaces. Windows the size of those in French cathedrals would have made the interior unpleasantly warm in the hot sun.

2. Milan Cathedral
Lombardy, Italy, 1386–1965

Nearly 600 years in the making, Milan Cathedral is Italy's largest church. Its vast west front mixes Gothic tracery, pinnacles, and ornament with several Renaissance-style windows and doorways, reflecting its lengthy construction period.

3. St. Barbara's Cathedral
Kutná Hora, Czech Republic, 1388–1905

Central European builders took Gothic architecture in new directions. One result was St. Barbara's Cathedral in Kutná Hora. By replacing conventional spires with pointed roofs, its designer created a unique and striking skyline.

4. Ely Cathedral
Cambridgeshire, UK, 1083–1375

Ely Cathedral was built on the site of a former abbey. Its octagonal lantern was constructed in the 14th century, after an earlier tower and nearby arches collapsed. This daring structure was only possible because the upper part of it is made of wood instead of stone.

5. Siena Cathedral
Tuscany, Italy, 1196–1348

Like many Italian Gothic churches, Siena Cathedral's interior is built of two types of stone—in this case, black and white marble. Its exterior has a mixture of pointed and semicircular arches.

5

6 7

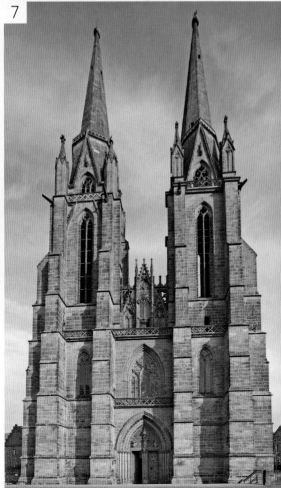

6. King's College Chapel
Cambridge, UK, 1446–1515

In 15th-century England, a style now known as Perpendicular Gothic became popular. It featured flattened arches and repeated vertical elements such as window mullions and pinnacles.

7. St. Elizabeth's Church
Marburg, Germany, 1235–1340

Several German cathedrals have a pair of towers topped with spires on their west fronts. The towers of Marburg are made of huge pieces of masonry, which project a sense of great power.

SECULAR GOTHIC BUILDINGS

Although the Gothic style was developed for churches, by the
later Middle Ages it was being used to construct secular buildings,
too. These structures tended to be centers of power, such
as palaces and law courts.

1. Belém Tower
Lisbon, Portugal, 1514–1519

Once the embarkation point for Portuguese
explorers, Belém Tower is at the entrance to
Lisbon harbor. With its carved oriel window and
corner turrets, its design marks the transition
from Gothic to the Renaissance style in Portugal.

2. Town Hall
Leuven, Belgium, 1439–1469

Richly carved parapets, arches, niches, and
statues show the amount of effort that the
authorities of 15th-century Leuven could afford
to lavish on their town hall. Distinctive spires
give this already tall building further height.

3. Cloth Hall
Ypres, Belgium, 13th century

With its Gothic belfry and rows of pointed
windows, the Cloth Hall in Ypres shows the
success of the Belgian builders in adapting
a church style for secular use. It was faithfully
restored after being damaged in World War I.

4. Palace of Justice
Rouen, France, 1499–1508

This building was designed to house France's
regional parliament and law courts. It combines
the filigree ornament of the Flamboyant Gothic
style and the Renaissance rectangular windows
that were becoming fashionable.

5. Doge's Palace
Venice, Italy, 14th century

An independent republic in the Middle
Ages, Venice developed its own style
of architecture. The Doge's Palace
features rows of Gothic arches and
multicolored masonry.

6. Copernicus House
Toruń, Poland, 14th century

The family of the celebrated astronomer Copernicus owned this tenement building. Although the main walls are brick-built, decorative black and white stonework creates swirling late-medieval Gothic tracery patterns.

7. St. Martin's Tower
Teruel, Spain, 1315–1316

The Aragonese St. Martin's Tower is an example of the Mudéjar style. It mixes Gothic and Romanesque window openings with a style of patterned decoration heavily influenced by the Islamic artistic tradition.

TIMBER-FRAMED BUILDINGS

Wood has long been a popular building material, especially for houses, which local craft workers could construct based on a timber framework without involving architects or other specialists.

For most of human history timber has been a critical building material. Its capacity to produce strong beams far lighter and thinner than stone meant that wood was often used for floors and roofs, even in areas without local forests, where it had to be carried long distances. In regions with abundant woodland, timber has often been favored for entire structures, ranging from North American longhouses to Chinese temples and palaces.

Timber structures have to be designed carefully to lessen the risk of rot and fire, but where these two threats are avoided, they can last for centuries. Most types of wood are soft enough to cut precisely when newly felled, and worldwide there are many different traditions for how to join timbers robustly without using iron nails, which were expensive to produce before the rise of coal-fueled industries.

HALF-TIMBERING

Much of medieval Europe followed a distinctive method of building in timber chunky enough to join together with wooden pegs, bracing the vertical and horizontal framing with diagonals

"Wood provides one of the most important, longest-lived, and most durable kinds of building material."

Paul Oliver, *Dwellings*, 2003

that prevented the building from folding sideways. Frames were built on the ground, from soft, new-felled wood, before being raised into place. The gaps between the timbers were then filled in—some with windows secured by shutters or (for the very rich) glass. Other gaps were filled with wattle and daub, a composite material of plant fibers and earth or animal dung. This was both easy to repair and a good form of insulation, helping to retain the precious warmth of the fire in winter. In some larger buildings, the timber frame was ornamented with elaborate patterns and carved motifs.

MIXED MATERIALS

The half-timbered style of house sometimes known as Upper Lusatian uses several types of structure in one. The ground floor combines stone walls and a timber frame with stout posts and plank infill, while the upper story has a conventional timber box frame.

Houses in the Upper Lusatian style are found in parts of Germany and the Czech Republic.

THE BALLOON FRAME

In the 19th century, after coal-fueled ironworking arrived in the US, an imported European tradition of timber framing came together with the use of powerful metal saws and cheap nails to produce a lighter, more economical version of timber-framed housing. This style, which remains in widespread use in America today, was so much lighter than the hefty timbers of older buildings that it came to be known as "the balloon frame."

LITTLE MORETON HALL

CHESHIRE, ENGLAND, 16TH CENTURY

This manor house in England was built in several stages between 1504 and 1610, for members of the rich Moreton family. Its highly decorative timber-framed structure is typical of parts of the west of England.

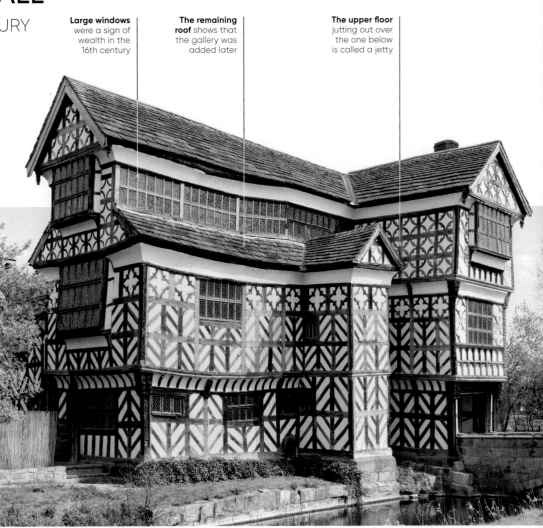

Large windows were a sign of wealth in the 16th century

The remaining roof shows that the gallery was added later

The upper floor jutting out over the one below is called a jetty

◀ **Decorative details**
Intricate patterns such as quatrefoils (four-lobed designs) and stylized foliage are combined with realistic carvings of animals like this dog. There are also architectural motifs like the miniature column.

◀ **Great Hall**
The main reception room would have been used for family meals and entertaining guests. It is a large, double-height room, well lit with generous windows, and has an exposed timber frame.

TIMBER-FRAMED BUILDINGS

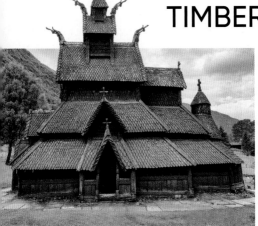

▲ **Stave church,** Borgund, Norway, 1180–1250
Named for their structure, stave churches have wooden posts and vertical wooden boards—known as staves—joined with interlocking tongues and grooves to form the walls. The Borgund church has a wooden shingle roof and four carved dragon heads.

▲ **Old Town Hall,** Bamberg, Germany, 1461
The impressive box frame of this 15th-century town hall was built on a medieval stone bridge. The strength of the wooden frame enables it to achieve a daring overhang on the masonry abutment beneath it.

▲ **Rue Martainville,** Rouen, France, 15th century
Rouen has several houses with attractive timber-frames in a mixture of close-studding and cross-braced designs. The amount of timber used and the large windows suggest that they were originally built as homes for wealthy traders.

CASTLES

Built to be strong and intimidating, and often situated in the most challenging locations, castles were among the most impressive buildings of the Middle Ages.

A castle is a fortified building, most often either the home of a lord, or a strategic military facility built by a monarch. From the 11th to the 15th centuries, castles became common all over Europe, as well as in places such as the eastern Mediterranean, as European armies invaded and attempted to retain their conquests. Under the feudal system, monarchs allocated large areas of land to lords, who in return agreed to supply knights and fighting men to the ruler in times of war. Castles provided strongholds for the lord, his family, and the fighting force under his command, but they were also designed to be comfortable homes in peacetime.

MADE FOR WAR

The first castles were made of wood, but by the early Middle Ages they had thick stone walls, which were designed to withstand attacks from battering rams, and were protected by a broad ditch or moat. They also had towers, which looked out over the surrounding countryside and served as platforms for archers. Castles were usually built in an elevated position on a hill or next to a river, which gave them a strategic advantage in war. They had numerous defensive features, among them drawbridges, gatehouses, and small windows that were difficult for enemies to target. With such levels of protection in place, and with a good store of supplies and a spring as a source of water, a medieval castle was able to withstand a long siege, which could last many months, provided they had a good commander and defenders.

SUITABLE FOR PEACE

For a war-obsessed aristocracy, a strong-looking castle was the ultimate status symbol. The architecture of castles often exaggerated their real defensive features. Inside were facilities for a luxurious life, including a grand hall, kitchens, store rooms, and private rooms for the owner and his family. In addition, they were outfitted with conveniences such as garderobes—lavatories that took human waste into the moat via chutes. Archaeologists have also discovered that some castles had large gardens, where food was grown and where the family could exercise. Despite these comforts and their apparent structural strength, the end came for castle-building when cannons became powerful enough to make tall stone walls a liability rather than a formidable defense.

◄ **Fortified entrance**
The entrance of Carisbrooke Castle, on the Isle of Wight, is protected by a narrow bridge and a portcullis (heavy grating), which slid vertically down from a slot above the arch. Archers could shoot at attackers from the towers on either side.

STRATEGIC LOCATIONS

Wherever possible, castles were built in a high position that afforded a good view of the surrounding area and made it difficult for enemies to approach. On flatter ground, they were often raised on artificial mounds, preferably by a river, which provided extra protection and could be diverted to form a moat.

Harlech Castle, Wales, stands on a hill overlooking the Irish Sea.

PEYREPERTUSE

FRENCH PYRENEES, 11TH CENTURY

The castle of Peyrepertuse stands on top of a steep crag 2,625 ft (800 m) above the surrounding countryside. Its main building contained lodgings for a lord or governor, and accommodation for a large military force when needed. The castle was rebuilt in the 13th century, when it became the property of the king of France.

CASTLE PLAN

The castle fits tightly on its long, narrow site. It has three walled sections, each of which could be defended separately. Its most recent western section, which includes the Chapel of Sant Jordi, was built by French king Louis IX (r. 1226–1270).

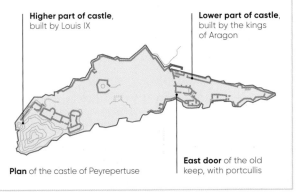

Higher part of castle, built by Louis IX

Lower part of castle, built by the kings of Aragon

Plan of the castle of Peyrepertuse

East door of the old keep, with portcullis

▲ Towers

Circular towers served as platforms from which archers could shoot in all directions. Some of the strongest parts of the castle, the towers also provided safe accommodation, and could be defended even when other parts of the building had been taken.

▲ High enclosure

Peyrepertuse was unusual in having two chapels. The chapel of Sant Jordi (in the left tower, above) occupies the highest point of the castle. It was built as a royal chapel by Louis IX in the western end.

End tower with an internal wall to the courtyard

The rocky outcrop deters attack

An internal wall separates the castle courtyards

Outer wall with walkway for defenders

Semicircular tower, used as a platform for archers

KEY **ELEMENTS**

Castles evolved from simple wooden structures that could easily be stormed by fire to stone fortifications able to withstand many months of attack.

DEFENSIVE FEATURES

The builders and engineers who designed medieval castles added ingenious features that helped those inside defend the building. Some of these features, such as murder holes, could take attackers by surprise; others were designed to intimidate the enemy.

▲ **Murder holes**
Defenders would drop heavy objects or pour boiling liquids onto enemies below from these openings in the roof of Bodiam Castle in England. Known as murder holes, they were situated above the entrance, where attackers were easy targets.

▲ **Portcullis**
A portcullis, such as this one at Caerphilly Castle in Wales, provided an extra layer of protection to castle gates. Made of wood and iron plates, it was strong enough to damage the head of a battering ram.

▲ **Crenellations**
Crenellated (gap-toothed) walls, such as these at Trujillo, Spain, were common to castles all over Europe. Archers could shoot through the gaps and then take cover behind the upright parts of the walls.

WALL TOWERS

As castle design developed, castles were given towers at each corner and along the lengths of their walls. These towers were used as look-outs and shooting platforms, and some contained inner rooms for soldiers on duty.

▲ **Square towers**
Early medieval castles usually had towers with straight sides. Those on the inner bailey wall at Dover Castle in England only had three sides—the forth was open to the inner courtyard. Although they were formidable, these walls could easily be attacked at the base.

▲ **Round towers**
Circular or semicircular towers, such as those above at Krak des Chevaliers in Syria, gave archers a wide range of directions in which to shoot. Building the towers on solid bedrock also protected them from being attacked at the base, which helped make the castle stronger.

▲ **Polygonal towers**
Some castles, such as Caernarfon in Wales, had towers with many sides. This made them stronger structurally and provided views over a broad area. This tower's numerous narrow openings were perfectly designed for archers, who could release volleys of arrows from a position of relative safety.

EUROPEAN **CASTLES**

Castles varied across Europe, each built to take advantage of its geographical site. They also developed over time, from the single-towered buildings of the 11th century to the multi-towered castles of later periods.

1. Eltz Castle
Germany, 12th century

Built high on a crag by a river, this well-defended castle housed several branches of the Eltz family. It was adapted over the centuries as it evolved from being a military fortress to a family home.

2. Muiden Castle
Netherlands, 14th century

A strong gatehouse and tall towers protect this Dutch castle, which was rebuilt in the 14th century and subsequently modified. Built in flat countryside, it makes good defensive use of its site near a river mouth, from which a broad moat flows to surround the entire building.

3. The Tower of London
England, 11th–13th centuries

The Tower of London was the most important castle of the medieval English kings. Its earliest part, the enormous White Tower, dates to the 1080s, and was designed for William I of Normandy, who conquered England in 1066.

"They stand like monumental pillars in the stream of time."

William Beattie, *The Castles and Abbeys of England*, c. 1880

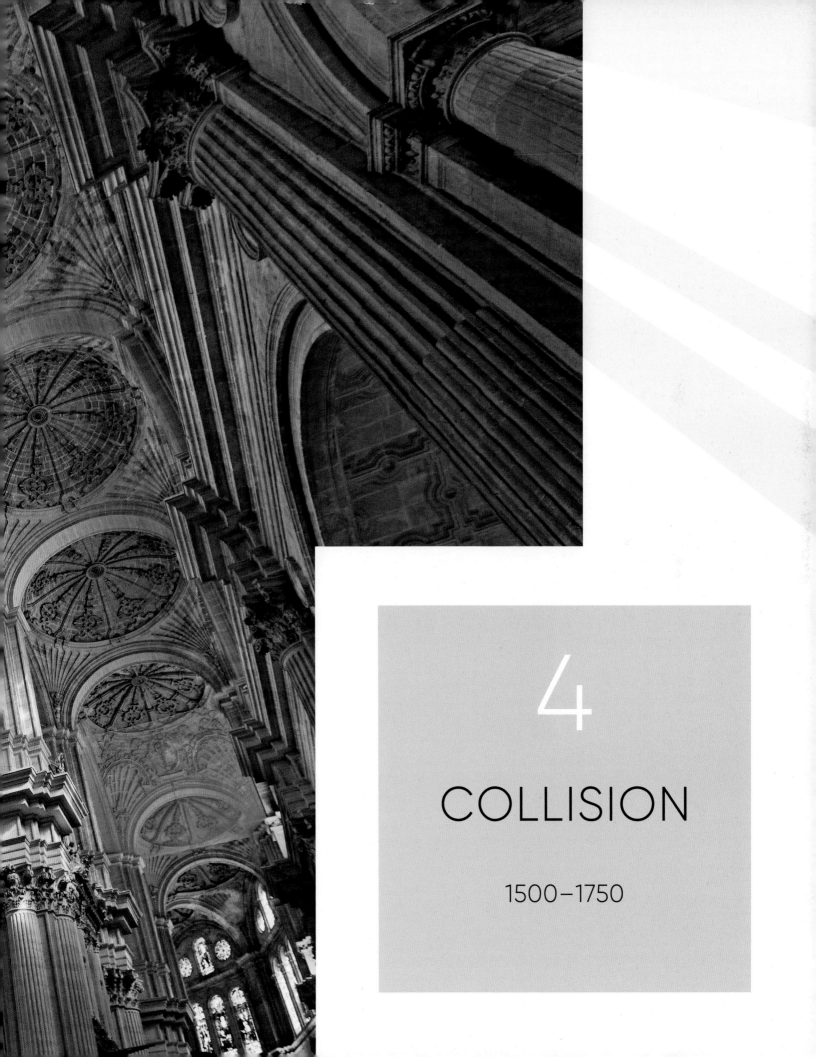

4

COLLISION

1500–1750

RUSSIAN ORTHODOX CHURCHES

Ecclesiastical architecture in Russia evolved from Byzantine roots and fused with foreign influences to create a unique style, characterized by onion domes and colorful ornamentation.

The earliest Russian churches, built after the region's conversion to Orthodox Christianity in the 10th century, were based on Byzantine models. Formed as cross-in-square designs, they were topped with a single dome with pointed, rather than rounded, arches. Built in wood or stone, many of these were destroyed during the Mongol invasions of the 13th century, and when strong Russian principalities reemerged in the 15th century, they rebuilt churches in a different form. Brick and masonry churches now had *kokoshniki* (curved corbel arches), while exterior galleries and bell towers gave them a turreted, almost pyramidal form. They were often highly ornamented with glazed ceramic tiles.

THE AGE OF DOMES
Italian architects such as Aristotele Fioravanti, who arrived in Moscow in 1475, brought a rational, geometric style, with new techniques including the use of solid bond masonry, which made it possible to build thinner walls. A more

◀ **Ornate domes and crosses**
The effusive exterior decoration of the Church of the Assumption in St. Petersburg is typical of Russian ecclesiastical style. Built in 1895, its five domes were the first in Russia to use aluminum.

familiar Russian style asserted itself with the introduction of tentlike roofs, extravagant multiple onion domes, and soaring verticals such as those of St. Basil's Cathedral in Moscow. The domes—which in extreme cases numbered 33 to symbolize the number of years in Christ's life—became a defining feature of Russian church architecture.

A PROLIFERATION OF STYLES
The tented roofs were declared uncanonical by Patriarch Nikon in the 1650s, leading to a return to rows of *kokoshniki* and rotunda-like churches with an octagon on cube design, such as his own New Jerusalem monastery in Moscow Oblast (see opposite). Foreign influence once more touched Russian church design in the reign of Peter the Great (1682–1725) bringing Baroque architecture with extensive stucco decoration and carvings. A more restrained version of the Baroque took root in northern Russia, exhibited by the Church of the Entry into Jerusalem in Totma (1794), with striking variants in Siberia influenced by East Asian styles, such as the "flaming" cornices and Buddhist, stupa-like form of the Church of the Intercession in Irkutsk (1719). Farther west, the later 18th century saw a return to a more austere style with the classically inspired structures of the new capital, St. Petersburg.

ICONOSTASIS
One of the key features of Orthodox churches, the iconostasis marks the division between the part of the church open to the congregation and the sacred area reserved for the clergy. It takes the form of a wooden or stone screen with three doors, and this partition is adorned with Christian icons, such as Jesus Christ, the Virgin Mary, and other saints, as well as with holy scenes.

Icons of Christ and saints set in tiers in an Orthodox church in Moscow, Russia

ST. BASIL'S CATHEDRAL

MOSCOW, RUSSIA, 1552–1561

The cathedral of Basil the Blessed was built on the orders of Czar Ivan IV "the Terrible" by the architects Barma and Postnik. Its extravagant layered shape and cylindrical form combine to create an ensemble that is unparalleled in Russian church architecture.

The orthodox cross tops the tower and domes

The tower sits right above the church's central chapel

Onion-shaped domes make it easier for snow and ice to fall off

Porch roof is triangular and pitched above the external gallery

▲ **Aerial view**
The nine domes of St. Basil's each sit above one of the cathedral's chapels. The bright candy-colored decor was added after a fire destroyed the original building, known as Trinity Cathedral, in 1583. The triangular-roofed bell tower dates from the 1680s.

RUSSIAN ORTHODOX BUILDINGS

▲ **Dormition Cathedral,** Moscow Kremlin, Moscow, Russia, 1475–1479
The five-apse Cathedral of the Dormition was built by Aristotele Fioravanti for Czar Ivan III and is one of the finest Renaissance-style churches in Russia. It served as the coronation venue for Russian czars for nearly 450 years.

▲ **Cathedral of the Assumption in the Trinity Lavra,** Sergiyev Posad, Russia, 1559–1585
Part of the Trinity Lavra of St. Sergius, the most important monastery in Russia, this church was begun under Ivan IV. The 20-ft- (6-m-) high walls of the monastery withstood a 16-month siege by Polish-Lithuanian troops from 1608–1610.

▲ **New Jerusalem Monastery,** Moscow Oblast, Russia, 1656–1698
Also known as the Resurrection Monastery, the site was chosen because it resembled the Holy Land. The interior was designed by Patriarch Nikon in 1656 to mirror various holy places in Jerusalem, including the Church of the Holy Sepulchre.

▲ **The Blue Mosque**
Officially known as the Sultan Ahmed Mosque, this Istanbul landmark derives its popular name from the hand-painted blue tiles that adorn its interior. It was built between 1609 and 1616.

OTTOMAN ARCHITECTURE

When the Ottomans captured Constantinople in 1453, they introduced a grand new style of imperial architecture—one that soon spread deep into Central Europe.

Originating in Anatolia (in present-day Turkey), the people known as the Ottomans were influenced culturally by both the Byzantines and the Seljuk Turks, who had previously ruled to the east. From the Byzantines, they learned that it was effective to use stone and brick together, and from the Seljuks they adopted the practice of topping square structures with domes. Both of these influences can be seen in the Hacı Özbek Mosque in Iznik (1333), the first known Ottoman single-domed mosque. The Ottomans also built mosques at Bursa (c. 1399), which had 20 domes, and at Edirne, where the Üç Şerefeli Mosque (1447), had an impressive dome that was 80 ft (24 m) in diameter.

CLASSICAL PERIOD
The Ottoman capture of Constantinople (present-day Istanbul) marked a new imperial phase of monumental architecture. The city's conqueror, Sultan Mehmet II, commissioned new mosques for the city. The earliest of these, the Fatih Mosque, was destroyed in an earthquake (and later rebuilt), but the second, the Beyazid Mosque (1505), still stands in its original form.

Like the Hagia Sophia (Constantinople's great Christian cathedral, which Mehmet converted into a mosque), the new mosque had a square plan and a vast central dome supported by semi-domes and buttresses. To this, the Ottomans added a courtyard and a külliye, a complex of buildings that included a madrasa (school), a hammam (bath house), a soup kitchen, a caravanserai (guest house), and several mausoleums. Külliyes became a feature of many subsequent mosques.

Ottoman architecture reached its peak in the time of Sultan Süleyman I (r. 1520–1566), who led his armies to the gates of Vienna. His chief architect, Mimar Sinan, designed and oversaw the construction of more than 370 buildings over a 50-year career, including aqueducts, fountains, palaces, and imperial mosques.

Reflecting an empire stretching to east and west, early Ottoman architecture reused Roman and Byzantine stone column shafts and decorative facings. By the 18th century, Turkish buildings had begun to take on European features, especially those of the Baroque and Rococo styles (see pp. 210–221).

> "Its dome rose to the highest point of the heavens."
>
> Tacizade Cafer Çelebi (1459–1515), Ottoman poet, on the Fatih Mosque

EMPIRE BUILDERS

The Ottoman dynasty was named after its founder, Osman I (r. 1299–1324), who led his Turkic people out of Central Asia to conquer much of what is now Turkey. His successors extended the empire into Central Europe, and Mehmet II (r. 1444–1446 and 1451–1481) defeated the 1,000-year-old Byzantine Empire in 1453.

Miniature depicting the Ottomans defeating a European army in 1396

SÜLEYMANIYE MOSQUE

ISTANBUL, TURKEY, 1557

Widely considered to be Mimar Sinan's masterpiece, the Süleymaniye Mosque is one of the largest and grandest mosques in Istanbul. Dominating the city skyline, it sits at the center of an extensive külliye complex, which includes gardens, hospitals, schools, shops, and several mausoleums.

SEMI-DOME STRUCTURE

Like many of Sinan's finest buildings, the Süleymaniye Mosque has a large central dome supported by a series of semi-domes. The design gives the building a sense of lightness, both inside and out.

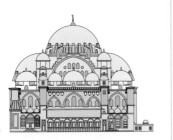

Cross-section of the Süleymaniye Mosque

▲ **Tomb of Sinan**

The modest tomb of Mimar Sinan lies just outside the mosque. The great architect lived until the age of 98, and designed buildings across the Ottoman Empire. These included mosques in Syria, Bulgaria, and Crimea, and a bridge in Bosnia-Herzegovina.

▲ **Mausoleum of Süleyman I**

The tomb of Süleyman I (the Magnificent), who reigned at the height of the Ottoman Empire's power, lies inside the grounds of the mosque. A large, octagonal structure with a peristyle of 24 columns, it was completed in 1566, the year in which the sultan died.

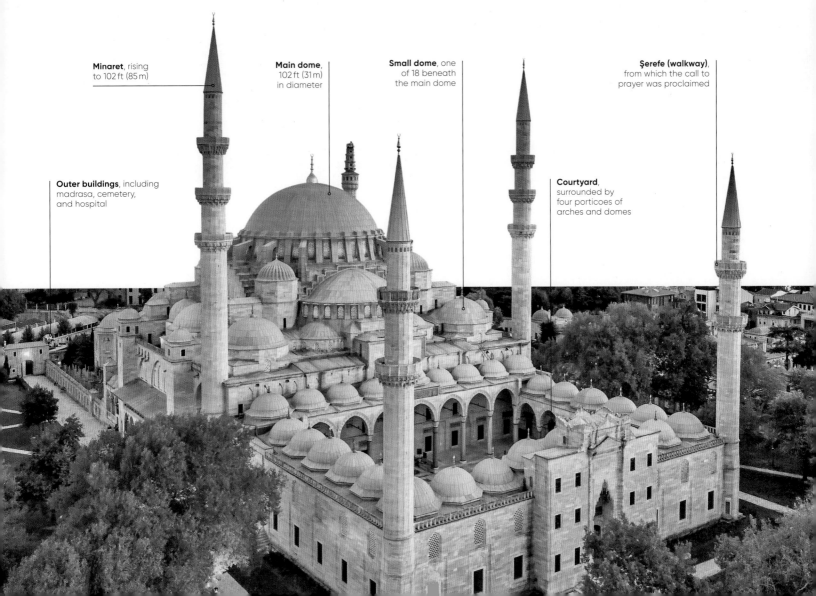

Minaret, rising to 102 ft (85 m)

Main dome, 102 ft (31 m) in diameter

Small dome, one of 18 beneath the main dome

Şerefe (walkway), from which the call to prayer was proclaimed

Outer buildings, including madrasa, cemetery, and hospital

Courtyard, surrounded by four porticoes of arches and domes

KEY **ELEMENTS**

At its height, the Ottoman Empire extended from Constantinople to Mecca, Baku, Algiers, and Budapest—a vast area in which Ottoman architecture retained its distinct identity.

MINARETS

Ottoman minarets are instantly identifiable, being typically tall and slender, with spike-like conical roofs. They usually have *şerefes* (wraparound balconies) near the top, from which Muslims were traditionally called to prayer.

◀ **Single minaret**
The Emperor's Mosque in Sarajevo was the first mosque to be built after the Ottoman conquest of Bosnia. Despite being at the western limit of the empire, it was built in classical Ottoman style and has a single minaret.

▼ **Multiple minarets**
Only large Ottoman mosques, especially those commissioned by sultans, had more than one *şerefe* per minaret. The Selimiye Mosque, in Edirne, Turkey, was commissioned by Sultan Selim II and has three *şerefes* on each of its four minarets.

DOMES

Like minarets, domes were distinctive elements of Ottoman mosques, and of Ottoman architecture in general. They tended to be shallow, less than a half circle in profile, and were typically covered in gray lead.

◀ **Domes and semi-domes**
Istanbul's New Mosque, which dates from the 17th century, has a large main dome, supporting semi-domes, subsidiary domes over its prayer hall colonnades, and small decorative domes on its buttresses.

ARCADED PORTICOES

The entrances of many mosques stood in courtyards that were flanked on three sides by arcaded porticoes. These courts were public spaces in which religious services were held, children had lessons, travelers were welcomed, and health care and charity were dispensed.

▲ **Alabaster mosque**
The courtyard of the Mosque of Muhammad Ali in Cairo, Egypt, is almost square, with arcaded porticoes topped with small domes running along all four sides. Many of the bays contain windows with decorative latticework.

▶ **Shelter from the weather**
Arcaded porticoes, such as these enclosing the courtyard of Mimar Sinan's great mosque in Istanbul, provided shade in summer and shelter from the wind and rain in colder months.

OTTOMAN TILING

The ceramic workshops of Iznik, 56 miles (90 km) southeast of Istanbul, began producing ceramic tiles for the Ottoman court in the early 16th century. Production increased with the surge of imperial building that took place under the direction of Mimar Sinan. Colorful Iznik tiles enlivened mosques, palaces, and public buildings across the empire. They showed off the luxurious use of skilled labor, and of wood burned to fire the tiles and their rich glazes.

▶ **Iznik tiles**
The Rustem Pasha Mosque in Istanbul, designed by Mimar Sinan, is famous for its beautifully patterned Iznik tiles in blue and turquoise. This small mosque contains more than 2,300 tiles, which are arranged in around 80 different nonfigurative patterns.

▲ **Cobalt blue**
The first Iznik tile makers were inspired by Chinese blue-and-white porcelain. Unlike porcelain, however, Turkish tiles were fritware, in which ground glass was added to clay to make white-colored pottery. The tiles were then dyed with blue ink.

▲ **More colors**
During the 16th century, the style of Iznik tiles became looser and more flowing. Tile makers introduced new colors, including sage green, red, and lighter shades of blue. The first building to have tiles with red in them was the Süleymaniye Mosque (see p.183).

▲ **Geometrical patterns**
Although tiling in mosques was initially limited to the mihrab (prayer niche) area, this restriction was soon lifted. The walls of the Rustem Pasha Mosque, for instance, were covered with colorful and mesmerizing geometrical patterns.

OTTOMAN BUILDINGS

Ottoman architects built many kinds of structure, including palaces, bridges, and bath houses, all of which had features in common with their mosques.

1. Haci Özbek Mosque
Iznik, Turkey, 1333

One of the earliest surviving Ottoman buildings, the Haci Özbek Mosque was built during the reign of Orhan, the son of Osman, the founder of the Ottoman Empire. Its single domed chamber remained a key feature of Ottoman architecture, but its Byzantine-style brickwork later fell out of favor.

2. Çemberlitaş Hammam
Istanbul, Turkey, 1584

The Ottomans gave their towns and cities countless public hammams (bath houses). The Çemberlitaş Hammam, with its series of domed steam rooms, may have been the work of Süleyman I's chief architect, Mimar Sinan.

3. Nuruosmaniye Mosque
Istanbul, Turkey, 1755

The Nuruosmaniye Mosque was the first significant building to be constructed in the 18th-century Ottoman Baroque style. European influences can be seen in radical innovations such as its horseshoe-shaped courtyard and abundance of decorative elements.

4. The White Tower
Thessaloniki, Greece, 15th century

This six-story cylindrical tower rises to a height of nearly 112 ft (34 m). Designed by Mimar Sinan, it was built on the site of an earlier Byzantine structure as part of the city's fortifications.

5

6 7

5. Mostar Bridge
Bosnia–Herzegovina, 1557–1566 (rebuilt 2001–2004)

One of the most elegant of all Ottoman structures, the Mostar Bridge soars 78 ft (24 m) above the Neretva River. The 17th-century Ottoman traveler Evliya Çelebi compared it to "a rainbow arch soaring up to the skies, extending from one cliff to the other."

6. Topkapi Palace
Istanbul, Turkey, 15th century

Six years after his conquest of Constantinople, Sultan Mehmet II began to build a grand palace. Serving as the center of imperial power until the mid 19th century, it was regularly extended to become a vast complex centered on four main courtyards.

7. Green Tomb
Bursa, Turkey, 1421

Built to house the remains of Sultan Mehmed I and his family, this hexagonal mausoleum is almost entirely clad in striking green-blue tiles. The tomb sits on a hill overlooking the other buildings of Bursa's Green Mosque complex.

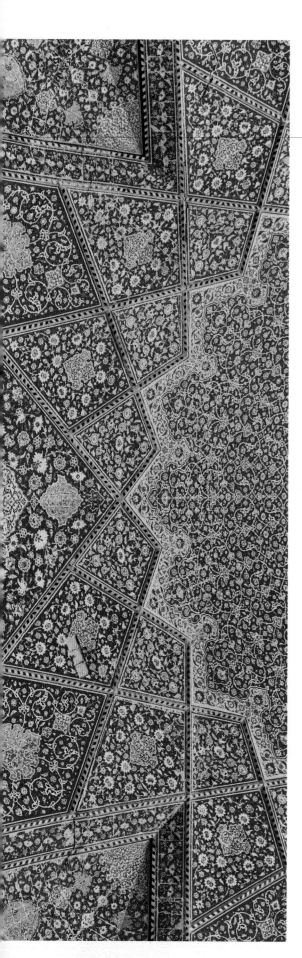

SAFAVID ARCHITECTURE

Shah Abbas I established the new Persian capital of Isfahan in 1588. With its dazzling array of Islamic buildings, the city was described as "half the world" in the contemporary proverb *Isfahan nesf-e jahan*.

Many rulers have left monuments to reflect the glories of their age, but fewer have created an entire city. One who did was Abbas I, the fifth of the Safavid shahs (kings), who reigned from 1588 to 1629, at the height of Persia's military, political, and economic power.

Although the city of Isfahan dates back to at least Sasanian times (see pp.48–49), it had been devastated and plundered, and its citizens slaughtered in their tens of thousands, on at least three occasions in the 14th and 15th centuries. Soon after his accession, Abbas decided to make the city his new capital, and appointed the philosopher, Islamic scholar, mathematician, and astronomer Sheikh Bahai as his chief architect to rejuvenate it.

HALF THE WORLD

In the hands of Abbas and Sheikh Bahai, Isfahan soon became a showcase of Islamic buildings. The focal point of the new capital was the vast public plaza known as the Maidan Naqsh-e Jahan (the Image of the World Square). This was three times as long as it was wide, deliberately mimicking the proportions of Solomon's Temple, which suggests that, for Abbas, Isfahan was a holy city. The large city square helped centralize power as it brought the three great powers of Persia together—the merchants, the clergy, and the shah himself.

> ## "... the epitome of Iran is Isfahan."
> **Persian scholar Mullah Salih Qazvini**, 1600s

The Maidan's northern arcade adjoined the city's vast bazaar, while its western side led to the royal gardens and the Ali Qapu Palace. On its eastern side stood the exquisitely decorated Sheikh Lotfollah Mosque, which was reserved for the shah and the women of the court. Finally, on its southern side, stood the Masjid-i Shah (Shah Mosque), a dazzling complex designed for public worship. The entire square was framed by arcades filled with shops, and was kept cool in summer by corridors of plane trees and channels of water.

BEYOND THE MAIDAN

After the death of Abbas I, two new buildings were erected. Abbas II built the Chehel Sotoun (Forty Columns) pavilion, whose 20 columns were reflected in the pool they stood beside, making it look as if there were 40 columns. His successor, Suleiman I, built the Hasht Behesht (Eight Heavens) pavilion—a two-story octagonal building with a cupola on top.

◄ **Dazzling display**
Built for the personal use of the women of the Safavid royal court, the modestly sized Sheikh Lotfollah Mosque features exquisite Islamic tilework. In the prayer hall, blue and gold tiles lead the eye inexorably up to the dome.

SAFAVID DYNASTY

Conquered by Arab Muslim armies in the mid 7th century, and later invaded by Seljuk Turks and Mongols from Central Asia, Persia (now Iran) finally reasserted its cultural identity in 1501 when Azerbaijani warlord Ismail (1487–1524) captured Tabriz, and proclaimed himself shah, founding the Safavid dynasty. Shah Abbas I, who moved the capital to Isfahan, in central Iran, was Ismail's grandson.

Shah Ismail, painted by Cristofano dell'Altissimo, c. 16th century

MASJID-I SHAH

ISFAHAN, IRAN, 1611–1629

Designed by architect Ali Akbar Isfahani, the Masjid-i Shah was the great public mosque of Shah Abbas's Isfahan. Its courtyard has four grand iwans: one serves as the entrance; one leads to the prayer hall; and two lead to madrasas (religious schools).

MAIDAN NAQSH-I JAHAN

The Masjid-i Shah has pride of place at the southern end of the Maidan Naqsh-e Jahan, but because the square is not aligned with the holy site of Mecca, the mosque stands at a 45-degree angle to the gateway, facing southwest. Visitors entering the mosque from the square have to turn right into the main court.

The Shah Mosque, facing Mecca

▲ **Dome**
The prayer hall is topped by a 177-ft-(54-m-) high dome. Raised on a drum, it has two shells with a 46ft (14m) gap between them. The dome is covered with blue and turquoise tiles, evoking the colors of a peacock's tail.

▲ **Winter prayer hall**
The mosque's two side iwans lead to a pair of low, rectangular rooms that serve as prayer halls in winter. Each is adorned with exquisite tiles arranged in geometric patterns of gold and deepest blue.

Madrasa, beyond the eastern iwan

Prayer hall, adorned with multicolored glazed tiles

Dome over the main prayer hall

Entrance iwan, leading from the Maidan Naqsh-i Jahan

Goldast, from which the call to prayer is announced

KEY ELEMENTS

Safavid architects drew heavily on Timurid traditions (see pp.142–143). They built primarily with brick, arranged their buildings around courtyards, topped their halls with domes, and decorated public areas with colorful tiles.

IWANS

The iwan was a Sasanian invention (see pp.48–49), but the Safavids made it a key element of their architecture. They developed a layout, particularly for mosques, in which four iwans opened out from a central courtyard, like gateways leading to the spiritual world.

▲ Main iwan
Built during the reign of Shah Abbas II, the Hakim Mosque has the characteristic four-iwan design. Otherwise, it is much simpler and less decorated than the mosques built under Abbas I.

GARDENS, FOUNTAINS, AND POOLS

Safavid Isfahan has been called one of the world's first garden cities. It had numerous planted areas that were designed for recreational use. These were typically dotted with pools and water features, which cooled the air and watered the plants and trees.

▶ Water feature
Fountains brought the soothing sound of water into Persian gardens. In the Chehel Sotoun gardens, four female figures hold up the heads of four lions, each of which is a waterspout.

▲ Beauty in symmetry
Of all the gardens that once graced Isfahan, only two have survived: those in the grounds of the Hasht Behesht pavilion, and these, known as the Chehel Sotoun Gardens.

PERSIAN TILES

As well as being beautiful, the elaborate tiles that covered the surfaces of mosques and other buildings also served a spiritual purpose: their abstract patterns were designed to focus the mind for divine contemplation.

▲ Haft rang tiles
The Safavids used *haft rang* (seven-colored) tiles. Previously, craftsmen had worked with single-colored tiles that had to be cut into pieces and assembled like mosaics. The new technique made it possible to paint directly on the tiles themselves.

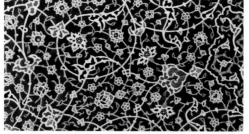

▲ Floral pattern
Artists specialized in decorating tiles with stylized plant forms. These motifs expressed fertility and abundance, and referenced the Tree of Life (also known as the Tree of Immortality) that is mentioned in the Qur'an.

▲ Secular tiling
Although they retained the Islamic tradition of decorating mosques and madrasas with repetitive, abstract patterns, the Safavids decorated their secular buildings with tiles depicting people in semi-realistic scenes—this was completely new.

SAFAVID BUILDINGS

Whether they were constructing mosques, palaces, bridges, or caravansaries, the Safavids used the same style of architecture for all of their buildings.

1. Pavilion of Ali Qapu
Isfahan, Iran, 1597

Overlooking the Maidan, the impressive gatehouse of the royal palace is known as the Pavilion of Ali Qapu, or the Sublime Gate. Its high balcony, fronting an eight-story building with a large central reception hall, served both as an entrance to the palace and as a place from which members of the court could watch people passing below.

2. Citadel of Bam
Bam, Iran, 16th century

First built by the Achaemenids around 579–323 BCE (see pp.44–47), the Citadel of Bam was a military garrison that commanded some important trade routes, including the Silk Road. It was rebuilt by the Safavids, complete with protective earthworks, to contain a city and what was known as the Four Seasons Palace.

3. Allahverdi Khan Bridge
Isfahan, Iran, 1599–1602

Also known as the *Si-o-se-pol* (The Bridge of 33 Spans), this bridge was the main crossing over the Zayanderud River in Safavid Isfahan. It has two levels of arcades, which once housed coffee houses, making it a popular meeting place as well as somewhere from which to watch boat races on the river below.

▲ **Islamic iwans**
The first example of Mughal architecture, the tomb of Humayun, was built in 1558. Following Islamic tradition, the mausoleum has domes, vaults, pointed arches, and iwans—arches that have a space underneath covered by half a dome.

THE MUGHAL EMPIRE

Although its best-known monument, the majestic Taj Mahal, has long been an icon of India, the Mughals and their distinctive architecture have their roots in Islamic Central Asia and Iran.

"The soul of Iran incarnate in the body of India."

René Grousset, French historian on the Taj Mahal, 1931

The mixing of the imported with the indigenous is characteristic of Mughal architecture. The debt that the Mughal style owes to Central Asia and Iran is evident in its earliest surviving buildings, such as the enormous mausoleum designed by Persian architects for Humayun (1508–1556), son of the founder of the Mughal dynasty. His tomb has a monumental iwan-style gateway, an Islamic-style dome raised on a drum, and a facade with a row of pointed arches that closely resembles the arcades of Isfahan in present-day Iran. The mausoleum even stands in a Persian-style garden arranged in four quarters. All of these Islamic features, however, are fused with local Indian elements, including the small domed pavilions known as chhatris and the use of red sandstone and white marble.

INDO-ISLAMIC GLORIES

Humayun's son, Akbar (1542–1605) built one of the most glorious examples of Indo-Islamic architecture in the form of his capital city, Fatehpur Sikri. Akbar was the greatest of the Mughal emperors and during his long reign,

he also invented his own religious movement, Din-i-ilahi, an amalgam of Islam, Hinduism, Jainism, and Zoroastrianism. When he died, he was laid to rest in an ornate mausoleum at Sikandra, in the suburbs of Agra. Akbar's mausoleum is approached by a gate with a huge iwan-style entrance, flanked by a pair of smaller iwan-style recesses, one above the other. The roof of the gate provides a platform for four white marble chhatri-topped minarets.

Akbar's grandson, who ascended the throne in 1628 as Emperor Shah Jahan, created a new capital at Delhi, where he built the Red Fort (named for its red sandstone outer walls) as his main residence. He also commissioned the city's impressive Jama Masjid (Friday Mosque). One of the characteristics of this period was an increase in the use of white marble, transported from quarries hundreds of miles away. The Red Fort complex includes several palaces built in white marble, and in Lahore, Shah Jahan ordered the construction of the white marble Moti Masjid (Pearl Mosque). Yet the most spectacular building he commissioned in this gleaming stone was the monument to his beloved wife, Mumtaz Mahal—the Taj Mahal.

DECLINE OF THE EMPIRE

Shah Jahan's reign ended when he became ill in 1658. When he died, he was entombed in the Taj Mahal next to his wife. After a dispute, the throne passed to his son, Aurangzeb, but under his leadership, the economy of the empire began to suffer. When Aurangzeb came to build a tomb for his wife, it was only about half the size of the Taj Mahal and poorly finished. The Mughal Empire's later rulers fell into religious intolerance, and oversaw its economic and political decline.

THE MUGHAL DYNASTY

India's great Muslim dynasty was founded by Babur (1483–1530), a conqueror from Central Asia who claimed descent from Genghis Khan. He called his empire the Mughal Empire in reference to his Mongol heritage. Although Muslim, the Mughals ruled a country with a large Hindu majority. The new rulers did not impose Islam on their subjects but encouraged people of different faiths to mix.

Emperor Shah Jahan (1592-1666) was the fifth Mughal ruler.

TAJ MAHAL

AGRA, INDIA, 1631–1653

Shah Jahan's monument to his wife, Mumtaz Mahal, is based on earlier tombs, with its iwans, octagonal chambers, and a great central dome. What elevates the Taj Mahal is the beauty of its proportions and symmetry, amplified by its magnificent setting.

GARDEN SETTING

Unusually for Mughal mausoleums, the Taj Mahal does not sit at the center of its garden, but at the back of it. This made it possible to build an especially long pool in front of it, in which the great white building is reflected. Behind and below the Taj Mahal is the Yamuna River, which also reflects the building. According to one story, Shah Jahan planned to build a corresponding tomb, in black marble, on the opposite bank of the river.

The gardens at the site symbolize Paradise.

▲ **Decorative inlays**
Many walls have inlaid patterns made of semiprecious stones such as carnelian, coral, jade, jasper, and onyx. As Islam prohibited representations of people and animals, the designs are based on plant forms.

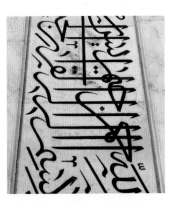

▲ **Qur'anic inscriptions**
Around the entrance portal is an inscription from the 36th sura of the Qur'an. It speaks of God's gifts to humanity on Earth and the promise of eternal life to the faithful. The writing is formed from inlaid jasper.

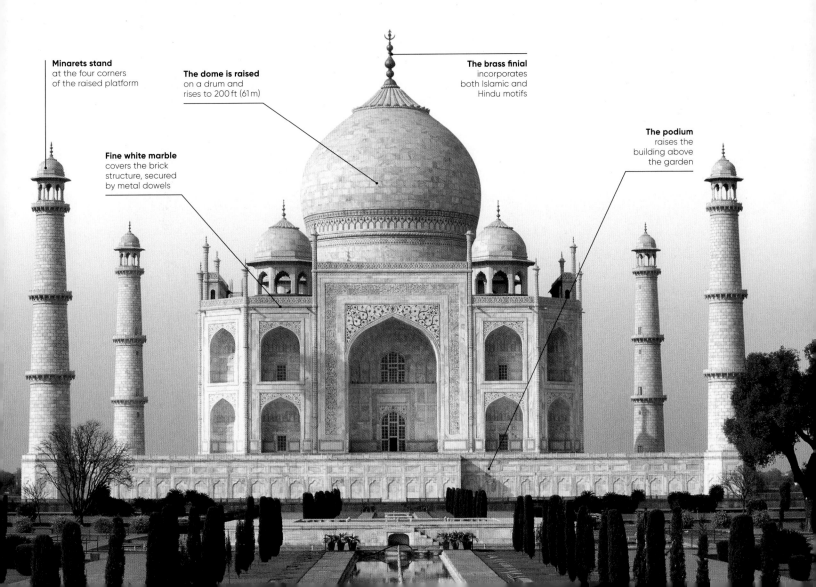

Minarets stand at the four corners of the raised platform

The dome is raised on a drum and rises to 200 ft (61 m)

The brass finial incorporates both Islamic and Hindu motifs

The podium raises the building above the garden

Fine white marble covers the brick structure, secured by metal dowels

KEY ELEMENTS

The architecture of Mughal India drew on and adapted Persian and other Islamic motifs to accommodate local preferences, materials, and techniques.

CHHATRIS

Originally used as canopies over tombs, chhatris are small pavilions on slender pillars with domed roofs. The earliest known example, which is in the western state of Gujarat, dates back to around 1160.

▲ **Rooftop corners**
A chhatri sits at each of the four corners of the roof of the Hall of Audience at the emperor Akbar's imperial capital of Fatehpur Sikri. Ornate carved brackets support the canopy.

◀ **Decorative dome**
Sher Shah Suri took control of the Mughal Empire in 1540. His tomb in Bihar stands on a square stone plinth in the middle of an artificial lake. It has a chhatri at each corner and around the dome.

JALI LATTICE SCREENS

Carved windows enable air and light to circulate within a building. Such screens were common in places like Egypt and Syria, where they were made of wood and known as *mashrabiya*, but in India, jali lattice screens were carved from stone or marble.

NEW MATERIALS

Mughal buildings employed two types of stone. Red sandstone was used extensively, notably in the red city of Fatehpur Sikri and at the Red Fort in Delhi. Marble was used more sparingly, except at the Taj Mahal, which is entirely covered in marble.

▲ **Marble carving**
The Tomb of Salim Chishti, a Sufi saint, is part of the Fatehpur Sikri palace complex and was built by the emperor Akbar between 1571 and 1580. Its veranda has a wall of finely carved marble jali panels set between columns and pilasters.

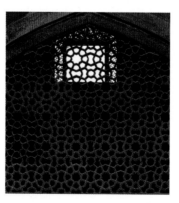

▲ **Geometric patterns**
Jalis typically use geometric patterns that can be repeated endlessly, as in this example from Humayun's Tomb in Delhi. Such patterns represent the infinity of the universe.

◀ **Red sandstone**
Agra Fort is also known as the Red Fort, like the fort in Delhi. Both derive their names from their extensive use of a red sandstone quarried in Rajasthan in northwest India. The stone takes its color from iron oxides in the earth.

MUGHAL BUILDINGS

Mughal building centered on the north of India, stretching further north to Lahore (in modern Pakistan) and south to Allahabad. Its great monuments are concentrated around Fatehpur Sikri and Delhi.

1. Humayun's Tomb
Delhi, India, 1566

Haji Begum, Humayun's widow, assembled the team of artisans who built this grand tomb for her husband. A turning point in architecture, it marked a clear synthesis of Indian and Persian traditions. It was also the first building in which red sandstone was used on such a scale. White marble covers the dome.

2. Tomb of Jahangir
Lahore, Pakistan, 1630

Jahangir, who ruled from 1605–1627, was the only surviving son of Akbar and the fourth Mughal emperor. Like other Mughal monuments, Jahangir's tomb has a podium, arcades, and four corner minarets, but he forbade the construction of a dome over his tomb.

3. Friday Mosque
Delhi, India, 1650–1656

Commonly known as the Jama Masjid, Delhi's great mosque was built by Shah Jahan as the centerpiece of his new capital. The imperial entrance is a massive iwan, and behind it there are three enormous domes.

"The dynasty and the empire itself became indisputably Indian."

John F. Richards, American historian on the Mughal Empire, 1995

ITALIAN RENAISSANCE

Renaissance architects revived the stylistic conventions of ancient Roman buildings and applied them in new contexts. The style flourished in Florence, Rome, and throughout Italy.

The term "Renaissance" literally means "rebirth." In architecture it refers to the conscious revival of the spirit and forms of ancient Roman buildings. This revival began in Florence around 1420, spreading throughout Italy during the 15th century. By the end of the 16th century, it had permeated most parts of Europe.

RENEWING THE ROMAN SPIRIT

The father figure of Renaissance architecture was Filippo Brunelleschi. He trained as a goldsmith, then took up sculpture, and only gradually turned to architecture, designing his first buildings when he was in his forties.

Brunelleschi is said to have visited Rome to study ancient buildings, but he did not try to imitate them closely. Rather, he absorbed their qualities and adapted them to the needs of his own time. He mastered the decorative vocabulary of Classical architecture and its sense of order and harmony, but his work typically has a feeling of graceful lightness rather than the massive strength associated with ancient Roman buildings.

Florence continued to be a major center of Renaissance architecture during the 15th century, but Rome was growing in importance, and from the early 16th century it assumed the lead. The key figure at this time was Donato Bramante, who was regarded by his contemporaries as the first architect to truly revive the majesty of ancient Roman buildings. His style was very different to Brunelleschi's, being weighty and solemn. More than any other architect, he exemplifies the ideals of the High Renaissance, the brief period when Italian art reached a peak of balance and nobility.

Many other Italian cities have outstanding examples of Renaissance architecture, and in the later 16th century some of the most momentous developments were outside the major art centers. In particular, Andrea Palladio, who worked mainly in and around Vicenza, created some of the most influential buildings in the history of architecture, admired for their air of effortless dignity and elegance. These include churches, palaces, and, most notably, villas in the countryside.

THE REDISCOVERY OF ROME

After the fall of the Roman Empire, the city of Rome deteriorated for almost a thousand years, becoming virtually a shanty town. The city's recovery began under Pope Martin V (r. 1417–1431). Much ancient statuary and architecture was unearthed, inspiring many artists, among them Maarten van Heemskerck, who made numerous drawings in the 1530s.

Roman ruins from the sketchbook of Dutch artist Maarten van Heemskerck

▶ **Antiquity revived**
Raphael designed the Villa Madama, Rome, for Cardinal Giulio de' Medici. The garden loggia was begun c. 1518 and is perhaps one of the loveliest attempts during the Renaissance to re-create the atmosphere of an ancient Roman interior.

> "The first who brought good and beautiful architecture to light."
> Andrea Palladio on Donato Bramante, *Four Books on Architecture*, 1570

PALAZZO FARNESE

CAPRAROLA, ITALY, BEGUN 1558

Also known as the Villa Farnese, this overwhelming building was created for the wealthy and powerful Farnese family, whose members included Pope Paul III. The foundations for a fortress on a pentagonal plan (popular in contemporary military architecture) were begun c. 1515, but the architect Giacomo da Vignola was commissioned to turn the site into a country mansion. It was still unfinished when he died in 1573.

Entrance facade of Palazzo Farnese

> "So noble and magnificent an edifice, marvellous in its site."
>
> Giorgio Vasari on the Palazzo Farnese, *Lives of the Artists*, 1568

Piano nobile, the principal storey, housing main rooms

▶ Spiral staircase

The most spectacular internal feature of the palace is the main staircase, which rises in a graceful spiral through three floors. It is crowned with a dome and richly decorated with frescoes by Antonio Tempesta, c. 1580.

VIGNOLA

Giacomo Barozzi (1507–1573), known as Giacomo da Vignola after the town of his birth, was one of the leading Italian architects of the 16th century. He worked mainly in Rome, and after Michelangelo's death in 1564, he succeeded him as architect of St. Peter's. In addition to his buildings, he is notable as the author of a highly successful textbook on architecture (1562).

An engraving of Vignola shows him holding architectural plans.

▲ Farnese pomp

The *Sala dei Fasti Farnesiani* (Room of Farnese Deeds), the palace's most famous room, is covered with frescoes (c. 1565) by Taddeo Zuccaro celebrating Farnese family history.

▲ Elegant courtyard

A circular courtyard was planned for the unfinished Farnese fortress. There is nothing fortresslike about the courtyard that Vignola created, however. It is one of his most elegant designs.

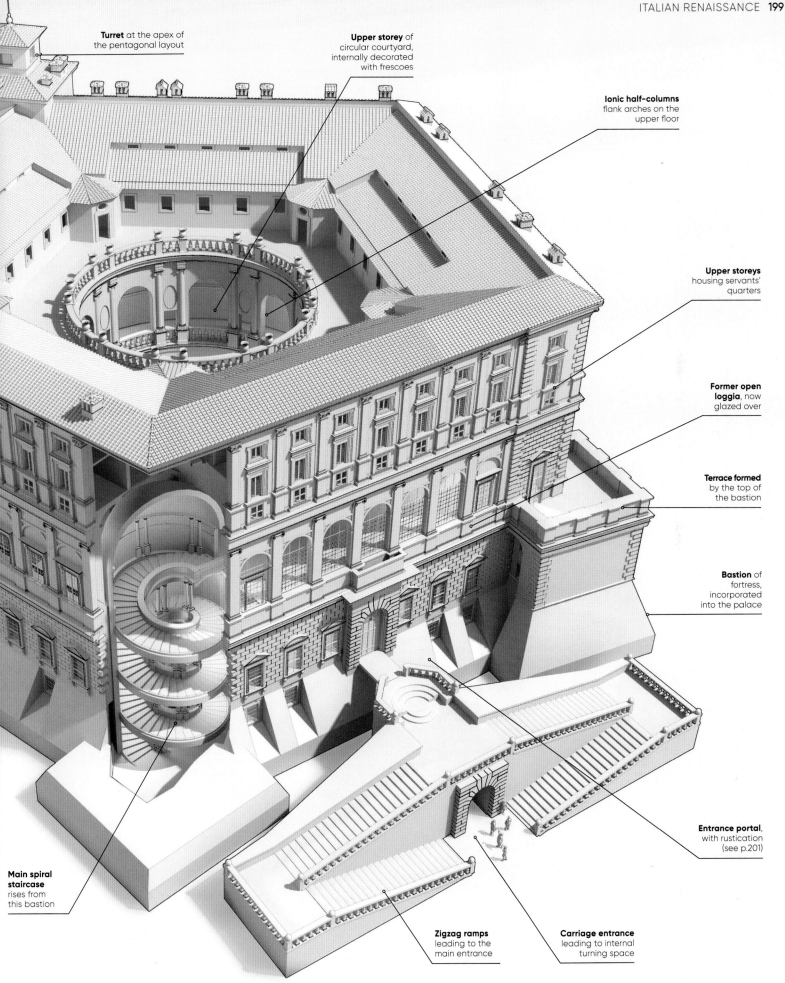

Turret at the apex of
the pentagonal layout

Upper storey of
circular courtyard,
internally decorated
with frescoes

Ionic half-columns
flank arches on the
upper floor

Upper storeys
housing servants'
quarters

**Former open
loggia**, now
glazed over

Terrace formed
by the top of
the bastion

Bastion of
fortress,
incorporated
into the palace

Entrance portal,
with rustication
(see p.201)

**Main spiral
staircase**
rises from
this bastion

Zigzag ramps
leading to the
main entrance

Carriage entrance
leading to internal
turning space

KEY ELEMENTS

The Classical architectural vocabulary inherited from ancient Rome—columns, arches, pediments, and so on—was flexible and adaptable, and Renaissance buildings embrace both epic grandeur and refined charm.

DOMES

The ancient Romans were the first great builders of domes. Although these fell from favor in medieval architecture, they returned during the Italian Renaissance. The largest examples are major feats of engineering as well as aesthetic triumphs.

CORNICES

A cornice is a horizontal ornamental strip that projects from a building, normally above a row of real or implied columns. On Renaissance palaces, cornices were often particularly rich and elaborate, so much so that in Florence there was at one time legislation about how far these decorative elements were permitted to project into the street.

▲ Papal splendor
The dome of St. Peter's in Rome was designed by Michelangelo, but it was unfinished when he died in 1564. Giacomo della Porta supervised its completion in 1590, making it steeper in outline than in Michelangelo's wooden model, perhaps to increase its structural stability.

▲ Engineering triumph
Brunelleschi invented special scaffolding and hoisting equipment to help create the huge dome of Florence Cathedral. Built between 1420 and 1436, it majestically dominates the city and is still the largest masonry dome in the world. The lantern at the top of the dome was begun in 1446, shortly before Brunelleschi's death.

▲ Revised design
After the death of Antonio da Sangallo the Younger, Michelangelo took over as architect of Rome's Palazzo Farnese (not to be confused with Caprarola's) in 1546, when the facade was nearly complete. His cornice was more imposing than the original design, increasing the visual impact of the building.

PEDIMENTED WINDOWS

Windows surmounted by pediments are among the most common features of Italian Renaissance architecture, especially in secular buildings. A favorite treatment in long palace facades is to alternate triangular and segmental pediments.

▶ Majestic palace
The windows of the Palazzo Farnese in Rome have alternating triangular and segmental pediments. Begun in 1515, the Palazzo was redesigned and enlarged in 1541–1546 by Antonio da Sangallo the Younger.

ARCADED COURTYARDS

Medieval monasteries often featured arcaded cloisters and the idea was continued in Renaissance churches. Arcaded courtyards also became a common feature of Renaissance urban palaces, offering a peaceful and protected space in contrast to the busy streets outside.

◄ Elegant harmony

Whereas the exterior of the Palazzo Medici in Florence (begun 1445) is massive and fortresslike, the courtyard is graceful and serene. The architect was Michelozzo di Bartolomeo, a favorite artist of the Medici family.

RUSTICATION

Used to create an effect of rugged strength, rustication describes stonework on a building's exterior that is cut with deep grooves between the blocks or given an exaggerated, rough texture. In Renaissance architecture it was typically used on palace facades to suggest power and authority. It was often only applied on the lower parts of the building in contrast with upper, smoother areas, but in some buildings it covers the whole wall.

Diamond rustication on Palazzo dei Diamanti, Ferrara

FACADE DECORATION

Although buildings in central Italy were often in a pure Classical style, in the north the Gothic tradition was still vigorous and there was a fashion for rich decoration on facades, creating a kind of fusion of medieval and Renaissance elements.

▲ Profuse ornament

Designed by Giovanni Antonio Amadeo, the Colleoni Chapel at Bergamo Cathedral (c. 1471–1475), is lavishly ornamented. A checkered surface of colored marbles is overlaid with a profusion of carved decoration.

▲ Exuberant carving

The Certosa di Pavia is a large monastery, begun in 1396. Work on it by many architects, sculptors, and painters continued well into the 16th century. The west facade (begun 1473) is covered with lively decoration.

ITALIAN RENAISSANCE BUILDINGS

The greatest achievements of Italian Renaissance architecture are found
in both religious and secular buildings. Although these share a basic
repertoire of Classical forms, they range in spirit from noble severity to
highly ornate exuberance.

1. Villa Rotonda
near Vicenza, c. 1565

In this, his most famous building, Andrea
Palladio gave equal prominence to all four
sides. It was built as a pleasure retreat
and has beautiful views in every direction.

2. Tempietto
San Pietro in Montorio, Rome, c. 1502

Bramante's tiny, circular church (whose
name means "little temple") marks the
place where St. Peter is said to have been
crucified. In spite of its small size, it has
remarkable grandeur and solemnity.

3. Pazzi Chapel
Santa Croce, Florence, begun c. 1442

Brunelleschi designed this chapel, but it
was completed about 15 years after his
death. Other architects might have had
a hand in finishing it, but it is regarded as
one of his noblest designs.

4. Medici Chapel
San Lorenzo, Florence, 1520–1534

This hauntingly somber room is a
mausoleum for various members of the
Medici family. It shows the unprecedented
freedom and inventiveness with which
Michelangelo used the forms of
Classical architecture.

5. Courtyard, Palazzo Ducale
Urbino, c. 1465

Designed by Luciano Laurana, this
graceful, dignified courtyard is the
architectural highlight of the palace of
Duke Federico da Montefeltro, one of
the most cultured of Renaissance rulers.

6

7

6. Library of St. Mark
Venice, begun 1537

This glorious work was praised by Andrea Palladio as "perhaps the richest building erected since ancient times." Designed by Jacopo Sansovino, it was not completed until after his death in 1570.

7. Palazzo del Te
Mantua, 1525–1534

The Palazzo was designed by Giulio Romano for Federico II Gonzaga, Duke of Mantua. It was a summer villa, intended for pleasurable days, not for living in. This is the imposing garden front.

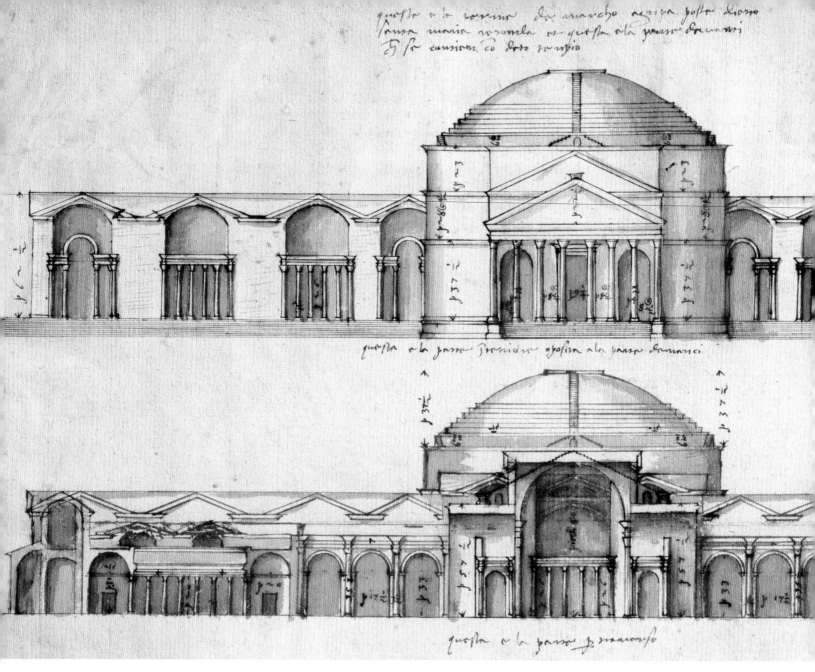

▲ **Architectural drawings**
More than 300 drawings by Renaissance architect Palladio have survived, both designs for his own buildings and records of ancient ruins. This is his imaginative reconstruction of the Baths of Agrippa in Rome. While architectural drawings from the Middle Ages are known, they did not become common until the Renaissance, when the production of paper greatly increased.

"The architect should be equipped with knowledge of many branches of study."

Vitruvius, *Ten Books on Architecture*, 1st century BCE

◀ **Egyptian architect**
A government official, as well as an architect, Senenmut rose from humble origins to enjoy high status. In this sculpture from his tomb (c. 1500 BCE), he is shown holding a rolled-up surveyor's cord.

THE ARCHITECT

Architecture goes back to our hunter-gatherer ancestors, but the idea of an "architect"—someone who specializes in designing buildings—is much more recent.

Many people are involved in producing a building—from the user and the person or institution paying for it through to the different craftspeople whose skills turn raw materials into architecture. Throughout history, large or complex projects have seen a variety of types of leader. The person most often recognized is the one who commissions and pays for the building, but stonemasons, administrators, artists, and scholars have all received credit for designing major buildings. The term "architect" arose in ancient Greece, was used in Rome, and came to something like its modern meaning in the Italian Renaissance, when competition between patrons produced a market for individual artistic "genius" in architecture, as it had in painting and sculpture.

ARCHITECTURE SCHOOLS

As industrial exploitation of fossil fuels spread in the 19th century, the amount and complexity of architectural construction rose sharply, and the first schools were set up to train architects to meet the rising demand for design work. Architects have since fulfilled varied roles as coordinators, advocates, visionaries, planners, and marketeers within the world of design and construction. The number of trained architects in the world today is in the millions, but most buildings worldwide are still built without the involvement of an architect.

ARCHITECTS AND CLIMATE ACTION

With uniquely broad training, encompassing technical, artistic, social, and ethical aspects of the built world, architects have a vital part to play in avoiding climate catastrophe. At the moment, 40 percent of all climate-changing emissions come from making and operating buildings. To reduce this to zero in just a few years requires cultural change and inspiring leadership, as well as technical development. Architects trained in the skills of analysis and persuasion are in a position to challenge the carbon-intense status quo, and advocate powerfully for a zero-carbon built environment.

▲ **Medieval architect**
In the Middle Ages, the architect and master mason were virtually synonymous. Such masons were not merely skillful craftsmen but honored professionals. Here, Hugues Libergier (d. 1263) is shown handsomely dressed on his tomb slab in Reims Cathedral, France.

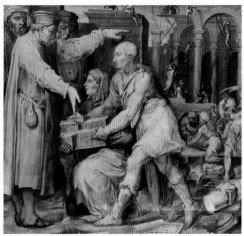

▲ **Architectural model**
Architects have made models of buildings since at least ancient Greek times, but few survive from before the Renaissance. In this fresco (1556–1558) by Giorgio Vasari, Brunelleschi and Ghiberti present a model of San Lorenzo, Florence, to Cosimo de' Medici.

DRAFTING

Before computers became common in the later 20th century, all architectural drawings were made by hand, often by specialized draftsmen. They traditionally worked standing up at large drawing boards or drafting tables. The boards usually had some kind of a mechanism to raise or incline the drawing surface. Drawing boards, though still in use, have now largely given way to computer-aided drafting (see pp.352–353).

Adjustable rules aid drafting

An engraving of a draftsman at work from 1893

THE RENAISSANCE BEYOND ITALY

In the 16th century, the Renaissance style of architecture spread throughout Europe. In some places, it mixed with older local styles; in others, it supplanted them.

The Renaissance style in architecture began to spread outside Italy around 1500, and within a century was well established in most of Europe. France was the first country to be strongly influenced, its wars in Italy from 1494 resulting in a counterinvasion of Italian culture. King Francis I (r. 1515–1547) was a great admirer of Italian art and brought leading Italian painters, sculptors, and architects to France to work for him, including Leonardo da Vinci.

Italian artists worked in many other countries at this time. Artists of various nationalities also visited Italy and returned to their own countries with an up-to-date knowledge of Renaissance art. One of the most notable was Spaniard Pedro Machuca, who spent several years in Rome before returning to Spain in about 1520. Having previously worked mainly as a painter, he then turned to architecture, and his palace of Charles V in Granada is a more imposing expression of the ideals of the High Renaissance than any surviving building of the same time in Italy.

THE INFLUENCE OF PRINT

Books and prints also enabled the spread of the Renaissance style. The first architectural books, published in the late 15th century, were scholarly treatises, written in Latin. In the 16th century, however, illustrated architectural books in modern languages began to appear, the most influential being by Sebastiano Serlio. Countless individual engravings were also used as a source of decorative motifs.

Such prints were abundantly used in England in the 16th century. Although some impressive Renaissance detailing had been used there by itinerant Italian artists early in the century, subsequent influence came mainly through the medium of engravings from France and the Low Countries. The detailing they inspired is sometimes crude compared with contemporary Italian work, but it can also have vigor and charm. A refined Renaissance architectural style did not arrive in England until the early 17th century, in the work of Inigo Jones, who made two lengthy visits to Italy.

◀ **Italians abroad**
The early-16th-century Sigismund Chapel at Krakow Cathedral in Poland, is one of the purest Renaissance works of its time outside Italy. It was designed by architect and sculptor Bartolomeo Berrecci, and several other Italian artists worked with him.

Conical roof
topped by lantern

SEBASTIANO SERLIO

Italian painter and architect Sebastiano Serlio (1475–1554) spent much of his career in France. He was the author of a treatise that played a key role in spreading knowledge of Renaissance architecture. Usually known by the abbreviated title *L'Architettura*, it was the first architectural treatise to be abundantly illustrated and was intended as a practical handbook. Published in parts from 1537, it was translated into several languages and frequently reprinted.

Sebastiano Serlio, by Bartolomeo Passarotti

CHÂTEAU DE CHAMBORD
CHAMBORD, LOIRE VALLEY, FRANCE, BEGUN 1519

Chambord is the greatest of the buildings commissioned by King Francis I, one of the outstanding art patrons of his time. It was perhaps designed by the Italian architect Domenico da Cortona, and Renaissance influence is apparent in its near-symmetry and many of its details. The spiky roofline, however, is medieval in spirit.

THE CENTRAL STAIRCASE

The most remarkable feature of the interior of Chambord is the double-helix staircase in the center of the main block. Rising from the ground floor to the roof terraces, its two spiral stairs twist one above the other around a central core. Its sophisticated geometry is characteristic of a period of proud and competitive intellectualism. The design is often attributed to Leonardo da Vinci, Francis I's favorite artist, who was paid to come to France, but died in the year that Chambord was begun

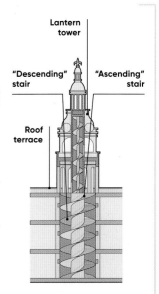

This section through the staircase shows its double-helix form.

▲ Chimney stacks
The ornate chimney stacks play a prominent part in the roofscape, the château's most distinctive feature, showing off the luxurious warmth of many fireplaces.

▲ Lantern tower
A lantern tower is one that has openings at the top, usually to admit light. Here, it stands over the central staircase. A fleur-de-lys tops the tower.

▲ Dormer windows
The facade is enlivened by dormer windows. The initials FRF stand for *François, Roi de France* (Francis, King of France). The pediment is adorned with fleurs-de-lys.

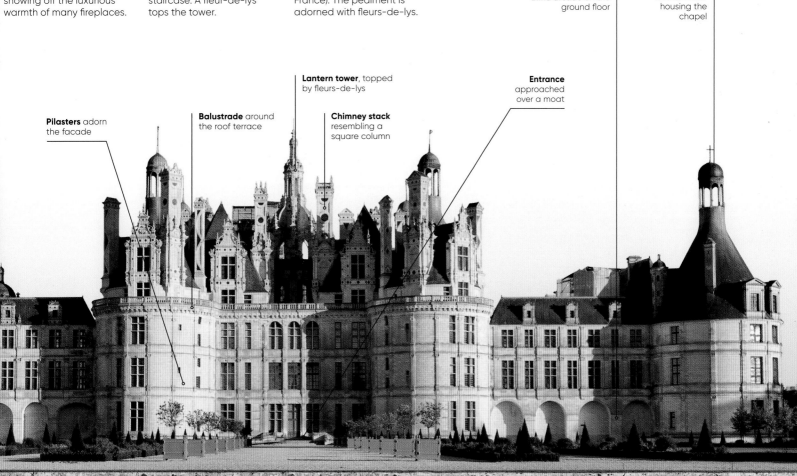

Pilasters adorn the facade

Balustrade around the roof terrace

Lantern tower, topped by fleurs-de-lys

Chimney stack resembling a square column

Entrance approached over a moat

Blind arcade on the ground floor

Round tower housing the chapel

KEY ELEMENTS

As Renaissance motifs and ideas were picked up outside Italy, designers used them with less obedience to invented rules. This greater freedom and exuberance is evident in their buildings.

STRAP WORK

In the 16th century, strap work was a popular form of decoration in architecture and other fields, particularly in northern Europe. It is a type of ornament using forms resembling strips of parchment or leather that have been elaborately cut, pierced, twisted, and interlaced.

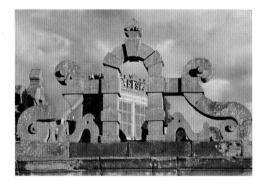

▲ Garden ornament
This vigorous strap work tops a garden wall at Hardwick Hall in Derbyshire, UK. Built in the late 16th century, Hardwick is one of several imposing country houses designed by Robert Smythson, the outstanding architect of the Elizabethan period.

▲ Whimsical head
Strap work is often combined with "grotesque" ornament, which typically involves whimsical human heads. This example is found on the facade of Audley End in Essex, UK, a huge country house whose construction began around 1603.

WENDEL DIETTERLIN

Printing presses, new to Europe, spread ideas and images at a new speed. German painter and engraver Wendel Dietterlin (c. 1551–1599) spent most of his life in Strasbourg. As a painter, he specialized in the decoration of buildings, but almost all of his work has been destroyed. He is mainly remembered for his book of engravings, *Architectura* (1593–1594). His unrestrained architectural fantasies were much used as sources by decorative artists.

Illustration from Dietterlin's book *Architectura*

LONG GALLERIES

Long, narrow rooms (often stretching the whole width of a building) were common features of major English houses in the 16th and early 17th centuries, and are also found in France. They allowed the wealthy residents to get enough exercise, even in the cold and wet of winter.

◀ Royal gallery
The Gallery of Francis I at the Château de Fontainebleau is one of the most impressive interiors of its time. The decoration was supervised by Italian artist Rosso Fiorentino.

STEEP ROOFS

In Italian Renaissance buildings, roofs tend to be hidden behind parapets, but in the rainier north, notably in France and Germany, steep roofs feature prominently. These often incorporate dormer windows, as well as decorative scrolls, urns, and even statues.

◀ Royal entrance
Built in 1528–1540 as a new main entrance for the Château de Fontainebleau in France, the Porte Dorée (Golden Gate) combines medieval structural forms with Italianate details. The architect was Gilles Le Breton.

RENAISSANCE BUILDINGS

In countries outside Italy, the Renaissance style was adopted in buildings of various kinds. The grandest were often those commissioned by royal patrons to show off their wealth and taste.

1

2

3

1. The Palace of Charles V
Granada, Spain, begun 1527

Spanish architect Pedro Machuca designed this palace for Holy Roman Emperor Charles V, who was also King Charles I of Spain. The massive, weighty style reflects Machuca's knowledge of contemporary buildings in Italy, specifically Rome, where he spent several years.

2. Banqueting House
London, UK, 1619–1622

Inigo Jones revolutionized English architecture, introducing a pure, Classical style to a country that had previously been little touched by Renaissance art. Jones was particularly influenced by the architect Palladio, whose work he had studied in Italy. The Banqueting House was originally a part of Whitehall Palace.

3. Friedrichsbau, Heidelberg Castle
Heidelberg, Germany, 1601–1607

The Friedrichsbau was designed by the architect Johannes Schoch and built for the Elector Palatine Friedrich IV, as part of the huge Heidelberg Castle, his ancestral home. It shows the rich ornamental detail characteristic of German Renaissance architecture.

▲ **Bronze colossus**
The baldachin is a huge bronze canopy over the high altar in St. Peter's, combining the arts of architecture and sculpture. It was designed by Bernini and made in 1624–1633.

BAROQUE

Dynamic and dramatic, the Baroque style was born in Rome in the early 17th century and spread throughout Europe, flourishing particularly in Roman Catholic countries.

The term Baroque is applied to a style of art and architecture that prevailed in much of Europe during the 17th century and into the 18th century, when it merged with the burgeoning Rococo style (see pp.218–221). There are strong links between Baroque art and the Counter-Reformation—a systematic campaign by the Catholic Church to reassert its authority in opposition to the spread of Protestantism. The visual arts were part of this campaign, because the Church realized that these arts could help bolster Catholics in their beliefs by appealing to their hearts and minds. As a result, Baroque painting and sculpture are often very emotional in tone, typically showing the agonies and ecstasies of the saints, and Baroque architecture departs from the feeling of massive repose typical of Renaissance buildings and creates instead a sense of drama and fluidity.

As well as being the center of the Catholic Church, Rome was at this time the artistic capital of Europe and it was here that the Baroque style emerged. Three great architects were mainly responsible for establishing it in the

> "Baroque architects preferred curves to straight lines and complex forms to those which were regular and simple."
>
> Anthony Blunt, *Baroque and Rococo: Architecture and Decoration*, 1978

city: Gian Lorenzo Bernini, Francesco Borromini, and Pietro da Cortona. Bernini was primarily a sculptor and Cortona primarily a painter; only Borromini was wholly dedicated to architecture. All three designed secular buildings, but did their most important work for the Church.

THE SPREAD OF BAROQUE

From Rome, the Baroque style spread to other parts of Italy and Europe, undergoing various modifications in response to different tastes, outlooks, and local traditions. It took root most firmly in other Catholic countries, and in some places (notably Spain and Latin America) it became more extravagantly ornate (see pp.222–223). However, in Protestant countries, such as England and the Dutch Republic, the style was usually considerably toned down. Germany was largely Protestant in the north and Catholic in the south, which was reflected in contrasting architectural preferences. Although Baroque architecture is often closely associated with religion, in France its most memorable expression was in a secular context—the glorification of the monarchy.

BERNINI

Gian Lorenzo Bernini (1598–1680) spent almost all his life in Rome, where he was the leading figure in the arts throughout most of his long career. He was the greatest sculptor of his time and an outstanding architect. Highly versatile and industrious, he had a huge impact on Rome's appearance through his buildings, fountains, and outdoor statuary.

A vivid self-portrait by Bernini shows his remarkable skill, although he painted only for recreation.

SANTI LUCA E MARTINA

ROME, ITALY, 1635–1650

One of the masterpieces of Pietro da Cortona, this was the first church to be designed and built in a Baroque style both externally and internally, and the first with a curved facade. Although officially completed in 1650, it was still not entirely finished when Cortona died in 1669.

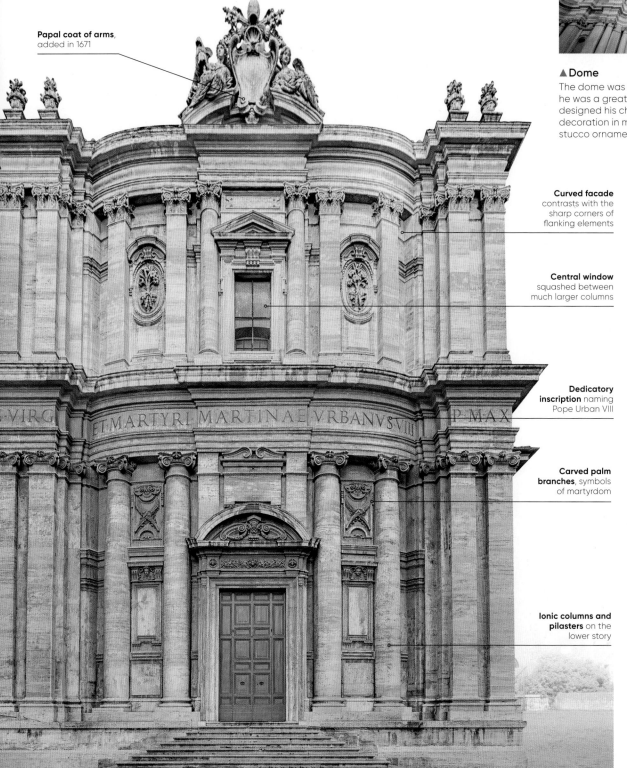

Papal coat of arms, added in 1671

Curved facade contrasts with the sharp corners of flanking elements

Central window squashed between much larger columns

Dedicatory inscription naming Pope Urban VIII

Carved palm branches, symbols of martyrdom

Ionic columns and pilasters on the lower story

▲ Dome

The dome was completed in 1666. Although he was a great painter, Cortona never designed his churches with painted decoration in mind. Here, the dome has rich stucco ornament by his pupil Ciro Ferri.

▲ Altar

The high altar, designed by Cortona but altered after his death, incorporates a marble sculpture of the Early Christian martyr St. Martina. The discovery of her remains in 1634 inspired the building of the church.

▲ Crypt

The crypt (or lower church) is in a richer style than the main building, using colorful marbles. It has an altar designed by Cortona containing the remains of St. Martina. Cortona himself is buried in the crypt.

KEY ELEMENTS

Baroque buildings usually convey confidence and vitality. Forms are often curvaceous and flow into one another rather than being clearly demarcated. There are also spectacular effects and complex spatial arrangements.

DOMES

With the huge examples at Florence Cathedral and St. Peter's in Rome, domes came back to prominence in the Renaissance, but they still remained fairly uncommon. During the Baroque period, however, they were built throughout Europe and also increased in variety, in terms of both external outline and internal arrangement and construction.

▲ Star-shaped dome
This masterpiece by Francesco Borromini in Sant'Ivo alla Sapienza in Rome has a highly inventive dome. Interpenetrating concave and convex forms create an undulating, starlike shape.

▲ Double domed
Santa Maria della Salute, Venice's greatest Baroque church, was designed by Baldassare Longhena. It features two domes: over the central space and over the high altar.

▶ Geometric beauty
Guarino Guarini, the architect of San Lorenzo in Turin (1668–1687), was a scholarly priest with a passionate interest in mathematics. His designs are geometrically complex: this dome has interlacing open ribs.

PALATIAL STAIRCASES

Following the example of Versailles, many great palaces were created in the Baroque age, and magnificent staircases were often some of the most conspicuous elements of these buildings. These staircases were not just imposing architectural features, but also statements of power, making a striking impression on visitors.

▲ Grand stairway
Balthasar Neumann, the greatest German architect of his time, was the principal designer of the Residenz Würzburg, built for the immensely wealthy Prince-Bishop of Würzburg. The staircase was constructed in 1737–1742 and the ceiling above was frescoed by Giambattista Tiepolo in 1752–1753.

FUSION OF THE ARTS

A recurring feature of Baroque art is the way painting, sculpture, and architecture are combined to form an overwhelming visual experience. This is usually in religious contexts, typically helping to create an ecstatic atmosphere, but it is also seen in secular art, where it sometimes incorporates landscape gardening.

▲ Heavenly ascent
In Braunau in Rohr Abbey in Germany, the high altar stucco group of the *Assumption of the Virgin* (1717–1723) by Egid Quirin Asam is set in an elaborate architectural framework. The angels bearing the Virgin to Heaven are partly gilded, and golden light streams down through a yellow glass window.

▲ Emotional fervor
The Gesù in Rome is the mother church of the Jesuits, who played a leading role in promoting Counter-Reformation ideas. The painting of the *Triumph of the Name of Jesus* (1674–1679) is by Giovanni Battista Gaulli. The stucco figures are by Antonio Raggi, a pupil of Bernini.

◄ Luxurious landscape
Louis Le Vau designed the sumptuous Chateau of Vaux-le-Vicomte (1657–1661) in France. Interior decoration was supervised by painter Charles Le Brun; the gardens were laid out by André Le Nôtre, the most famous of all specialists in his field.

BAROQUE BUILDINGS

Baroque architecture was initially confined to Italy, but by the end of the 17th century, France was challenging for artistic leadership. In the 18th century, Central Europe also came to the fore.

1

3

2

1. Karlskirche
Vienna, 1716–1737
This is the masterpiece of Johann Bernhard Fischer von Erlach, the greatest Austrian architect of his time. The giant columns were inspired by Trajan's Column in Rome.

2. Santa Susanna
Rome, 1597–1603
Carlo Maderno's facade is regarded as a herald of the Baroque style. Earlier church facades had been essentially flat, but here the decorative detail is concentrated around the central doorway, making it appear to thrust outward.

3. Basilica della Collegiata
Catania, Sicily, c. 1767
This facade, notable for its pronounced concavities, was designed by the Polish-born architect Stefano Ittar. The church is one of many in Sicily that were rebuilt after a powerful earthquake in 1693.

4. Weltenburg Abbey
Germany, 1716–1735
With a relatively plain facade but one of the most sumptuous interiors among German Baroque churches, Weltenburg Abbey is the joint creation of the Asam brothers (Cosmas Damian and Egid Quirin), who also worked as a sculptor and painter respectively.

4

5. Hall of Mirrors, Palace of Versailles
France, 1678–1689
Mirrors, candles, and gilding made this spectacular room probably the brightest artificially lit interior ever seen to that date, backing up Louis XIV's claim to be the "Sun King."

6. St. Paul's Cathedral
London, 1675–1710
Designed by Sir Christopher Wren, this is the greatest English building of its time. The most conspicuously Baroque features are the two towers, which recall Borromini. Wren never visited Italy, but he knew some of Borromini's buildings through engravings.

7. San Carlo alle Quattro Fontane
Rome, begun 1638
This church, with its accompanying monastic buildings, was Francesco Borromini's first independent commission, but the facade was not built until 1665–1667, at the end of his life. The undulating forms create a sense of movement that is typical of his work.

ST. PETER'S BASILICA

ROME, ITALY, BEGUN 1506

St. Peter's, perhaps the most venerated Catholic church, replaced an Early Christian building that had stood on the site for more than a thousand years. After many changes of plan and architect, the basilica was consecrated in 1626.

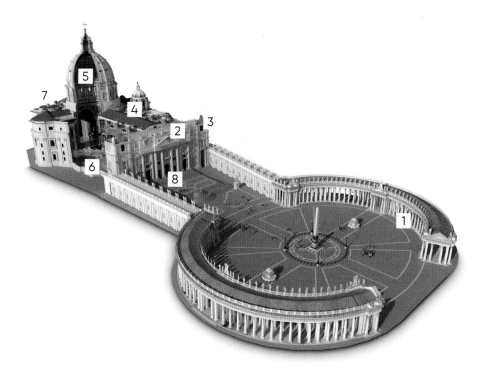

1. Colonnade

The last major external addition to St. Peter's is a majestic colonnade (1656–1667), which forms an oval piazza in front of the building. Simple in conception but immensely imposing in effect, it was designed by Gian Lorenzo Bernini.

2. Portico

The cavernous entrance portico or vestibule (1608–1612) was designed by Carlo Maderno, who regarded it as one of his finest works (he had it specifically mentioned on his tomb). Five huge doorways lead from the portico into the church.

3. Scala Regia

Rising at the right of the entrance portico is the *Scala Regia* (Royal Staircase), which connects St. Peter's to the papal palace. It was remodeled into its present form by Bernini in 1663–1666, narrowing as it rises, to exaggerate its length and height.

4. Nave

Carlo Maderno became architect to St. Peter's in 1603, and the nave was built to his design in 1609–1616. The lavish marble enrichment was designed by Bernini and carried out by a team of assistants from 1647.

5. Dome interior

The dome was completed in 1590. Its interior is decorated with mosaics (1603–1612) designed by Giuseppe Cesari (also known as Cavaliere d'Arpino). God is depicted at the summit, with Jesus, various saints, and angels below.

6. Baldachin

This enormous construction, made of gilded bronze, forms a canopy over the high altar. It stands at the center of the building, directly under the dome. One of Bernini's most inventive creations, it was made in 1624–1633.

7. Cathedra Petri

Bernini designed a spectacular setting (1657–1666) for the Cathedra Petri (Chair of Peter), a wooden throne said to have been used by St. Peter. It is theatrically lit by a window of yellow glass with a dove representing the Holy Spirit.

8. Entrance facade

Designed by Carlo Maderno, the facade was built in 1607–1612. In 1637, work began on the addition of bell towers (designed by Bernini), at each end of the facade, but these were demolished before completion because of structural problems.

4

5

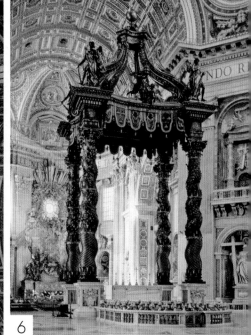

6

7 8

ROCOCO

Originating in France and spreading round much of Europe, the graceful Rococo style initially appeared in the applied arts, but soon expanded into architecture and interior design.

The Rococo style was both a development of and a reaction against the Baroque. Both styles share a love of curving forms, but while Baroque buildings are typically grand, Rococo designs are lighter, and often playful. At its purest, Rococo architecture is mainly confined to interiors, where this kind of treatment is most suitable, but some exteriors, too, have a graceful charm that embodies the Rococo spirit.

ARTISTIC FLAMBOYANCE

By the end of the 17th century, the showy style exemplified by the Palace of Versailles was beginning to go out of fashion. This was partly a matter of finances: Louis XIV's wars had depleted the royal treasury and weakened the French economy in general, so materials such as marble and precious metals tended to be replaced by more modest alternatives. At the same time, large ceremonial rooms began to give way to smaller, more comfortable interiors, to which a more informal and intimate style was appropriate. Rococo decoration is often asymmetrical, with flowing lines and motifs typically based on shell-like forms.

The Rococo style emerged in Paris around 1700, initially in applied arts such as furniture and textiles. By this time, Paris was taking over from Rome as a center of taste, and the new fashion gradually spread to other countries. This was largely due to the extensive availability of engraved designs, but also to the travels of French artists. Outside France, the style flourished most vigorously in Central Europe, particularly in Germany. In most places, Rococo art was predominantly secular (and often mildly erotic in spirit), but in Germany and Austria the style was gloriously adapted to religious buildings.

In France, Rococo was at its peak from about 1730 to 1755. In the 1760s, architectural taste began to turn toward the severity of Neoclassicism. However, in Central Europe, Rococo continued to be the dominant style until the end of the century, in some places virtually untouched by the Neoclassical tide.

Segmental cornice over the windows

THE QUEEN OF ROCOCO

Madame de Pompadour (1721–1764), Louis XV's most famous mistress, has been dubbed "the Queen of Rococo" because of her role as a leader of fashion during the heyday of the style. She had several residences, of which her favorite was the Hermitage at Fontainebleau, an exquisite building designed by Ange-Jacques Gabriel.

Madame de Pompadour, as portrayed by Jean-Marc Nattier in 1746

Flat panel in the predominant pink color

AMALIENBURG HUNTING LODGE

MUNICH, GERMANY, 1734–1739

The Amalienburg Hunting Lodge was commissioned by the Elector Karl Albrecht as a gift for his wife Maria Amalia, after whom it is named. It was designed by French architect François de Cuvilliés.

▲ Hall of Mirrors

The building's central room is perhaps the most enchanting of all Rococo interiors. The doors, mirrors, and windows are set in an inventive framework of putti (chubby infants), garlands, and other motifs in stucco-work overlaid with silver foil.

▲ Bedchamber

The one bedroom in the building was designed for Maria Amalia. Stucco and woodcarving help to create a delicate harmony of lemon and silver. The portraits on either side of the bed depict Maria Amalia (right) and her husband (left).

▲ Kitchen

Apart from the Hall of Mirrors, the largest room in the building is the kitchen, where game birds were cooked. It is lavishly decorated with Delft tiles imported from the Netherlands, which depict various birds and flowers.

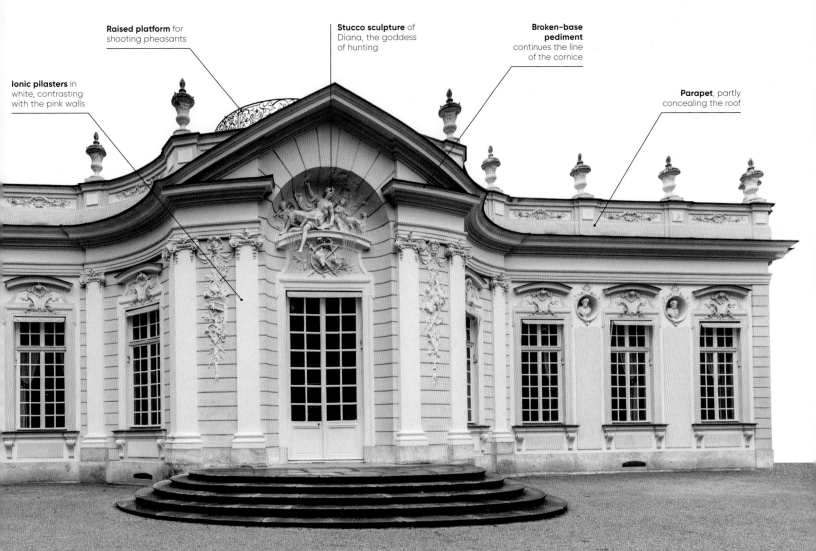

Raised platform for shooting pheasants

Stucco sculpture of Diana, the goddess of hunting

Broken-base pediment continues the line of the cornice

Ionic pilasters in white, contrasting with the pink walls

Parapet, partly concealing the roof

KEY ELEMENTS

Rococo is essentially a style of decoration, expressed at its highest level through exquisitely delicate craftsmanship. Lightness of spirit prevails, even in religious art.

PLAYFUL THEMES

Rococo ornament is sometimes purely abstract, but it often has elements based on the natural world. These include figures, both human and animal, which are typically involved in cheerful activity.

▲ Monkey room
Scenes in which monkeys are dressed and act like humans were a distinctive feature of Rococo art. This detail (1737) is from an entire room devoted to such scenes at the Château de Chantilly, France.

▲ Chinoiserie
In the Rococo period, there was a fashion for imitating Chinese art, usually in a whimsical rather than a serious spirit. This example is a detail of wallpaper (c. 1770) in the Geelvinck Hinlopen House in Amsterdam.

PASTELS AND WHITES

Overall lightness of tone is one of the hallmarks of the Rococo style. The dominant impression in interiors is of whites and pastels, often embellished with gold or silver.

◀ Extreme refinement
This detail of a ceiling in the palace of the Marquis of Pombal at Oeiras in Portugal shows remarkable subtlety in its handling of pale colors to create an ethereal effect.

VIRTUOSO STUCCO-WORK

The 18th century was one of the great ages of stucco—a type of plaster (usually reinforced with various additives) that was used for both the internal and external decoration of buildings. With it, artists created both ornamental details and figurative sculpture.

▲ Ornamental stucco
Stucco-work was often a family trade. This frothy example was created by Joseph Schmuzer, working with his son Franz Xaver Schmuzer. It frames a painting by Matthäus Günther at Rottenbuch Abbey, in Bavaria, Germany.

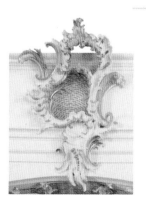

◀ Figurative stucco
Balanced daintily on one foot, this cherub is part of the lavish decoration of Zwiefalten Abbey, Germany. It was probably made by the sculptor Johann Joseph Christian, who decorated much of the church.

SHELL-LIKE FORMS

The term "Rococo" derives from the French word *rocaille*, which described a type of ornament, often used for fountains and grottoes, in which the irregular, curving forms typically suggested shells. Such curves are considered central to the Rococo style, and shell-like forms were frequently used in furniture, silverware, and other fields of the applied arts. S- and C-shaped curves were particularly popular.

Free-flowing curves exemplify the Rococo style.

ROCOCO BUILDINGS

Although aspects and echoes of the style can be found throughout Europe, it is in France and Germany that Rococo architecture is seen in its purest and most memorable form.

1. Chinese House
Potsdam, Germany, 1755–1764

This strikingly ebullient building was constructed for Frederick the Great, King of Prussia, for the park surrounding his Sanssouci Palace. Designed by Johann Gottfried Büring, it was primarily a colorful garden ornament, but it was also used as a setting for minor social events.

2. Hôtel de Soubise
Paris, France, 1736–1739

This oval room, the Salon de la Princesse in the Hôtel de Soubise, is regarded as one of the summits of Rococo art. Designed by Germain Boffrand, it is elegant and supple, but also firmly controlled, as a series of undulating forms merge into one another.

3. Pilgrimage Church of Wies
Steingaden, Germany, 1746–1754

This is one of the masterpieces of German Rococo. Externally, the church is fairly plain, but internally it is a radiant vision in white and porcelain-like colors. It was designed by Dominikus Zimmermann, and the extensive painted decoration is by his brother, Johann Baptist Zimmermann.

CHURRIGUERESQUE

A highly ornate offshoot of Baroque, the Churrigueresque style flourished in Spain and subsequently Latin America from the late 17th century to the late 18th century.

The term Churrigueresque can be used very loosely to refer to the late Baroque and Rococo periods as a whole in Spanish architecture. More precisely, however, it describes a variant style of Baroque that developed in Spain and its North American colonies. Characterized by the use of extremely dense and florid surface ornament, the style is named after the Churriguera family of artists, who were some of the first to adopt it.

Churrigueresque style first appeared in interior settings, particularly in the large, elaborate altarpieces characteristic of Spanish churches at the time. These altarpieces usually had architectural frameworks, and one of the distinctive features of the style, particularly in its early days, is the use of columns with twisting, corkscrew shafts. These are known as barley-sugar columns or, more formally, *salomónicas* (Solomonic columns). Another distinctive type of column (or pilaster) that later became more prominent was the *estípite*, which tapers toward the base, like an inverted obelisk.

From interior woodcarving and stuccowork, the style expanded into exterior stone carving. This was usually reserved for specific features, such as doorways or towers, rather than applied to buildings as a whole. The style was popular mainly in central Spain (Madrid and Salamanca, for example) and the south (notably Granada and Seville), although one of the most imposing examples is the cathedral facade at Santiago de Compostela in the far northwest of the country. In the early

> ## "... the wildest of all orgies of over-decoration ..."
>
> **Nikolaus Pevsner** on the extremes of the Churrigueresque style, *An Outline of European Architecture*, 1945

18th century, the style began to appear in the Spanish colonies. It reached its most extreme form in Mexico, where the underlying architectural forms were sometimes almost completely obscured by a riot of ornamentation.

FROM ORNAMENT TO ORDER

In the mid 18th century a reaction began to grow in Spain against such exuberant decoration. By this time, the Neoclassical style was coming to the fore and its ideals of order and clarity were totally at odds with Churrigueresque profusion. The growth of Neoclassicism was closely linked with the spread of art academies, several of which were founded in Spain in the second half of the 18th century: Madrid (1752) and Barcelona (1753) were the first. Mexico City followed in 1782. These institutions valued following rules above freedom of expression; to them the Churrigueresque style represented artistic degeneracy, and by the end of the century it had completely died out.

◀ **Altar of the Kings**
The main altarpiece of Mexico City Cathedral is one of the most sumptuous and complex of all Churrigueresque works. It was designed by Jerónimo de Balbás and made in 1718-1737.

JOSÉ BENITO DE CHURRIGUERA

José Benito de Churriguera (1665-1725) was an architect and sculptor who came to prominence in 1689, when he won a competition to design a funeral catafalque (a platform for displaying a coffin) for Marie Louise, wife of King Charles II of Spain. This has not survived, but its appearance is recorded in an engraving. Churriguera designed several buildings but is best known as the creator of large and elaborate altarpieces.

This engraving shows Churriguera's catafalque for Queen Marie Louise.

CHURCH OF SANTA PRISCA AND SAN SEBASTIAN

TAXCO, MEXICO, 1751–1758

Financed by wealth from local silver mines, this is the most splendid Mexican building of its time. The architect Diego Durán Berruecos oversaw the construction, but it is not clear if he was the designer.

Lantern of the dome, glimpsed behind the facade

Twin bell towers, lavishly decorated

Windows framed by foliate surrounds

Heavy decoration on the frontispiece masks underlying Classical orders

▲ **Decorative sculpture**
A huge relief of the Baptism of Christ is flanked by statues of the church's patron saints, Prisca (left) and Sebastian (right), set between pairs of *salomónicas* (twisted columns).

CHURRIGUERESQUE BUILDINGS

▲ **Santiago de Compostela Cathedral,** Santiago de Compostela, Spain, 1075
Spain's most important pilgrimage church was expanded and embellished over centuries. This huge, profusely ornamented western facade (1738–1750) was designed by Fernando de Casas y Novoa.

▲ **Sacristy of the Cartuja (Charterhouse),** Granada, Spain, 1732
Part of a Carthusian monastery, this is the most luxuriant example of a Churrigueresque interior. The plasterwork was undertaken in 1742–1747; the identity of the designer is uncertain.

▲ **Palace of San Telmo,** Seville, Spain, 1672–1754
Originally a naval academy, this building was designed by Leonardo de Figueroa. It is predominantly fairly restrained in style, but the entrance portal (finished in 1754) is a magnificent example of Churrigueresque.

INUIT ARCHITECTURE

The Inuit of the North American Arctic and Greenland dealt with their extreme environment by building houses that conserved heat while making the most of the limited resources available.

The High Arctic habitat of the Inuit is a harsh environment, and little vegetation grows in the extreme climate. In Greenland's three-month summer, the average temperature is 46°F (8°C), while in midwinter it can plummet to as low as -58°F (-50°C). Descended from the Thule people, who migrated to the east Arctic around 1000 CE, the Inuit traditionally survived by moving seasonally in search of food—fishing, or hunting for seals, walrus, whales, and polar bears.

Inuit architecture was shaped by the Inuits' seminomadic lifestyle, responding both to their critical need for warmth, and an unusual range of building materials. They had no trees for wood, little useful stone (nor tools to shape it), and, until modern times, no metal tools, and so they relied on knives made of walrus or whale ivory.

INUIT HOUSES

The most compelling need was for warmth. In summer, and on hunting expeditions, the Inuit used a tent called a tupiq. Made from sealskin canvas stretched over a whalebone frame, these tents could easily be taken down and moved. In other seasons, a larger, sunken structure called a qarmaq provided shelter. These were originally built of turf, with upper layers of skin or canvas stuffed with heather. Later, the Inuit adapted qarmat to make them more robust, forming the core of permanent settlements. They also built igloos—dome-shaped chambers made of compacted snow to give insulation. Inside an igloo, fur-lined walls and oil lamps kept the temperature comfortable. All Inuit houses had to be adapted to their Arctic environment. Low or sunken entrances, tightly covered with sealskin, kept out wind or snow and retained hot air.

Following overhunting and overfishing by industrial societies, many modern Inuit have had little choice but to adopt a more settled lifestyle, moving into towns to live in wooden, European-style houses. Most of the qarmat have now been dismantled for their valuable whalebone frames, but the old architecture is a source of cultural pride, and construction techniques (particularly of igloos) are passed on to preserve Inuit heritage. Inuit knowledge of home-building in the High Arctic provides vital lessons for modern architects on how to adapt buildings to extreme cold.

> "Their very livelihood depended solely on dealing with the landscape every day."
>
> Alootook Ipellie, quoted in *Inuit Art: An Introduction*, 1998

IN CONTEXT

In the 1950s, the Canadian government relocated almost 100 Inuit from northern Quebec to Cornwallis Island in the High Arctic, where they claimed the hunting would be better. The move was partly due to construction of the Distant Early Warning Line, a defense infrastructure project. Unfamiliar with local conditions, the Inuit suffered terrible hardships. The government later set up a fund to compensate their families and, in 2010, issued a formal apology.

This man was among the 92 Inuit moved to the northern resettlement location.

TUPIQ

NUNAVUT, CANADA, 1000–1960s

During the summer months, Inuit hunters would travel in search of prey. The tupiq's lightweight driftwood frame and outer canvas, made from sealskin or caribou hide, meant that it was easy to dismantle and move to a new location.

A central pole of brushwood holds up the tupiq

Rocks weigh down the tupiq against the wind

The entrance can be covered with a flap of skin

The walls are made from sewn strips of stretched caribou skin

Interior lit and heated with animal-oil lamps

▲ Interior
Like all Inuit dwellings, the tupiq is designed for warmth. Its circular plan minimizes heat loss, and furs are spread on the ground inside to create a cozy space for communal living. Warmth from people's bodies is also conserved.

INUIT BUILDINGS

▲ Winter qarmaq, Uummannaq, Greenland, 1925
In some settlements, traditional qarmat were adapted to form permanent structures. Partly sunken, and built with turf and small stones, these qarmat provided the Inuit community with warmth and security during the winter months.

▲ Winter igloo, Canada, 21st century
For centuries, traveling Inuit built igloos like this, with snow that had been compacted by the wind. They laid blocks of snow in a spiral curving inward, with thinner blocks at the top to reduce the weight of the roof. Some igloos could reach 10 ft (3 m) in height.

▲ Wooden houses, Narsaq, Greenland, 1950–1980
In the later 20th century, many Inuit were rehoused in European-style wooden houses. These were brightly painted, and traditionally the colors were used to indicate an association: blue was for fishing; yellow for doctors; and red for churches and schools.

AMERICAN COLONIAL

During the 17th and 18th centuries, settlers from a handful of European countries made their mark on the rich architectural tradition of the land that was to develop into the United States.

When European colonizers arrived in North America they brought with them architectural styles and building methods, which they mixed and matched to fit local conditions. Their settlements were typically small and isolated, on the seaboard of a vast continent inhabited by diverse peoples. Learning from each other and from Indigenous traditions, the colonizers adapted their own architectural norms to meet the needs of life in a very wide range of climates, local resources, and ecosystems.

INDIGENOUS INFLUENCES

The oldest surviving colonial buildings in mainland North America date from the early 17th century and were erected by Spanish settlers in the southwest, in what is now New Mexico. These were mainly constructed of adobe (sun-dried brick)—a material that had already been used for centuries by Indigenous peoples—and the buildings were generally plain and rugged in appearance, with almost no ornamentation. There are several impressive churches in this vein.

EUROPEAN IMPORTS

In the northeast (New England), where the British were the chief colonizers, houses were the main type of building. These were usually built of wood, which was abundant, rather than brick or stone, and were similar in appearance to contemporary examples in England.

Apart from the Spanish and British, Dutch and French colonizers also uprooted Indigenous populations. The main Dutch settlement was New Amsterdam, renamed New York after it was taken over by the British in 1664. The vast area colonized by the French (known as New France) extended from Canada to the Gulf of Mexico, with New Orleans in Louisiana being the main architectural center. The British territories included the most densely populated and economically prosperous region adjoining the eastern coast, and in 1763, after a series of wars, France ceded its territories to Britain.

By this time, numerous substantial colonial towns and cities were flourishing in America, supported in many places by agriculture dependent on the labor of enslaved people, growing cash crops for exportation to Europe. In prosperous areas, designers began to create more ambitious buildings, based on sophisticated ideas from Europe. Imitation was made easier by the availability of illustrated architectural books, of which the most influential in America was James Gibbs' *A Book of Architecture* (1728). In more remote regions, however, buildings often retained something of the character of folk art.

COLONIAL ARCHITECT

Peter Harrison (1716–1775) was the outstanding architect in colonial America. Born in England, he settled in Newport, Rhode Island. He married a wealthy heiress, so he had no need to earn money from his designs, which he usually provided free. His architectural knowledge came mainly from books, but there is nothing amateurish about his buildings, which are imposing and impeccably detailed.

Francis Malbone House (1760) in Newport, Rhode Island, is probably Harrison's design.

CAPTAIN WILLIAM SMITH HOUSE
CONCORD, MASSACHUSETTS, c. 1692

In spite of alterations, additions, and renovations, the Captain William Smith House (named after a former owner) retains much of its original character as a colonial New England dwelling: sturdy and unpretentious.

Rear extension, added around 1900

Plaster cove cornice, a rare example of this feature

Large brick chimney, centrally placed

Roof tiles, originally wooden, but replaced with asphalt

▲ Clapboarding
Clapboards or weatherboards are overlapping horizontal wooden boards covering the outer walls, and sometimes roofs, of buildings. They are a very common feature in American colonial architecture.

The windows are mid 18th century in style

Pedimented doorway, added c. 1750

AMERICAN COLONIAL BUILDINGS

▲ Abram Ackerman House, Saddle River, New Jersey, 1704
The most distinctively Dutch feature of this Dutch-style colonial house is the roof, with its curving slopes and overhanging eaves. The supporting posts are later additions, however, and there is also a single-story extension to the left.

▲ Parlange Plantation, Pointe Coupée Parish, Louisiana, c. 1750
This French-style house was built by enslaved people on a sugar plantation. Because of the threat of flooding, the lower story is built of brick, while the upper story, with its shaded porch, is constructed from wood and other lighter materials.

▲ San Esteban del Rey Mission, Acoma, New Mexico, c. 1630-1640
This is the best surviving example of early colonial Spanish architecture. Following Indigenous tradition, the unadorned, adobe (mud-brick) walls are very thick, which helped keep the interior cool during the heat of the day and retain warmth at night.

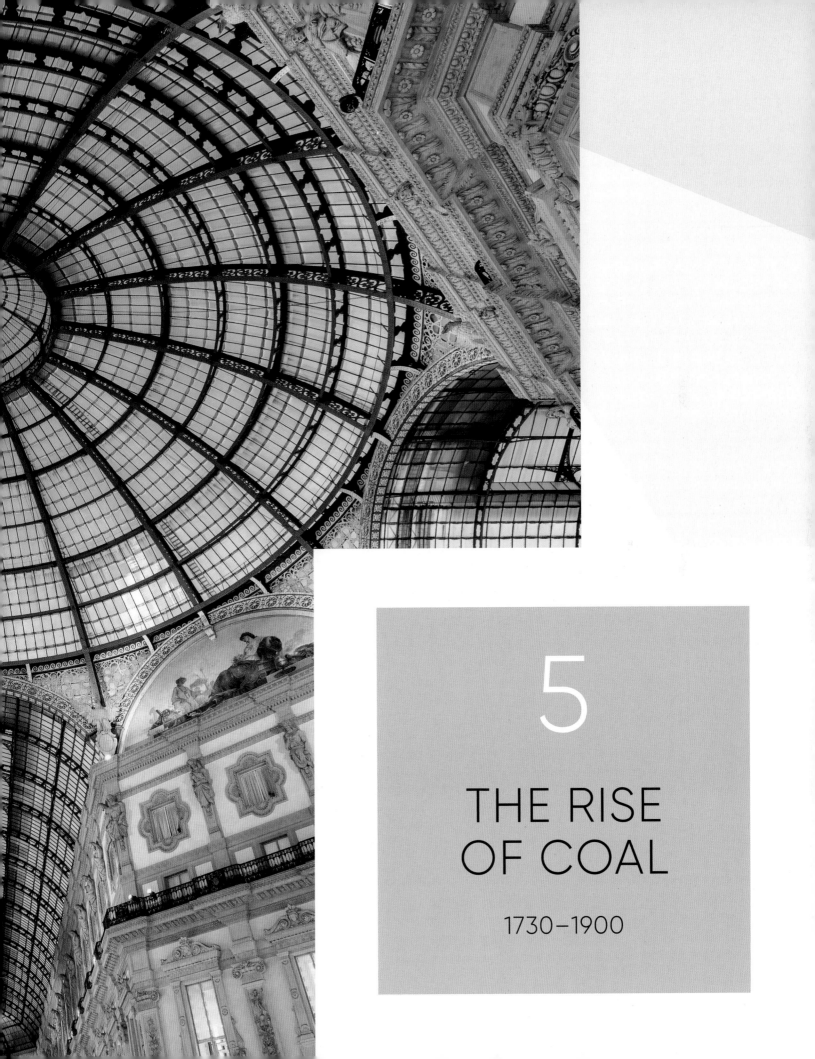

5

THE RISE
OF COAL

1730–1900

NEOCLASSICAL

The Neoclassical style evolved during a turbulent period of wars and revolutions in Europe, but it was also the age of the Enlightenment, when knowledge and refinement were highly prized.

The Neoclassical movement was a dominant force in European culture from the latter part of the 18th century to the early 19th century. It permeated all of the arts, from architecture and painting to fashion and design, taking very different forms in each of these fields. At its simplest, it was an attempt to recapture the spirit and the glory of ancient Greece and Rome. There had been other revivals of this kind, most notably the Classicism of 17th-century France, but the new movement had a very different character.

UNEARTHING THE PAST

Neoclassical architecture was shaped by a number of factors. In part, it developed as a reaction to the perceived excesses of previous styles, namely the bombastic display of the Baroque (see pp.210–217) and the fussiness of the Rococo (see pp.218–221). This coincided with a growing interest in the Classical world. Discoveries at the ancient sites of Herculaneum and Pompeii captured the public's imagination, especially since there

was an element of secrecy about them. At Herculaneum, for example, there was a museum near the site, but illustrated books about it were banned, and artists were not allowed to sketch any of the finds, so a genuine mystique surrounded the place. However, the architectural ruins of Pompeii and Herculaneum proved a less powerful inspiration than the frescoes that were unearthed, which prompted architects such as Robert Adam and Joseph Bonomi to develop a "Pompeian" style of interior design.

Another great source of inspiration was the lavish, illustrated studies of the ancient world that were published from the mid 18th century onward. Some of these were sponsored by learned bodies, such as the Society of Dilettanti, whole others were written by enthusiastic amateurs. Marc-Antoine Laugier was a Jesuit priest, but his *Essai sur l'Architecture* (1753) directly influenced the style of Soufflot's Panthéon (see pp.232–233). Translated into English and German, it became one of the seminal texts of the Neoclassical movement.

ARCHAEOLOGICAL DISCOVERY

In the 18th century, interest in the Classical world was heightened by two major archaeological finds. The Roman towns of Herculaneum and Pompeii, both of which had been buried during the eruption of Mount Vesuvius in 79 CE, were rediscovered in 1738 and 1748 respectively. The excavations revealed a wealth of art from the ancient world.

Remains of the Forum, the most important building in Pompeii

▶ **Grandeur**
The Neoclassical style could evoke grandeur, power, and glory, making it the ideal style for the military monuments of the 18th century. One of these was the Brandenburg Gate, Berlin, commissioned in 1788 by Frederick II of Prussia.

> "Let us learn from the ancients how to submit the rules to genius."
>
> Charles-Louis Clérisseau, assistant to US president Thomas Jefferson, 1778

THE PANTHÉON

PARIS, FRANCE, 1757–1789

The Panthéon was the first great masterpiece of French Neoclassical architecture. It was designed by Jacques-Germain Soufflot, who was inspired by St. Paul's Cathedral in London. He combined monumentality with the structural lightness of Gothic to create a new and striking style—one that theorist Marc-Antoine Laugier described as "the first example of perfect architecture."

Street view of the Panthéon

▲ **Pediment**

The allegorical sculptures on the pediment were designed by David d'Angers. They show Liberty handing laurel crowns to the central figure of the Nation, who awards them to famous generals, statesmen, politicians, and scientists.

▲ **Columns**

The portico is supported by three huge columns. These are surmounted by elaborately carved Corinthian capitals and a fine entablature of architrave, frieze, and cornice.

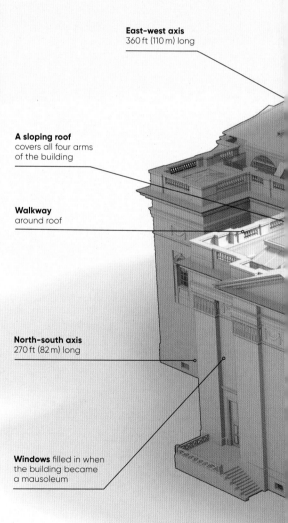

East-west axis
360 ft (110 m) long

A sloping roof
covers all four arms
of the building

Walkway
around roof

North-south axis
270 ft (82 m) long

Windows filled in when
the building became
a mausoleum

ST. PAUL'S CATHEDRAL

Built between 1675 and 1710, St. Paul's Cathedral in London was designed by Sir Christopher Wren, who was commissioned to rebuild more than 50 churches after London's Great Fire of 1666. Made of Portland stone in the English Baroque style, it has a lead-covered dome that rises to a height of 365 ft (110 m). It is still the second largest church in the UK, after Salisbury Cathedral.

St. Paul's Cathedral, one of the great landmarks of London

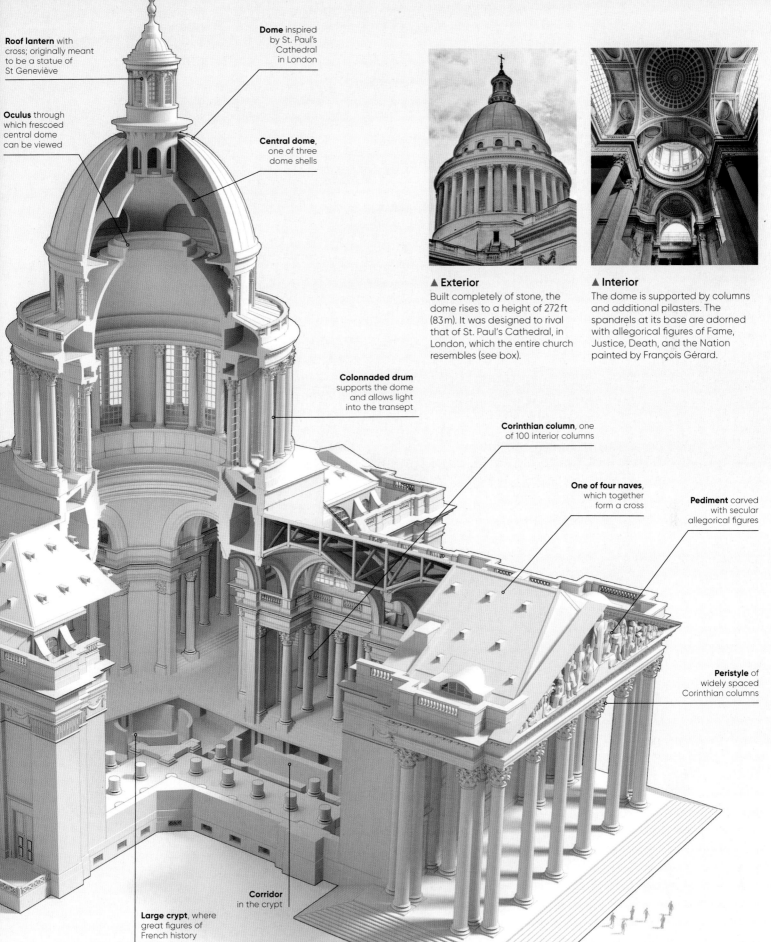

Roof lantern with cross; originally meant to be a statue of St Geneviève

Oculus through which frescoed central dome can be viewed

Dome inspired by St. Paul's Cathedral in London

Central dome, one of three dome shells

Colonnaded drum supports the dome and allows light into the transept

Corinthian column, one of 100 interior columns

One of four naves, which together form a cross

Pediment carved with secular allegorical figures

Peristyle of widely spaced Corinthian columns

Corridor in the crypt

Large crypt, where great figures of French history are buried

▲ **Exterior**
Built completely of stone, the dome rises to a height of 272 ft (83 m). It was designed to rival that of St. Paul's Cathedral, in London, which the entire church resembles (see box).

▲ **Interior**
The dome is supported by columns and additional pilasters. The spandrels at its base are adorned with allegorical figures of Fame, Justice, Death, and the Nation painted by François Gérard.

KEY **ELEMENTS**

Neoclassical architects drew inspiration from many sources, and significant variants of the style developed over the years. From the very first, however, it established a repertoire of forms and techniques, and these became its defining characteristics, used by the greatest architects of the day.

DOMES

Neoclassical domes varied greatly in style, often departing considerably from ancient models. Their internal construction could be very complex, and frequently consisted of two or three separate shells. These shells strengthened the dome, and gave artists more opportunities to add sumptuous decoration and color.

COLONNADES

A colonnade is a row of columns supporting an entablature and usually one side of a roof. In the 18th century, colonnades became prominent features of front porticoes. When deployed on all sides of a building, they became what is called a "peristyle."

▲ Capitol dome
The US Capitol dome is made of cast iron, but is painted to look as if it is made of stone and timber, like the rest of the building. Inside, it is decorated with scenes from American history.

PALLADIANISM

An influential Classical revival occurred in 16th-century Italy, thanks to the work of architect and theorist Andrea Palladio. Using his knowledge of ancient Rome and his studies of Vitruvius (c. 70 BCE–15 CE), Palladio developed a graceful style of design, which found its fullest expression in a series of villas in the Vicenza region of Italy. The ideals of "Palladianism," as it became known, gained particular favor in England, where they were taken up by Inigo Jones (1573–1652) and Lord Burlington (1694–1753).

Chiswick House, in the UK, was designed by Lord Burlington. Completed in 1729, it was based on Palladio's Villa Capra, near Vicenza, Italy.

▲ Greek portico
The Altes Museum, in Berlin, is Karl Schinkel's masterpiece. Its prime feature is its magnificent stoa—a Greek style of portico, which is shallow in depth but fronted by a long colonnade. Its graceful columns are Ionic.

PEDIMENTS

An innovation of the ancient Greeks, the pediment was a triangular section of masonry that lay above a temple's entrance and served to support its roof. For the Romans, pediments were largely decorative features, which they added to the doorways and windows of all kinds of buildings.

▲ **Window pediment**
Neoclassical pediments were placed over doors and windows as well as above grand entrances. This example is from the Archbishop's Palace at Syracuse, Sicily.

▲ **Spectacular tympanum**
Commissioned by Napoleon Bonaparte in 1806 as a monument to his victories, La Madeleine in Paris was later converted into a church. Its pediment features a fine sculpture of The Last Judgment by Philippe Lemaire. Looking up at the sculpture, Christ presides in the center: the elect are ushered up by angels on the left, and the damned are sent to Hell on the right.

CLASSICAL DECORATION

Neoclassical architects adorned their buildings with a wide variety of motifs. These ranged from imposing allegorical figures on military monuments to purely ornamental details on more modest structures.

◀ **Victory arch**
As a symbol of France's military glory, the Arc de Triomphe in Paris was covered with plaques and friezes celebrating the heroes of the Napoleonic Wars. It was also studded with decorative panels of patera (rosettes).

▲ **Bronze quadriga**
Triumphal arches were often topped by a quadriga—a chariot drawn by four horses. The quadriga above the Brandenburg Gate in Berlin is driven by Victoria, the Roman goddess of Victory.

◀ **Stone festoons**
Carved garlands of fruit or flowers, known as "festoons," were often added to Neoclassical facades. The festoons on the Sainte-Geneviève Library, Paris, hang in curved swags, which are tied at the end with trailing ribbons.

NEOCLASSICAL BUILDINGS

At its grandest, the Neoclassical style expressed political and military power. However, it also embodied grace, and its symmetrical forms reflected the Greek passion for geometry, reason, and science.

1

3

2

1. Arc de Triomphe
Paris, France, 1806–1836

Loosely based on a Roman triumphal arch, this imposing monument was commissioned by Napoleon Bonaparte to celebrate his military victories. He did not live to see it completed, but his cortège passed through it after his death.

2. Jefferson Memorial
Washington, D.C., 1939–1943

The style of this elegant memorial to America's third president, Thomas Jefferson, was inspired by Rome's Pantheon and by some of Jefferson's own designs. It is inscribed with famous Jefferson quotations, praising democracy, republicanism, and the rights of the individual.

3. Monticello
Charlottesville, Virginia, 1772

Thomas Jefferson designed this plantation house for himself. Inside, he abandoned symmetry in favor of a more practical layout. Like the Greeks and Romans, Jefferson seems to have seen no contradiction in enslaving people while writing about liberty and reason.

4. Palace Square
St. Petersburg, Russia, 1819–1829

Facing the Winter Palace, this bow-shaped range of buildings, designed by Karl Rossi, served as administrative offices. At its heart is a triumphal arch celebrating Russia's victory over Napoleon in 1812.

4

5. Vendôme Column
Paris, France, 1806–1810

Modeled on Trajan's Column in Rome, this column was built to commemorate Napoleon's victory at Austerlitz in 1805. It is topped by a statue of Napoleon dressed as a Roman emperor.

5

6

7

6. British Museum
London, UK, 1823–1847

With its massive colonnade and portico of 44 Ionic columns, Robert Smirke's masterpiece is a fine example of Greek Revival style. Behind its facade the museum had cutting-edge technologies for providing clean air.

7. Museo del Prado
Madrid, Spain, 1785

Designed by Juan de Villanueva, one of the pioneers of Spanish Neoclassicism, the Museo del Prado was constructed to showcase Spanish art. A statue of artist Diego de Velázquez was added to the entrance in 1899.

▲ Masterclass in glass
Joseph Paxton, an engineer who specialized in greenhouses, used plate glass to make a huge prefabricated building that could be erected quickly. The result was the Crystal Palace of 1851.

▲ Jewels of light
Despite the expense of making glass in medieval conditions, the wealthiest religious institutions could afford very large amounts of beautiful, high-quality glass, such as that seen in the stained-glass windows of Chartres Cathedral in France.

"The important thing is the play of reflections and not the effect of light and shadow, as in ordinary buildings."

Ludwig Mies van der Rohe, pioneer of using glass in architecture in his designs from c. 1920

GLASS

Methods of making glass have changed radically over the centuries. Once a luxury material for the richest, cheap heat from coal made glass affordable on a whole new scale.

Glass is made by heating sand with other substances (particularly lime and sodium carbonate) to a very high temperature. It has a long history, and although the Romans were probably the first to use it in buildings, their skills were lost when the Roman Empire fell.

A VERSATILE MATERIAL

People discovered how to make window glass again in the early Middle Ages, but it was not fully transparent at that time. It was made by spinning a piece of hot, semi-molten glass mixture until it formed a disk. Although the center of the disk was spoiled because it bore the mark of the spinning tool, the glassmaker cut the rest of the glass into small pieces and bound them together with strips of lead and iron bars to make a window—a method that was labor intensive. Because firewood was slow-growing and costly, windows were extremely expensive and were only fitted to high-status buildings such as churches, palaces, and mansions.

As production methods improved, larger quantities of glass were made, and windows became bigger and completely transparent. In the 17th and 18th centuries, such windows were fitted to buildings in prosperous cities, including London and Amsterdam, but the glass still had minor imperfections, such as variations in thickness, which produced ripple effects when it was viewed from certain angles.

The quality and size of glass plates improved through the 19th century in energy-rich industrial countries, with prices continuing to drop. Glass appeared in the homes of the poor and in large quantities in exhibition halls, stations, and shopping centers.

In the mid 20th century, large sheets of cheap plate glass of very high quality became possible with the float glass process, which allows the liquid glass to pool completely flat on a bath of molten tin. Entire buildings could now be clad cheaply in high-quality glass, producing a crystalline look that many architects fell in love with.

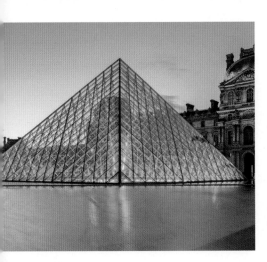

▲ **Old and new**
Built in 1988, the glass pyramid in the courtyard of the Louvre in Paris shelters the entrance to the lobby below. Its architect, I. M. Pei, designed it to make a strong, modern impression without obscuring the historic buildings around it.

▲ **Glassy reflections**
The Shard, in London, built in 2009–2012, is a 72-story skyscraper that is covered in 11,000 panes of glass. Architect Renzo Piano wanted this cladding to reflect the sky, so the building would change its appearance throughout the day.

CHANGES TO KILNS AND FUEL

Glass was traditionally made in wood-burning furnaces, but in the early 17th century, English glassmakers began to use coal, which was cheaper. They discovered, however, that coal smoke darkened the glass. To resolve this, they built bottle-shaped kilns with tall chimneys and vents at the bottom to create a strong draft. They then placed lids on the pots holding the glass mixture to keep out the smoke.

Wood-fired glass, as shown here, was plagued with bubbles, distortion, and discoloration.

THE GEORGIAN TERRACED HOUSE

In a period of rapid urban growth, Georgian terraces provided elegant, dense housing for the newly affluent of 18th-century Britain and Ireland.

The greatest transformation in the history of world architecture began with the brick terraced houses of 17th-century London. These were the first buildings where cheap coal heat came to transform what buildings were made of and how they operated. Up to this point, heat was an expensive resource, harvested from slow-growing trees. Now, cheaply mined coal—and later other fossil fuels—made heat cheap, and labor increasingly expensive.

This transformation was immediately evident in the terraced houses of the Georgian period. (The term "Georgian" refers to the four British monarchs—George I to George IV, 1714–1830—whose reigns marked the high point of the style.) The Georgian terraced house's big glass windows were made with coal heat, as were its fired brick walls, resistant to weather and fire, and its iron railings, balconies, and lamp standards. Numerous fireplaces warmed the inhabitants using more cheap coal, delivered directly through an iron hatch in the sidewalk

"Howses and buildings fitt for the habitacons of Gentleman and men of ability."

License granted to Inigo Jones for his terraces in Covent Garden, 1630s

into an underground coal bunker. Even the street lighting that became widespread from 1800 was powered by coal gas. Up until then, the world had been terrifyingly dark at night.

THE BIRTH OF MODERNITY

Georgian terraced houses are widely seen as timeless classics—elegant leftovers of a world that valued beauty. In reality, their Classical proportions represented a longing for order in the face of global change. Many of their residents made their fortunes from Britain's ever-expanding empire, and British cities were growing at an explosive rate—thanks to the new cheap, durable building techniques—raising concerns over the destruction of the countryside.

Large numbers of poorer people were sucked into the cities to work as domestic servants, and a new scale of urban poverty emerged, in which tens of thousands of people lived in unsanitary, crowded conditions with high levels of criminality and exploitation. Even for the poor, however, cheap bricks and the first generations of building regulations were beginning to reduce the risk of the kind of catastrophic fires that had been all too familiar in medieval cities built of wood and thatch.

MATHEMATICAL RATIOS

The harmonious appearance of the terrace house stems from the English version of Palladianism. One of the earliest examples dates from the 1630s, when Inigo Jones built London's first square of terraced houses for the Earl of Bedford, basing his design on the Classical style of Palladio's town houses. The emphasis on symmetry increased still further in the following century, when Classical pattern books became widely available for the general builder.

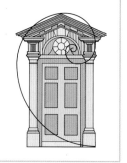

Diagram of a classically proportioned Georgian door, based on Fibonacci's Golden Ratio (drawn as a spiral)

BEDFORD SQUARE

LONDON, UK, 1775–1783

This fine four-storied terrace was designed to comply with Georgian building regulations. The doorways are particularly ornate, with their bands of ashlar and their decorative Coade-stone (an artificial stone) moldings.

▲ Fireplace
All of the rooms, except a few in the garret, had fireplaces, which were small and had to be cleared out regularly. They were not just for heating, but also for making tea, which had recently become fashionable.

Living rooms with large windows on the second floor

Servants' rooms with small windows in the garret

Mass-produced bricks

Coade-stone molding on keystone

Ashlar masonry blocks with decorative keystone

Street-level steps up to the entrance and down to the basement

GEORGIAN TERRACED HOUSES

▲ 10 Downing Street, London, UK, 1682–1684
Home to British Prime Ministers since 1735, Downing Street's distinctive look is due to the renovations carried out by Kenton Couse in 1766–1775. He added the blackened brick bays and a narrow, black-oak door (which is now made of blast-proof steel).

▲ Merrion Street, Dublin, Ireland, 1762–1792
Built in one of the most fashionable quarters of Dublin, Merrion Street is a picture of elegance. The terrace's uniformity is broken up by variations in the size and design of the fanlights and windows, and today by the colors of the doors.

▲ St. Leonard's Place, York, UK, 1828–1842
These private residences date from the end of the Georgian period. They are stuccoed, and feature a "palace-front"—in which several houses appear to form a unit—this one (center) complete with pilasters, a central pediment, and an extended porch.

INDUSTRIAL ARCHITECTURE

By the 19th century, coal-powered steam engines, furnaces, and kilns were rapidly changing the world, making it possible for architects to use materials such as iron, steel, and glass on a entirely new scale.

Coal changed everything. A typical coal miner in the 19th century could produce 2,500 times more energy each year than a medieval farmer, so countries that had either large reserves of coal or the money to buy it from elsewhere could make use of almost limitless heat energy. Iron, steel, glass, lime, and ceramics had all been used for thousands of years, but when slow-growing wood had to be burned to produce these materials, they were used sparingly. Now, thanks to coal heat, entire bridges could be made just from iron, and buildings from iron and glass. Britain was at the heart of this first wave of industrial revolution.

In just decades, industries such as the textile industry went from production in the home, powered by hand, to mass-production in large water-powered mills, followed by enormous coal-powered mills. Intense competition between factory owners made it worth spending money and time on finding improvements, such as bigger open spaces,

THE INDUSTRIAL REVOLUTION

British society was transformed during the Industrial Revolution, when steam power and mechanization stimulated trade and increased prosperity. In 1838, statesman Benjamin Disraeli described the UK as "the workshop of the world," and the truth of his claim was confirmed by the splendor of wares on show at the Great Exhibition of 1851, which was staged, fittingly, in Joseph Paxton's Crystal Palace.

Contemporary watercolor of the Nantyglo Ironworks in Wales

▲ The Forth Rail Bridge
Built by engineers Sir John Fowler and Sir Benjamin Baker between 1883 and 1890, this famous Scottish bridge once boasted the longest, single cantilever span in the world. Its construction was made possible by improvements in the steel-making process pioneered by Sir Henry Bessemer (see p.251).

improved lighting, better ventilation, and a lower fire risk. Huge warehouses and growing networks of docks had to be built to store and transport ever-larger quantities of goods, and keeping track of transactions and activities across an aggressively expanding empire required a sizable workforce. Clerical staff no longer fit into a single room in a merchant's city home, and instead required specially built office premises.

Meanwhile, housing large populations of laborers within a short walk of the factories they worked in presented both a need and a money-making opportunity. Slums were rapidly constructed, but from the 1840s, increasingly effective local government action imposed minimum standards on private landlords, and living conditions gradually improved.

The Industrial Revolution magnified both the beauty and the horrors of cities. Railroads brought terminus stations and viaducts into city centers, and public buildings grew in size and diversity, but the pollution from coal-fired industry and domestic grates turned cities black, damaged the health of their inhabitants, and sowed the seeds of today's climate crisis.

"Engineer's architecture, at once costly and offensive and full of pretension."

Augustus Pugin in his criticism of Brunel's Temple Meads station, 1843

ST. PANCRAS STATION

LONDON, UK, 1868

The railroads were the greatest technological development of the industrial age, and by the 1840s there was a near mania for adding more stations to the network. The complex of new buildings at St. Pancras, designed by Sir George Gilbert Scott and William Henry Barlow, was by far the most spectacular of these.

Midland Grand Hotel, with 250 bedrooms, designed by Sir George Gilbert Scott

Clock tower similar to the one housing London's Big Ben

Brick and stone brought by train from the areas the station served

St Pancras station at dusk

> "The skeletal transparency of the ... vault added a futuristic, magic dimension to the stunning space..."
>
> M.Trachtenberg and I. Hyman, *Architecture: from Prehistory to Post-Modernism*, 1986

Arcaded Gothic windows with polished granite shafts

▲ Cellars

St. Pancras was built with an underground level that was designed to receive and store the huge number of beer barrels that arrived at the station. Its cast-iron columns were spaced to match the arrangement of a typical brewer's warehouse.

▲ Arch structure

Most train sheds were built with costly, complex wrought iron trusses that pulled inward against the thrust of the arch. Here, the ends of the arch were connected with an iron band running under the platforms, making the arch cheaper and faster to build.

▲ Roof

The train shed was the first part of the station to be built (1865–1868). It was designed by William Henry Barlow, and its 55-ton ribs were supplied by the Butterley Iron Company. At the time, its single-span roof was the largest in the world.

Glazed central section of 18,000 self-cleaning panes

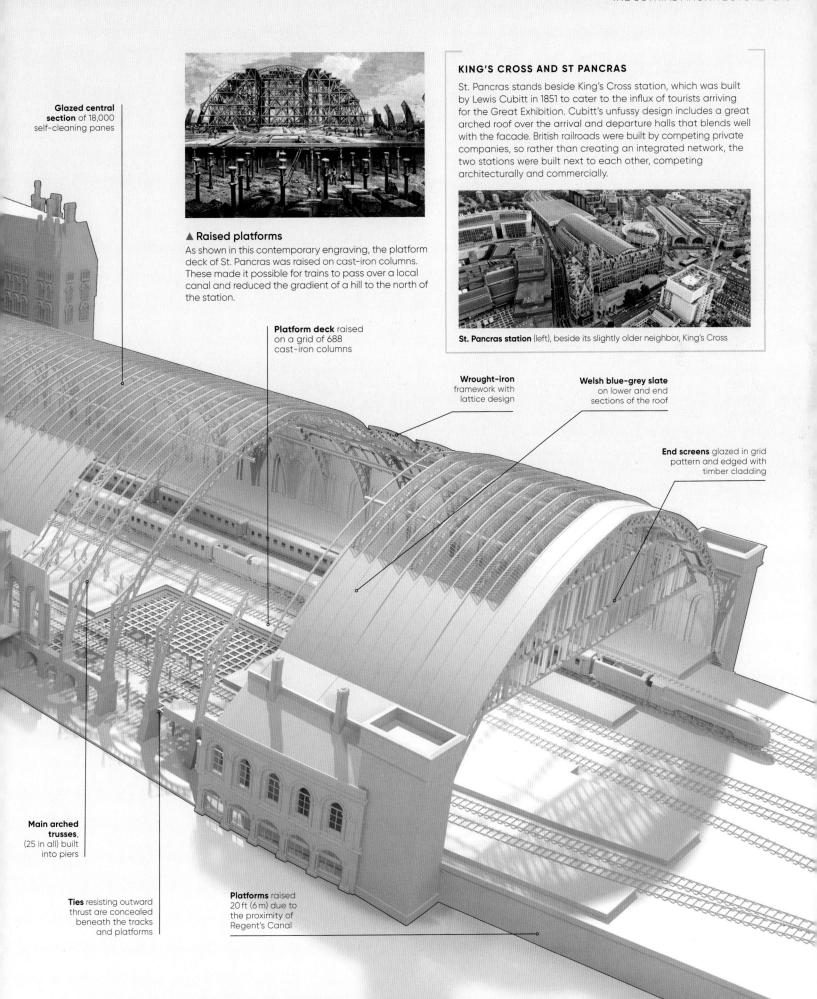

▲ **Raised platforms**

As shown in this contemporary engraving, the platform deck of St. Pancras was raised on cast-iron columns. These made it possible for trains to pass over a local canal and reduced the gradient of a hill to the north of the station.

KING'S CROSS AND ST PANCRAS

St. Pancras stands beside King's Cross station, which was built by Lewis Cubitt in 1851 to cater to the influx of tourists arriving for the Great Exhibition. Cubitt's unfussy design includes a great arched roof over the arrival and departure halls that blends well with the facade. British railroads were built by competing private companies, so rather than creating an integrated network, the two stations were built next to each other, competing architecturally and commercially.

St. Pancras station (left), beside its slightly older neighbor, King's Cross

Platform deck raised on a grid of 688 cast-iron columns

Wrought-iron framework with lattice design

Welsh blue-grey slate on lower and end sections of the roof

End screens glazed in grid pattern and edged with timber cladding

Main arched trusses, (25 in all) built into piers

Ties resisting outward thrust are concealed beneath the tracks and platforms

Platforms raised 20 ft (6 m) due to the proximity of Regent's Canal

KEY **ELEMENTS**

During the Industrial Revolution, changing methods of production inspired new attitudes toward design. Long-revered historical styles came into controversial collision with new wonder materials. Some of the solutions that are most admired today were found ugly and bizarre by critics at the time.

ENERGY-HUNGRY MATERIALS

The Industrial Revolution was driven by improvements in the production of strong, durable materials such as brick, glass, and iron. The groundbreaking iron bridge at Coalbrookdale, for example, was made possible by Abraham Darby's discovery of a method of smelting iron with coke in 1709, and producing wrought iron became easier after Henry Cort devised his "puddling" process in 1784 (see p.250).

▼ Brick

New viaducts and aqueducts were built primarily of brick. The Ribblehead Viaduct in the UK, for example, has 24 tapered piers and arches made of red brick faced with limestone masonry set in lime mortar.

▲ Iron

Ironbridge in the UK takes its name from its 100-ft-(30-m-) wide bridge—the first made of cast iron. As molten iron cast into molds like this turned out to be brittle, wrought iron (hammered into shape) was used until steel became affordable in the late 19th century.

▲ Glass

During the early Victorian era, there was a boom in building huge glasshouses, to house plants brought back from all over Britain's growing empire. The Palm House, built in 1844–1848 at the Royal Botanic Gardens in Kew, London, is a beautiful example.

▲ Terra-cotta

In the late 19th century, terra-cotta supplanted stucco as a prestige decorating material. In the UK, it figured prominently in Dale House in Manchester (above), and in London's Victoria and Albert Museum, Natural History Museum, and Harrods department store.

LARGE SCALE

The Industrial Revolution saw hundreds of thousands of people join huge workforces that were crammed into communal buildings such as mills, factories, and warehouses. Designed for efficiency, these buildings had minimal decoration.

▲ Victorian factory
Most factories of the time were plain, rectangular blocks, like this one in Birmingham's jewelry quarter. Large windows were a priority, since providing artificial lighting indoors was still a major problem at this time.

▲ Huge interior
Built by Joseph Craven in 1869, Dalton Mills was said to be the largest textile mill in Yorkshire, in the UK. It specialized in producing worsted, and housed more than 2,000 employees. Its vast colonnaded interior was crammed with workers who operated the steam-powered production line.

EXPOSED MATERIALS

After the 1850s, when costs came down, cast iron became regarded as a cheap, utilitarian material, and was used even for temporary or prefabricated structures.

◄ Iron columns
Supremely graceful yet entirely practical, the Reading Room in Paris's National Library is Henri Labrouste's masterpiece. Nine ceramic, light-reflecting domes, each with its own oculus (aperture), are supported by just 16 slender iron columns that measure only 1ft (0.3m) in diameter.

▲ Skeletal frame
Architects Deane and Woodward designed the interior of the Oxford University Museum as a huge, glass-covered courtyard. Its ironwork frame is minimal, which allows light to flood in through the glass to illuminate the exhibits.

◄ Metal walkways
Shad Thames, near Tower Bridge in London, was originally home to a complex of wharves and warehouses. These handled a vast array of imported goods, making it essential for traders to have easy access to the lofty stores.

INDUSTRIAL BUILDINGS

During the Industrial Revolution, architects were proud of the strength and beauty of their new building materials. Some made virtues of exposed metalwork—which was widely considered ugly at the time—while others courted controversy by building enormous structures that seemed to have only the minimum of support.

1

3

2

4

1. No. 3 Covered Slip at Royal Navy Dockyard
Chatham, UK, 1838

In its day, the No. 3 Covered Slip at Chatham Dockyard was the largest wide-span timber structure in Europe. With its gigantic cantilever roof, designed by shipwright Sir Robert Seppings, it proved that wood was far from obsolete as an industrial building material. Today, it is part of an extensive maritime museum.

2. Eiffel Tower
Paris, France, 1889

Built by Gustave Eiffel to commemorate the centenary of the French Revolution, the Eiffel Tower was the centerpiece of the 1889 Exposition Universelle (World's Fair). It was reviled at the time—some dubbed it "the iron lady" or "a hollow candlestick"—but it has since become a world-famous symbol of Paris.

3. Clifton Suspension Bridge
Bristol, UK, 1831–1864

Designed by Isambard Kingdom Brunel, this elegant suspension bridge spans 702 ft (214 m) across the Avon Gorge. Brunel won the commission in 1831, but work was halted by local riots and not completed until after his death. Its chains were recycled from Brunel's Hungerford Bridge in London, which had just been demolished.

4. Neptune's Staircase
Caledonian Canal, UK, 1803–1822

Built by Thomas Telford and consisting of eight separate locks, this is the longest staircase lock in the UK. It lifts boats 64 ft (20 m) up and over a hill in the Scottish Highlands.

5. Saulnier Mill
Noisiel, France, 1865–1872

Originally a watermill, designed by Jules Saulnier, this is now the Menier Chocolate Factory. It was the first building in the world to be built with its metallic structure fully on display. It is covered with ceramic tiles.

6. Pontcysyllte Aqueduct
Wrexham, UK, 1795–1805

This is the longest aqueduct in the UK and the highest canal aqueduct in the world. Designed by Thomas Telford and William Jessop, it was built to carry the Llangollen Canal over the Dee River in Wales.

7. Santa Justa Street Elevator
Lisbon, Portugal, 1900–1901

This famous attraction carries passengers seven stories up, to a wrought-iron viewing platform with views of the city. The original system was steam-powered, but has since been replaced by an electric engine.

▶ **Structure on show**
The 1,083-ft- (330-m-) high Eiffel Tower in Paris opened in 1889. Made of prefabricated components that were brought to the city center for assembly, it demonstrated the huge potential of iron as a building material.

IRON AND STEEL

Producing iron and steel requires a huge amount of heat energy, but fossil fuels made it possible to make these versatile, powerful materials in ever-larger quantities.

Iron was first used by the Hittites of ancient Turkey around 1200 BCE, and the Chinese used it in some of their pagodas in the 9th century CE. However, iron only became widely used in construction in the 18th century, when two inventions made it possible for iron-makers to mass-produce reliable iron components using coal heat: the coke-fired blast furnace, which replaced its charcoal-fed predecessor; and a process known as "puddling," whereby iron is strengthened by being stirred inside a furnace. The latter solved the problem of iron being brittle (if cast directly into a mold) and removed the labor-intensive strengthening method of hammering it into shape.

A significantly greater amount of iron could be produced using coal rather than with the limited and slow-growing supply of firewood. For example, if Britain's iron production in 1850 had used wood charcoal instead of coal, almost all of England would have had to be covered in woodland to supply enough of it. Thanks to coal and mass-produced iron

components, builders were able to raise all kinds of tall, wide, or wide-roofed structures. These included mills, bridges, railroads, and factories, which in turn sped up the rate of industrialization in Europe and the US. By the end of the 19th century, the potential of iron was obvious, and was spectacularly embodied by the Eiffel Tower in Paris, made entirely of iron.

THE COMING OF STEEL

In the 1880s, steel joined iron in being coal-made and much more affordable. Steel is iron that contains a measured amount of carbon, which gives it extra strength. It soon became a widespread default option—strong, versatile, long-lasting, and well-understood by engineers and insurers—and was used to build suspension bridges and skyscrapers.

Today, over a billion tons of new steel is manufactured each year for use in construction, producing almost two billion tons of carbon dioxide emissions. This amounts to around four percent of all human emissions.

THE BESSEMER PROCESS

British scientist Sir Henry Bessemer, using ideas first formulated by the iron-maker Robert Mushet, patented a process for removing impurities from iron that made it possible to produce steel in large quantities. The process, which he announced in 1856, involved blasting air through the molten metal to oxidize the impurities, which then separated from the iron. The process took place in a pear-shaped furnace known as a Bessemer converter.

A Bessemer converter, depicted by Fritz Gehrke

▲ **Girders and cables**
Suspension bridges, which are some of the largest structures in the world, are designed so their road decks hang from steel-reinforced cables attached to towers and anchor points. New York's Brooklyn Bridge, built in 1883, also has steel girders in its deck.

▲ **Supporting arches**
Large train stations need wide roofs that have no supporting columns, which would get in the way of the tracks. Built in 1854, London's Paddington Station has enormous iron arches, some spanning 102 ft (31 m), providing space for several parallel platforms.

▲ **Unconventional angles**
Designed by Zaha Hadid, the Eli and Edythe Broad Art Museum in Michigan, US, exemplifies the way in which steel came to represent progress and futuristic vision in the 20th century. It features unusual angles, folds, and inclined walls, as well as reflective cladding.

▲ **Interior color**
William Butterfield's most ambitious commission, All Saints in London, was built to promote the ideals of the Cambridge Camden Society. Its interior is ablaze with colorful murals, marbles, and mosaics.

GOTHIC REVIVAL

In the 18th and 19th centuries, Europeans took a new interest in the medieval world—popularized in part by the historical novels of Sir Walter Scott—and particularly in its Gothic style of architecture.

The Gothic Revival began in the UK, where it became linked with religious reform, but it soon spread to continental Europe, and then to the US and Asia. Its earliest examples were often a mixture of the authentic and the fantastical: at Strawberry Hill, for example, novelist Horace Walpole built a make-believe castle for himself, in which the fireplaces (and the headboard of his own bed) were based on genuine medieval tombs. However, as the 19th century progressed, the revival took a more serious tone, which was partly due to a rise in the demand for churches in fast-growing industrial cities with increasing religious diversity.

EUROPE AND BEYOND
In 1818, a British government commission recognized that there was a critical shortage of churches, and sponsored a major building program. The new churches were usually of low quality, but standards improved after the Oxford Movement, founded in 1833, began to promote a more elaborate, high-church service, and argued for a similarly inspiring architecture. William Butterfield's ground-

> "Gothic is not only the best, but the only rational architecture."
>
> John Ruskin, *The Stones of Venice*, 1854

breaking All Saints church, in Margaret Street, London, was an early answer to this demand. Completed in 1859, it became the model for a style of architecture known as High Victorian Gothic. Butterfield published further influential designs in *The Ecclesiologist*, the journal of the Cambridge Camden Society, which promoted Gothic church architecture. Meanwhile, revivalist architect Augustus Pugin found fame with a series of books in which he argued that Gothic was the only acceptable architecture for a truly Christian nation.

From the UK, the revival spread to France, where its leading light was Eugène Viollet-le-Duc, and to the US, where it inspired the Carpenter Gothic style. Applied to timber buildings, Carpenter Gothic was far removed from the European models of church architecture. St. Andrew's Church in Prairieville, Alabama (see p.255), for example, is uniquely American, but also unmistakably Gothic.

STRAWBERRY HILL
Owned by Horace Walpole, the writer of the first Gothic horror novel, *The Castle of Otranto* (1764), Strawberry Hill was designed to have what Walpole called an air of "venerable gloom." The approach to Gothic detail is selective rather than historically accurate: Strawberry Hill could not be mistaken for a real medieval building.

Walpole's Gothic Revival mansion

Victoria Tower, originally the tallest square tower in the world

PALACE OF WESTMINSTER

LONDON, UK, 1870

Built to replace the old Houses of Parliament, which were destroyed in a fire in 1834, the Palace of Westminster was designed in the Gothic style by Charles Barry. It was a bold choice, since British state institutions were traditionally built in the Classical style.

BUILDING A PALACE

Charles Barry won the competition to design the new Houses of Parliament. However, he was not a Gothic specialist, so he commissioned Augustus Pugin to work with him, which proved to be a masterstroke. Barry concentrated on the exterior, harmoniously combining spires and turrets into an unforgettable new skyline, while Pugin took charge of the Gothic detailing inside.

Sketch of Charles Barry's design for the central tower of the Palace of Westminster

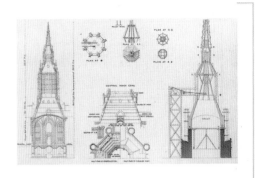

Belfry containing hour bell and four quarter bells

▲ Elizabeth Tower
Renamed after Queen Elizabeth II, the clock tower, which was designed by Augustus Pugin, houses the bell known as "Big Ben." At the date of the tower's completion (1859), the clock was the most accurate of its kind in the world.

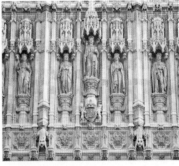

▲ Victoria Tower
The Victoria Tower is the entrance through which the British monarch enters Parliament. Barry decorated it with a series of lavish carvings, including a group of statues featuring Queen Victoria flanked by her parents.

Spire covered in cast-iron roof tiles

Central tower, designed to be a ventilating chimney, part of one of the world's first artificial ventilation schemes

Steeply pitched Gothic roofs

Multiple rows of windows with pointed arches

River facade largely symmetrical, like a Classical country house

Clipsham stone from Rutland

The four-faced clock points in four directions

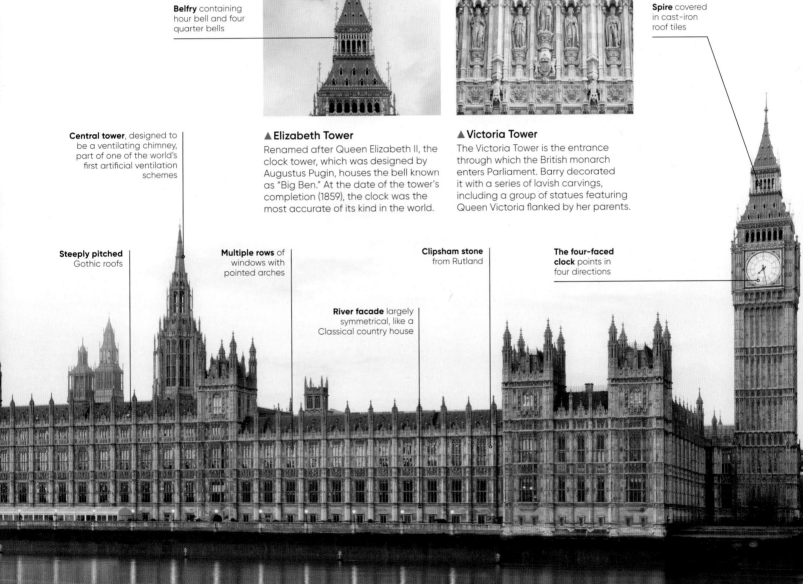

KEY ELEMENTS

Many Victorian architects found themselves drawn to medieval architecture for its religious associations, its structural ambition, and its flexible rules.

▶ **Mock medieval**
Sir George Gilbert Scott's jewel-like memorial to Prince Albert, in London, is an enlarged medieval shrine. Without iron, it would not be able to stand up—the sideways thrust of the arches would push over the slender piers.

SPIRES AND TOWERS

The Gothic Revival took place during the Railway Age, when train stations and luxury hotels became common features of the landscape. Architects gave these large, expansive buildings elements that were traditionally associated with churches, such as lofty spires and steeples.

▲ **Spectacular station**
The Chhatrapati Shivaji Railway Terminus in Mumbai, India, has a ribbed, octagonal dome surmounted by a giant statue of Progress as its centerpiece. It also has four large turrets, which are topped by domes and spires.

ARCHES

Cheap energy from coal meant that iron and glass were available on an unprecedented scale. Victorian Gothic architects explored their architectural potential, while also using the full catalog of earlier building materials.

▲ **Iron and glass**
Built by architects Deane and Woodward in 1855–1861, the Museum of Natural History in Oxford reflects the latter's passion for Pugin. Pointed arches abound both inside and out, and the glass roof is supported by cast-iron columns. The wrought-iron spandrels between the arches feature different species of tree.

▲ **Wood**
Horace Walpole placed wooden arches above doorways, fireplaces, and even bookcases in his "plaything house" of Strawberry Hill (see p.252). The bookcase arches were designed by John Chute, who modeled them on Wenceslaus Hollar's illustrations of Old St. Paul's Cathedral in London.

POLYCHROMY

Gothic revivalists were keen to emulate the colorful appearance of medieval churches, and preferred the color to come from the building materials themselves. Whereas medieval masons had built with the materials most easily transported to the site, trains and steamships allowed Victorian architects a much wider choice of materials.

Polychromatic brickwork in Butterfield's Keble College, Oxford

1

2

GOTHIC REVIVAL BUILDINGS

Gothic architecture was used for many churches and, despite objections from some, for secular buildings, too.

4

1. Midland Grand Hotel
London, UK, 1868–1876

Commissioned by the Midland Railway Company, the Midland Grand Hotel is Sir George Gilbert Scott's secular masterpiece. Its design is both opulent and eclectic, incorporating Gothic motifs from English, French, and Italian sources.

2. St. Paul's Cathedral
Melbourne, Australia, 1880–1891

St. Paul's Cathedral was designed primarily by William Butterfield, one of the stalwarts of the Gothic Revival. Its interior features rich polychrome effects, including tiles by the English tile manufacturer Maw & Co.

3. Trinity Church
New York, NY, 1839–1846

Trinity Church is celebrated for its soaring spire, which made it the tallest building in the US until 1869, and the tallest building in New York until 1890. The church was designed by British-American architect Richard Upjohn.

4. St. Andrew's Church
Prairieville, Alabama, 1853

An intriguing example of the American Carpenter Gothic style, St. Andrew's Church has pointed windows, a steeply-raked roof, and a series of vertical projections that resemble slender buttresses.

3

"I seek antiquity not novelty. I strive to revive not invent."

Augustus Pugin, in a letter to the poet John Bloxam, 1840

BEAUX ARTS

Lavish and often swaggeringly imposing, the Beaux-Arts style was well suited to an age of opulence on both sides of the Atlantic.

The Beaux-Arts style, which flourished in the late 19th and early 20th centuries, is named after the École des Beaux-Arts in Paris, which asserted a powerful claim to be the 19th century's world capital of art. Beaux Arts is characterized by bold, orderly planning of large, complex buildings clad externally in repetitive Classical motifs, and was associated with the teaching of the École, where many leading architects trained. Most Beaux-Arts buildings were major public structures, such as government offices and train stations.

CITY REBUILT

Paris was a particularly fertile ground for the Beaux-Arts style, since the city experienced a building boom in the second half of the 19th century. From 1853, Baron Georges Haussmann, a civil servant, masterminded a radical modernization of the city's structure, sweeping away cramped, winding medieval streets and replacing them with long, straight, wide boulevards. Prominent buildings were placed at the intersections of the main boulevards,

> "A triumph for our dear city of Paris."
>
> **Albert de Lasalle**, journalist, reporting on the inauguration of Garnier's Opéra, 1875

and served as landmarks in the new urban landscape. The grandest of these buildings was the Paris Opéra, which since 1989 has been formally known as the Palais Garnier, in honor of its architect, Charles Garnier. Garnier had a brilliant start to his career when he was awarded the prestigious Prix de Rome as a student at the École, but he was still relatively unknown when, at age 35, he won an open competition to design the new opera house. The building is renowned for its exuberantly festive style, but it is also notable for its careful planning (a priority in École des Beaux-Arts teaching) which allows it to function smoothly for both performers and audience.

BEYOND FRANCE

Outside France, the Beaux-Arts style flourished most vigorously in the US. Numerous American architects trained at the École, including such illustrious figures as Richard Morris Hunt, Charles Follen McKim, and Henry Hobson Richardson. The style continued to be popular into the 1920s, although some critics deemed it to be out of touch with the modern world. In 1908, for example, Frank Lloyd Wright referred to its products as "Frenchite pastry." The Great Depression of the 1930s finally made the style's conspicuous extravagance outmoded.

ÉCOLE DES BEAUX-ARTS

The École Nationale Supérieure des Beaux-Arts, as it is formally known, can trace its origins back to the founding of the Académie Royale de Peinture et de Sculpture in 1648. However, it did not become a separate institution until 1793, as part of the administrative reforms of the French Revolution. In 1816, it moved to its present location, on the left bank of the Seine, opposite the Louvre.

The Palais des Études, one of several buildings that make up the École.

PALAIS GARNIER

PARIS, FRANCE, 1861–1875

The exterior of the Palais Garnier (the Paris Opéra) was completed in 1867, but work on the interior was interrupted by the Franco-Prussian War of 1870–1871. The building was formally inaugurated on January 5, 1875.

◀ **Grand staircase**
The most spectacular part of the interior is the staircase—a place to see and be seen. The stairs themselves are made predominantly of white Italian marble and have a wealth of sculptural and painted decoration.

▲ **Dancing figures**
The most famous part of the building's sculptural decoration is *The Dance* (1866–1869), created by Jean-Baptiste Carpeaux. Although the version now on the facade is a replica, the original is on display in the Musée d'Orsay.

▲ **Center of the facade**
Garnier used a variety of colors and materials to create an extraordinarily sumptuous effect. The bust in the roundel—made of gilt bronze—is a portrait of Mozart, one of eleven composers featured on the facade.

Gilt bronze sculptural group *Harmony*

Pediment carving called *Architecture and Industry*

Dome, surmounted by the figure of Apollo

Pediment carving called *Painting and Sculpture*

Gilt bronze sculptural group *Poetry*

Masks of Comedy and Tragedy above the cornice

KEY ELEMENTS

In the Beaux-Arts style, the elements of Classical architecture are typically handled with freedom and inventiveness. Projecting and receding surfaces and the use of varied materials create a rich interplay of forms and different colors.

ARCHITECTURE PARLANTE

The phrase "architecture parlante" is French for "speaking architecture," and conveys the idea that the function or identity of a building can be clearly expressed by its appearance. More generally, it encompasses the notion that decorative elements should be closely connected to a building's purpose.

▶ Inscriptions

One way to proclaim a building's function is to give it bold inscriptions. This example is on the James A. Farley Building, formerly New York's main branch of the United States Postal Service. Designed by McKim, Mead, & White, it was built in 1911–1914.

▲ Nautical allusions

The voluptuously ornate New York Yacht Club Building was designed by Whitney Warren, and opened in 1901. One of its windows resembles the stern of an 18th-century ship; carved fish and wavelike forms similarly evoke the sea.

▶ The Glory of Commerce

This enormous allegorical sculpture, designed by Jules Coutan and unveiled in 1901, adorns the facade of Grand Central Terminal in New York. Its central figure, Mercury, was the Roman god of commerce and travelers.

TRADITIONS REFRESHED

Beaux-Arts architects drew on many sources, particularly the buildings of ancient Rome, as well as Renaissance and Baroque forms. However, they used these sources with imagination and panache, expressing in the new buildings some of the technical innovation and industrial production that underlay them.

▲ **Pediment and loggia**
The facade of the Art Institute of Chicago combines a Roman-inspired pediment with a Renaissance-style loggia in a strikingly bold way. The building was designed by the Boston firm Shepley, Rutan, and Coolidge.

▲ **A modern palazzo**
The University Club of New York, designed by Charles Follen McKim, is reminiscent of an Italian Renaissance palace. However, it differs from its forebears in the placement of its windows and in its use of multiple balconies.

▲ **Baroque influence**
Designed by Charles Girault, the Petit Palais was built for the Paris Exposition Universelle (World's Fair) of 1900. Its rich, flowing forms recall Baroque architecture, but the sheer effervescence of its decoration is new.

PIONEERING TECHNOLOGY

Although Beaux-Arts architects often looked to the past for inspiration, they also embraced new technology, particularly the use of iron and glass, which came of age as building materials in the 19th century.

▲ **Internal courtyard**
In 1832, Félix Duban was appointed architect to the École des Beaux-Arts. He designed various parts of the complex, including this courtyard in the main building. The roof was completed in the 1870s, after Duban's death.

▲ **Glass giant**
Built as an enormous exhibition space for the Paris Exposition Universelle (World's Fair) of 1900, the Grand Palais has the largest glass roof in Europe. The building's principal architect was Charles Girault.

THE WORLD'S COLUMBIAN EXPOSITION

In 1893, a World's Fair was held in Chicago to celebrate the 400th anniversary of Christopher Columbus's first voyage to the Americas. Known as the World's Columbian Exposition, it included 14 large buildings designed by leading architects of the day, and served as an influential showcase for the Beaux-Arts style. At the time, some commentators believed that Beaux-Arts buildings would have a civilizing effect, but Modernists were appalled; Frank Lloyd Wright wrote that this "grandomania" would set American architecture back "at least 50 years."

The Administration Building, designed by Richard Morris Hunt, at the World's Columbian Exposition

BEAUX-ARTS BUILDINGS

Grandiose and often ornate, the Beaux-Arts style was expressed mainly in large, prestigious, and costly public buildings, such as government offices, museums, libraries, law courts, and train stations.

1

2

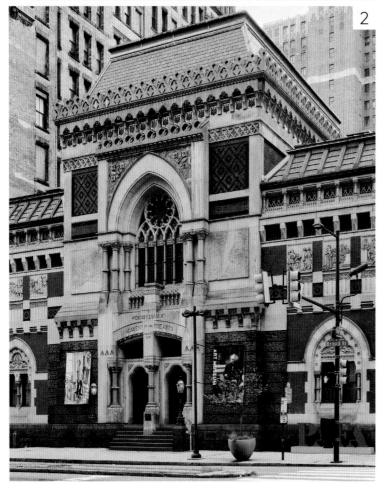

3

4

1. Boston Public Library
Boston, MA, 1887–1895

Designed by Charles Follen McKim, the Boston Public Library is often described as the first fully fledged Beaux-Arts building in the US. McKim based its design on the Bibliothèque Sainte-Geneviève in Paris.

2. Pennsylvania Academy of the Fine Arts
Philadelphia, PA, 1871–1876

Although essentially Gothic in style, this building's punchy reinterpretation of historical precedent is comparable with Beaux-Arts architecture. Designed by Frank Furness, it houses the oldest art school in the US.

3. Alberta Legislature Building
Edmonton, Canada, 1906–1912

Designed by Allan Merrick Jeffers, the Alberta Legislature Building is one of the most imposing Canadian buildings of the period. It has a particularly impressive dome.

4. Musée d'Orsay
Paris, France, 1897–1900

Now one of Paris's most important museums, the Musée d'Orsay was originally a train station, the Gare d'Orsay. After closing in 1939, the station was put to various uses before opening as a museum in 1986.

5. Pont Alexandre III
Paris, France, 1896–1900

The most exuberant of the Seine River bridges, Pont Alexandre III was inaugurated to coincide with the huge Paris Exposition Universelle (World's Fair) of 1900.

5

6

7

6. Metropolitan Museum of Art
New York, NY, 1894–1902

The Metropolitan Museum was designed to
be a palace of art to rival the museums of
Europe. Its entrance facade was the final work
of architect Richard Morris Hunt, and was
completed by his son, Richard Howland Hunt.

7. Teatro Colón
Buenos Aires, Argentina, 1889–1908

The most famous opera house in South
America, the Teatro Colón was designed by
Francesco Tamburini and completed by other
architects after his death. Its acoustics make
it one of the best concert halls in the world.

MĀORI ARCHITECTURE

The carved *wharenui* meeting houses of New Zealand are a source of cultural pride for the Māori, and a storehouse of knowledge about their past.

The Māori, who settled in Aotearoa (New Zealand) from the 12th century, traditionally lived in *kāinga* (villages) or *pā* (fortified settlements). Their buildings were typically either *wharepuni* (sleeping houses), which tended to be plain and were made of timber, bulrush, tree fern, and bark, or *paketa* (storehouses), which were sometimes elaborately carved. However, when Europeans arrived in New Zealand in the early 1800s—bringing Christian missionaries with them and buying up Māori land—the Māori needed new places in which they could meet to discuss their challenges. The result was the *wharenui* (large house), also known as the *whare whakairo* (carved meeting house), built using some European construction techniques that were adapted to serve the new building type.

OLD TRADITIONS, NEW METHODS
In the 1840s, using new materials such as nails and sawed planks, Māori builders modified the traditional *wharepuni* to create their new meeting houses. These were built in the traditional gabled style, with large porches,

or *whakamahau*, at the front, where meetings could take place. They were also elaborately decorated and furnished inside and out with statues of Māori ancestors and heroes, creating a building that was both the center of a living community and an embodiment of the past. Many houses were named after ancestors of the *iwi* (tribe) or *hapu* (tribal subdivision), their long rectangular shape symbolizing an outstretched body, with the *tāhuhu* (ridge pole) representing the backbone. In the late 19th and early 20th centuries, many of these meeting houses became centers of Māori religious and political movements.

Although knowledge of traditional Māori crafts declined in the early 20th century, Māori culture has since undergone a renaissance. A New Zealand Māori Arts and Crafts Institute was established at Rotorua in 1966, and since then *marae* (traditional Māori meeting grounds, which often feature *wharenui*) have been incorporated into school enclosures and even shopping centers. The Māori style of architecture, which reaches back to the time of the ancestors, remains very much a living tradition.

◀ **Ancestral faces**
The lavishly decorated Te Whare Rūnanga meeting house at Waitingi contains many carved wooden panels (*poupou*) that represent ancestors, histories, and legends.

RESISTANCE TO COLONIZATION

From the 1840s, the strong sense of cultural self-awareness that the *wharenui* symbolized became a focus for Māori resistance to European colonial rule. Religious leaders, such as Te Kooti, built meeting houses across New Zealand, following the style that was developed for houses such as Te Hau-ki-Tūranga. The tradition was revived in the late 20th century.

A self-portrait of Raharuhi Rukupō, carver of the Te Hau-ki-Tūranga meeting house.

TE WHARE RŪNANGA WHARENUI

WAITANGI, NORTH ISLAND, NEW ZEALAND, 1940

Built to commemorate the centenary of the Waitangi Treaty between Māori chiefs and the British Crown, the Waitangi meeting house has carvings that represent the unity of all Māori, rather than the ancestor of one particular *iwi*.

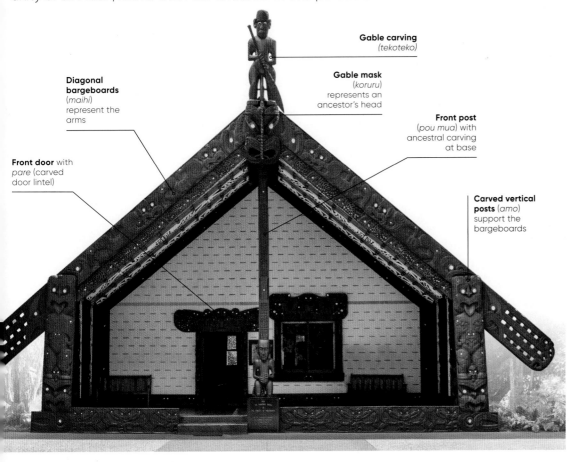

Gable carving
(*tekoteko*)

Gable mask
(*koruru*)
represents an
ancestor's head

**Diagonal
bargeboards**
(*maihi*)
represent the
arms

Front post
(*pou mua*) with
ancestral carving
at base

Front door with
pare (carved
door lintel)

**Carved vertical
posts** (*amo*)
support the
bargeboards

▲ **Richly decorated interior**
The interior of the *wharenui* is filled with decorative detail. Supporting the *tāhuhu* (ridge pole) is the *poutokomanawa* (carved centre post), with an ancestral figure at its base. The ceiling rafters (*heke*) are representative of the ribs of the body.

▲ **Latticework panels**
Alternating with the carved wooden panels that line the walls of the *wharenui* are latticework panels (*tukutuku*), traditionally woven by Māori women using the leaves and stalks of indigenous plants. Motifs include the lozenge and step patterns seen here, among others.

MĀORI BUILDINGS

▲ **Eripatana Te Waiti,** North Island, 1884
Built by the followers of Te Kooti, prophet of the Māori Ringatū movement, the Eripatana *wharenui* is unusual in being largely painted rather than carved. It is one of several meeting houses that were built on Te Kooti's instructions in the Te Urewera region.

▲ **Te Ika ā Māui,** Ratana Pa, North Island, 1914
The name of this meeting house means "the fish of Māui", a reference to the story of the demi-god, who pulls the North Island from the sea when fishing. The building has the typical diagonal bargeboards and carved upright posts but lacks a central front post.

"The *whare whakairo* isn't a building so much as an ancestor ... filled with other ancestors."
Damian Skinner, *The Māori Meeting House,* 2016

ECLECTICISM

The 19th century was an age of revivals. Styles from earlier periods were resurrected or reinvented, leading to an eclectic and lively combination of architectural forms.

Styles have always blended and mixed through history, especially at moments of change. What happened in 19th-century industrial countries was on a new scale, however. With colonial empires bringing awareness of the diversity of architectural styles worldwide, and with very rapid technological change in their own architecture, European and North American clients and architects had difficult decisions to make about which historical precedents their buildings should draw on.

From the early years of the 19th century, it was clear that different architectural styles could coexist and flourish side by side. There was a widespread belief that specific styles were more suitable for certain types of institution, such as Classical for public buildings and monuments, and Gothic for religious foundations, but these views were not firm. Sometimes, there were heated debates when a prestigious commission was involved, and in some cases, such as for the British Houses of Parliament, competitions were held to decide on which style should be employed, rather than which architect.

Slowly, barriers were broken down. Architects were given greater freedom to choose their style—or, alternatively, to "adulterate" a chosen style by combining it with elements from a different historical tradition.

The choice of a period style did not necessarily entail a slavish regard for historical accuracy. At Neuschwanstein, for example, King Ludwig II of Bavaria built a medieval fantasy using the latest construction materials and techniques. The castle was also fitted out with every modern convenience—including central heating, flushing toilets, and a state-of-the-art electric bell system for summoning servants.

EXOTIC TASTES

Some of the most remarkable examples of eclecticism resulted from the vision, or whim, of a wealthy patron rather than an architect. The original Pavilion at Brighton in the UK, for instance, was a relatively conventional Palladian building until the Prince Regent was given some Chinese wallpaper and insisted on adding "Oriental" features to the place. By 1808, he had developed a new enthusiasm for Indian styles, before changing his mind again and opting for James Wyatt's plans for a Gothic exterior. These might have gone ahead, but Wyatt died, so the Prince turned to John Nash, who managed to blend these disparate elements successfully. The result is an outlandish concoction of domes, minarets, and pagodas, which horrified many of his contemporaries, but is now much loved.

◄ **Hybrid style**
Rio de Janeiro's Municipal Theatre is a fusion of designs by the joint winners of an architectural competition in 1903—Francisco Passos, the son of the mayor, and Frenchman Albert Guilbert. Both were inspired by Charles Garnier's Paris Opéra.

ECLECTIC ENSEMBLES

In the 19th century, wealthy patrons had no qualms about juxtaposing structures of very different styles. At the German palace of Schwetzingen, for example, the gardens featured a Chinese bridge, a Roman fortress, and a Turkish-style mosque. Designed by Nicolas de Pigage, the mosque was purely ornamental and never served any religious purpose. Instead, it has been used as a military hospital, a meeting place for an Islamic academy, and as a setting for a Mozart opera.

Pigage's Red Mosque at Schwetzingen Palace, Germany

NEUSCHWANSTEIN CASTLE

HOHENSCHWANGAU, GERMANY, 1868–1886

This is the ultimate fairytale castle. King Ludwig II of Bavaria masterminded its design, visualizing the place as a romantic, medieval dreamland. He adorned his castle with scenes from German legends, identifying himself with the swan-knight Lohengrin, and adding references to the operas of his hero, Richard Wagner.

Gothic and Byzantine-style
tall, slim towers

Large foundations
built on a stone outcrop

Romanesque
bifora and trifora window openings

Ornamental,
non-defensive, overhanging battlements

▲ **Fit for a king**
The Throne Room has the gilded opulence of a Byzantine basilica, although its immediate influence was actually All Saints Church at the Residenz (Royal Palace) in Munich. The room expressed Ludwig's idea of kingship—he even intended to replace the altar with a throne.

ECLECTIC BUILDINGS

▲ **Church of Santa Teresa,** Madrid, Spain, 1928
Originally built for the Carmelite Order, this is now a parish church and nursing home. It has Neo-Gothic battlements—inspired by the fortress in St. Teresa of Ávila's book, *Las Moradas*—combined with a Byzantine-style dome with polychrome tiles.

▲ **Sezincote,** Moreton-in-Marsh, UK, 1805
The first major example of the "Indian style" in the UK, and the inspiration behind the Brighton Pavilion, Sezincote was designed by Samuel Pepys Cockerell, who was Surveyor to the East India Company.

▲ **The Royal Pavilion,** Brighton, UK, 1815–1823
The design of the Pavilion evolved over several decades, but was completed by John Nash when he was working as personal architect to the Prince Regent (later George IV). The final version was an exotic blend of Chinese and Indian elements.

ARTS AND CRAFTS

A reaffirmation of the principles of the Gothic Revival, or a nostalgic reimagining of an idealized agrarian past, the Arts and Crafts movement reflected an unease about coal-fueled industrialization.

Rejecting the grandeur of Neoclassicism and the Beaux Arts, the architects of the Arts and Crafts movement, such as Philip Webb and William Lethaby, endorsed a return to vernacular materials and designs inspired by nature. They reacted against the squalor caused by the Industrial Revolution, and sought to revive craftsmanship, organized through guilds of tradesmen. They were also inspired by the ideals of artists and critics such as Augustus Pugin, John Ruskin, and William Morris.

People who could afford to buy into this utopian vision of society commissioned manor houses in the countryside, or lodges in the new suburbs being built on the edges of cities. The most successful architects won commissions to design school buildings, art galleries, and other philanthropic institutions. Turning their backs on the darkness and pollution of the factories and the slums that clogged Victorian towns, architects such as Charles Voysey and Baillie Scott designed their houses to take best

advantage of the natural landscape and the sun. They also added large fireplaces and cozy inglenooks, which residents could retreat to as inclement weather and the seasons dictated. The influence of the Arts and Crafts movement can be seen in the model housing designs of Parker and Unwin, which shaped the urban landscape of new towns such as Letchworth Garden City, Hertfordshire, UK, and Hampstead Garden Suburb, London, UK. However, these were ideal examples, and a solution to the problem of housing the masses, and the broader sociopolitical agenda of the Arts and Crafts, remained unrealized.

THE NEXT GENERATION

Arguably the most significant influence of the Arts and Crafts movement was on a new generation of architects that were working internationally at the beginning of the 20th century. In the US, its legacy can be seen in the Prairie School houses of architects such as Frank Lloyd Wright and Walter Burley Griffin, or the work of the Greene brothers in California. Meanwhile, in Scotland, Charles Rennie Mackintosh turned its more picturesque elements into an unapologetically urban, industrial language, employing materials such as steel, concrete, and plate glass.

◀ **Natural forms**
The stained-glass windows at Blackwell, in the UK, were designed by Baillie Scott. The house benefits from its southwest-facing prospect overlooking the water and fells of the Lake District.

WILLIAM MORRIS
A well-known socialist thinker, William Morris was also an artist and designer. Collaborating with the Pre-Raphaelites, he founded Morris & Company to design and sell fabrics, wallpaper, and furniture. He also set up the Society for the Protection of Ancient Buildings in 1877, which campaigned for the sympathetic repair of historic buildings.

William Morris, photographed in 1887

THE RED HOUSE

BEXLEYHEATH, UK, 1859–1860

William Morris commissioned Philip Webb to design a house for himself and his wife at Bexleyheath, near London. Both men saw it as an opportunity to transform their ideas about craft and design into a manifesto built of unassuming red brick and tile. For Morris, "a beautiful house" was the greatest work of art.

PHILIP WEBB'S DESIGN

Morris and Webb collaborated on every detail of the house, from the garden layout to the furniture and wallpaper. They placed the windows according to internal convenience rather than external appearance, and set the fireplaces centrally to conserve heat. The stairs led up to hallways that were crowned with exposed oak beams and brick archways.

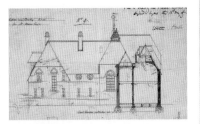

Philip Webb's plan for the Red House, drawn in pen and ink with watercolor

◄ **Window detail**
The somber Gothic interior of the house is animated by hand-painted glass by Pre-Raphaelite artist Edward Burne-Jones.

▲ **Rustic fireplace**
The red brick of the exterior is reflected in internal details such as the fireplace in the north-facing Drawing Room. The Latin inscription above the fireplace reads *Ars longa vita brevis* (Art is long, life is short).

Red brickwork and tiles give a rustic appearance

Pointed arches show a Gothic influence

Medieval-style well fed water to the kitchen

Sash windows placed to catch the morning sun

KEY ELEMENTS

Arts and Crafts architects paid careful attention to every aspect of a building, from its place in the landscape to its interior furnishings. Every detail was of equal importance.

CRAFTSMANSHIP

Revealing the care with which something is made tells an important story about the honesty and virtue of its creator. As Morris said: "Have nothing in your houses that you do not know to be useful, or believe to be beautiful."

LOCAL MATERIALS

In reaction to the mass production that defined the Industrial Revolution, Arts and Crafts architects believed that the materials of their buildings should reflect the history and traditions of their surroundings.

▲ **Undressed stone**
The entrance of Ernest Gimson's Stoneywell (see opposite) reveals how the variation of texture in undressed stone or brickwork greatly enhances the visual interest of a building.

▲ **Different colored facings**
Juxtaposing different kinds of brick enlivens the facade of Standen House in the UK. Designed by Philip Webb, the house also uses local tiles and sandstone.

▲ **Light and dark**
In the drawing room at Blackwell, in the UK, Baillie Scott used contrasting tones of light and dark to emphasize transitions between rooms used for different purposes at different times of day.

VERNACULAR INFLUENCE

Using vernacular construction techniques went hand in hand with a design philosophy that prioritized local materials and labor. The ideal Arts and Crafts house represented a work of art that restored the status of local craftsmen as designers in their own right.

▶ **Tall chimneys**
Designed by Walter Brierley, Goddards, Surrey, in the UK has tall chimneys, which improve the draft of the fireplaces, making it easier to warm the principal rooms. To store heat, the chimney flues are built into internal walls made of brick or stone.

▶ **Long, sloping roofs**
Folly Farm, in the UK, was designed by Edwin Lutyens. Asymmetric, sloping roofs extend close to the ground, while dormer windows bring light to the upper floors. Windows at the gable ends illuminate the principal rooms.

ARTS AND CRAFTS BUILDINGS

By the beginning of the 20th century, the Arts and Crafts movement had made a lasting mark on architecture, establishing itself chiefly in the UK and the US.

1. Stoneywell
Leicestershire, UK, 1899

Built on an outcrop of exposed rock in Charnwood Forest, Stoneywell is constructed from local stone and appears to spring organically from the geology of its site. The house was designed by Ernest Gimson for his brother Sydney and his family.

2. Glasgow School of Art
Glasgow, UK, 1896–1909

Charles Rennie Mackintosh's masterwork exploits its location at the top of Garnethill, overlooking Glasgow and the Clyde valley to the south. The main studio spaces are lit by large north-facing plate glass windows. The building was equipped with electric light, and an innovative warm air ventilation system that was built into a "spine wall" running the length of the plan.

3. All Saints' Church
Herefordshire, UK, 1901–1902

Emulating the lifestyle of the Gothic master builders, William Lethaby lived on the site while he supervised the construction of All Saints'. Beneath a thatched roof is an unreinforced concrete vault, showing the complex relationship leading Arts and Crafts architects had with new technologies.

4. Nathan G. Moore House
Oak Park, Illinois, 1895

Built near his own home in the Chicago suburb, Frank Lloyd Wright embellished his Prairie style with mock-Tudor half-timbering on the upper stories at his client's request. Unhappy with the results, Wright remodeled the house after a fire in 1922.

ART NOUVEAU

At once functional and futuristic, Art Nouveau—"new art"—was a self-conscious attempt to find new forms, inspired by nature, for the new technologies of a world reshaped by fossil fuel industries.

Art Nouveau was an exuberant and radical reimagining of architecture and the decorative arts that flourished from the last decade of the 19th century up until World War I. Art Nouveau architects relied on the expressive use of materials such as iron, glass, and ceramics to generate an astounding visual richness and complexity. Their buildings were dynamic in form and broke away from the static and staid historicist architecture popular at the time. Known as Jugendstil (young style) in Germany, Modernisme in Spain, and Secession in Austria, suggesting a clean break with the past, Art Nouveau rapidly spread across Europe and beyond. It was popularized by the growth of international trade exhibitions and by the proliferation of design magazines.

A TOTAL WORK OF ART
Art Nouveau first took root in Belgium and France, inspired by Chinese and Japanese art and by 19th-century design reform movements such as the English Arts and Crafts (see pp.266–269). Its pioneers included the architects Victor Horta, who designed several important

> "We must clothe modern ideas in modern dress."
> **Charles Rennie Mackintosh**, Address to The Glasgow Art Institute, 1893

buildings in Brussels, including the Hôtel Tassel, and Hector Guimard, whose skeletal iron-and-glass canopies are still a distinctive feature of many Paris Métro stations. Meanwhile, in Barcelona, the delirious inventions of Antonio Gaudí drew inspiration from Gothic art and the work of 19th-century French architect Eugène Viollet-le-Duc, creating a mythic vision of nature wrought in the materials of the modern era. The movement also reached the US, where Louis Sullivan, the "father of skyscrapers," applied sumptuous ornamentation to his office buildings and banks.

Underpinning Art Nouveau was the idea that a building's structure, facade, interior design, furniture, and decoration should all coalesce to produce a Gesamtkunstwerk, or "total work of art." In this it represented the first genuinely modern movement in architecture. However, its dramatic blooming was short-lived. By 1910, Art Nouveau was beginning to be seen as indulgently decadent, its sinuous contours belonging to a bygone age. After its brief heyday, its decline was hastened by the outbreak of World War I.

EXPOSITION UNIVERSELLE
Showcasing technical achievements, and attracting some 50 million visitors, the 1900 Exposition Universelle, in Paris, was notable for its lavish array of work by Art Nouveau designers, including Victor Horta, Otto Wagner, and Hector Guimard. Heralding the new century, it reflected the popularity of Art Nouveau, and marked the high point of the style's critical appeal.

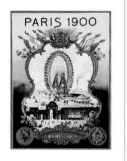

Poster advertising the 1900 Exposition Universelle

HÔTEL TASSEL

BRUSSELS, BELGIUM, 1893

Widely recognized as the first true Art Nouveau building, the Hôtel Tassel was a town house designed by Victor Horta for scientist and professor Emile Tassel. Its style evokes swirling plant forms and spatial fluidity.

The symmetrical structure blends in with neighboring buildings

▲ **Metal balcony**
Horta was fascinated by the pliability of wrought iron, which he crafted into ornamental balcony details that mimic flowing vegetation.

The windows have a membrane-like delicacy

Smooth facade made of light and subtly darker bands of limestone

▲ **Organic stone columns**
When designing the columns, Horta invented a new kind of form that evokes a sense of fluidity, suggesting that the stone is somehow melting.

Cornice between the entrance and the large oriel window

Double doors set in a sculpted, symmetrical frame

▶ **Interior staircase**
Exquisite, tendril-like motifs distinguish the iron staircase. These extend to the decoration of the painted walls and tiled floors, elevating the interior into a total work of art.

KEY **ELEMENTS**

Art Nouveau architects, inspired by their technical properties, made flamboyant use of materials such as iron, glass, and fired ceramics, made newly affordable by cheap coal heat.

FACADES

The facades of Art Nouveau buildings tended to be vigorously modeled and embellished. Colorful mosaics, stained glass, terra-cotta, and metalwork all contributed to the often fantastical compositions.

MATERIALS

Art Nouveau architects used a range of decorative materials, including tiles, stained glass, and wrought iron. Iron, in particular, proved to be perfect for bringing their ideas to life, enabling them to blur the distinction between natural and artificial forms.

◄ Metalwork
The influence of European Art Nouveau can be seen in the bronze-plated, cast-iron ornamentation around the windows of the Carson, Pirie, Scott and Company Building in Chicago. The building was designed by Louis Sullivan in 1899.

▲ Bones and scales
Known locally in Barcelona as the House of Bones, Antonio Gaudí's dragonlike Casa Batlló of 1904 combines skeletal stone elements with a richly hued skin of broken ceramic tiles.

► Stained glass
Osvald Polivka used vibrant stained glass in his redesign of the facade of the former Novak department store in Prague. Built in a historicist style in 1878, Polivka remodeled the building in 1901.

◄ Giant heads
Greatly inspired by the Viennese Secessionists, Russian architect Mikhail Eisenstein designed some 20 buildings in the Latvian capital, Riga. He specialized in producing highly sculpted facades.

WHIPLASH CURVE

With its origins in Islamic, Japanese, and Rococo art, the whiplash curve has a long history. In the late 19th century, its sinuous, asymmetrical lines became emblematic of Art Nouveau. The term "whiplash" was first used to describe a woven fabric panel that was designed in 1895 by German artist Hermann Obrist: it depicted the stylized roots and stem of a cyclamen flower.

The entrance of the Castel Béranger, Paris

1

ART **NOUVEAU** BUILDINGS

At the end of the 19th century, Art Nouveau had reached the height of its popularity. By then, it had spread from Europe as far as Mexico, and had influenced the designs of numerous exquisite buildings.

1. Gran Hotel Ciudad
Mexico City, Mexico, 1899
Originally a department store, and then converted into a hotel, the Gran Hotel Ciudad shows Art Nouveau at its most dramatic. Its highlights include a breathtaking, Tiffany-style stained-glass roof designed by Jacques Gruber. The entire roof was imported from France.

2. Hill House
Helensburgh, Scotland, UK, 1904
Designed for publisher Walter Blackie, Hill House is Charles Rennie Mackintosh's domestic masterpiece. Synthesizing the heft of a Scottish baronial castle with the delicacy of an Art-Nouveau interior, it is an unusual hybrid of robust and florid forms.

3. Majolica House
Vienna, Austria, 1898
Otto Wagner's Majolica House takes its name from the majolica (glazed earthenware tiles) that cover its facade—the floral design of which was inspired by the early Vienna Secession. The facade is practical as well as beautiful: it can be washed down with fire hoses, to combat the heavy coal soot that coated facades in all industrial cities.

4. Abbesses Métro station
Paris, France, c. 1900
Hector Guimard designed a series of entrances for Parisian Métro stations, including this version with an elegant fan shaped glass awning resembling a dragonfly's wing. It is supported by curvaceous cast iron columns fashioned to look like plant stems.

2

3

4

LA SAGRADA FAMILIA

BARCELONA, SPAIN, 1882–

This Roman Catholic church is the masterwork of Antoni Gaudí, who spent the last 40 years of his life on the project. A freely expressive design inspired by medieval Gothic, La Sagrada Familia remains incomplete.

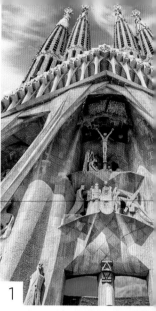

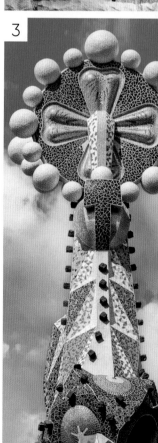

1. Passion facade

The north entrance is through a portal in the facade, a vast wall topped by four spires and adorned with sculptures depicting the Passion of Christ, from the Last Supper to his Crucifixion and entombment.

2. Sculptures

Working more than 100 years after Gaudí began the building, Josep Maria Subirachs sculpts in a bold, dramatic style. His figures are almost cubist in form, often with angular heads and faceted limbs.

3. Finials

The spires' twisted, organic forms terminate in a riot of applied color that picks out carved symbols, such as the cross and the bishop's ring. The finials are covered with mosaics made from broken tiles.

4. Nave

Gaudí's columns are fluted at the base and smooth-sided higher up, where the polygonal cross-section becomes circular. The columns branch out like trees toward the top, to form clusters of slender branches that support the vault.

5. Stained glass windows

Following the general plan outlined by Gaudí, the artist Joan Vila-Grau began work on the stained-glass windows for the naves. Using abstract patterns of saturated color, Vila-Grau created the vivid light that suffuses the interior.

6. Vault detail

The jagged edges, where each concave compartment adjoins the others, creates the effect of a series of starbursts. The curves of the vaults reflect the light from above, illuminating the interior of the church.

7. Slender spires

Emphasized by the pattern of openings and carvings that extend from top to bottom, the slender spires create a striking profile as they rise majestically above the center of Barcelona. Eighteen spires are planned altogether.

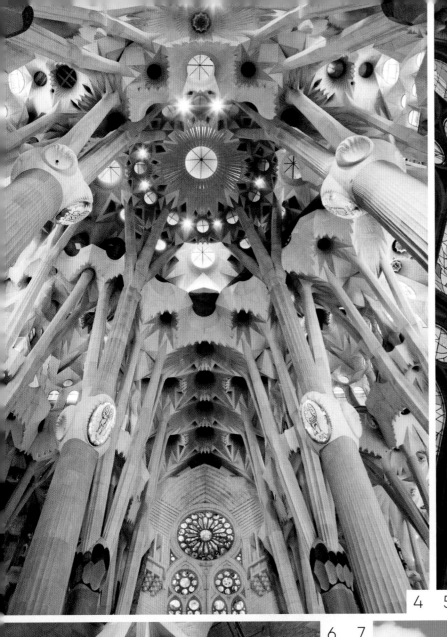

4 5

6 7

► **New heights**
Originally housing the headquarters of the
F. W. Woolworth Company, the Woolworth
Building in New York was built between 1910
and 1913. Clad in limestone and terra-cotta,
it has 60 stories (half in its base and half in
its tower) and rises to 792 ft (241 m).

SKYSCRAPERS

The first skyscrapers were built in the US in the 1880s, but it was only after World War II that they spread to dominate the skylines of the world's major cities.

Fossil fuel-driven industry flourished in the US through the 19th century, with rapid developments in iron, steel, elevators, and services such as plumbing removing limits on the useful height of buildings. On valuable sites in the center of America's leading cities, it became profitable to build ever higher.

Built at a time when architects liked their buildings to refer back to earlier architecture, the first generations of skyscrapers set their designers a tough challenge: no one had ever built anything remotely like them before. Architects drew inspiration from tall buildings such as Gothic cathedrals and bell towers, but in all but the most skilled hands these styles could end up looking awkward.

The freer architectural languages of Art Nouveau and Art Deco proved valuable in liberating 1920s skyscrapers from ill-fitting historical designs, and after World War II, the glass-clad skyscraper became a lastingly influential shorthand for investment, internationalism, and "progress."

RACE TO THE TOP

Since the first skyscrapers were built, there has been intense competition for the prestige of constructing the highest building in the world, with a long-standing competition between New York and Chicago, giving way to a series of Asian holders, and now to the Burj Khalifa in Dubai, at 2,717 ft (828 m).

While reasonably dense cities offer sustainability advantages over dispersed suburbs designed for cars, the competition for the title of "world's tallest building" now looks like a luxury of the fossil-fuel age. Building such high structures requires very large amounts of environmentally devastating steel and concrete, and the preference for an all-glass facade makes air-conditioning systems work wastefully hard when the sun shines.

If societies are to reach net-zero carbon, the world's rich need a new goal to aspire to. It is not the "world's tallest building" that is needed, but the "world's most sustainable tall building."

BUILDING A SKYSCRAPER

A skyscraper needs deep foundations that reach down to (and sometimes into) the bedrock. These support the building above ground, which is usually a network of vertical columns and horizontal girders made of steel. Smaller steel beams form a grid to support each of the floors, which are made of concrete. The windows and the outer, nonstructural walls are attached to this framework.

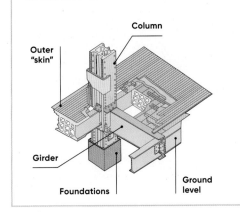

Column

Outer "skin"

Girder

Foundations

Ground level

▲ **Early skyscraper**
Due to its awkward, triangular site, New York City's Flatiron Building (1902), designed by Daniel Burnham, is shaped like a domestic iron. Like most early skyscrapers, it has three main sections: a base, a column, and a decorative top.

▲ **Gardens in the sky**
Architects are increasingly developing ways of greening their buildings. The towers of the Bosco Verticale (Vertical Forest) in Milan, Italy (2007–14), house as many trees and smaller plants as could be grown in 32,2900 sq ft (30,000 sq m) of land.

▲ **Symbolic form**
The headquarters of China Central Television in Beijing (2008) has a unique slanting-arch form with smooth outer surfaces. Its architects, Rem Koolhaas and Ole Scheeren, wanted the building to symbolize the energies at work in contemporary society.

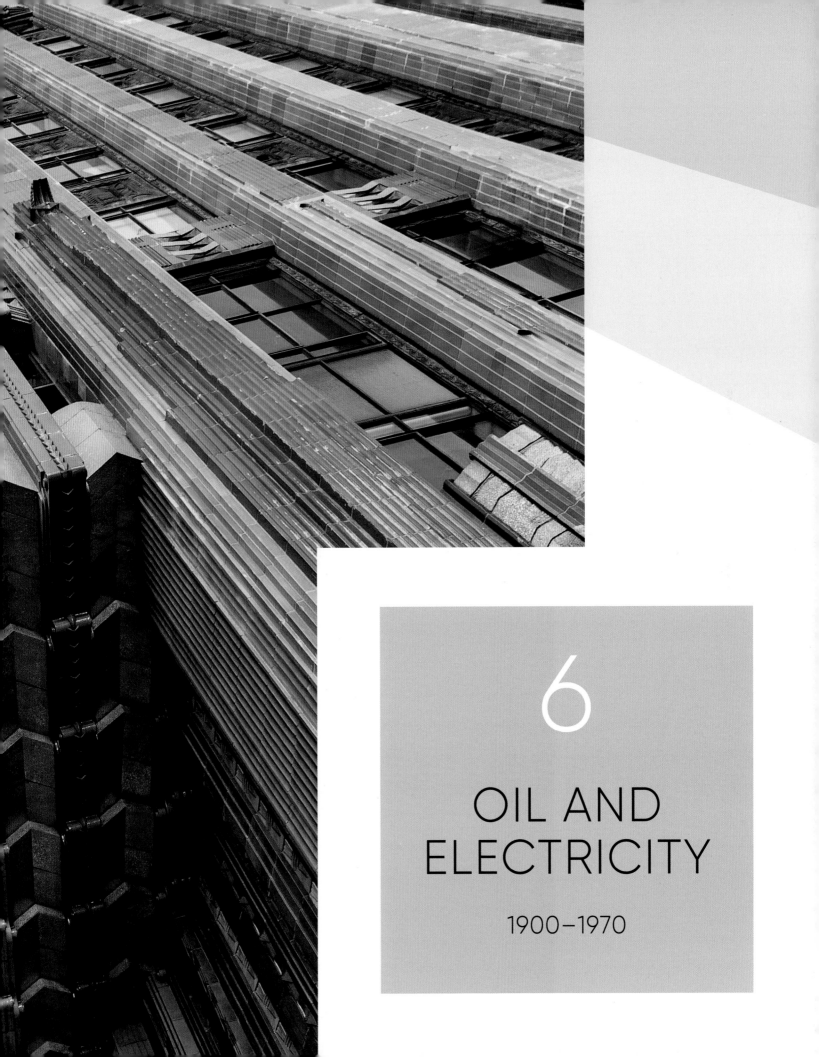

6

OIL AND ELECTRICITY

1900–1970

HISTORICISM

As fossil-fueled industry reshaped the world in the 19th and early 20th centuries, many architects looked to the past to find appropriate styles for a global building boom.

With new materials and technologies changing the ways in which buildings were made and how they functioned, architects—especially those from Europe and North America—began to plunder the history of architecture for motifs and styles that could give legitimacy to structures that might otherwise be dismissed as ugly, utilitarian, or mere engineering. This approach became known as Historicism.

COLONIAL BUILDINGS

The challenge of finding an appropriate architectural language was especially acute for buildings in the European colonial empires. A large proportion of 19th-century colonial architecture was relatively modest and functional, built quickly and cheaply using components that had been mass-produced in European factories. This enabled the colonial powers to expand their industrial base in the regions that they controlled, while forcing local populations into unskilled work and extracting raw materials from their land.

There were also commissions for important, prominent buildings, designed by European architects. These buildings represented an opportunity not only to display the wealth and technical skill required to build large, complex structures, but also to portray an idealized or propagandistic version of the colonizers' role.

The architectural style chosen could be used to send a message. European Classical architecture was a common choice, recalling the Roman Empire and carrying an implicit message of bringing "Western civilization" to lands whose rich cultures were categorized as inferior by European ideologies of the time. Gothic architecture was also chosen on occasion, often for churches built to support Christian missionary activity.

WEST MEETS EAST

In other cases, such as in India, new buildings offered European architects the chance to signal some level of engagement with the colonized region's own cultures, blending Western planning and construction techniques with elements of architectural ornament that evoked local traditions. Many of these grandiose buildings, built with the intention of serving generations of colonial rulers, have long outlived the empires that produced them. Their architecture recalls the contradictions and complexities of colonial histories that still have enormous impact worldwide.

◄ **Facade detail**

The Museum of Islamic Art in Cairo, Egypt (1902), was built in a Historicist style recalling Egypt's Mamluk era. The facade has traditional Islamic motifs and elements, such as polychromatic stonework, geometric decoration, and carved wooden screens.

INSPIRATION OF THE PAST

The early 17th-century tomb of Nithar Begum, set in the gardens of Khusro Bagh in Allahabad, India, typifies Indian Mughal architecture. Built from red sandstone and raised on a plinth, its walls feature arches and niches, with four chhatri (umbrella-shaped pavilions) surrounding the main dome. Elements of Mughal architecture were incorporated into colonial buildings to create a new style based on the reinterpretation of these traditional forms.

Historicism incorporated details of older styles, such as Mughal architecture.

VICEROY'S HOUSE

NEW DELHI, INDIA, 1929

As the centerpiece of New Delhi, this fusion of Indian and Edwardian architecture, now known as Rashtrapati Bhavan, epitomizes colonial-era grandeur. Its upper-class British architect Edwin Lutyens believed he was correcting flaws in Indian architecture by introducing European ideas and motifs.

> "New Delhi was to be a subliminal [ad] of the might of the Raj."
>
> **Suhash Chakravarty**, "Architecture and Politics in the Construction of New Delhi," 1997

▲ Chhatri pavilions
Traditionally ornamental canopies above tombs in Mughal architecture, chhatri are dome-shaped pavilions, held up here by distinctive elephant columns. These key decorative elements animate the roofline.

▲ Column order
Lutyens designed a new column order for the building, based on Greek or Roman columns, but with stone bells hanging at each corner, said to be inspired by Indian temple bells.

▲ Central dome
Influenced by the dome of the Pantheon in Rome, Italy, a huge central dome forms the great focus of Lutyens' design. It is decorated with elephant head sculptures and jalis, traditional latticed screens or windows.

Chhajja, deep overhanging cornices, provide shade from the sun

A central dome unifies the composition

Chhatri pavilions decorate the roofline

Jalis, traditional openwork screens, adorn the dome

Delhi Order of columns designed to incorporate Indian motifs

Extensive facade of red and cream sandstone

KEY **ELEMENTS**

The Historicist architecture of the late 19th and early 20th centuries was characterized by attempts to find historical precedents for technically unprecedented buildings.

THE BATTLE OF THE STYLES

Architects in this period were equipped with greater technical powers than any earlier generation, thanks to the might of fossil-fueled industry. Most used their new powers to indulge in fantasies of reviving past styles and reproducing them on a grander scale.

▼ Neo-Baroque
Designed by Belgian architect Paul Belau in Neo-Baroque in 1914, Cuba's Gran Teatro de La Habana was commissioned and funded by Spanish immigrants. Adorned with statues representing benevolence, education, theater, and music, its articulated facade displays key Baroque elements.

▲ Neo-Gothic
Overlooking the Danube River, Imre Steindl's 1904 Hungarian Parliament Building in Budapest is a symphony of pinnacles, spires, and arches, anchored by a huge central dome. Partly inspired by the British Houses of Parliament, it embraces the Neo-Gothic style as an expression of national identity.

▶ Mamluk revival
Alfonso Manescalo's 1902 Museum of Islamic Art in Cairo, Egypt, draws inspiration from the rich architecture of the Mamluk Sultanate, which ruled over Egypt from 1250 to 1517. In the late 19th century, the style experienced a popular revival.

▲ Beaux Arts
Grand Central Terminal in New York exemplifies the popularity of Neoclassicism and the Beaux-Arts style in the US. Opened in 1913 and based on the concept of a Roman triumphal arch, the terminal's imposing main facade was envisaged as a gateway to New York.

HISTORICIST BUILDINGS

Western-trained architects were educated in the use of historical styles, and applied this learning very literally wherever they worked. The results border on fantasy, and range from stunning to disconcerting.

1. Kuala Lumpur Station
Kuala Lumpur, Malaysia, 1910

Designed by British architect Arthur Benison Hubback, this station mashes together south Asian architectural motifs, including a vivid assortment drawn from Indian Mughal architecture, with little respect for specifically Malaysian traditions.

2. São Paulo Municipal Theatre
São Paulo, Brazil, 1911

Brazilian architect Ramos de Azevedo's theater is designed with Neoclassical flamboyance, modeled on the Paris Opéra building. The development of Neoclassicism in South America reflected a desire to imitate European archetypes—the Brazilian architect had originally studied in Belgium.

3. Tribune Tower
Chicago, Illinois, 1925

By the 1920s, Neo-Gothic skyscrapers were common in US cities, and the Tribune Tower was a lavish example of so-called "American Perpendicular." Featuring gargoyles and buttresses, its top section is modeled on the tower of Rouen Cathedral in France.

4. Peace Palace
The Hague, the Netherlands, 1913

Resembling a Renaissance town hall with its imposing bell tower, the Peace Palace was the outcome of an international competition held in 1905 and won by French architect Louis M. Cordonnier. Its clear Historicist design looks backward rather than forward.

"You can't escape the influence of architectural history."

Richard Meier, interviewed in *Architectural Digest*, 2013

▲ **The rise of concrete**
Designed by Auguste Perret in 1923, Notre-Dame du Raincy in Paris is a highly original, modern reworking of a Gothic church. Its lofty barrel vault and slender columns are made of reinforced concrete rather than stone.

NEW EXPERIMENTS

In the early 20th century, a new generation of architects began to radically reshape architecture, dispensing with historic models and embracing the possibilities of technology and modernity.

Galvanized by developments in engineering, construction technology, and building materials, a group of architects, who became known as Modernists, devised a new style of architecture that rejected the prevailing Historicist models. Their ambition gained momentum after World War I, when many people believed that the world should be rebuilt, and that architecture could accelerate a wider, social transformation. At the time, traditional hand-craftsmanship was giving way to fossil-fuel-driven mass production, and experiments with materials and building techniques were making it possible for architects to design innovative new structures. The Modernists' style was based on the maxim "form follows function." This, they believed, was the best guide to serving the needs of the age.

NEW POSSIBILITIES

Reinforced concrete was a key Modernist material. Its use had been growing since the late 19th century, but it was usually concealed behind more acceptable facing materials, such as

"New synthetic substances— steel, concrete, glass—are actively superseding the traditional raw materials of construction."

Walter Gropius, *The New Architecture and the Bauhaus*, 1925

stone or brick. In 1903, French architect Auguste Perret built a reinforced-concrete apartment building in Paris. Victorian experiments with glass were also influencing Modernists. In 1914, German architect Bruno Taut built a glass pavilion in Cologne, and rhapsodized about the material's extraordinary potential. Being stronger, steel replaced iron in structural frames, leading to the construction of ever taller buildings, including skyscrapers (see pp.276–277).

The rise of Modernism as a style was clearest in central Europe, where fossil-fuel-powered industrialization started later and moved faster than it had in Britain. Whereas British architects had decades to adapt, technological and social changes hit other European countries at a thrillingly disruptive speed. Young designers leapt to figure out what these changes meant for new buildings. Re-creating the language of medieval cathedrals and Renaissance palaces suddenly seemed a ridiculous way to use architecture's new capabilities. The materials of modernity promised a new architecture that would eclipse all the styles of history.

THE DEUTSCHER WERKBUND

Established in 1907 to promote new forms of German design, the Deutscher Werkbund was an association of architects, artists, designers, and manufacturers. Its motto was *Vom Sofakissen zum Städtebau* (From sofa cushions to city buildings), showing the expansive range of its interests. A precursor to the Bauhaus, it became a significant force in the development of modern architecture, with members including Peter Behrens, Walter Gropius, and Bruno Taut.

A Deutscher Werkbund exhibition poster

FAGUS FACTORY

ALFELD, GERMANY, 1911

Designed by Walter Gropius and Adolf Meyer, the Fagus Factory, which manufactured shoe lasts, was one of the most influential buildings of the early Modernist period. Its large glass panels created a unprecedented sense of openness and lightness, which Gropius described as "etherealization."

◄ Glazed facade
For the very first time, a facade was made entirely of glass. Its success led to the development of the glazed curtain wall, which became a key feature of Modernist buildings.

► Entrance
Plain, yellow-brick walls are stripped of decoration, making their texture and color the main focus of attention.

▲ Staircase
Made of concrete and finished with a crisply detailed balustrade, the main staircase is set in a glass stair tower. Bathed in natural light, it provides a focal point for the building and animates the facade.

Glazed corners stand free of load-bearing structures

Metal panels conceal concrete floor slabs

Ranks of windows create the illusion of a floating curtain wall

Recessed brick pillars accentuate the facade

A smoke stack rises 66 ft (20 m) above the forge

Brickwork conceals a load-bearing frame

KEY ELEMENTS

Early Modernist architects had in common a sense that new technical possibilities required a new architecture, but their ideas on what that should look like varied widely.

MODERNIST FEATURES

The term "Modernist" was not used by most of these architects before World War I, but their diverse experiments shared an interest in structure, material, and expression. Rather than recycle history, they planned a new kind of architecture that was shaped by the challenges of the times.

▲ **Cuboid forms**
Frank Lloyd Wright's Unity Temple in Chicago, completed in 1908, sought to turn exposed concrete into dignified religious architecture. It has functional, rectilinear features and flat roofs that were usually associated with factories and warehouses.

▼ Glazed facades
Designed by Walter Gropius, the Bauhaus in Dessau, Germany (1926), is an icon of Modernism. Its vast expanse of glazing ushered in an architectural style that was dedicated to openness.

▲ **Minimal ornamentation**
Designed by Adolf Loos, who wrote an essay on the relationship he saw between ornament and crime, the Looshaus in Vienna has a plain facade. It exemplifies his belief that cultural progress depended on eliminating ornament from everyday objects.

FORM FOLLOWS FUNCTION

American architect Louis Sullivan wrote in 1896 that "form shall ever follow function." He meant that a building's shape should be generated primarily by the spaces inside it—and, shortened to "form follows function," his words became an influential slogan for Modernist architects. Sullivan was a pioneer in skyscraper design, and had to break with established norms in order to develop a new style of architecture.

Louis Sullivan, the "father of Modernism," photographed in 1890

MATERIALS

Materials that had been known for millennia—including glass, steel, and concrete—became cheap and abundant in this period, thanks to fossil fuels. Architects raced to find compelling aesthetic expressions of their qualities, seeking to break with the past and express the spirit of the modern age.

◀ **Glass**

Bruno Taut's prismatic Glass Pavilion was built for the 1914 Deutscher Werkbund Exhibition in Cologne. It explored the properties of glass, which at the time was undergoing a manufacturing revolution.

▲ **Brick**

Although brick was a traditional building material, it was embraced by the early Modernists. Hans Poelzig's chemical plant in Lubán, Poland, featured vast brick walls punctuated by rectangular and arched windows. Constructed in 1911–1912, it was conspicuously severe-looking.

▲ **Steel**

Stronger than iron, and therefore capable of making higher, lighter structures, steel became the material of choice for architects designing frames for very tall buildings. The Old Colony Building in Chicago was one of these. Designed by Holabird and Roche and completed in 1894, it was one of the first skyscrapers.

▶ **Reinforced concrete**

Auguste Perret was one of the first architects to explore the aesthetic and intellectual potential of exposed concrete architecture. Built in 1904, his apartment building in Paris has decorative features set into its concrete facade.

EARLY MODERNIST BUILDINGS

The imaginative scope of the early Modernists, and their dedication to experimenting with new materials, is reflected in their huge range of pioneering buildings, which included factories, churches, and concert halls.

1

3

2

1. Villa Steiner

Vienna, Austria, 1910

With its sparsely embellished white stucco facade, the Villa Steiner, designed by Adolf Loos, is a seminal early Modernist building. Inside, it is organized on the basis of what Loos called *Raumplan*—space designed according to function.

2. Turbine Factory

Berlin, Germany, 1909

Designed by Peter Behrens to house a steam-turbine factory, this monumental building calls to mind ancient temples. It embodies the industrial power that was changing society at the time.

3. Notre-Dame du Raincy

Paris, France, 1923

Built to commemorate the dead of World War I, this stunning church by Auguste Perret marked a significant advance in the use of concrete. Its facade has a complex tessellated pattern that evokes medieval tracery.

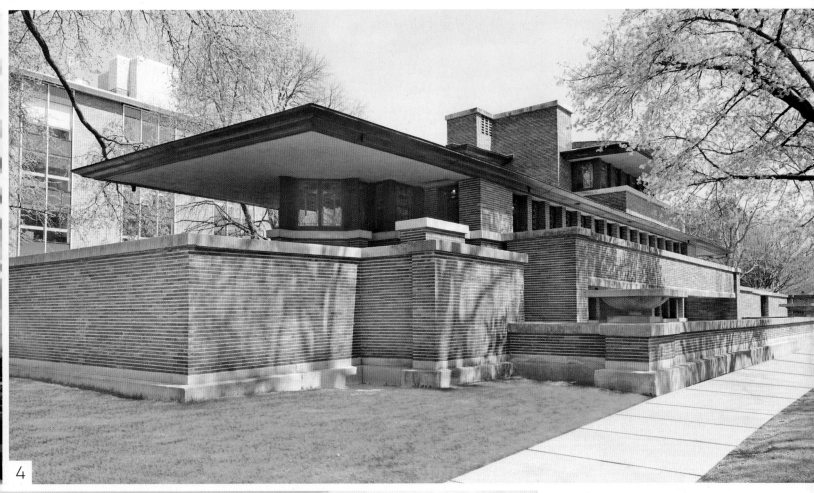

4

5

4. Robie House
Chicago, Illinois, 1909

Robie House is widely considered the finest example of Frank Lloyd Wright's uniquely American Prairie School style. It has cantilevered roof eaves; continuous bands of glazing; and long, thin Roman bricks, all of which reminded Wright of the prairie landscape

5. Centennial Hall
Wroclaw, Poland, 1913

Centennial Hall, designed by Max Berg, proved that reinforced concrete could be used to build large and dramatic structures. Designed as a multipurpose building with a capacity to seat 6,000 people, it is still in use today.

FUTURISM

Driven by feverish worship of youth, speed, and destruction, Futurism envisioned entirely new buildings and cities that could only be achieved by rejecting historical styles and methods.

Emerging in Italy during the first decade of the 20th century, the avant-garde art movement of Futurism was so enraptured by modernity that it believed it was necessary to completely break with the past. For the Futurists, fossil-fuel-powered developments like the motor car, the airplane, and rapid industrialization demonstrated humanity's dominance over nature. In Italy, where the presence of the past and influences from the natural world had long been mined for inspiration, the Futurists advocated wholesale destruction, followed by a modern rebirth.

THE FUTURIST CITY

Of all the arts, it was on architecture that Futurism had the greatest impact. Futurist thinking on architecture and urbanism was outlined in the *Manifesto of Futurist Architecture* in 1914. It is widely thought to have been written by the Italian architect Antonio Sant'Elia. Building on the 1909 *Manifesto of Futurism* by Filippo Tommaso Marinetti, a poet and one of the movement's founders, Sant'Elia's manifesto argued against the historical idea of architecture as something permanent and enduring. Instead, it outlined

how each generation would need to redesign the city anew to meet its own needs. Sant'Elia's designs in his 1914 conceptual work *La Città Nuova* (*The New City*) are some of Futurism's most enduring depictions, prophesying a city of skyscrapers and transportation networks that made a complete break with the urban styles and architecture of the past.

SPEED, TECHNOLOGY, AND VIOLENCE

While the Futurists were fierce and compelling in conveying their ideas in manifestos, the movement was relatively short-lived. It was also largely confined to Italy—with the exception of a parallel movement in Russia, which lasted until the 1917 revolution.

Many of Futurism's proponents advocated war due to what they saw as its "cleansing" ability to bring about the cultural reset they desired. Many, including Antonio Sant'Elia, were killed after enthusiastically signing up to fight in World War I. The movement's obsession with violence would see it take a darker turn. In 1919, Marinetti coauthored the *Fascist Manifesto* with Alceste de Ambris. Marinetti's death in 1944 is generally considered to mark the end of the Futurist movement.

> "Architecture is breaking away from tradition: it must start over from scratch."
>
> Antonio Sant'Elia, *Manifesto of Futuristic Architecture*, 1914

◀ **Prophetic visions**
Depicting towering skyscrapers and raised railroad bridges, Mario Chiattone's work *Ponte e Studio di Volumi* presented a modern city grounded in function, efficiency, and technology. Its influence remains clear on new buildings even now.

A CHANGING WORLD

Although Futurism's approach and ideology were extreme, they were grounded in real architectural developments and were prophetic. In the United States, the first skyscrapers had been completed at the turn of the century In Europe, meanwhile, Tony Garnier had already proposed a prescient vision of the modern, industrialized city in his work *Cité Industrielle*, in 1917.

Skyscrapers by the industrial architect Albert Kahn transformed Detroit's skyline.

LA CITTÀ NUOVA

MILAN, ITALY, 1914

A set of speculative drawings by Antonio Sant'Elia, *La Città Nuova* was exhibited in Milan in 1914. Although the city was never built, the drawings had a lasting impact. When Europe was rebuilt after World War II, the idea of the Futurist city still preoccupied Modernist architects. Decades later, it was even cited as inspiration for Ridley Scott's 1982 film *Blade Runner*.

Elevators travel outside buildings in separate towers

Stepped apartments, made possible by reinforced concrete, allow for balconies

Rapid transport is integrated on overlapping levels

Suspended walkway hanging from steel truss

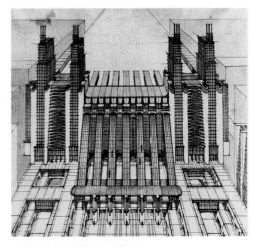

▲ **The epitome of efficiency**

Prioritizing function and autonomy, the Futurist city was conceived as being highly mechanized. Transportation hubs and multilevel traffic circulation were viewed as a means of increasing efficiency.

FUTURIST BUILDINGS

▲ **Monument to the Fallen,** Como, Italy, 1933

Based on drawings by Antonio Sant'Elia, Giuseppe Terragni's World War I memorial was commissioned by Mussolini's National Fascist Party. It echoes proposals for Futurist skyscrapers.

▲ **Lingotto Fiat Factory,** Turin, Italy, 1916–1923

A truly Futurist work focused on efficiency, Giacomo Mattè-Trucco's car factory was designed around a helical concrete ramp to aid a smooth production line. The roof is used as a test track for new cars.

▲ **Futurist Pavilion,** Turin, Italy, 1928

Painter and sculptor Enrico Prampolini designed this geometric pavilion for the *Esposizione del Valentino,* It demonstrates the Futurists' interest in modern, geometric forms drawn from styles such as Cubism.

CONSTRUCTIVISM

Expressively combining geometric forms with modern, industrial materials, Constructivism evolved in post-revolutionary Russia as a utopian new vision of architecture.

Emerging from the Constructivist art movement founded in 1915 by Russian artists Vladimir Tatlin and Alexander Rodchenko, Constructivist architecture embodied a radical new concept of modernity. Russian society was in a state of turmoil in the aftermath of World War I and the 1917 Russian Revolution, and Constructivist architects proposed a futuristic new style of architecture for the people.

Constructivist architecture was to favor mechanistic and geometric forms, avoid applied decoration, and use the latest industrially produced materials—notably concrete, steel, and glass. Throughout the 1920s and '30s, in response to the ambitions of the communist regime, Constructivist architects designed buildings and urban spaces aimed at bringing about social and cultural change.

PIONEERING ETHOS
An early, extremely influential Constructivist project was Tatlin's Tower (see below), a dramatic proposal for a 1,312 ft (400 m) tower based on a double spiral with a revolving cube, pyramid, and cylinder, all suspended in a skeletal steel frame. Although it was never built, its pioneering ethos set the tone for subsequent developments. Among the leading Constructivist architects were Ilya Golosov, Moisei Ginzburg, and Konstantin Melnikov, who designed the Soviet Pavilion for the 1925 Paris Exposition of Decorative Arts, popularizing the Constructivist style.

TRANSFORMING SOCIETY
The Constructivists envisaged a better future, driven by industrialization and collectivism, for the people of Russia, many of whom still lived on the land in almost medieval conditions. Buildings that came to symbolize their vision included department stores, newspaper offices, and mass housing, along with infrastructure projects, such as dams and power stations. The Narkomfin Building (see opposite), for example, was an attempt to create a new model for mass housing. Yet despite achieving many of its architectural and social aims, Constructivism had fallen out of political favor by the mid 1930s, supplanted by a regressive Stalinist form of Neoclassicism that went on to dominate the architecture of the Soviet Union for most of the 20th century.

> "To create a union of purely artistic forms for a utilitarian purpose."
>
> Vladimir Tatlin, *The Work Ahead of Us*, 1920

◀ Melnikov's House
This house in Moscow, which architect Konstantin Melnikov designed for himself and his family in 1929, is considered an innovative masterpiece. The design is based on two intersecting cylindrical towers that are studded with hexagonal windows.

TATLIN'S TOWER
Vladimir Tatlin's proposal for a grand, monumental tower to commemorate the Third International Communist Congress was to be erected in Petrograd (now St. Petersburg) after the Bolshevik Revolution of 1917. Although it was never built, the tower's design set the tone for subsequent Constructivist buildings.

Model of the Monument to the Third International, Moscow, 1919

RUSAKOV WORKERS' CLUB

MOSCOW, RUSSIA, 1928

With its strong geometric forms, dramatic cantilevered structure, and juxtaposition of concrete and glass, the Rusakov Workers' Club designed by Konstantin Melnikov was revolutionary in style. It epitomized the Constructivist ideal of creating a new form of social, utilitarian architecture for working people.

Expansive glazing opens up the building

Reinforced concrete allows the auditoriums to cantilever out

Geometric forms create a dramatic interplay between concrete and glass

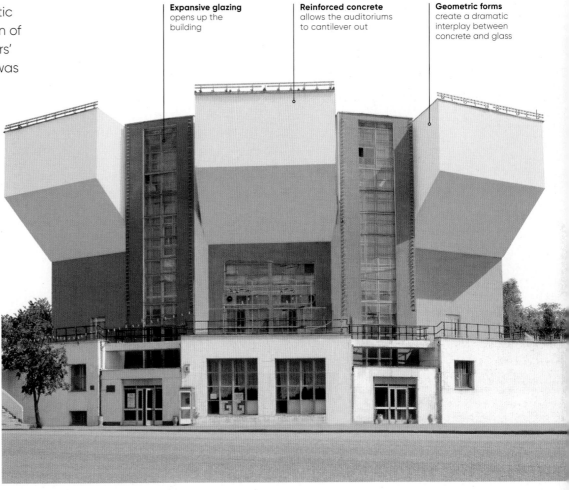

▲ **Interior**
Workers' clubs represented a new type of building for collective social, educational, and cultural activities. The Rusakov Workers' Club (now refurbished) houses a trio of theaters that can either be used separately or as one large theater.

CONSTRUCTIVIST BUILDINGS

▲ **Zuev Workers' Club,** Moscow, Russia, 1929
Designed by Ilya Golosov, this building has a large, cylindrical, glazed staircase that intersects with stacked rectangular units, creating a dynamic structure. A sequence of club rooms and open foyers lead to an 850-seat auditorium.

▲ **Derzhprom (the State Industry Building),** Kharkiv, Ukraine, 1928
The very first "Soviet skyscraper," and the largest single structure in the world when it was completed in 1928, Derzhprom is a massive, city-like complex of office towers that are linked together by a system of aerial walkways.

▲ **Narkomfin Building,** Moscow, Russia, 1930
This long block of apartments raised on pilotis (columns) is linked to a smaller block of communal facilities, including a crèche, laundromat, library, and gymnasium. Narkomfin was an experimental social housing project that aimed to encourage collective living and foster a sense of community.

◄ Bare bricks
Grundtvig's Church in
Copenhagen, Denmark,
blends Gothic height
with plain geometric
form, shaped from
millions of local yellow
bricks. The soaring west
facade is reminiscent
of a church organ.

EXPRESSIONISM

Focusing on individual vision rather than tradition or rationality,
Expressionist architects adopted new materials and styles to
create buildings that explored the limits of artistic expression.

Expressionist architecture developed as part of
an avant-garde artistic movement in Germany
during the first decades of the 20th century.
Seeking to free themselves from traditional,
realist conventions, Expressionists saw art as a
means of expressing inner, emotional truths in
an authentic and vibrant manner. In architecture,
they believed in looking beyond the confines of
conventional building materials and techniques.
However, although their innovative proposals
often pushed the boundaries of what was
possible, the movement was short-lived.

MATERIAL EXPERIMENTATION
Some Expressionists were particularly interested
in glass, which had been used for the windows
of the rich for centuries, but had only come to
be cheap enough to use for whole buildings
since the rise of coal-fired glass production. For
German architect Bruno Taut, glass buildings
were nothing short of utopian, and in 1914 he
unveiled his multicolored Glass Pavilion for the
Deutsche Werkbund Exhibition in Cologne. Around
the same time, German-American architect
Mies van der Rohe produced designs for Berlin's
first skyscraper. Although his proposals were
never built, his futuristic blueprints—of curving,
angular buildings with curtain walls made entirely
of glass—were a prescient vision of a time when
such buildings would become commonplace.

> "The architect
> must carry ... all the
> deep feelings and
> sentiments for which
> he wants to build."
> Bruno Taut, *City Crown*, 1919

Given its focus on individuality, Expressionism
had no formal principles, so Expressionist
buildings were highly eclectic and varied. In
Germany, the style was often associated with
the jagged, angular sets that were seen in films
such as *The Golem* (1920) and *Nosferatu* (1922).
However, as technology improved, monolithic
concrete shapes became more common.

By the mid 1920s, the popularity of the
movement had begun to wane, and many
architects were turning to more functional
building styles. Then, in 1933, when the Nazis
came to power, "degenerate" Expressionist art
was outlawed in Germany. Nevertheless, the
idea that architecture should be more dynamic
and have an emotive force outlived the original
Expressionist movement, which has since been
revived numerous times worldwide.

IN CONTEXT

Many Expressionists had been soldiers in World War I,
and had initially supported the war effort, believing
it would pave the way to a bright new future. After
their experiences, however, they used art both to
portray the horrors of war and to reimagine
society. One such soldier was German
architect Erich Mendelsohn, who
planned futuristic buildings
in the trenches.

Sketch of an industrial
building by Erich Mendelsohn

Design similar to
Mendelsohn's Red
Flag textile factory,
Leningrad

The dome lets light into the telescope

Shaft houses vertically mounted optical telescope

Brickwork covered in stucco forming curved shapes

The basement contains a laboratory where light is analyzed

EINSTEIN TOWER
POTSDAM, GERMANY, 1921

Designed by Erich Mendelsohn, this observatory, with its dynamic, curved form, was named after Albert Einstein. Although reminiscent of a futuristic ocean liner, Mendelsohn is said to have been unable to explain it, saying that it arose out of an unknown urge.

CROSS SECTION

The Einstein Tower was designed to house a solar telescope that was used to confirm Einstein's general theory of relativity. Sunlight entered the telescope through the domed roof and was directed down into a basement laboratory where it was analyzed. Although it was designed to be made out of reinforced concrete, the building was eventually made of bricks, which were covered in stucco. The change of material made the building more susceptible to damage.

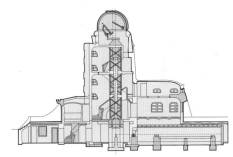

The Einstein Tower, viewed from the side

EXPRESSIONIST BUILDINGS

▲ **Monument to the Revolution,** Germany, 1926
Built in memory of socialist revolutionaries Karl Liebknecht and Rosa Luxembourg, Mies van der Rohe's stark Berlin memorial, with its rough brick wall finish and cantilevered slabs, hinted at their brutal murder. It was demolished by the Nazis in 1935.

▲ **The Goetheanum,** Switzerland, 1919
Rudolph Steiner's Goetheanum is a sculpted concrete form that was designed to reflect the spiritual concerns of the Anthroposophy movement, that Steiner founded. It is named after the great German author Johann Wolfgang von Goethe.

▲ **The Chilehaus,** Hamburg, Germany, 1924
Fritz Höger's angular and sharp-edged Chilehaus is a reminder that Expressionists also used traditional materials. A ten-story office building, it is an example of "Brick Expressionism," and features complex and exposed brick detailing and ornamentation.

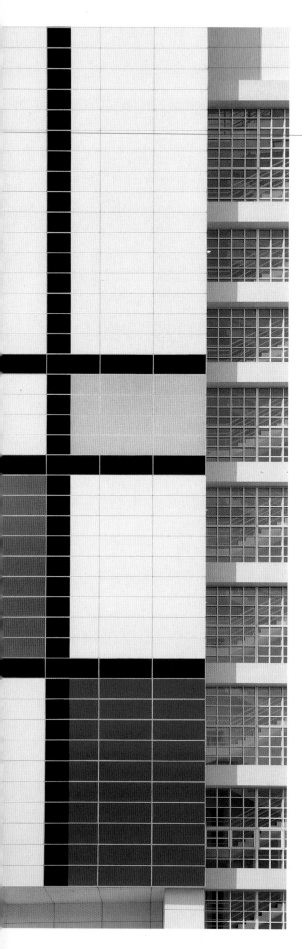

DE STIJL

A style restricted to just a few forms and a limited palette of colors, De Stijl represented an attempt to create a universal and ideal architecture by paring it down to its key elements.

De Stijl (Dutch for "The Style") was a movement founded in The Netherlands in 1917 by a group of artists and architects. Rejecting the emotive and organic style of Expressionism that was popular at the time, proponents of De Stijl aimed for simplification and abstraction. They did not regard De Stijl as merely aesthetic, but thought that simplification was the way to reach their idea of truth, stripped of anything superfluous or changing. They believed that they could create true harmony with perfect geometrical arrangements.

LINES, PLANES, AND COLOR

The guiding principles of De Stijl were deliberately restricted and simplistic. Works in the style, whether art, furniture, or architecture, were to be made up of planes and volumes that were square or rectangular, bounded by horizontal and vertical lines. These geometric forms could intersect, overlap, or be arranged in asymmetrical, grid-like patterns. Colors were also restricted. Apart from black, white, and gray, only the three primary colors (red, blue, and yellow) were to be used.

The best-known examples of De Stijl are the paintings of one of its founders, the Dutch artist Piet Mondrian. After exploring Impressionism

and Cubism for a while, Mondrian turned to geometric forms in pursuit of a utopian, spiritual idea of universality and harmony. This approach to art and design was informed by the wish for transformation and regeneration after the horrors of World War I.

SIMPLICITY AND MINIMALISM

Although there is only one building that is regarded as a true De Stijl work, the Rietveld Schröder House in Utrecht (see opposite), the style's emphasis on minimalism, proportion, and primary colors had a profound influence on Modernist architecture in the following decades, not just in the Netherlands but also further afield. The European Modernists' pursuit of machinelike, efficient functionalism agreed with De Stijl's pared-down aesthetic—they, too, believed that it was essential to simplify forms and colors in order to strip architecture down to its bare essentials.

The iconic Bauhaus style drew inspiration from De Stijl, particularly in the field of graphic design. So, too, did the International Style, a Functionalist form of Modernism spearheaded by Swiss-French architect Le Corbusier, which often incorporated De Stijl's geometric, gridded forms and use of color.

◀ **Replication of Mondrian's work**
To mark the 100th anniversary of De Stijl in 2017, the facades of Richard Meier's City Hall in The Hague were painted in the style of Piet Mondrian's *Composition* paintings, with bold rectangles of red, blue, and yellow.

A MOVEMENT IN MANY ARTS

Although its principles were perhaps best suited to paintings and works on paper, designers also explored De Stijl in many other media. They did not just experiment with it in architecture, but also applied it in innovative ways to furniture, as seen on the right in Rietveld's famous *Red and Blue Chair*. Here, he tried to accommodate the straight lines and angles of De Stijl with the demands of human ergonomics.

Red and Blue Chair, Gerrit Rietveld, c. 1919

RIETVELD SCHRÖDER HOUSE

UTRECHT, THE NETHERLANDS, 1924

Gerrit Rietveld followed De Stijl's strict rules in every detail of his Rietveld Schröder House—even the windows can only open as far as 90 degrees, a right angle. The house is considered to be the only true De Stijl building.

> "Nothing is more concrete, more real than a line, a color, a surface."
>
> Theo van Doesburg, *Art Concret*, 1930

Clean horizontal and vertical lines

The corner window on the top floor opens on both sides

Primary colors used alongside white, black, and gray

DE STIJL BUILDINGS

▲ **Café de Unie,** Rotterdam, Netherlands, 1924–1925

This café caused outrage when it first opened because its straight lines, geometric shapes, and primary-colored facade made it look so different from the more decorative neighboring buildings.

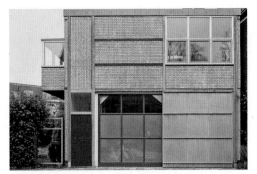

▲ **Garage mit Chauffeurswohnung,** Utrecht, Netherlands, 1927–1928

An early project by Gerrit Rietveld, this garage and apartment was designed as a prototype for an industrialized architecture. It shows the hallmark De Stijl use of geometry and color.

▲ **House Theissing,** Utrecht, Netherlands, 1958–1960

Named after its owner, House Theissing was one of many private projects by Gerrit Rietveld. Although built nearly 30 years after the official end of De Stijl, it adopted the style's colors and geometric forms.

MODERNISM

With the technical advancements allowed by coal-fired industry and a new focus on outwardly expressed functionalism, Modernism arose amid the cultural upheaval in Europe following World War I.

For Modernism's chief propagandist, Swiss-French architect Charles-Édouard Jeanneret (better known as Le Corbusier), the postwar aesthetic of fast cars, faster airplanes, and elegant ocean liners inspired an architecture of unapologetic functionalism. This new style was structurally and materially efficient, clean, technologically advanced, and unencumbered by the tired symbolism that had characterized the 19th-century "battle of the styles"—which pitted Gothic architecture against Classical.

FOSSIL-FUEL ARCHITECTURE

The age-old rules of architecture were blown away by fossil-fuel energy: concrete, steel, and glass became cheap, and powerful new central heating systems made it comfortable to have open-plan rooms, and large heat-leaking windows, even in cold winters.

In 1926, Le Corbusier outlined his "five points of modern architecture": rules for building in the fossil-fuel age. Load-bearing pilotis or a grid of columns (1) permitted the "free" placement of walls and partitions (2), while facades unencumbered by structure (3), with horizontal windows to admit more light and frame views of nature (4), were enhanced by gardens on rooftops (5). For Le Corbusier, Walter Gropius (founder of the influential Bauhaus design school), and the other architects of the Congrès Internationaux d'Architecture Moderne (CIAM), these tenets represented immutable principles that placed their work in direct opposition to the fashions of the past.

Yet despite American architect Philip Johnson canonizing the new architecture as the "International Style" at an exhibition in New York in 1932, aggressive global marketing of materials and services probably did more than architectural connoisseurship to spread the architecture of concrete, steel, and glass around the planet. As the 20th century wore on, various splinter groups developed, breaking the strict rules of the early Modernists and moving away from its puritanical style with a diversity of approaches.

FUNCTIONALISM

In his 1927 book *Toward a New Architecture*, Le Corbusier declared that "a house is a machine for living in," reflecting an ideology where architecture was no more or less than the sum of its functional parts. This notion applied at every scale—for example, the human body could be reduced to a series of precise measurements to inform the design of furniture, bathrooms, and kitchens.

The Dom-ino construction scheme used repeating modular concrete elements.

▶ **Masterclass in modernity**
The extensive glazing on the facades of the new Bauhaus school in Dessau, Germany, symbolized modernity and openness, but it leaked heat so badly that the pipes froze even when the heating was on.

"The new times demand their own expression."
Walter Gropius, 1913

VILLA MAIREA

NOORMARKKU, FINLAND, 1938–1941

Supportive of Alvar Aalto's design philosophy, which sought to reconcile Modernism with the landscape and environment of Finland, Maire and Harry Gullichsen asked the Finnish architect to treat the design of their summer house, Villa Mairea, as a personal design experiment. The result is a domestic retreat that invites the forest into the interior.

Villa Mairea

◄ Bringing the outside in

Villa Mairea's entrance canopy is split into two levels, admitting horizontal light like layers of cloud. Small circular windows framed in bronze form part of the door and reflect the dappled light into the interior.

◄ Warm welcome

A dominant feature of the living area, the fireplace evokes the comfort of the traditional domestic hearth. The shape of the white plaster surround alludes to the curtain-like forms of the Northern Lights (aurora borealis).

Front view

Chimney for one of five fireplaces in the villa

Large, angled bay windows project from facade

Timber facades of teak and Finnish pine on some parts of the exterior

Slate used on some lower sections of the building

Asymmetrical entrance porch with projecting canopy

Thin wooden poles emulate the forest surrounding the villa

Rear view

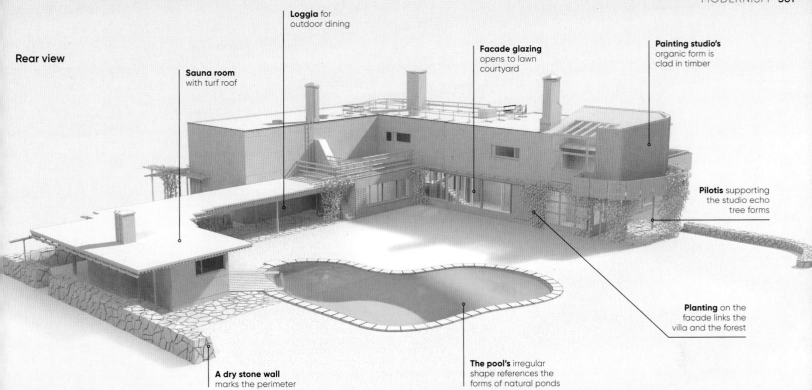

Loggia for
outdoor dining

Sauna room
with turf roof

Facade glazing
opens to lawn
courtyard

Painting studio's
organic form is
clad in timber

Pilotis supporting
the studio echo
tree forms

Planting on the
facade links the
villa and the forest

The pool's irregular
shape references the
forms of natural ponds

A dry stone wall
marks the perimeter

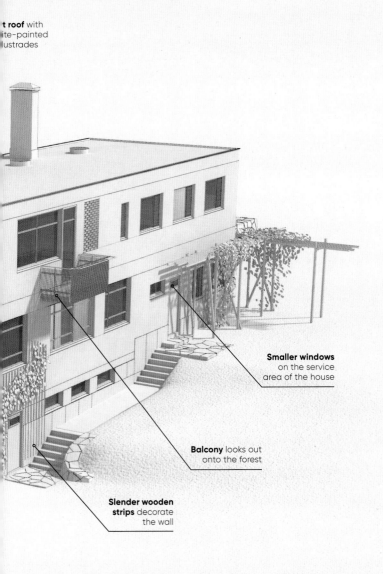

t roof with
te-painted
ustrades

Smaller windows
on the service
area of the house

Balcony looks out
onto the forest

**Slender wooden
strips** decorate
the wall

◄ Forest steps
The clusters of vertical
poles lining the staircase
mirror and exaggerate
the vertical lines of the
birch forest outside. The
bottom tread is larger
than the rest, hovering
above the tiled floor as
an invitation to ascend.

"We should work to make
things simple, good, and
without decoration, things
that are in harmony with
the human being..."

Alvar Aalto, speech to RIBA (Royal Institute of British Architects), 1957

KEY **ELEMENTS**

The early Modernists were concerned with codifying an appropriate set of rules that would set the new architecture apart from the stylistic confusion of the 19th century. Over time, this grew to include its own idiomatic motifs, such as organic sculptural forms cast in concrete, and exposed steelwork.

FORM FOLLOWS FUNCTION

Rather than focusing on external appearance as an end in itself, Modernist architects believed that an authentic form could be derived from a building's internal functional arrangement. They rejected ornamentation in favor of a more direct expression of construction and exposed material finishes.

▼ Artful form
Frank Lloyd Wright conceived of the journey through the Guggenheim Museum as a continuous ramp for viewing art. The resulting concrete helical (spiral) form overlooks Fifth Avenue in New York.

▼ Centre stage
At Helsinki University of Technology in Finland, Alvar Aalto used the shape of the red brick and copper-clad auditorium to create a distinctive landmark and amphitheater at the center of the parkland campus.

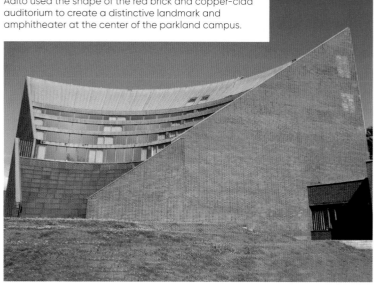

FACADE AS SKIN

Modernist architects treated the facade as the skin of a building, admitting light and air, and conserving heat or coolness. Wall to wall glazing permitted wide views and projected an image of modernity, realized by the seemingly limitless availability of fossil-fuel energy powering air conditioning and electric light.

◄ Sunshade
Completed in 1943, the new Ministry of Education by Lúcio Costa was the first Modernist building in Brazil. Its north elevation is covered with a concrete screen of fins, known as a brise-soleil, to protect the glass facade from the heat of the sun.

FREE-PLAN SPACE

The Dom-ino system of a grid of concrete columns made Le Corbusier's *plan libre* (free plan) possible, so the placement of interior furniture and partitions was unimpeded by vertical structure. Some architects took the idea further, moving the columns to the outside to create truly open-plan spaces within.

◀ See-through

Philip Johnson's Glass House in Connecticut frames landscape views through its structural steel facade. The "rooms" are defined only by furniture and screens, with the exception of the brick bathroom and fireplace.

▼ Exoskeleton

Mies van der Rohe used steel girders on the roof of Crown Hall, at the Illinois Institute of Technology in Chicago, instead of interior columns. The space, lit by large, high windows, is an apt studio for trainee architects.

USE OF MATERIALS

The Modern Movement made no apology for the utilitarian use of mass-produced industrial materials such as concrete, steel, and brick. These materials were cheap and plentiful, and enabled rapid construction.

▲ Concrete construction

The National Assembly of Bangladesh is built in gray concrete, with bands of white marble that catch the light and emphasize the pattern of the form. Triangular, circular, and rectangular openings puncture the facade, revealing the human activity within.

▲ Ship-like form

Le Corbusier's prototype residential community, Unité d'Habitation, floats above the French landscape, with stacked duplex apartments interlocking around central "streets" or corridors. The roof (shown here) is given over to leisure.

INFLUENCE ON URBAN DESIGN

From Le Corbusier's radical proposal to rebuild central Paris, France, with a series of cruciform towers, to his design for a new city at Chandigarh, India, to Oscar Niemeyer's design for Brasília, Brazil, the language of Modernism—concrete slab blocks, towers, and "streets in the sky"—would go on to influence the design of cities around the world. The new cities made provision for the rapidly rising number of cars.

Brasília became Brazil's capital in 1960, after it was built from scratch to a radical urban plan featuring Modernist buildings.

MODERNIST BUILDINGS

Outstanding works of the Modern Movement translated its utopian ideals—the improvement of society—into buildings that promised a better future to those who lived and worked in them.

1

3

2

1. Barcelona Pavilion
Barcelona, Spain, 1929 (rebuilt 1986)

Designed as a temporary pavilion for the 1929 International Exhibition, the intersecting planes of polished marble, onyx, travertine, and reflecting pools of water combined to erase traditional boundaries between inside and out.

2. Seagram Building
New York City, NY, 1958

Mies van der Rohe's corporate masterwork is clad in bronze and steel mullions, with a public plaza fronting Park Avenue. Its groundbreaking indoor climate-control technology includes air conditioning and luminous ceilings.

3. Paimio Sanatorium
Paimio, Finland, 1932

The curved lines of Alvar Aalto's sanatorium for the treatment of tuberculosis reveal a familiar Modernist nautical influence. The bedrooms face south, as do the sun terraces at the end of the wing, which were originally open-air.

4

4. Engineering Building
University of Leicester, UK, 1963

On a constrained site, James Stirling and James Gowan turned functionalism into a personal aesthetic of red brick, tile, and patent glazing. The workshops are topped by prism-shaped rooflights designed to catch the north light.

5. Palace of Assembly
Chandigarh, India, 1963

Marrying the everyday and the extraordinary, Le Corbusier's parliament building has a columned courtyard with brise-soleil-lined offices and a portico on the outside, and a chamber like a cooling tower in the center.

5

6

7

6. National Congress of Brazil
Brasília, Brazil, 1960

Brazil's two legislative chambers sit on either side of the twin administrative tower blocks in Oscar Niemeyer's expression of democracy: the Senate under the inverted bowl, and the Chamber of Deputies under the larger dish.

7. Phillips Exeter Academy Library
Exeter, New Hampshire, 1972

For Louis Kahn, the story of a library was the journey of a book to the light. A top-lit central atrium orients the reader among the bookshelves; from there, books can be taken to the oak reading desks on the facade.

VILLA SAVOYE

POISSY, FRANCE, 1929–1931

One of the pivotal designs of the great Swiss-French architect Le Corbusier, the Villa Savoye was commissioned by the Savoye family as a weekend country retreat, not far from Paris. It celebrates the use of fossil fuels in architecture.

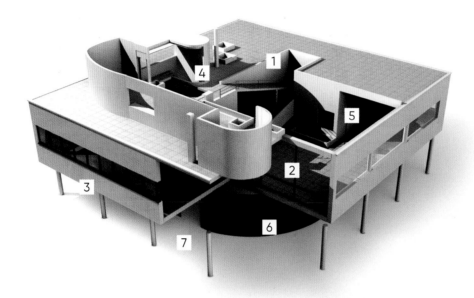

1

2

3

1. Ramp to the roof
As well as stairs, the main levels of the villa can be reached via gently sloping ramps that cut through the house and open up interesting views. This one leads up toward the roof terrace at the top of the building.

2. Internal space
One area of the house flows seamlessly into the other, without solid dividing walls. This kind of open plan was made possible by powerful central heating—fireplaces require enclosed rooms.

3. Strip windows
Large strip windows provide fine uninterrupted views in all directions from the main rooms. The walls above them appear to have no visible support as the weight is borne by the pilotis (narrow pillars) beneath.

4. Spiral staircase
The white curves of the skillfully molded concrete stairs are thrown into relief by black rails and uprights. They reflect the color scheme that runs throughout the villa, where dark doors and window frames form a contrast to the plain white walls.

5. Living area
The main living room is uncluttered and connects seamlessly with part of the roof garden by means of a full-height glass wall and a sliding screen of glass. Abundant fossil fuels were used in the glass's manufacture and in warming the space, given its rapid heat loss.

6. Service room
The curved glass facade of the ground floor contains rooms for the chauffeur and maid, and the garage. The paved area beneath the main house was exactly the right curvature for the owner's car—a 1927 Citroën—to be driven around.

7. Clean, uncluttered lines
The plain, unadorned pilotis leave open space beneath the building for a central block containing the maintenance and service rooms of the villa. The living areas are on the floor above the pilotis.

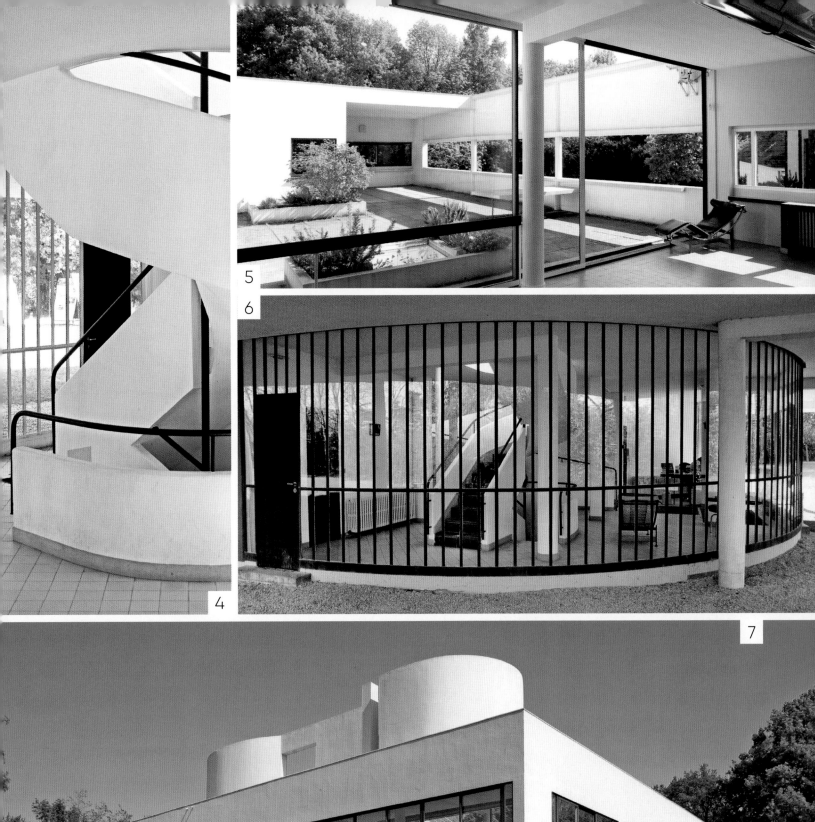

ART DECO

The bold geometry and decoration of Art Deco began in the theater sets and design of 19th-century France and became synonymous with the glamour of America's Roaring Twenties.

Art Deco emerged in the first decade of the 20th century, when it was becoming clear that the historical styles of architecture could not keep up with the pace and scale of change brought about by fossil-fuel-powered industrialization. New York skyscrapers looked silly in ill-fitting historical costumes, and the rushing technology of elevators, cars, and electric lighting brought new possibilities to architecture. Art Deco sought new images for the thrilling new world, drawing on everything from new materials and new art movements to the excitement over fresh archaeological finds in Egypt and Mesoamerica.

MODERN OPTIMISM
Art Deco grew in popularity as it optimistically built on the past rather than rejecting it, and embraced new materials and construction methods—in particular, reinforced concrete. For example, the Théâtre des Champs-Élysées in Paris, designed in 1913 by Auguste Perret, used reinforced concrete to create a strikingly plain form decorated with sculptural reliefs that drew

on Greek myths. This was a stark departure from the highly fluid and organic style of Art Nouveau, which was still at its peak in France.

Emerging as a symbol of progress and luxury during the great age of American skyscraper design, Art Deco was also embraced by those looking to make a bold mark on the skyline. At first, it occupied the glamorous new worlds with which it is still synonymous: movie theaters, hotels, and first-class travel. But part of the style's optimism about social progress was that beauty should not be confined to the privileged few, so it soon appeared everywhere from apartment buildings to industrial warehouses as a means of elevating the everyday.

GLOBAL INFLUENCE
Art Deco flourished in Europe and the US during the 1920s and '30s. However, the rise of the International Style in Europe, with its standardized, ornament-free design, and the Great Depression in the US saw Art Deco become more subdued, and its dominance ended with World War II. Nevertheless, it found popularity around the world as a symbol of modernity and progress without the cultural baggage of other architectural styles. Far from simply adopting Western designs, Art Deco often fused with local architectural traditions. As a result, by the mid 20th century it had become one of the first truly international styles.

◀ **Inspired by nature**
Designed by Claud Beelman in 1930, the Eastern Columbia Building is an Art Deco landmark of Los Angeles. Its entrance, as well as much of its exterior, is adorned with highly stylized sunburst and nature motifs in gold and blue terra-cotta.

DECORATIVE ARTS
In 1875, the French government gave craftspeople such as furniture makers, jewelers, and glass workers the official status of "artist," marking a new golden age for the decorative arts. In 1925, the Exposition Internationale des Arts Décoratifs et Industriels Modernes was held in Paris—and it is from this event that Art Deco derived its name. The Expo celebrated not just architecture, but modern design in everything from housewares and fashion to lighting and sculpture.

A wall lamp on the Bacardi Building in Havana shows how Art Deco buildings were often total works of art.

CHRYSLER BUILDING

NEW YORK CITY, NY, 1928–1930

Designed by William Van Alen for the automobile pioneer Walter Chrysler, the Chrysler Building was the tallest building in the world for almost a year after it was completed in 1930. The 77-story tower reaches 1,047 ft (319 m) up into Manhattan's skyline. This was thanks to a late addition during construction— a dazzling spire with a metallic sunburst-patterned crown, all clad in recently trademarked Nirosta stainless steel.

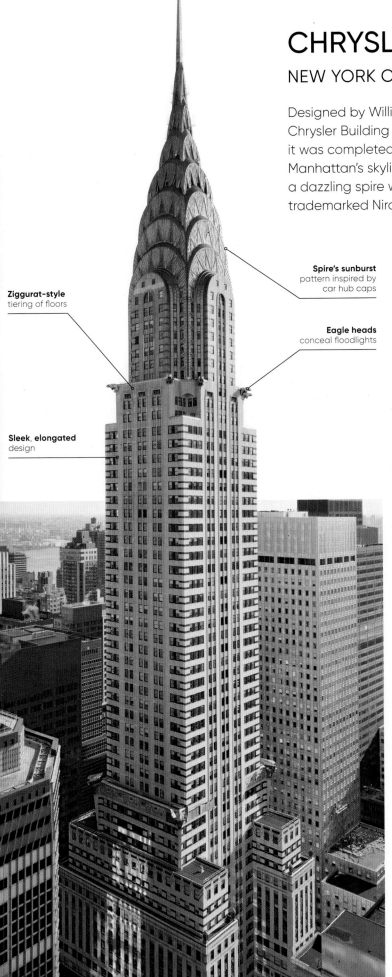

Ziggurat-style tiering of floors

Sleek, elongated design

Spire's sunburst pattern inspired by car hub caps

Eagle heads conceal floodlights

▲ **Automobile motifs**
On the tower's exterior, traditional forms of ornamentation were adapted with motifs from cars, such as hub caps and the winged hood ornaments used on Chrysler cars at the time.

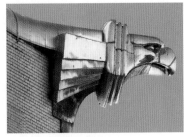

▲ **American gargoyles**
Making reference to the gargoyles typically used to decorate Gothic cathedrals, the tower's 61st floor features a series of projecting metal eagle ornaments that proudly reference America's national bird.

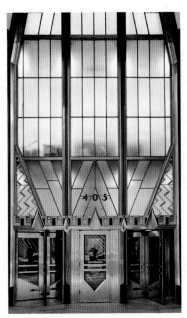

▲ **Geometric glazing**
The grand entrance to the tower is declared by a large area of symmetrical, geometric glazing with chevron and zigzag motifs, typical of Art Deco patterning. A decorative metal frieze separates the glazing from the doors below.

"It quickly became the symbol of big city glamour, excitement, and style."

David Stravitz, *The Chrysler Building*, 2002

KEY **ELEMENTS**

Since it evolved in different countries, Art Deco became highly eclectic and varied, but its designs were united by a core set of visual motifs. These cues, in particular the use of bold, repeating geometric patterns, made the style instantly recognizable, not just in architecture but across art and design.

STRAIGHT LINES

Art Deco's use of straight lines and geometric shapes was informed by avant-garde movements in the arts, such as Cubism. As well as creating a building's underlying form, these straight lines and sharp edges were also incorporated into sculptural reliefs, ornamentation, and patterns to create complex, multilayered facades.

▲ Classical influence
The India Assurance Building in Mumbai uses Classical influences and straight lines to grand effect, with monumental columns; ribs; and large, sword-bearing sentinels.

◄ Nautical influence
At the Musée de la Mer aquarium in France, a feeling of verticality is emphasized by narrow slits and glazing in the angled section above the entrance, which protrudes like the prow of a ship.

THE ART DECO CAPITAL

After New Zealand's devastating earthquake in 1931, architects working on Napier's reconstruction used numerous styles, but none was more prevalent than Art Deco. Such a high concentration of this architecture prompted Napier to be known as the "Art Deco Capital of the World." Designers often drew on Indigenous traditions to produce Art Deco styles with a local twist, so in New Zealand, Art Deco motifs were interwoven with Māori adaptations, along with Egyptian, Aztec, and Maya designs.

Māori-inspired kōwhaiwhai patterns in plaster decorate Napier's ASB Bank

"No more poverty, no more ignorance, no more disease. Art Deco reflected that confidence, vigor, and optimism."

Robert McGregor, *Art Deco Architecture*, 2010

CURVED LINES

The sleek, aerodynamic forms of cutting-edge cars, planes, and ocean liners were a rich source of visual inspiration for Art Deco. The approach was so popular that it gave rise to a later sub-style called Streamline Moderne, which typically favored plainer, curving forms over excessive decoration.

◀ Curved walls

The Hoover company's factory in London was elevated with color and ornament with the intention of improving the lives of its workers.

▲ Circular details

The Cassis apartment building in France features simple facades with porthole windows and curving, ocean-liner-style balconies.

ORNAMENTATION

While some early Modernist architects believed that architecture had outgrown decoration, Art Deco embraced it wholeheartedly. The plain geometric surfaces of its buildings created a blank canvas for conveying a sense of glamour, luxury, and progress through both historic and modern motifs.

▲ Ancient Egypt

The discovery of Tutankhamen's tomb in 1922 sparked a trend for ancient Egyptian motifs. Sunbursts, lotus flowers, eagles, and gods abounded, as on the Egyptian Theatre in DeKalb, Illinois.

▲ Mesoamerica

450 Sutter Street in San Francisco is indicative of the influence of the exoticism of Mesoamerica on Art Deco, which was popularized through archaeological discoveries.

▲ A stylized natural world

Rather than mimicking the organic forms of nature, Art Deco's plants and animals were highly stylized, as seen in the symmetrical bird pattern on the Marine Building in Vancouver.

▲ Geometric shapes

The geometric metal screens on the Parkview Square offices in Singapore are typical of the interlocking, repeating patterns of much Art Deco design.

ART DECO BUILDINGS

As Art Deco spread, it proved an adaptable style. While some designers explored stripped-back geometric forms, others embraced luxurious ornamentation and color.

1. Fiat Tagliero Building
Asmara, Eritrea, 1938

This gas station, built under the Italian colonial occupation of Eritrea, expresses the excitement many felt for the new technologies of oil, evoking ships and airplanes in its form.

2. Cincinnati Union Terminus
Cincinnati, Ohio, 1933

The plain, geometric exterior of this train station conceals a vast rotunda ceiling in gold above the main concourse. Around the base of the striking ceiling is a colorful mural depicting industrial workers.

3. Art Deco hotels
Miami, Florida, 1930s

As affordable air conditioning made Florida's humidity livable, Miami boomed. South Beach was transformed with rows of colorful hotels designed in a stripped back, Streamline Moderne style of Art Deco.

4. Café Groppi
Cairo, Egypt, 1925

Designed for the Swiss chef Giacomo Groppi, Café Groppi in Cairo's Talaat Harb Square features an almost Classical exterior, with clean lines and a "crowning" top story. The entrance way is decorated with intricate mosaic tiling.

5. Eastern Columbia Building
Los Angeles, California, 1930

With a stepped form that leads up to a "crown" at the building's peak, this apartment building, clad in turquoise and gold terra-cotta, represented a luxurious vision of Los Angeles living.

5

6 7

6. Central Market
Phnom Penh, Cambodia, 1937

Phnom Penh's boldly colored, stepped central market was a key part of modernizing and expanding the city to cope with a large increase in population in the 1930s. A central dome lined with stepped openings evokes a historic temple.

7. Masonic Hotel
Napier, New Zealand, 1932

Colorful glazed letters on a grand canopy announce the name of this Art Deco hotel. Along one side of the building, pergolas reference the hotel that had stood on the site until it was destroyed in the 1931 Napier earthquake.

▲ **Monumental style**
Built for the 1936 Olympic Games in Berlin, the vast Olympic Stadium was an architectural propaganda project for the Nazis, which embodied all the hallmarks of Stripped Classicism.

STRIPPED CLASSICISM

Long schooled in Classical architecture, many European architects of the early 20th century responded to the turn away from ornament by simplifying classicism rather than abandoning it.

Incorporating the motifs and proportions of Classical architecture, Stripped Classicism rose to prominence in the 1920s and '30s. As the name suggests, decorative features such as moldings, ornament, and other details were stripped away, leaving only a starkly simplified version of recognizable Classical forms. This austere version of Classicism was used by totalitarian and democratic regimes alike, often for expressions of political, military, or civic authority. It was frequently employed by governments to design official buildings, war memorials, and utility works.

Throughout history, Classical architects have experimented with ways to reduce ornament for both aesthetic and economic purposes. The origins of Stripped Classicism lie in the work of Neoclassical architects from the late 18th and early 19th centuries, such as Étienne-Louis Boullée, John Soane, and Karl Friedrich Schinkel. With its pared-down yet still familiar

> "Architecture is a sort of oratory of power by means of forms."
>
> Frederick Nietzsche, *Twilight of the Idols*, 1888

Classical imagery, Stripped Classicism was developed in parallel with early Modernism. It reflected a more conservative response to the unsettling forces of modernization in the interwar years, and became the default style for institutional buildings around the world.

EARLY PIONEERS

An early example of Stripped Classicism in Europe was the Embassy of Germany in St. Petersburg, designed by Peter Behrens in 1912. French-American architect Paul Philippe Cret was another leading proponent, and the style flourished across the US in the 1930s, marking a fresh start under President Roosevelt's New Deal—a set of measures designed to combat the impact of the Great Depression.

Stripped Classicism took hold in Europe in the 1930s, attracting the totalitarian regimes of Germany, Italy, and Soviet Russia. The Zeppelin Field near Nuremberg, designed by Hitler's architect Albert Speer, used Classical elements in tandem with modern technology, such as lighting and sound, to choreograph grandiose political and military spectacles. Adopting the architecture of Stripped Classicism meant such regimes could invoke the power of modernity to represent an idealized future, while reinventing the past. Following World War II, the style fell out of favor and, though briefly revived during the 1960s, it still has contentious associations.

EXTREME REGIMES

In the 1930s, totalitarian regimes across Europe, from Nazi Germany and Fascist Italy to Stalin's Soviet Union, used Stripped Classicism as the approved style for government buildings. As an embodiment of Western Classical civilization, its pared-down features suggested modernity and progress, while its often vast scale was calculated to intimidate, typified by Zeppelin Field, used for Nazi rallies in Nuremberg.

Stripped Classicism forms an ominous backdrop to a Nazi rally at Zeppelin Field.

PALAZZO DELLA CIVILTÀ ITALIANA

ROME, ITALY, 1938–1943

Known as the "Square Colosseum," the Palazzo della Civiltà Italiana was conceived by Fascist leader Benito Mussolini as the centerpiece of Esposizione Universale Roma (EUR), a new suburban district in Rome designed to host the subsequently aborted 1942 World's Fair and celebrate 20 years of Fascism.

▲ Facade
Polished travertine stone used in ancient Roman architecture clads the concrete structure. A "seamless" facade was contrived to make the building seem as if it was made of solid stone.

► Inscription
An excerpt from a speech by Mussolini glorifying the Italian people is inscribed on all four sides of the building.

▲ Arched form
The repeated arches were inspired by the Roman Colosseum, indicating Mussolini's romanticized vision of Classical civilization. His architects used them to create a powerful symbol of authority.

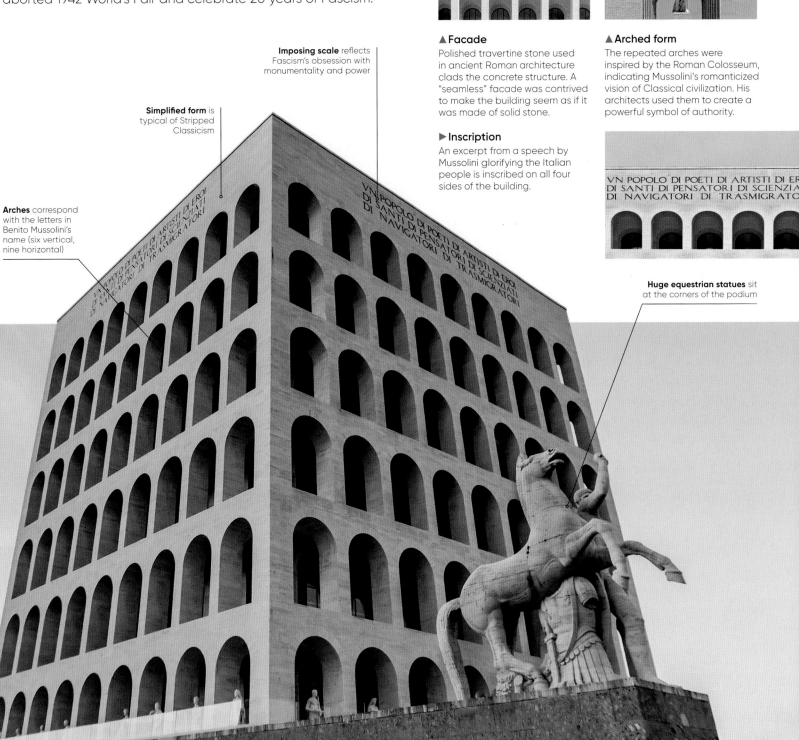

Imposing scale reflects Fascism's obsession with monumentality and power

Simplified form is typical of Stripped Classicism

Arches correspond with the letters in Benito Mussolini's name (six vertical, nine horizontal)

VN POPOLO DI POETI DI ARTISTI DI EROI DI SANTI DI PENSATORI DI SCIENZIATI DI NAVIGATORI DI TRASMIGRATORI

Huge equestrian statues sit at the corners of the podium

KEY ELEMENTS

Through the use of overscale, repetitive elements, austere detailing, and monumental facing materials such as stone, Stripped Classicism cultivated a sense of timelessness and permanence.

FACADES

Based on Classical proportions and symmetry, facades were typically plain and formal, with decoration and ornament removed or pared-down. The scale of buildings was generally monumental in order to convey civic or military authority, or, in more extreme cases, to instill a sense of disquiet.

▲ **Symmetrical facade**
Designed by Stripped Classicism pioneer Paul Philippe Cret, the Federal Reserve Board Building in Washington, D.C., boasts a rigorously symmetrical and sparsely detailed facade. Clad in white Georgia marble, it is typical of Cret's late work.

▲ **Golden ratio**
The facade of Casa del Fascio, Como, Italy, is based on the "golden ratio," when a form divides into a rectangle and a square that will combine to establish a ratio of 1:1.61.

MATERIALS

Traditional materials gave a sense of solidity, gravitas, and permanence. Marble and stone were sculpted and carved in bas relief, or augmented with uplifting inscriptions. Metal and glass were used more sparingly as visual and functional counterpoints, adding subtle details to facades.

▲ **Solid stone**
The Parliament of Finland building in Helsinki was designed by Johan Sigfrid Sirén. Kalvola Red granite was used to clad the building, giving it a feeling of weight and authority befitting a national parliament. Fourteen columns with Corinthian capitals are symmetrically arranged along the main facade.

▲ **Metal details**
Built on Hitler's orders in 1936 by architect Werner March, the Olympic Stadium in Berlin, Germany, exemplified Stripped Classicism, with metal Olympic rings hung from a pair of stone pylons. Metal was often used to emphasize features, but they tended to be understated, in keeping with the spirit of asceticism.

▲ **Bas-relief sculpture**
An American eagle sculpted by Alfred-Alphonse Bottiau forms the colossal centerpiece of Château-Thierry American Monument in Aisne, France—a World War I memorial for American servicemen. The sober symbolism worked into the stone in bas-relief is intended to be timeless and enduring.

STRIPPED CLASSICISM BUILDINGS

Despite its political popularity with tyrannical regimes, the simple forms and motifs of Stripped Classicism proved a versatile style for a range of civic buildings, including libraries, power stations, and war memorials.

1. Olympic Stadium
Berlin, Germany, 1936

Conceived by Hitler as a space for sporting spectacles in the manner of a Roman arena, the Olympic Stadium in Berlin embodied both the architectural and political tenets of the Nazi regime. It has since been remodeled as an athletics and football stadium.

2. Stockholm Public Library
Stockholm, Sweden, 1928

Dominated by a cylindrical volume containing a rotunda, the library's combination of pure geometric forms and unadorned exterior won international admiration. It reflected architect Gunnar Asplund's interest in synthesizing Neoclassical and modern elements in a major civic building.

3. Bankside Power Station
London, UK, 1952

Stripped Classicism gave powerful expression to the huge scale and modernizing ambitions of utility buildings, such as power stations. Containing 4.2 million bricks, Bankside was a streamlined "cathedral of power" on the Thames waterfront, generating electricity for London. It was converted into the Tate Modern in the 1990s.

4. Thiepval Memorial
Thiepval, France, 1932

Commemorating more than 72,000 missing servicemen who died in the Battle of the Somme, this monument by British architect Sir Edwin Lutyens is based on a series of interlocking memorial arches. Constructed from brick and Portland stone, it rises majestically over the French countryside.

MID-CENTURY MODERN

The abstract symbols and sculptural forms of mid-century design anticipated a bright and airy future, where ever-cheaper oil powered new technologies to bring every comfort and convenience.

As the austere concrete, steel, and glass of European Modernism became the new norm rather than the exception, wealthy patrons in the US sought architects who could offer a more optimistic vision—one that reflected the economic prosperity and optimism prevailing in the decades following World War II. The influence of Scandinavia was never far away: the work of architects like Alvar Aalto and Arne Jacobsen, which showed empathy for the needs of ordinary people, resonated more with the mid-20th-century American psyche of liberal individualism than the continental European form-follows-function approach. With an emphasis on low-level lighting, organic forms, and materials evocative of the natural world, this new architectural language was glamorous and optimistic.

THE NEW MODERNISTS

Finnish-American Eero Saarinen was the son of architect Eliel Saarinen, first dean of the United States' influential Cranbrook Academy of Art in Michigan. Eero's innovative use of plastic, precast concrete, and stainless steel to form sweeping parabolic curves ensured that his designs, from armchairs to airport terminals, presaged the high-tech future he envisaged. In his design for a new terminal at John F. Kennedy International Airport (JFK) in New York, Saarinen interpreted the sensation of flying as a pair of reinforced concrete shells resembling

a pair of wings taking to the air. Other Mid-Century Modern pioneers, like husband and wife Charles and Ray Eames, sought to make good design more accessible. Their bold designs, influenced by contemporary abstract art, were both practical and relatively economical to reproduce, making use of prefabricated components and new materials such as fiberglass and molded plywood.

The translation of Modernist principles into consumer product was particularly evident in the Case Study House Program, sponsored by *Arts & Architecture* magazine, which ran from 1945 until 1966. Featuring houses designed by Richard Neutra, Charles and Ray Eames, Eero Saarinen, Craig Ellwood, and Pierre Koenig, this project grew out of an idealistic vision to develop prototype affordable family housing. Perhaps inevitably, the results often had more in common with one-off luxury villas than realistic models that might be replicated. Nonetheless, the houses were immortalized as icons of postwar American culture.

Mid-Century Modern was an architecture of excess. The glass walls that blurred the boundaries between inside and outside characterized many examples and relied upon advances in building servicing, from air conditioning to electric light. But in the land of plenty that was mid-century America, the energy required was cheap and abundant.

◀ **Soaring vision**
Saarinen's vision for the new Trans World Airlines terminal at JFK was one of unconfined spaces flowing from exterior to interior, where clear sight lines and ease of movement mirrored the exciting possibilities opened up by trans-continental aviation.

EAMES HOUSE

SANTA MONICA, CALIFORNIA, 1949

Charles and Ray Eames's home, also known as Case Study House No. 8, was an attempt to apply the logic of assembly not only to the design of a building, but also to the organization of daily life. In Charles's words, the house was designed to be "a natural product of the business of life itself."

▲ Natural contrast

A backdrop of eucalyptus trees softens the light and fragments the geometric make up of the facade. Nature is also reflected on the interior, where the rear wall of the living room, running on to the south-facing terrace, is lined in eucalyptus wood.

▲ Efficient structural details

The naval-ladder-like staircase demonstrates the "honest" use of materials (based on their properties) and the potential of prefabricated lightweight components, reflecting the assembly-line production process of cars and aircraft.

▲ Panel pattern

The main elevations are made up of steel-framed glass and insulated fiberboard panels, arranged in a geometric abstract composition like a Piet Mondrian canvas. Sliding panels of translucent plastic afford shade and privacy.

SIMPLE STRUCTURE

The 200-ft- (60-m-) long site was excavated into a slope behind a row of eucalyptus trees, embedding the house in its natural setting. The ground slab and retaining wall are constructed from reinforced concrete, onto which two-story steel frames were erected to support the walls and roof. The main structural elements were assembled on site in a single day, highlighting the advantages of using prefabricated materials.

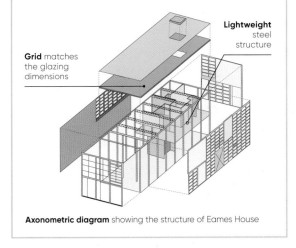

Lightweight steel structure

Grid matches the glazing dimensions

Axonometric diagram showing the structure of Eames House

Eucalyptus trees provide shade for the house

Living area opens out onto a sheltered, south-facing terrace

Thin walls and extensive glazing make underfloor heating ducts essential

Colored panels reflect contemporary abstract art

The structure is expressed on the facade

KEY **ELEMENTS**

Mid-Century Modern buildings are characterized by abundance—of materials, energy, and resources. To those who could afford it, this architectural style was the future.

FREE EXPRESSIONIST FORM

Away from the postwar austerity and demand for rapid reconstruction that prevailed in Europe's major economies, architects like Eero Saarinen were able to exploit the full potential of new materials and innovative engineering techniques to create more original architectural forms.

ARTIFICIAL LIGHT

Transparency by day was to be complemented by better illumination at night. A ready supply of cheap energy, along with more profligate use of expensive materials and fittings, encouraged architects to pay more attention to the design of elegant interior lighting.

▲ **Tentlike terminal**
At Dulles International Airport, Saarinen used concrete to form skeletal-shaped columns and billowing roof shells, like a vast nomadic tent. Passengers arrived under the canopy by car, then were transported to the aircraft in "mobile lounges."

◀ **Reflecting light**
Poul Henningsen's Artichoke pendant light hangs in the lobby of Arne Jacobsen's SAS hotel in Copenhagen, Denmark. Henningsen and Jacobsen were employed by Danish manufacturer Louis Poulsen to design a series of glare-free lamps to direct light more purposefully.

INTERIOR DESIGN

An important feature of Mid-Century Modern architecture is the continuity of design, from building elements—such as walls lined in timber, or polished stone—to the interior design of furniture and textiles.

▲ **Show home**
Craig Ellwood's Bobertz House, in California, is as much a furniture showroom as a house, with its redwood walls, cork floor, concrete block fireplace, white shiplap ceiling, and hanging pendant lamps.

▲ **Perfect fit**
White marble walls washed with toplighting, floating ceilings, planes of glass extending the interior to the garden; Saarinen's signature tulip table and chair set befit his design for the Miller family, in Indiana.

▲ **Bold prints**
The striking shapes and colors of mid-century exteriors were echoed by the textiles within, such as those printed by Marimekko, a Finnish company founded in 1951 by Viljo and Armi Ratia.

MID-CENTURY MODERN BUILDINGS

From the Case Study House Program to Saarinen's airport terminals, Mid-Century Modern buildings are exceptional for their individualism, mirroring the sociopolitical context of mid-century America.

1. Kaufmann House
Palm Springs, California, 1946

Hovering roof planes are juxtaposed against the rugged desert landscape of Palm Springs. The facade slides away, opening up to a manicured lawn and pool. Vertical aluminum fins reflect the desert sun into the interior, giving architect Richard Neutra's framing of views and space a cinematic quality.

2. Gateway Arch
St. Louis, Missouri, 1965

Designed by Eero Saarinen in 1948, this polished, stainless steel parabolic arch is 630 ft (192 m) high, opening to the western sky. The profile of the monument reflects the weather and sunlight, appearing almost as an ephemeral vision in the landscape.

3. United Nations Headquarters
New York, NY, 1951

Officially designed by a committee including architects from 10 different countries, the UN Secretariat and General Assembly most closely resemble the original designs of Brazilian architect Oscar Niemeyer, though the omnipresent Le Corbusier would claim principle authorship.

4. Stahl House
Los Angeles, California, 1960

In Pierre Koenig's iconic stage set for the Hollywood high life, a swimming pool floats over the city below, and the lights of the city are reflected in the all-glass walls of the partly cantilevered pavilion. An open fireplace in the center of the plan counteracts the cool night air.

CRITICAL REGIONALISM

With the rise of Modernism, some architects sought to combine the latest building methods with traditional materials and crafted details, acknowledging the unique qualities of landscape and cultural context.

The architects who favored the approach that became known as Critical Regionalism embraced Modernism's new technology, but they rejected the globalized, universal approach described as the "International Style." The Modernist architect Le Corbusier (see p.298) regarded the building as like a machine, but Critical Regionalists thought of architecture as a social habitat. Critical Regionalism was not intended to be a collage or pastiche of older architecture. It engaged with modern processes of construction and the benefits of industrial production while stressing the importance of creativity, a building's purpose, and location.

ARCHITECTURE OF PLACE

Critical Regionalist architects adopted lessons from vernacular building traditions. They sought to reflect a deeper understanding of regional landscapes and climates, preferring architectural solutions that worked in harmony with the local environment rather than against it. The characteristics of any particular site provided Critical Regionalist architects with an opportunity to root a structure in its context. They considered the approach to a building

or the view from its windows as ways of extending a person's architectural experience of both a building and its surrounding area. Central to this approach was consideration of the local climate, so that buildings would respond daily to the light and seasonally to the weather. As well as creating meaningful engagement with the landscape, it meant that buildings were less dependent on energy-hungry mechanical heating, ventilation, cooling, and lighting.

REGIONAL VARIATION

Critical Regionalism encouraged architects and builders to collaborate on an equal footing, and it also celebrated personal expression. Architects such as Carlo Scarpa, Mario Botta, Sverre Fehn, and Álvaro Siza Vieira assimilated and reinterpreted western Modernism to ensure the continuity of regional building culture. Other architects, including Egyptian Hassan Fathy, Mexican Luis Barragán, Sri Lankan Geoffrey Bawa, and Indian Charles Correa, sought to adapt the lessons of Modernism to the unique vernacular building traditions and climates of their own communities.

◀ **A sense of place**
In his 1962 Nordic Pavilion for the Venice Biennale, Norwegian Sverre Fehn used two layers of 2½in (6cm) concrete beams to bring the atmosphere of a misty Scandinavian sky to the Mediterranean.

A CRITIQUE OF GLOBAL CULTURE

The theorist Kenneth Frampton defined Critical Regionalism as "an architecture of resistance," in opposition to the placelessness he perceived in the Modern movement and Postmodern reactions to it. In response to what the philosopher Paul Ricoeur termed "universal civilization," Frampton called for the creation of "a place-oriented culture" that would prioritize physical context, climate, light, and form above abstract symbolism or aesthetics.

The Jawahar Kala Kendra Arts Center in Jaipur echoes the tiered form of an Indian stepwell.

BOA NOVA TEAHOUSE
LEÇA DA PALMEIRA, PORTO, PORTUGAL, 1963

The Atlantic coast north of Porto forms the dramatic backdrop to the Boa Nova Teahouse by local architect Álvaro Siza Vieira. The restaurant is approached by white, stone-clad steps and platforms that are cast into the surrounding rocks.

▲ **Framing the horizon**
Horizontal windows frame the ocean views, and projecting eaves lined in red afzelia wood extend the interior into the landscape while shielding diners from the bright afternoon sky.

The terra-cotta roof reflects local vernacular construction

Clerestory windows admit daylight and frame views of the horizon

A concrete plinth is embedded within the rocky outcrop

Projecting eaves form sheltered thresholds to the landscape

CRITICAL REGIONALIST BUILDINGS

▲ **Kandalama Hotel,** Dambulla, Sri Lanka, 1995
The rainforest envelops the concrete frame of Geoffrey Bawa's masterpiece, which is set against granite cliffs overlooking the Kandalama Reservoir. The hotel's lobby, staircases, and terraces are all open-air, in celebration of the tropical light and climate of Sri Lanka's hill country.

▲ **Canova Museum,** Possagno, Italy, 1957
The role of light is paramount in Carlo Scarpa's extension to the Neoclassical sculpture gallery in Possagno. Trihedral corner windows in the High Hall cast light onto the walls and sculptures inside, while a lower trapezoidal gallery steps down to a pool of water that reflects dappled sunlight onto the ceiling.

▲ **New Gourna Village,** Luxor, Egypt, 1952
A new settlement was planned by Hassan Fathy in order to relocate the population of Old Gourna away from the archaeological site of Luxor. He drew on local traditional building methods and involved the future community in the design process so they could take ownership of their new town.

▲ Corduroy concrete
American architect Paul Rudolph came up with a way of casting concrete in ridges, which workers then bashed with hammers to produce an exciting, rocky texture.

▲ Curved frame
Designed by Brazilian architect Oscar Niemeyer, the Cathedral of Brasilia has a hyperbolic-curve-shaped roof of fiberglass supported by 16 identical concrete pillars. Each weighs 90 tons, and together they evoke Jesus Christ's crown of thorns.

"Believe me, the sweetest music you will ever hear is 'concrete' on your own site."

Denys Lasdun, British architect, 1914–2001

REINFORCED CONCRETE

Concrete is the defining material of architecture and infrastructure in the modern world. Humans use more of it than of any other substance apart from water.

Concrete is made up of cement, sand, gravel, and water. Mixed together, they form a sludge that can be poured into any shape of mold—known as the formwork—where they will set into a stonelike mass. Usually, steel bars are placed inside the formwork before the concrete is poured, producing reinforced concrete. The resulting material has the strength of stone when compressed, and the strength of steel against pulling and twisting forces. It is also relatively fire-resistant.

ADAPTABLE MATERIAL

Reinforced concrete allows architects to design buildings in almost any shape they like, with big, column-free internal spaces, substantial overhangs called cantilevers, and enough strength to allow roads to pass over or through a building. A common feature of 20th-century architecture was the expression of excitement at the remarkable powers the new material had given to designers, and the better new world they believed they were building.

Modernist Le Corbusier was a pioneer in the use of reinforced concrete, exemplified in his iconic Unité d'habitation building (see p.326).

As the 20th century progressed, this cheap, strong, versatile material became a universal norm in industrialized countries, and in the 21st century, its use continues to expand rapidly—especially in countries with high levels of urban growth, such as China. Nonetheless, it has drawbacks. Neglected concrete can corrode, and structures tend to "creep" as they eventually buckle under the weight of a building.

AN UNCERTAIN FUTURE

In recent years, a critical problem has come to light: concrete produces very high carbon emissions to make the cement that holds it together. Experiments in removing the carbon emissions from concrete production are underway, but it seems certain that sustainable alternatives will need to be found for most applications where concrete is currently the leading building material (see pp.362–369).

▲ Draped canopy
Designed by Álvaro Siza Vieira for the 1998 Lisbon World Expo, the Portuguese National Pavilion looks out onto the harbor in homage to Portugal's maritime past. Two porticoes support a 230-ft- (70-m-) long concrete canopy that is just 8 in (20 cm) thick.

▲ Climate control
As part of Le Corbusier's new concrete city at Chandigarh in India, the High Court of Punjab and Haryana (1951-1965) has a double roof. This shades the building from the sun, protects it from monsoon rains, and allows cooling air to circulate.

CEMENT PRODUCTION

The crucial material that binds concrete is cement, a gray powder made by heating limestone and adding other minerals. Cement is very similar to the lime that bonded ancient Roman concrete and medieval mortars, but is produced at hotter temperatures. Heating limestone and burning fossil fuels for cement production creates high levels of carbon dioxide. These emissions make up around eight percent of all climate-change emissions.

Cement production factory

BRUTALISM

The years after World War II saw a global outpouring of expressive, technically daring concrete architecture that aimed to serve all the needs of humanity: Brutalism was a powerfully self-assured style.

Technology seemed to give new superpowers to architects practicing in the 1960s. Brutalism's key materials—concrete, steel, and glass—had been known for centuries, but until the spread of cheap fossil fuels, they had all cost too much heat energy to use on a grand scale. Now, they were affordable and all-changing.

Whereas older buildings had been produced in straitjackets of vertical brick walls, reinforced concrete could now be engineered into almost any shape. Old buildings had relied on windows for ventilation and lighting, but now, thanks to cheap coal-powered electricity, new technologies could pump fresh air at a uniform temperature and humidity into any room. Along with powerful electric lighting, these advances meant that buildings could be supersized, and rooms could also function underground.

Not only old buildings but whole cities were deemed unsuited to modern life. The rapid rise of car ownership in many countries led to the rethinking of city design around new roads and parking structures. Older buildings seemed, to many, to be technically obsolete and a waste of valuable city space. Plans were drawn up to

> ## "One of the greatest ever flowerings of human creativity and ingenuity."
>
> Barnabas Calder, *Raw Concrete: The Beauty of Brutalism*, 2016

replace much of the worn-out old building stock with more efficient, denser cityscapes. Many cities around the world pushed through new office complexes, ever-larger shopping malls, and slum clearance and housing schemes on an unprecedented scale.

LOVED AND HATED

Architects were working to create a new world. Their excitement at the magic of concrete shines out of Brutalist buildings, with parts overhanging each other just because they could. Chunky spaces hovered exhilaratingly over fragile-looking glass boxes, and roads and walkways criss-crossed the city at any height, just as Antonio Sant'Elia had foretold in his Futurist drawings (see pp.290–291). Designers wanted to celebrate the wonder material that made all this possible, not conceal it behind old-fashioned brick or stone. In Brutalism, concrete is proudly displayed, its texture recording forever how the building was made.

The scale of the movement's global success ultimately attracted an enormous backlash. From the late 1960s, mass-demolition in cities met with widespread opposition, and the economic turmoil of the 1970s led many to feel that the ambition and expansiveness of Brutalism had been a nightmarish mistake.

BRUTAL SCHOOL

The first building to be publicized as "Brutalist" was a school in Hunstanton, UK, which was completed in 1954. Architects Alison and Peter Smithson refused to hide not only the concrete and steel the school was made of, but even the electric cables and piping that ran across the surfaces. It was a controversial building: aesthetically powerful and durable, but—some felt—rather tough-looking for a school.

Exposed framework of Smithdon High School, Hunstanton, Norfolk

NATIONAL THEATRE

LONDON, UK, 1964–1976

Architects Denys Lasdun & Partners worked with some of the great theater directors of the age to design London's National Theatre. A masterpiece of Brutalist architecture, with its proudly exposed concrete structure, the building is home to three theaters, as well as other vast public spaces.

PERFECT VIEWS

Inside, the National Theatre's big auditoriums and well-equipped stages posed a huge challenge for the engineers as they required large spaces without columns that would spoil the view or get in the way of the actors. The building's public areas—its foyers and terraces—were also built on a grand scale, and the different levels and walkways help it blend in with its urban setting.

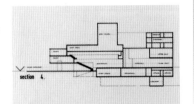

This cross-section of the National Theatre shows the huge voids within.

▲ Concrete achievement

The architects and builders took enormous care to ensure that the concrete carried the beautiful imprint of the rough-sawed wooden molds (formwork) into which it had been poured.

▲ Indoor public space

The spirit of generosity in 1960s architecture is embodied in foyers much bigger than was usual for a theater, allowing the public, even non-theater-goers, to relax and mingle amid elegant columns.

Light gray concrete echoes the color of nearby buildings

The lack of a main entrance makes the building feel part of the city

A larger fly tower projects up from the tiered structure

Overhanging terraces wrap around the building

Below ground is a parking garage

KEY **ELEMENTS**

Concrete was the defining feature of Brutalism, generally exposed to view on at least parts of Brutalist buildings, and underpinning the scale, shapes, and functionality of whole new building types that became common in the postwar decades.

HIGH-RISE HOUSING

Reinforced concrete structures, combined with affordable electricity to run elevators, made it possible to build dense housing higher than had been seen before. Similar-looking new housing blocks went up all around the world. Building high meant that more people could live in improved conditions, with heating, plumbing, great views, and a handy trash chute. In subsequent decades, some of these plans developed a bad reputation for social problems and technical difficulties.

◄ Hot house
Trellick Tower in London, UK, has a boiler house atop its elevator tower, advertising for miles around that residents of this 31-story building were enjoying the latest comfort technologies.

◄ ▲ Global style
Similar techniques led to buildings being built around the world, often with too few adaptations to local tradition and climate. The added air conditioning units on this building in Cairo, Egypt (left), suggest it was not designed to provide enough shade from the hot sun. Meanwhile, in cold winters, like those of Belgrade, Serbia (above), apartments were chilly and damp despite heavy use of fossil-fuel central heating.

CAMPUS ARCHITECTURE

The economic boom that many countries experienced after World War II supported ambitious new programs of education, health, and welfare. Many countries expanded their universities, building proudly forward-looking campuses. For some nations, this was part of the process of forging new identities as they won independence from colonial powers; for others, it demonstrated a commitment to equality and modernity. University campuses were often seen as opportunities to try out new ideal-city concepts for the age of cars and concrete.

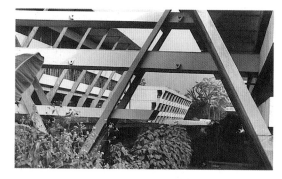

▲ Cool and shade
At the University of Ife in Nigeria, Brutalist structural ideas were used to produce cooling shade, along with plenty of outside spaces for conversation and reflection.

▲ Inside out
The excitingly expressive campus exterior of Canada's University of Toronto, Scarborough, reflects the shapes of its different internal spaces.

NEW METHODS, NEW POSSIBILITIES

Inspired by the mass-production of cars, Brutalist architects experimented with new ways of building that would cut costs and increase production. They took advantage of new structural options and utilities, incorporating a much wider range of facilities into the same big, complicated building. Flushed with success, architects began to imagine not only new buildings but new cities, and new ways to live in them.

▼ **Cross-section of a city within a city**
New technologies meant that large crowds at the Barbican Arts Centre in London, UK, could see and safely breathe in cinemas, theaters, and concert halls buried beneath apartment buildings, far from natural light and air.

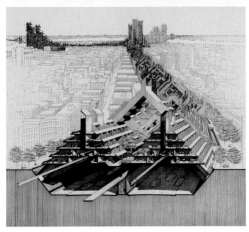

◄ **Underground roads**
Reinforced concrete was so strong that architects invented ideas for topping new road projects with entire linear city districts, as seen in this plan of the Lower Manhattan Expressway in New York, which was never completed.

▶ **Prefabrication**
Factory mass-production lowered prices and improved quality in many products. Architects tried to exploit the same phenomenon by developing mass-produced building kits, such as this one being assembled in the USSR.

BRUTALIST BUILDINGS

Most cities on Earth have some example of Brutalist architecture. Thanks to global magazines and faster, cheaper travel, new ideas and techniques spread fast and far and wide.

1

2

3

4

1. Casa del Portuale
Naples, Italy, 1968–1980

Brutalist architects avoided using architectural decoration. Instead, as seen in this dockworkers' building, they used the versatility of reinforced concrete to compose the necessary elements of the structure into spectacular sculpture.

2. Terminal 1, Charles de Gaulle airport
Paris, France, 1974

With oil prices dropping sharply in the postwar decades, aviation expanded rapidly. Huge new air terminals were built in a futuristic style. French architect Paul Andreu's Terminal 1 brings together cars, trains, and planes in one elegant hub.

3. Museum of Art
São Paulo, Brazil, 1968

Lina Bo Bardi's museum exudes excitement at the ability of reinforced concrete to span very large distances. The stunning lack of columns beneath the building opens up a sheltered public space.

4. Hotel du Lac
Tunis, Tunisia, 1973

A growing postwar global tourist industry led to a boom in modern hotels, many of which used the memorable shapes of Brutalist architecture as part of their appeal. This hotel uses concrete cantilevers to have more rooms at the top, with better views, than further down.

5. La Concha Motel
Las Vegas, Nevada, 1961

Growing technical understanding gave architects ever more options. The shape of this motel's roof shell is a very efficient way to engineer a vault far thinner than earlier examples.

6. Indian Institute of Management
Ahmedabad, India, 1974

Although concrete set the tone for Brutalism worldwide, brick remained, for many, a durable and expressive material. US architect Louis Khan's careful composition of spaces and surfaces is evident in his design for this Indian campus.

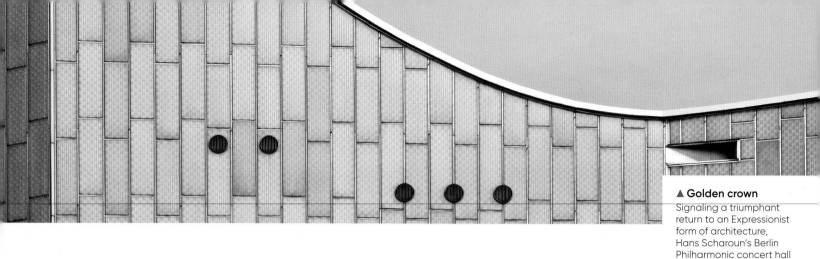

NEO-EXPRESSIONISM

As the ideal of a rational, functional Modernism lost its grip after World War II, some architects returned with new vigor to experimenting with expressive and dynamic forms.

Beginning in the 1950s, Neo-Expressionism was the resurgence of a more individualistic and stylized approach to architecture that harked back to the original Expressionist movement of the 1920s. Its return formed part of a general shift away from the functional, utilitarian Modernism that had dominated architectural thought for the preceding half century, and had neglected what many considered to be the more "human" aspects of architecture, such as experience and emotion.

NEW FORMS
If the Expressionist architects of the 1920s often had visions that went beyond what they could achieve with existing building materials and technology, Neo-Expressionists were able to take advantage of numerous developments in engineering and construction to push the boundaries of architecture. Reinforced concrete, with its sculptural possibilities, continued to capture the imaginations of architects such as Jørn Utzon, Eero Saarinen,

> "The purpose of architecture is to ... enhance man's life on Earth."
> **Eero Saarinen**, 1959

and even the Modernist Le Corbusier. Advances in the use of metal and glass, combined with the dawn of computer-aided design (CAD) in the 1970s, made it possible for architects not only to solve complex engineering problems, but also to generate entirely new forms that might otherwise have been impossible.

Neo-Expressionism did not emerge from the same political climate as Expressionism, when forward-thinking architecture was regarded as a means of achieving a socialist utopia. Rather, it coincided with a new era of commercial confidence and individualism in many parts of Europe and the US, which brought a renewed appreciation for the role of architecture as a powerful symbol and branding tool. This was in many ways the start of the global trend for "iconic" architecture that continues to this day, and is manifested less in everyday buildings such as houses, than in large-scale cultural projects, such as museums, galleries, music venues, and even shopping centers.

BLOBITECTURE
In the 1980s, a series of experiments into blob-like architectural forms led to an entire sub-style known as Blobitecture. Inconceivable without the help of computer-aided design techniques, the dynamic, undulating facades of these blob-shaped buildings were entirely unprecedented, and were often inspired by natural, organic forms.

Roof made of steel and glass panels

The Sage Gateshead by Norman Foster

Terrace overlooking Sydney Harbor

SYDNEY OPERA HOUSE

AUSTRALIA, 1959–1973

One of the most distinctive pieces of architecture in the world, Danish architect Jørn Utzon's expressive Sydney Opera House is based on a cluster of soaring concrete shells, which are both a visual and technological marvel.

▲ Interior foyers
The foyers atop the building's massive base are illuminated by large areas of glazing beneath each shell-like form, and offer dramatic views across Sydney Harbor.

▲ Ribbed shells
While the exteriors of the shells are clad in small tiles, their undersides reveal the huge precast concrete ribs that provide them with additional strength.

▲ Timber ceiling
The expressive nature of the building is not just confined to its exterior; the stage and auditorium are enclosed by richly sculpted walls and timber ceilings.

SEGMENTS OF A SPHERE

The technical design of the Opera House's roof initially caused enormous challenges, as each segment was originally planned as a slightly different shape. Utzon made a breakthrough when he realized that if each of these shells were made from a single plane, such as the surface of a sphere, the construction and engineering processes could be streamlined, making it easier to calculate both the forces and production.

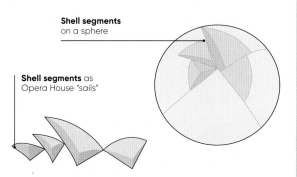

Shell segments on a sphere

Shell segments as Opera House "sails"

The Sydney Opera House shells cut from an imaginary sphere

Shells evoke sails in the harbor

Structure made of over 2,000 precast shell segments

Glass walls supported by vertical steel mullions

Outer skin of over one million ceramic tiles

KEY ELEMENTS

Neo-Expressionists designed buildings to both convey and provoke emotions, using materials that were best suited to express affecting ideas on a large scale.

METAPHORIC ARCHITECTURE

Freed from the idea that buildings should reflect the purposes they serve, Neo-Expressionists returned to designing buildings that were potent symbols—of everything from private emotions and experiences to the characters of companies or entire cities.

▲ **Taking flight**
This winglike terminal at JFK Airport, in New York City, was originally designed to be a strong branding symbol for airline TWA.

▲ **Lotus Temple**
This Bahà'í House of Worship, in Delhi, India, was designed to resemble a giant lotus flower. Its concrete "petals" are clad in white marble and create dome-like spaces for the interior, which is open to all.

▲ **Soaring spire**
Stretching as though for the heavens, the dramatic "wings" of Iceland's Hallgrímskirkja, completed in 1986, mimic the country's columnar basalt formations.

▲ **Boat hull**
The upturned hulls of wooden boats inspired the shape of the debating chamber of the Scottish Parliament building in Edinburgh, Scotland.

ECCENTRICITY

Like the Expressionism that preceded it, Neo-Expressionism gave architects the freedom to express their ideas in radically new and different ways that were not tied to any particular style or set of rules or principles.

NEW FORMS

Part of Neo-Expressionism's power came from its architects' determination to create curving, blob-like, and often gravity-defying forms that had never been seen before.

▲ **Criss-crossing walkways**
Surrounding the performance space with a network of walkways creates a dynamic experience for audiences at Hans Scharoun's Berlin Philharmonic concert hall. The design experiments with acoustics and lines of sight.

▲ **Underground art gallery**
The Amdavan ni Gufa in Ahmedabad, India, is covered by a series of reinforced cement domes. Designed by Balkrishna Doshi, the domes resemble bubbles and tortoise shells, and are covered in mosaics made from tiles and broken crockery.

▲ **Friendly alien**
Known locally as "the friendly alien," the blob-like Kunsthaus Graz, an art museum in Austria, is composed of blue acrylic panels. Built in 2003, it is an entirely unfamiliar, technologically advanced form that still looks futuristic today.

NEO-EXPRESSIONIST BUILDINGS

Neo-Expressionism quickly spread around the world, its increasingly ambitious forms capturing the public's imagination. The most famous Neo-Expressionist buildings are iconic and built on a grand scale.

1. Vitra Design Museum
Weil am Rhein, Germany, 1989

Designed in collaboration with Günter Pfeifer, the sculptural form of Frank Gehry's first building in Europe mixes white plaster with titanium-alloy plating, and curved forms with angular shapes.

2. Liverpool Metropolitan Cathedral
Liverpool, UK, 1962–1967

A stained-glass lantern finished with a crown-like form of metal pinnacles tops this boldly modern cathedral designed by Sir Frederick Gibberd. It offers a contemporary take on the traditional form of the spire.

3. Chapel of Notre-Dame du Haut
Ronchamp, France, 1955

Considered to be an early example of Neo-Expressionism, or even proto-Postmodernism, this church was a radical departure from the earlier Modernism for which Le Corbusier is known. Its thick and sweeping walls and roof show a fascination with the sculptural potential of concrete.

METABOLISM

Proposing organic, skeletal, alien megastructures composed of prefabricated components, Metabolism pushed the new possibilities offered by architecture to its limits in the 1960s and '70s.

Metabolist architecture was conceived as a radical solution to the exponential growth of the Japanese economy in the 1950s and '60s. Influenced by the visionary plans of their mentor Kenzō Tange, a group of young Japanese architects, including Kiyonori Kikutake, Kisho Kurokawa, and Fumihiko Maki, proposed a new approach to architecture that befitted the rapidly evolving society around them. Kenzo Tange's Boston Harbor project of 1959, developed by his students while Tange was at the Massachusetts Institute of Technology, was the inspiration for his Tokyo Bay master plan of 1960. Both projects envisioned "megastructures" that were designed to extend their respective cities over neighboring bodies of water. These structures were not simply large buildings—they were gigantic frames that could house entire towns, and could grow and evolve according to the needs of their citizens.

Tange likened the megastructure to the human body, which constantly renews and replenishes itself through its various circulatory, respiratory, and nervous systems. His aspiration

> "Human society [is] a continuous development from atom to nebula."
>
> **Kiyonori Kikutake**, Metabolist manifesto of 1960

was to develop a new "method of linking the various functions of the city" to build a more organically efficient whole. This included redesigning roads and public transit systems to connect public facilities to residential areas and other parts of the city more effectively.

EXPENDABLE BUILDINGS

Although it remained unrealized, Tange's vision inspired a generation of architects who worked on the problems of urban expansion. These included the British Archigram group, who developed the "Plug-In City" concept, and Paul Rudolph, who proposed a linear megastructure above New York's Lower Manhattan Expressway (see p.329). For a while, it seemed as is if the megastructure offered a viable alternative to the orthodoxy of Modernism, which, by the 1960s, had become the official style of the postwar, reconstructed Anglo-American world.

In Japan, Tange and other architects adapted the principles of the megastructure to design individual buildings that could be constructed both immediately and within the constraints of preexisting infrastructure. They used primary structures as formworks onto which they added modules or capsules, typically clustering them together around circulation and service cores.

FLEXIBILITY AND GROWTH

Completed in 1967 on an awkward triangular site in Ginza, Tokyo, Tange's prototype Metabolist structure was a 187-ft- (57-m-) high service tower, housing a staircase, elevators, kitchens, and toilets, onto which prefabricated glass offices could be plugged in, removed, or replaced as required. The building proved to be too difficult and too expensive to modify, however, and so it still stands in its original configuration today.

The Metabolist Shizuoka Press and Broadcasting Center

NAKAGIN CAPSULE TOWER

TOKYO, JAPAN, 1970–1972

Kisho Kurokawa's aspirational residential building in Tokyo was made of two towers that rose from a plinth of street-level shops and offices. Its 140 prefabricated capsules, each containing a futuristic micro-home, were plugged into the towers and were designed to be replaced after 25 years.

▶ Futuristic interior
Inside the capsules, gloss-white walls, porthole windows, and spaceship-like interfaces all alluded to a futuristic world in which a person's every need could be met by advanced technology.

ADDITIVE FORM

The Nakagin Capsule Tower was the world's first "capsule" building intended for permanent use. Its prefabricated homes were bolted to concrete circulation cores, which tapered upward, implying the possibility of unlimited future extension. However, the tower was poorly maintained and was demolished in 2022.

The Nakagin Capsule Tower under construction in the early 1970s

Exposed circulation cores emphasize the movement of people and services

Capsules affixed in various orientations

Porthole windows allude to ship or aircraft design

METABOLIC BUILDINGS

▲ Habitat 67, Montreal, Canada, 1967
Moshe Safdie's early proposals for a model apartment complex included 1,000 prefabricated modular units supported by a structural exoskeleton. However, his design evolved until the units clustered into self-supporting stacks shaped like ziggurats.

▲ Culture Hall, Yamanashi, Japan, 1966
Composed of 16 cylindrical service cores supporting horizontal decks of accommodation, Tange's press and broadcasting center includes a printing press and radio and television stations. Although designed for future expansion, it was enlarged only once, in 1974.

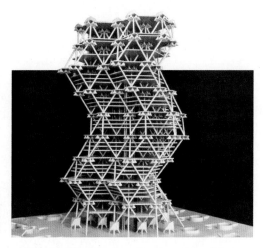

▲ Plan for City Tower, Philadelphia, PA, 1950s
Louis Kahn and Anne Tyng's unrealized project for a 30-story skyscraper in Philadelphia is notable for its experimental non-perpendicular, tetrahedral space frame. It fulfilled Kahn's desire to create "a continuous structure worthy of being exposed."

7

CRISIS AND HOPE

1970 ONWARD

MINIMALISM

Shaped by the radicalism of abstract art and the development of more sophisticated construction technologies, Minimalism pares architecture down to qualities of form, materials, and light.

Inspired by simple geometric forms, a limited palette of materials, and a reductive approach to detailing, Minimalism focuses on a narrow range of qualities. An offshoot of Modernism, it originated in early 20th-century modern art movements, with artists such as Piet Mondrian, and Josef Albers, as well as Kazimir Malevich, whose work had a profound influence on the development of abstract art. A key pioneer of Minimalist architecture was architect Mies van der Rohe, who fled Nazi Germany in 1937 to work in the US. He coined the phrase "Less is more," which became a defining statement for Minimalist architects. It describes a tactic of arranging the various parts of a building to create an impression of extreme simplicity, by enlisting every element and component to serve multiple visual and functional purposes.

A MINIMALIST AESTHETIC

During the mid 20th century, Minimalism was given further impetus by Modernist architects' preoccupation with rational and efficient structures, and the development of increasingly sophisticated construction technologies, which

made it possible to produce large sheets of glass and "fair-faced concrete"—a smoother, lighter type of concrete that could act as a finished surface. Glass and concrete became linked to the Minimalist aesthetic, along with planar forms and pure use of color, as seen in the buildings of Mexican architect Luis Barragán. Influenced by Mexican rural life, with its rich hues, raw materials, and relationship with light and landscape, Barragán's Minimalist style contrasted with the more precisely engineered and mechanistic style of Mies van der Rohe.

PERFECTING SIMPLICITY

Though primarily linked to modern architectural and artistic movements, Minimalism also has deeper historical roots. The concept of formal and material simplicity is seen in many cultures, especially in Japan, evoked in the philosophy of Zen, Haiku poetry, and the notion of "wabi-sabi," which values the innate properties of plain, unadorned objects. Through the work of Japanese architects such as Tadao Ando and Kengo Kuma, Minimalism attained new heights of austere sophistication, helped by the high standards of the Japanese construction industry. In an increasingly chaotic world, the fundamentals of Minimalist architecture have proved to be enduring. They appeal to the human desire for calm space, the reassurance of solid, simple materiality, and the chance to contemplate and connect with nature.

◀ **Monochrome facade**
White ceramic panels make up the striking monochrome facade of the Suntory Museum of Art in Tokyo, remodeled by Kengo Kuma in 2007. The panels control light and connect the internal space to the garden outside.

ORIGINS OF MINIMALISM

Minimalism had its origins in the modern art movements of the early 20th century, which marked a radical shift away from representational painting to abstraction. Key to this transition was the work of Russian artist Kazimir Malevich. His 1915 painting *Black Square*, often described by experts as the "zero point of painting," was a pivotal work, its stark tonal and geometric simplicity becoming a touchstone for a new way of seeing that had a profound influence on architecture.

Black Square is considered the first artistic attempt to use abstract shape and form over a depiction of reality.

Planar (flat-sided) forms are typical of Minimalist geometry, creating simple, rectilinear spaces

Timber screens at street level add a contrasting, more rustic texture

Bold wall colors recall the paintings of Mexican artist Jesús Reyes Ferreira

CASA GILARDI

MEXICO CITY, MEXICO, 1976

Characterized by its elementally simple forms and inspired by Mexican vernacular architecture, Casa Gilardi was the final project of Luis Barragán. His carefully composed interaction of light, shade, color, and texture contrived to create different sensations as people moved through and around its spaces.

◄ **Interior**
Casa Gilardi's austere interior contains a small, shallow pool, framed by blue and red walls, which draw the eye through the space. The walls extend vertically to a skylight above that bathes the pool in natural light.

MINIMALIST BUILDINGS

▲ **Neue Nationalgalerie,** Berlin, Germany, 1968
Mies van der Rohe's concept of "less is more" is epitomized by his Minimalist gallery in Berlin. Little more than a platform topped with a precisely detailed roof supported by steel columns, it still commands its site and has a strong civic presence.

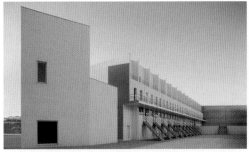

▲ **Bouça Social Housing,** Porto, Portugal, 1977
Drawing on the simple forms of traditional Iberian housing, Álvaro Siza Vieira's housing plan consists of four parallel four-story, white rendered blocks. These are made up of different combinations of duplex units, connected to the ground by external stairs.

▲ **Hyogo Museum of Art,** Hyogo, Japan, 2002
Characteristic of Tadao Ando's Minimalist oeuvre, the Hyogo Museum of Art is an imposing composition of concrete, stone, steel, and glass. Ando designed the building to act as a neutral backdrop for the vibrant modern art it was created to house.

HI-TECH ARCHITECTURE

Toward the end of the 20th century, Hi-Tech architecture promised limitless light and air; almost weightless structures floating over boundless space, all controlled and serviced by the latest in building technology.

Although they became famous for pioneering open-plan office interiors, Hi-Tech architects set out to reshape not only offices but also homes, art galleries, shops, and airports with a new kind of structural and material efficiency. Norman Foster, Richard Rogers, Michael and Patty Hopkins, Nicholas Grimshaw, and Renzo Piano advanced a new and exciting aesthetic of steel, glass, and concrete. These materials could span greater distances than ever before and improve transparency in buildings to make them look lighter and more efficient. They also highlighted the parts of buildings that are usually kept hidden. Rogers and Piano designed the Pompidou Centre, for example, so the electrical, transportation, and ventilation systems were exposed on the outside of the building, making it look like a gigantic pipe organ.

FUNCTIONAL EFFICIENCY

The possibilities afforded by glass, steel, and concrete seemed infinite. At Stansted, UK, Norman Foster designed a new kind of airport

> "I have always felt we should use the technology of the age we live in for the improvement of mankind."
>
> **Nicholas Grimshaw**, Hi-Tech architect

terminal with glass walls, so travelers could see their aircraft from the moment they entered the building. This simple idea shaped the design of a whole generation of airports, including Hong Kong International, Beijing Capital, Madrid Barajas, and London Heathrow Terminal 5. Later, advances in computer-aided technology revolutionized the very forms that architects could design, enabling them to standardize components for assembly on building sites anywhere in the world.

This material and functional efficiency came at the cost of a great deal of energy. Glass is thermally less efficient than an insulated wall, so buildings with large areas of glass require more energy to heat or cool. Likewise, air conditioning and fluorescent lighting, supplied through service voids in ceilings and floors, consume a great deal of electricity. It is only in recent years that these energy costs have been fully understood, and architects and engineers are starting to come to terms with the need for radical change in architecture to reduce the energy costs of buildings.

THE AESTHETICS OF BUILDING UTILITIES

American Modernist Louis Khan famously said: "I do not like ducts, I do not like pipes. I hate them really thoroughly, but because I hate them so thoroughly, I feel they have to be given their place." The architects of the Hi-Tech movement turned this idea on its head; rather than hiding them, they showcased the technologies that they used to keep their buildings powered and comfortable.

Utilities exposed on the facade of the Lloyd's Building, London

POMPIDOU CENTRE

PARIS, FRANCE, 1971–1977

Rising to 10 stories, the Pompidou Centre is an immense modern arts complex at the heart of Paris. Its ground level was initially designed to be a forum that opened out onto the public piazza, but this proved to be technically incompatible with the concept of a perfectly controlled environment, isolated from the atmosphere outside.

PLAN OF THE POMPIDOU CENTRE

Trusses span the depth of the plan, ensuring that the interior floor plates are free from the vertical structure. This open plan allows for flexibility in the design of touring exhibitions. Visitors are taken to each level by escalators on the facade of the building. The roof is dotted with the numerous air-handling units that are needed to maintain the atmosphere of the interior, which is hermetically sealed.

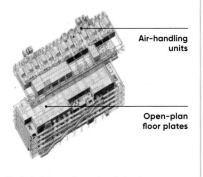

Exploded three-dimensional drawing of the Pompidou Centre

▲ **Color-coded utilities**
Utilities are exposed on the facade and are color-coded according to function: blue for air; yellow for electricity; green for water; and red for escalators and elevators.

▲ **Tube escalator**
Visitor circulation is highly visible. Escalators encased in glass snake up the building's facade, offering views across the piazza.

▲ **Periscope ducts**
Nearly half of the Centre lies underground. These spaces, which include car parking and storage areas, are ventilated by huge, periscope-like ducts.

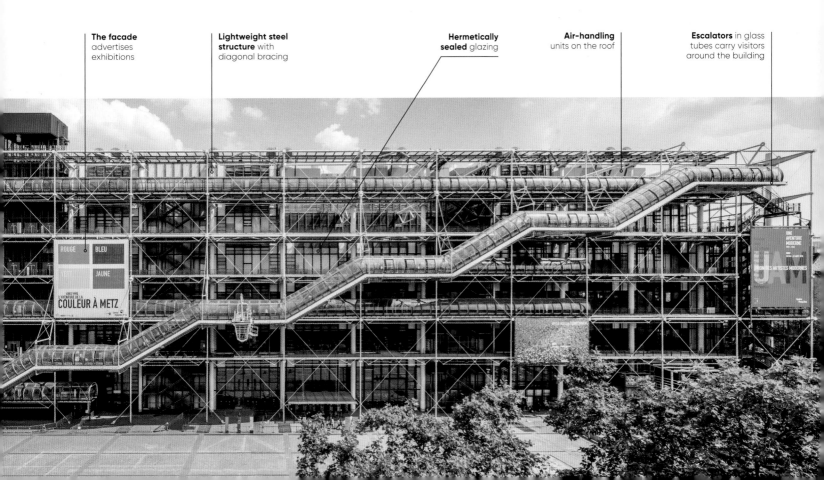

The facade advertises exhibitions

Lightweight steel structure with diagonal bracing

Hermetically sealed glazing

Air-handling units on the roof

Escalators in glass tubes carry visitors around the building

KEY **ELEMENTS**

Space frames, stainless-steel sheeting, billowing facades, pipes and ducts—the dynamic forms of Hi-Tech architecture were a rejection of the stability of the past.

CELEBRATING STRUCTURAL SYSTEMS

Hi-Tech architects accentuated the visual expression of structural forces in their design of individual building components, such as steel beams. These could be scaled to different sizes or tapered, depending on the direction of stress and the size of the load.

▲ **Statement beams**
Yellow steel branches bolted to concrete plinths lift 236-ft-(72-m-) long gull-wing beams in Richard Rogers' Barajas Madrid International Airport, Spain. The beams in turn hold an undulating, bamboo-lined roof canopy above the concourse.

TRANSPARENCY

The development of patent glazing technology, new glass sealants and coatings, and the manufacture of bespoke components made it possible for architects to design ever more transparent walls, revealing the interior of a building to the outside world.

APPLIED ENERGY

Hi-Tech architecture exploited the possibilities afforded by new and more powerful light fixtures and HVAC (heating, ventilation, and air conditioning) technologies. These services were integrated seamlessly into the fabric of buildings, but the demand for greater flexibility increased the amount of power that was needed to operate them.

▲ **Structure and utilities**
Branching, treelike columns supporting the roof of Norman Foster's Stansted Airport, in the UK, contain electrical cables, air-conditioning, and lighting. They also connect the service spaces beneath the terminal with the main concourse above.

▲ **Ventilation shafts**
Oversize, funnel-shaped ducts at the foot of Richard Rogers' 50-story Leadenhall Building in London give it an almost animalistic quality. They are a reminder of the huge amounts of energy that glass skyscrapers require.

▶ **Open-plan**
Clad in mirrored glass that reflects its surroundings, the Willis Faber & Dumas Building, a three-story insurance headquarters in Ipswich, UK, is planned on a grid of concrete columns. With almost no internal subdivisions, it pioneered the concept of the open-plan office.

◀ **Industrial look**
A Hi-Tech interpretation of Charles and Ray Eames' house in Santa Monica, Hopkins House in London amplifies the industrial aesthetic. The tubular steel frame is encased in sheets of glass and steel, and has Venetian blinds for privacy.

1

HI-TECH BUILDINGS

Monuments to the technological optimism of the late 20th century, Hi-Tech buildings have an almost ageless quality, emphasized by their light structures and polished, reflective surfaces.

2

3

1. British Pavilion Expo 92
Seville, Spain, 1992

A temporary structure assembled largely from prefabricated components, Nicholas Grimshaw's steel pavilion featured walls of billowing polyester fabric and stacked shipping containers. Sail-like polyester panels on the roof filtered sunlight into the interior.

2. Sainsbury Centre for Visual Arts
Norwich, UK, 1978

More like an aircraft hanger than an art gallery, the Sainsbury Centre combines all of its public functions into one 443-ft- (135-m-) long space. It is enclosed by a steel space frame, which contains all of the building's utilities, bathrooms, kitchens, and storage areas.

3. Somerville College
Oxford, UK, 1967

Working with engineer Ove Arup, Philip Dowson created a cutting-edge precast concrete structure for the Wolfson Building at Somerville College. The bedrooms all have projecting window seats, which form a grid of glass boxes on the facade of the building.

4. Lloyd's Building
London, UK, 1986

The headquarters of Lloyd's of London takes many of the ideas developed for the Pompidou Centre in Paris (see p.343) and incorporates them into a 14-story open-plan office with a 196-ft- (60-m-) high atrium at its center. Its six external towers contain stairs, elevators, and bathrooms.

4

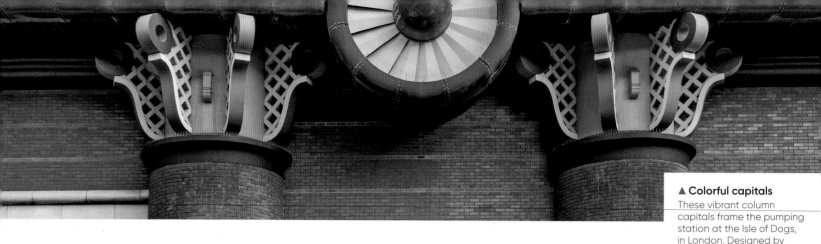

▲ **Colorful capitals**
These vibrant column capitals frame the pumping station at the Isle of Dogs, in London. Designed by John Outram, it is finished with curving latticework forms that reference a Classical temple.

POSTMODERNISM

Eclectic and excessive, the playful and colorful designs of Postmodernism were a bold riposte to decades of Modernist functionalism, challenging the very notion of "good taste."

> ## "Less is a bore."
>
> Robert Venturi, *Complexity and Contradiction in Architecture*, 1966

Postmodernist architecture developed as part of a forceful reaction against Modernism, which had dominated architecture and art for decades. By the 1960s, however, Modernism's popularity had started to wane, and it was beginning to be perceived by some as austere and elitist. Modernists, it seemed, prioritized function over human life and experience, and they were felt to have severed architecture from its rich and meaningful history.

As a movement, Postmodernism was broad, encompassing wider culture and all of the arts. Architecturally, it describes several styles, such as Neo-Expressionism (see pp.332–335) and Deconstructivism (see pp.356–359), that were united in their rejection of Modernist orthodoxy. Together, they formed a movement that was defined by its pluralism and diversity.

A RETURN TO THE PAST

One of the Postmodernists' most impactful moves was the return to explicitly referencing architectural motifs of the past in new buildings. Modernists had rejected historical architectural styles and symbols, believing that a modern, advanced future needed a new way of representing itself that rejected the old. Postmodernists, by contrast, took a renewed interest in the styles and ornamentation of the past, using them in a free, almost collage-like manner. This amounted to a revival of Historicism (see pp.280–283), which referenced the appearance of older buildings as well as their approach to planning and urban design.

SYMBOLISM AND MEANING

Modernists were also felt to have stripped architecture of its ability to communicate anything beyond a narrative of technological or social progress. For Postmodernists, this narrative—along with its utopian belief in changing the world for the better—had failed. It was simply one way of seeing the world among many others, each of which was equally valid.

Postmodernists embraced the commercial and the everyday as being an equally valid form of aesthetic appreciation as so-called high art. They rejected Modernist elitism, which had deemed only certain approaches worthy. Postmodern architecture was rich with layers of meaning open to many interpretations.

Humor and irony were also a key part of the Postmodernists' approach—they liked to play with preconceived notions of what a building should look like and mean. This game-playing would sometimes be obvious, such as putting a giant hat on a building, but it could also be more highbrow, challenging the assumptions and meanings of established styles such as Classicism.

THE DEATH OF MODERNISM

Postmodernism in architecture was largely defined by American historian Charles Jencks, who put a specific date to the "death" of Modernism. For Jencks, this was the demolition of the Pruitt Igoe apartment complex in St. Louis, Missouri, on July 15, 1972. Designed in 1954 by Minoru Yamasaki, to Modernist ideals of housing, Pruitt Igoe was made up of 33 buildings, all 11 stories high. Jencks saw its demolition as the failure not only of a single apartment complex, but of the social and aesthetic project of Modernism as a whole.

The demolition of Pruitt Igoe began in 1972, but the final building did not fall until 1976.

NEUE STAATSGALERIE

STUTTGART, GERMANY, 1977–1984

A key example of Postmodern architecture, this gallery was designed by British architect James Stirling. Blending Classical architectural forms in pale sandstone with colorful, geometric accents, the gallery borrows from the monumental urbanism of historic cities to create a richly varied sequence of spaces.

"The shapes of a building [are] ... likely to be rich and varied in appearance."

James Stirling, quoted in *Writings on Architecture*, 1998

▲ Central atrium
James Stirling united the interior and exterior of the museum at its central atrium. This large, circular space, decorated with columns, architraves, and gables, creates an architectural landscape rich in historical reference.

▲ Color coding
Color is used throughout to denote function. The entrance has bright red doors with a zigzagging blue steel canopy overhead. All the windows are green, and circulation routes are marked with pink and blue steel pipes.

◄ Galleries
Inside the galleries themselves, chunky concrete columns have been erected in both historic and modern styles. This design feature plays with the notion of the monumental, despite the small size of some of the rooms.

Traditional sandstone creates a sense of the monumental

Historic and modern materials are juxtaposed

Colorful accents are used to denote specific functions

Steel piping marks continuous walkways around the building

KEY ELEMENTS

Postmodernism was often defined by excess—in color, form, and meaning. This celebration of architecture's joyful side proved controversial after the far more understated Modernism.

COLOR

Bold and playful colors featured prominently in much Postmodernist architecture, ranging from bright, primary colors that recalled the work of Dutch artist Piet Mondrian to more pastel shades, such as pink and avocado.

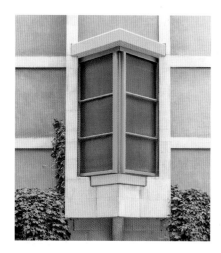

▲ **Colorful window frames**
Bright green frames enliven the windows of this 1987 extension of the Clore Gallery at Tate Britain in London, UK. Designed by Stirling, Wilford, and Associates, the new gallery wing was controversial due to its blend of modern and historic styles.

▲ **Internal design**
The interior of the Judge Business School in Cambridge, UK, was designed by British architect John Outram in a riot of color and ornamentation. Its chunky, classically inspired columns carry the building's modern utilities and ducting.

▲ **Striking facade**
Designed by American architect Michael Graves, the Portland Building in Oregon provided a striking departure from the Modernists' minimal skyscrapers. The distinctive exterior of the building incorporates large-scale decorative flourishes, with abstracted columns, pediments, and friezes above a teal-colored podium.

COMPLEXITY AND CONTRADICTION

Postmodernists would often take a magpie approach to a new design, enjoying the contrasts created by blending forms and styles from different eras, and drawing on the building's surrounding site and context as a source of inspiration.

◀ **Open facade**
This classically proportioned stone facade of the British Embassy in Berlin, Germany, designed by Stirling, Wilford, and Associates, is disrupted by the brightly colored metal shapes that burst from its center. This bold feature creates a blatant clash of the old and the new.

▶ **Multiple forms**
Designed by American architect Michael Graves, Denver's Public Library in Colorado is made up of an eclectic cluster of forms, each clad in a different shade of pastel-colored masonry. The design makes this single, large building look like several smaller buildings grouped together.

CLASSICISM REINTERPRETED

Postmodernists reinterpreted and reframed the meaning of many historical architectural styles, blending them with modern materials in lively and unexpected ways. One of their greatest influences was Classicism.

◄ Blended styles

American architect Charles Moore created a lively combination of Classical facades and colonnades in the Piazza d'Italia, a public square and fountain in New Orleans. His Classical forms are reinterpreted in modern materials such as stainless steel.

► Giant column

An oversized Ionic column protrudes from the center of the M2 building in Tokyo, Japan. Designed by Japanese architect Kengo Kuma, the building merges glass and metal forms with features that look as if they have come from an Italian temple.

► Classical design

Designed to improve the lives of its residents, the features of Les Espaces d'Abraxas, a social housing complex in the suburbs of Paris, France, were based on those of Classical buildings. The building was designed by Spanish architect Ricardo Bofill.

▲ Roof detail

550 Madison Avenue in New York is considered the world's first Postmodern skyscraper. Designed by Philip Johnson and John Burgee, it is topped with an outsize, broken Classical pediment, and has a grand, arched entrance covered in rhombus tiles.

POSTMODERNIST INFLUENCES

Married American architects Robert Venturi and Denise Scott Brown had a strong influence on Postmodernism. Their books *Complexity and Contradiction in Architecture* and *Learning From Las Vegas* contributed to a wider understanding of Postmodernism, especially its relationship to ornamentation and symbolism. They also promoted the acceptance of vernacular architecture in the United States on a par with "designed" architecture.

The Vanna Venturi House, designed by Venturi for his mother, is considered the first Postmodern building.

PLAYFULNESS AND HUMOR

Postmodernists often made use of humor and playful architectural forms to give buildings character and make them more relatable. This was a way of undermining the perceived elitism of Modernism.

▲ "Crumbling" stonework

Revealing the illusion of the modern construction methods that support a building's more historic-looking stonework, these "collapsed" areas of the Neue Staatsgalerie in Stuttgart, Germany, act as a visual joke—playing with expectation versus reality by creating the impression of a wall falling apart.

▲ Wizard's hat

The entrance of the headquarters of the Walt Disney Animation Studios in California, designed by Robert A. M. Stern Architects, is topped with a large wizard's hat. Boldly and playfully, it references the people inside and what they do for a living.

POSTMODERNIST BUILDINGS

Although a relatively short-lived movement, Postmodernism was associated with a new era of commercial building, seen in skyscrapers and offices that sprang up during economic booms.

1. Petronas Towers
Kuala Lumpur, Malaysia, 1998

The work of César Pelli, an Argentine-American architect, the design of these two towers incorporated Islamic motifs. Its cross-section is based on an Islamic symbol known as Rub el Hizb, or the Islamic Star (shaped as an octogram).

2. Kyoto Concert Hall
Kyoto, Japan, 1995

A cluster of contrasting forms combine in this building by Japanese architect Arata Isozaki. Its varied forms include a large, black cylinder that houses an entrance foyer, and a circular ramp leading to the performance hall.

3. Chiat/Day Offices
Los Angeles, California, 1991

This office building by Frank Gehry incorporates a large-scale sculpture of a pair of binoculars, by Claes Oldenburg and Coosje van Bruggen. It frames the entrance to a parking garage and contains two conference rooms.

4. KSIS (MI6) Building
London, UK, 1994

Merging the industrial-style architecture of power stations with Aztec pyramids, the MI6 building by British architect Terry Farrell is an example of Postmodernism at its most monumental, boasting steep stone facades alongside large expanses of green glass.

4

5 6

5. Amoreiras Towers
Lisbon, Portugal, 1985

Controversial for the impact
it made on Lisbon's skyline, this
iconic development by Tomás Taveira
features numerous Postmodern motifs,
such as oversize columns in glass, and
geometric ornamentation.

6. Taipei 101
Taipei, Taiwan, 2004

The stacked form of this skyscraper in
Taiwan evokes the shape of a traditional
pagoda, with eight segments finished in
green-toned glass. In Chinese culture, the
number eight symbolizes prosperity and
good fortune.

▶ **Virtual design**
This CAD drawing of a proposed television center in Seoul, South Korea, was made by British-Italian architect Richard Rogers in 1996. Although the drawing went through several subsequent revisions, it provided a three-dimensional view of what the finished structure would look like.

CAD

Computers and computer-aided design (CAD) programs have transformed the ways in which architects work—from conceiving and visualizing buildings to optimizing the use of materials.

For hundreds of years, architects designed buildings entirely by hand, developing rough sketches into more detailed construction drawings. Today, while hand drawing still has a place in architecture, computers have streamlined the design process. They enable architects to build more complex structures and to share realistic images of their designs with clients and the wider public.

DIGITAL ARCHITECTURE

Computers were first used in architecture in the 1960s for completing complex engineering calculations. In 1963, a computer program called Sketchpad made it possible for users to draw, move, and change objects on their computer screens. From this tentative start, CAD became more sophisticated, and by the 1990s, architects were using it to push the boundaries of what they could design. Many of these designs were incredibly complex, but they were easy to model and visualize digitally.

COMPUTER MODELING

Today, CAD has become the new language of architecture. Using a combination of powerful software tools, cloud computing, and advanced graphics, architects can model, design, and visualize buildings quickly and creatively. Long before the first concrete is poured, they can estimate the operational and environmental efficiency of any building, structure, or space.

The most recent development in digital architecture is Building Information Modeling (BIM), which focuses on all aspects of building design. Through BIM software packages, all kinds of data about a building's structure, cost, services, and energy use can be assimilated and shared between architects, building contractors, and engineers. This enables architects to optimize the design process and to monitor a building's performance over time. Crucially, it also gives them an insight into which aspects of a building will need to be serviced or updated.

BUILDING INFORMATION MANAGEMENT

Traditionally, architects designed buildings using two-dimensional drawings, such as plans, elevations, and sections. CAD enabled them to work in three dimensions, but BIM added a fourth dimension—namely, time. It provides a step-by-step account of how a building will fare over time, from each stage of its construction to each year of its life as a finished structure.

An architect at work using BIM

▲ **Sketchpad**
Developed in 1963 by American computer scientist Ivan Sutherland, Sketchpad was the first computer program to have a graphical user interface. Although extremely basic by today's standards, it marked the start of the era of CAD in architecture.

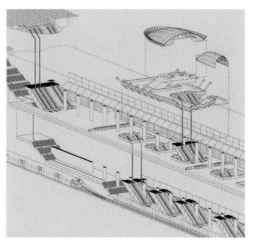

▲ **Piece by piece**
This CAD image of Canary Wharf Underground Station in London was made by British architects Foster + Partners in the 1990s. As its design progressed, each part of the structure could be isolated, analyzed, and modified on screen.

▲ **Design without limits**
Created by Zaha Hadid Architects, this image of a proposed neo-futuristic Performing Arts Center in Abu Dhabi shows how architects can design fantastical structures using CAD. The building is currently under construction.

GUGGENHEIM MUSEUM BILBAO

BILBAO, SPAIN, 1997

Set on a riverside site, the Guggenheim art museum is a landmark of its era. Architect Frank Gehry used computer software and hand-built models to create architecture of intense drama and exhilarating complexity.

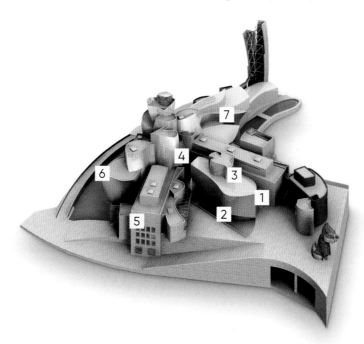

1. Stepped approach
From a public plaza, visitors make their way down a broad stairway to the entrance, a feature that overcomes the height difference across the museum's site, located between the Nervión River and the higher city level.

2. Titanium cladding
The building is clad in a shimmering epidermis of titanium, a material which is extremely strong and resistant to weathering. Changing color in different light conditions, the wafer-thin sheets of titanium resemble rippling fish scales.

3. Central atrium space
Like the nave of a cathedral, the soaring central atrium forms the dramatic heart of the building. Elevated walkways bring visitors in and out of it, offering a variety of standpoints to observe the artwork on display.

4. Permanent galleries
The museum contains 19 galleries, with several designed to house permanent artworks, such as Richard Serra's monumental spiraling steel sculpture *The Matter of Time*, which occupies the building's largest gallery.

5. Connection to the city
Within the central atrium, large expanses of glazing frame panoramic views of the city. As an iconic piece of modern architecture, the success of the museum helped transform Bilbao into a popular tourist destination.

6. Expressive structure
Rather than being a neutral backdrop for art, the Guggenheim's varied array of gallery spaces are often as dramatically expressive and sculptural as the works they were designed to house, with the architecture becoming, in effect, a work of art.

7. Sculptural forms
The museum's distinctive, dynamic forms were achieved by first creating rough, hand-built models, which were then precisely digitized using computer software—originally designed for use in the aerospace industry—capable of modeling complex curves.

4 5 6

7

DECONSTRUCTIVISM

Characterized by jagged, irrational formal arrangements, Deconstructivist buildings challenged the idea of architecture as stable forms, embracing unpredictability and dynamism.

An extension of the Postmodernist and Neo-Expressionist movements of the 1980s and '90s, Deconstructivism challenged fundamental ideas about architecture. The design of buildings had long been ruled by concepts of harmony and function, reinforced in particular by the Modernist movement. Deconstructivists rejected this and embraced the idea that people—and the buildings and cities they lived in—were unpredictable and disordered. What if, instead of attempting to dictate a way of living, buildings could reflect the more unstable, chaotic nature of everyday life?

CHALLENGING MEANING

"Deconstructivism" combines Constructivism, a style of Modern architecture popular in Russia in the 1920s and '30s, and Deconstruction, a method of literary analysis developed by 20th-century French philosopher Jacques Derrida. Derrida rejected the idea of "true" meaning in language and suggested that, in fact, meaning was derived from contrasts.

This philosophy became the basis of a new, Deconstructivist architecture, which questioned some conventional architectural patterns, such as the need for a strict divide between the interior and exterior, and that certain rooms should go next to one another. This gave rise to the characteristic Deconstructivist "clashing" aesthetic.

This new approach met with criticism, and many Deconstructivist buildings stoked debates of "form versus function." Some critics argued that the architect's artistic vision was prioritized over comfortable, usable spaces.

MOVEMENT AND EXPERIENCE

Deconstructivist architects were interested in how people occupied and moved through buildings. They considered architecture not just as a static backdrop, but as something dynamic, and often looked beyond the building to its relationship with the wider site or city. American architect Bernard Tschumi, portrayed this as a form of "choreography." His seminal 1976–1981 work *The Manhattan Transcripts* used diagrams and film techniques to portray New York locations as stage sets on which everyday life took place. In her early works, Iraqi–British architect Zaha Hadid used overlapping lines of movement or geometry to form the basis of a building's formal arrangement, criss-crossing and colliding to dramatic effect.

> "Any relationship between a building and its users is one of violence."
>
> Bernard Tschumi, *Architecture and Disjunction*, 1996

◀ **Subversion**

At Daniel Libeskind's Jewish Museum in Berlin, Germany, the idea of a staircase is subverted. The stairs end at a blank wall, with slanted concrete beams above. Their function is lost and instead, they symbolize the Jewish lives cut short by the Holocaust.

CONCEPTION

The term "Deconstructivism" was coined at the MoMA's 1988 "Deconstructivist Architecture" Exhibition in New York. Curators Philip Johnson and Mark Wigley grouped seven architects whose work they felt radically subverted architectural form, but not all of them liked being labeled Deconstructivists.

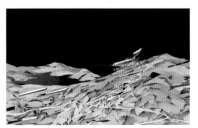

Zaha Hadid's work *The Peak Leisure Club* (1983) was featured at the exhibition.

VITRA FIRE STATION

WEIL AM RHEIN, GERMANY, 1990–1993

This fire station in Germany, now an exhibition space, was the first major work built by Iraqi-British architect Zaha Hadid and was a key piece in defining Deconstructivism. Its soaring, jagged forms, described as "movement frozen," were inspired by the sudden rush of activity that would occur when the fire sirens went off.

▲ Raw finish
The fire station is built entirely from concrete to emphasize the many angled, geometric planes. The concrete is left exposed both inside and out, with minimal finishes.

▲ Parallel lines
The Deconstructivist ethos is seen in every detail. This staircase has several parallel handrails. Their course is not interrupted by any landing areas.

▲ Geometric angles
Bathrooms and changing areas are geometric, with jagged edges and sloping walls. Strips of lighting emphasize the gaps between the building planes.

ZAHA HADID PAINTINGS

Few architects have done more to define Deconstructivism than Zaha Hadid. She expressed bold urban visions and master plans in vast painted canvases, inspired by 1920s Russian Constructivism. Her 1983 proposal *The Peak Leisure Club* in Hong Kong existed only as a set of stylized, highly geometric artwork, but it placed her at the forefront of a new stylistic movement.

Hadid's original painting shows the angular form upon which the Vitra Fire Station was based.

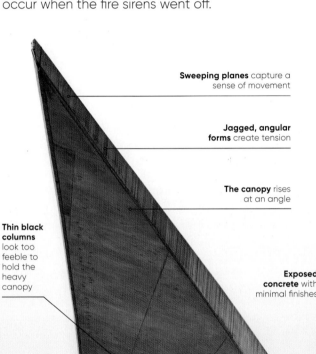

Sweeping planes capture a sense of movement

Jagged, angular forms create tension

The canopy rises at an angle

Thin black columns look too feeble to hold the heavy canopy

Exposed concrete with minimal finishes

A steel-framed glazed wall houses the fire engines

KEY **ELEMENTS**

Deconstructivist buildings were showy, photogenic and intriguing, and people began to believe that they could generate tourism, the so-called "Bilbao effect."

DISORDERED GEOMETRIES

Rejecting the idea that buildings could be neatly divided according to their uses, Deconstructivists avoided symmetry, order, and clarity and created complex formal arrangements that looked almost random.

▲ **Clashing geometry**
The iconic Guggenheim Museum by Frank Gehry in Bilbao, Spain, is characteristic of Deconstructivist clashing geometries. Its titanium-clad exterior evokes a ship, while the foyers take on unusual, disordered forms.

DYNAMIC SURFACES OR "SKINS"

The extravagant shapes of Deconstructivist buildings made them hard to engineer and expensive to build, with large amounts of carbon-intense steel and concrete required to fulfill the designer's vision.

▲ **Folding structure**
Sweeping upward from the adjoining plaza, the curving walls and ceilings of Baku's Heydar Aliyev Center in Azerbaijan defy the traditional compartmentalization of buildings, favoring a singular, dramatic formal gesture instead.

EXPOSED MATERIALS

Deconstructivists often left building materials, typically concrete, steel, and glass, in their raw, exposed state, to emphasize the geometric qualities of their buildings.

◀ **Concrete exterior**
At the MAXXI in Rome, Italy, the curves of the concrete exterior give a material often considered heavy and permanent a sense of dynamism.

▲ **Metal framework**
A metal grid frames the entrance to Wexner Center for the Arts in Columbus, Ohio. Evoking scaffolding, it conveys incompleteness and potential.

DISRUPTING CONVENTIONS

Deconstructivists were not interested in the usual approaches to a building's form or context. Instead, they questioned why rules about how to build existed in the first place.

▲ **Steel and glass extension**
This rooftop extension to a Falkestrasse law office in Vienna, Austria, disrupts a historic building with a jagged extension in steel and glass. It broke local planning regulations and was only permitted because the mayor considered it a work of art.

DECONSTRUCTIVIST BUILDINGS

The distinctive, signature styles pioneered by Deconstructivist architects were soon in high demand, particularly for large-scale cultural projects, such as museums and galleries.

1. Port Authority Building
Antwerp, Belgium, 2009–2016

The dominance of this extraordinary extension to a historic building is characteristic of the Deconstructivists' preoccupation with bold contrasts. Perched on a monolithic concrete support, the glass-covered structure bursts from the roof of the existing building.

2. Parc de la Villette
Paris, France, 1984–1987

The large, open areas of this Parisian park are dotted with a series of 26 bright red follies, designed to be used in a variety of ways. The park was planned as a leisure space without any historical or traditional references.

3. Museum of Pop Culture
Seattle, WA, 1995–2000

The crumpled metallic facades of this museum in Seattle by Frank Gehry demonstrate the Deconstructivists' preoccupation with manipulating the exterior surface of a building. The effect that Gehry creates is to make the scale, interior arrangement, or even purpose difficult to deduce from the outside.

4. Imperial War Museum North
Manchester, UK, 1997–2001

The first building by Daniel Libeskind in the UK boasts a dramatic, aluminum-clad facade. In this museum, the architect's highly narrative approach is translated into three large "shards," designed to represent a world shattered by conflict.

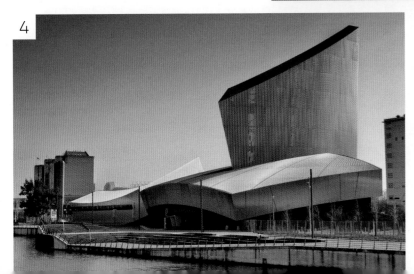

POETICISM

Architectural design relies on the imagination: it is impossible to fully describe the quality of a space before it is built. Every building, with its particular materials and site, will feel different.

The creation of atmosphere is often incidental to the function of a building, but sometimes fundamental to the intention of the architect. The way a building is experienced—the "architectural promenade" or journey from exterior through the interior—can be curated through the manipulation of light, materials, and temperature to establish a mood that may change to reflect the time or weather.

The fabric of buildings also changes with time: materials age, timber is smoothed and worn by human touch, and rain and wind erode brick, stone, and concrete. This aging process can influence the design: different elements may be selected for their durability, intended to be replaced, protected from, or deliberately exposed to weathering.

NARRATIVE THROUGH DESIGN
Contemporary architects such as Peter Zumthor, Steven Holl, Kengo Kuma, and Wang Shu all focus on atmospheric and temporal qualities in their work. They are less interested

"Buildings which have a strong impact always convey an intense feeling of their spatial quality."

Peter Zumthor, *Architecture and Urbanism*, 1998

in functional expression and more concerned with how their architecture might tell a story about a particular place or a particular set of circumstances.

Peter Zumthor's buildings, for example, reflect a deep personal association with the landscape and architecture of his native Switzerland. He describes his approach to spatial design as "a bit like the tempering of pianos perhaps, the search for the right mood, in the sense of instrumental tuning and atmosphere as well." This "mood" is most evident in his designs for spaces intended to be places of reflection—chapels, galleries, and museums that reveal the past.

In their concern for detail, the passage of time, the creation of enclosure, spatial experiences, and sensations, the work of architects such as Zumthor serves as a reminder that buildings are fundamentally not just technological artifacts, but are also the settings for human life.

ENGAGING THE SENSES
Holistic design must take all of the senses into account. Materials have a tactile quality—rough or smooth, cold or warm—and a person's sense of temperature is affected by both convection of the air and radiation. The eye adjusts quickly to bright light but slowly to darkness, while different volumes of space lined in different materials have different acoustic properties. Understanding the sensual impact of spaces can transform design.

Stone and water engage the senses at Peter Zumthor's Therme Vals, Switzerland.

SHELTER FOR ROMAN RUINS

CHUR, GRAUBÜNDEN, SWITZERLAND, 1986

Three timber-framed structures designed by Peter Zumthor enclose the excavated walls of a Roman settlement, mirroring the Roman plan. Lined in timber lamella louvers, they let in sound, light, and air but keep out wind and rain. Box skylights illuminate the interior during the day; the louvered facades glow when lit at night.

▲ **Thresholds between spaces**
Access to the shelter is via four steps enclosed by a cantilevered steel porch. Similar connections are made between the timber structures, forming a spatial journey of enclosure and exposure.

Facade is lined with timber lamella louvres

Box skylights constructed from steel sheet

The windows align with the Roman ruins

▲ **The visitor's journey**
A lightweight steel bridge takes visitors through the enclosed space, over the ruins. Flights of folded steel steps descend to the excavated rooms in the interior.

POETIC BUILDINGS

▲ **Zinc Mine Museum,** Sauda, Norway, 2016
Here, laminated timber structures support three enigmatic plywood boxes perched on a valley wall. Designed by Peter Zumthor, and inspired by the old mines, the boxes are covered with jute (fiber) mesh and resin. They house a museum, café, and toilets.

▲ **Church of the Light,** Ibaraki, Japan, 1989
A crucifix of light illuminates the concrete interior of this church. The concrete shell is 15 in (38 cm) thick, creating a silent, enclosed space. Designed by Tadao Ando, this is an architecture of contrasts: solid and void, dark and light, secular and sacred space.

▲ **Kiasma Museum of Contemporary Art,**
Helsinki, Finland, 1998
A void between two masses forms Steven Holl's lobby, where a curved ramp draws the visitor to galleries beyond. Light scoops, clerestory windows, and translucent glass modulate incoming daylight.

RETROFIT ARCHITECTURE

The construction and running of buildings is, today, responsible for around 40 percent of climate-changing emissions by humans. The world of architecture is gearing up for massive changes.

A few visionaries have warned since the 1960s that global fossil fuel consumption is pushing the world toward ecological crisis, but since 2000, understanding of the human impact on climate and nature has rapidly deepened and spread. Many countries and organizations have pledged to operate with no net carbon emissions in just a few decades, which requires a huge reduction in the amount of energy and emissions associated with both the making and running of buildings.

The quantity and size of buildings being constructed has shot up with the increased use of coal, oil, and gas energy around the world. In just three years, from 2011 to 2013, China used 7.3 billion tons of concrete—far more than the 5 billion tons the US, the world's richest country, used throughout the 20th century.

While many struggle with the scale of the challenge, a growing number of talented and committed architects, engineers, and clients are rushing to figure out how to move away from the carbon-intense materials and building practices of the construction industry. New approaches to architecture may have the power to avert climate catastrophe. The profession is at the start of its most radical revolution yet—fossil fuels are gradually being replaced by renewable energy, and a gentler, more circular economy is evolving to reduce the destructively excessive extraction of materials.

Until a new range of materials and techniques emerges, however, the best thing to make tomorrow's buildings from is today's buildings.

RETROFIT FIRST

The architectural world is coming to recognize that demolishing and replacing an existing building is no longer a sign of progress but an admission of creative failure, with a high carbon cost. Replacing a substantial city building can create tens of thousands of tons of carbon emissions. By keeping as much as possible of an existing building, the huge emissions produced in making brick or concrete and steel for foundations and structure are avoided.

The other great advantage of retrofitting existing buildings is that almost all of them currently waste a lot of fossil-fuel energy. Heat leaks through gaps and conducts through walls, requiring far more heating in winter or air conditioning in summer than if the building was well insulated and more airtight. As heatwaves intensify, many existing buildings will need more shading for their windows to prevent the rooms inside from getting dangerously hot.

Even now, money, effort, and carbon emissions are habitually spent demolishing and rebuilding existing buildings. In a climate emergency, it makes sense to keep them and improve their energy performance. The result will be sustainable, varied, and beautiful cities.

◀ **Reinvention**

Most of the structure of Quay Quarter Tower, a 1970s office building in Sydney, Australia, was retained during its refurbishment, saving 8,800 tons of carbon dioxide that would have been released with the use of new concrete and steel. The building was given a completely new facade and profile (see box p.364).

WASTE IN CONSTRUCTION

The cement industry is responsible for 8 percent of all human CO_2 (carbon dioxide) emissions. CO_2 remains in the atmosphere for centuries, so the emissions produced by a building's construction will long outlast it. When a concrete building is demolished, a robust, fire-resistant structure becomes low-quality rubble. The new building's construction then produces enormous carbon emissions.

The demolition of a Brutalist-style parking garage in Bath, UK, 2022

GRAND PARC

BORDEAUX, FRANCE, 2019

Architecture awards normally go to expensive new buildings, but architects Anne Lacaton and Jean-Philippe Vassal won multiple awards for their imaginative improvement of an unremarkable social-housing building—at half the cost of replacing it. The refurbishment created additional, light-filled living spaces.

EXTENDED APARTMENTS

During refurbishment, existing apartments were left undisturbed, except for the alteration of front windows to doors for accessing the new winter garden. This avoided displacing residents, who remained in their homes, and kept relationships between neighbors intact. The addition took just 12 to 16 days per apartment, and rents have remained stable despite the increase in square footage. The large amounts of concrete and steel in the original building have been retained, avoiding the carbon cost of replacing them.

▲ Before
The existing building was an ordinary 1960s apartment building of the sort that is very often demolished and replaced with a new structure, displacing all of its previous residents.

▲ Winter gardens
The extra room produced by the extension can be used for whatever purposes the residents choose, with screens open in warm conditions or closed for winter warmth, and with a balcony beyond it.

A typical apartment shown before and after the addition of the winter garden at Grand Parc

Precast concrete slabs and columns extend the depth of the apartments by 12½ ft (3.8 m)

Varied forms and splashes of color seen from outside hint at the resident's lives within, giving a sense of diversity and humanity

Strong continuous horizontals and crystalline materials give a sense of order and a kind of chilly beauty

External elevator shafts on rear of building

Materials used include concrete, metals, glass, and polycarbonates, which, although carbon-intense, are cheaper

KEY **ELEMENTS**

The best retrofit projects combine well-implemented technical improvements and a strong aesthetic vision. Architects and cities alike profit from the variety achieved by working with what is already there.

IMPROVED PUBLIC REALM

Retrofit should not stop with the building. By rethinking how we use our street spaces, we can make our cities less vulnerable to flooding and heatwaves, safer for pedestrians and cyclists, less polluted, and far more beautiful for those who live there.

ENHANCED PERFORMANCE

When an older building is admired and of high quality, it is possible to produce considerable improvements in the energy efficiency of the building while respecting its architecture. In order to achieve the level of carbon reduction required, almost every existing building must receive performance improvements.

◄ Putting cars first
This image from 1978 shows Eerste van der Helststraat, a street in Amsterdam, choked with vehicle traffic—a smelly, bleak, and dangerous environment.

▼ Pedestrian priority
By prioritizing pedestrians and cyclists, and planting trees, the same street has today been transformed into a place where people want to linger and relax.

EXPANSION AND IMPROVEMENT

Retrofit does not need to conserve the look of the existing building or prevent expansion. Quay Quarter Tower, Sydney, is considerably larger after the retrofit and has gained a new appearance in both its shape and the details on its facade. The new facade also takes into account the need to keep sunshine from overheating the north side of the offices.

Before **Retained structure** **After**

The new profile retains the core structure.

▲ Optimal energy efficiency
A fine Brutalist office building in Connecticut, by Marcel Breuer, has been converted into Hotel Marcel: the US's first hotel to achieve Passive House certification—an assessment that identifies buildings using almost no energy for heating or cooling.

RETROFIT BUILDINGS

Retrofit can involve better insulation, rethinking existing spaces, or adding solar paneling. If users are willing to be cooler in winter and hotter in summer, this can also reduce carbon footprint and energy bills.

1. Private house
Uzbekistan, c. 1970 (21st century)
This home has been retrofitted with enough solar panels to supply all the energy needs of the household while also producing excess to sell to the government. Electricity-generating solar panels are an efficient way of reducing fossil-fuel consumption, and can be installed on most roofs, new or old.

2. New Court, Trinity College
Cambridge, UK, 1825 (2016)
Even amid famous historic architecture, it is often possible to make sensitive changes that hugely improve insulation and reduce heat loss to air leaks. Using huge technical expertise, this building was upgraded to save 80 percent of its carbon emissions.

3. Cedar Court
Glasgow, UK, 1960s (2016–2019)
In a city that has demolished much of its 1960s high rise housing, this building was one of a few to be retrofitted instead, hugely increasing the quality of life of its residents and reducing their carbon emissions, while also retaining, rather than wasting, the concrete and steel of the building.

"The greenest building is ... one that is already built."

Carl Elefante, AIA President, 2018

SUSTAINABLE ARCHITECTURE

The race is on to meet the world's need for new buildings without using ecologically disastrous materials such as concrete, steel, plastics, and aluminum.

It is conceivable that ever-more sophisticated levels of technology will fix the problem of climate change, while allowing people to continue living in much the same way that they do now. New technologies, however, tend to have a counterproductively high carbon cost to implement. The most promising directions in sustainable architecture so far are those that look not only at how buildings operate but also at how they are constructed, where they are built, and the materials they are made from. Redesigning ways of living and of building together is the path to sustainability.

A GUIDE TO THE FUTURE

When looking for low-energy, zero-carbon building materials and techniques, the best guide might be older architecture, built without cheap fossil fuels and using materials and techniques in ingenious ways that are far more sustainable than those regarded as the norm today.

The best sustainable architecture does not return to the past, however, but learns lessons selectively. With renewable electricity sources, sophisticated materials science, and advanced electronics, traditional materials can be used in improved ways: from computer-calculated bamboo structures to architect Yasmeen Lari's redesign of a widely used Pakistani rural stove to substantially reduce its fuel use.

Many of the most sustainable buildings of new architecture have emerged outside the regions that led the rise in fossil-fueled architecture. As a result, the people who are doing most to fight fossil-fuel dependency are often from countries that have contributed the least to the problem of climate change. It is time for the rich world to learn lessons from those skilled in so-called "lower" technologies.

HABITS VERSUS NEEDS

Since the 1920s, energy-hungry technologies like air conditioning and central heating have spread around the world. Glass towers in Dubai, flooded with hot sunshine, are cooled by mighty air conditioners; similar-looking buildings far closer to the poles are overheated through icy winters. This costs an enormous amount of fossil-fuel energy.

Shedding the habits of 150 years of fossil-fuel dependency is not easy—a cooler interior in winter or a warmer one in summer may feel uncomfortable at first, and it is hard to unlearn associations between shiny, new buildings and a sense of investment and progress. But as people grow accustomed to embracing creative sustainable solutions, the beauty of economy and modesty becomes compelling, and even thrilling, promising a more balanced, cleaner, and greener world on the other side of the climate emergency.

◀ **Creative sustainability**

Architecture made of traditional materials, as at Bali's Green School, do not need to be old-fashioned or unambitious. Good design can produce buildings that are as exciting and beautiful as they are sustainable.

BAMBOO

One of the fastest-growing plants, bamboo takes carbon out of the atmosphere and forms strong, light stems that can be used as a renewable, highly sustainable building material. In areas where it grows abundantly, it has been used in construction projects for thousands of years. It is now used widely, both in its natural state and in industrially engineered forms that work like glued, laminated wooden beams.

Bamboo, which is actually a grass, is as strong as timber.

THE ARC GYMNASIUM

GREEN SCHOOL, BALI, 2008

The Green School, Bali, has worked to ensure that its buildings live up to its low-carbon, circular economy ideals. The architecture draws on the materials and some of the techniques of traditional Indonesian architecture, updated with modern engineering expertise. The results have attracted worldwide admiration.

WORLD'S GREENEST GYM?

The famous roofline of the Sydney Opera House is made of steel-reinforced concrete and fired and glazed tiles, all requiring huge fossil-fuel heat inputs to make, transport, and erect. The Arc Gymnasium produces an equally beautiful result using a tiny fraction of the energy inputs, and on a much lower budget. If, one day, the Arc is no longer needed, its ribs and roofing can simply disappear back into the soil.

Front and side elevations show multiple arches and gridshell design.

◄ Gridshell design

The strength of the lightweight roof is partly due to the gridshell design: the bamboo lattices are laid in two directions in opposite curvatures for a column-free interior and a structure able to flex in storms.

◄ Bamboo tiling

The use of locally grown materials with minimal industrial processing throughout has meant very low energy inputs. Materials can be renewed using local craft skills and little or no carbon emissions.

Bundles of bamboo form arches spanning 62 ft (19 m)

Open sides for natural ventilation let in cooling breezes from any direction

Vents allow hot air to escape and cooler air to circulate

Bamboo arches reach a height of 45 ft (14 m)

The steep roof provides good run-off for heavy monsoon rains, and creates deep shade

KEY **ELEMENTS**

The most sustainable materials are locally sourced and used to moderate excesses of heat and cold with minimal energy inputs. This means that sustainable architecture looks very different depending on where it is built.

LOW-ENERGY COMFORT

Rather than use large amounts of energy from fossil fuels for cooling, shading a building's windows from direct sunlight can increase comfort in hot climates. In cold places, better insulation and interior surfaces that prevent loss of radiated heat can make a significant reduction in the amount of heating required.

▶ Designing for heat
In their buildings at the Rwanda Institute for Conservation Agriculture, the design team have integrated shading for windows and used thick walls of rammed earth, which retain some of the cool of the night during the day. They even used stone foundations, rather than the carbon-intense concrete that is more commonplace worldwide.

BAREFOOT ARCHITECTURE

Yasmeen Lari was Pakistan's first female architect. After a very successful career, she helped with emergency housing following a 2005 earthquake and became persuaded that architects should be helping ordinary people, not the richest few. Since then, she has helped tens of thousands to house themselves in very low-carbon homes of bamboo, earth, and thatch. Lari describes her community-focused approach as "Barefoot Social Architecture."

Lari focuses on natural materials and local skills.

LOW-CARBON MATERIALS

A good reference for low-carbon building materials is to look back to the pre-fossil-fuel periods of architecture. Before cheap coal made concrete and steel affordable, people built with earth, timber, bamboo, straw, or local stone.

▲ A house of straw
In one fairy tale, building in straw is made to sound foolish, but in fact straw is a good insulator and stores carbon removed from the atmosphere when it was part of a fast-growing grain plant. This building combines a timber frame with straw-bale infill, which will be plastered to increase its durability.

▲ Who needs concrete?
Concrete is an extremely versatile building material, but, as Webb Yates Engineers, a UK practice, have shown with this 36-ft (11-m) stone beam, lightly reinforced with steel, it is possible to make an excellent structural material without emitting lots of carbon by cooking stone into cement.

SUSTAINABLE BUILDINGS

Many designers and builders worldwide are working to be more sustainable, but a radical rethink of materials and a revolutionary new approach to architecture is still needed.

1. Earth masonry village school
Sindh, Pakistan, 2012

Designed by Yasmeen Lari, this school is raised to withstand floods, which the area was badly hit by in 2005. It is made of bamboo, mud, and lime—materials that are low cost and leave no carbon footprint.

2. Cork House
Eton, Berkshire, UK, 2013–2019

In an attractive garden, Matthew Barnett Howland with Dido Milne and Oliver Wilton have designed a small, carbon-negative house of expanded cork. The cork insulates the interior and is held together by gravity rather than glues or other treatments that would make it hard to recycle.

3. Massive stone social housing
Toulouse, France, 2011

In France, Gilles Perraudin is bringing back stone construction for ordinary buildings, such as this social housing project made from limestone blocks. Turning stone into cement has a high energy and CO_2 cost; natural stone only needs energy to quarry and transport it.

DIRECTORY

▲ **The entrance** to the Mycenaean Treasury of Atreus

DIRECTORY OF BUILDINGS

PYRAMID OF KHUFU

Giza, Egypt, *see pp.26–27*

ZIGGURAT OF UR

Nasriyah, Iraq, *see p.19*

TOMB OF RAMOSE

Luxor, Egypt, c. 1350 BCE

Ramose was the Vizier under pharaohs Amenhotep III (r. 1390–1353 BCE) and Akhenaten (r. 1353–1336 BCE) of the 18th Dynasty. His large, private tomb (numbered "TT 55") is one of the finest in the Valley of the Nobles, adjacent to Luxor's Valley of the Kings.

The design of the tomb shows an important stage in the transition between the traditional, formal artistic styles of the early New Kingdom and the freer style under Akhenaten. Some of the earlier wall paintings were defaced after the change of religious observance under Akhenaten to the worship of one sole god (the Aten, or sun-disk). A roof collapse rendered the tomb inaccessible, preventing more paintings suffering a similar fate after the pharaoh's religious revolution was overturned.

The "T"-shaped tomb, though unfinished, is still impressive, with a greater density of wall decoration than most noble tombs, including an image showing Akhenaten and his wife Nefertiti bestowing a gift of gold on Ramose.

TEMPLE OF AMEN-RA, KARNAK

near Luxor, Egypt, *see pp.32–33*

TREASURY OF ATREUS

Mycenae, Greece, c. 1350–c. 1250 BCE

Built by the Mycenaean civilization, the Treasury of Atreus *tholos* (beehive-shaped tomb) consists of a 118-ft- (36-m-) long *dromos* (passageway) leading to a domed burial chamber. For more than 1,000 years, it was the largest dome ever built. The monumental doorway lintel weighs 132 tons, and was decorated with geometric relief plaques. On each side of the entrance were once Minoan columns of green marble with spiral and zigzag carvings.

The main chamber is made up of 33 courses of corbeled (overhanging) blocks polished smooth. Around 50 ft (15 m) in diameter, it is the largest corbeled dome in the world. A short passageway leads to a secondary chamber cut into the bedrock for the actual burials; the main chamber was probably used for rituals in honor of the dead. The tomb was later known as the Tomb of Agamemnon, after the king in Homer's *Iliad*, whom the ancient Greeks believed to be the king of Mycenae.

THE FIRST TEMPLE OF HERA

Paestum, Italy, c. 550 BCE

The oldest of the three Greek Doric temples at Paestum, the First Temple of Hera was nicknamed "the Basilica" by 18th-century antiquarians for its resemblance to that type of Roman civic building, with its absence of pediments and colonnades in the center of the building. Measuring 177 ft (54 m) by 82 ft (25 m), the temple stands at the highest point of the town. Its rectangular shape is formed of 9 rows of 18 tapered limestone columns which bulge at the top to create the illusion of straightness.

The temple's structure was bisected inside, possibly indicating the worship of more than one god or indicating two aspects of Hera, the goddess of marriage and childbirth. Artifacts found suggest Hera's connection to the site. The later Second Temple of Hera (see pp.42–43) is also at Paestum, Italy.

PALACE COMPLEX OF PERSEPOLIS

Shiraz, Iran, *see p.45*

▲ **The Tomb of Ramose** in the Valley of the Nobles

▲ **Made of multi-colored glazed brick,** these decorative panels from the Palace of Darius show a pair of winged lions with bearded human heads.

PALACE OF DARIUS

Susa, Iran, c. 518 BCE

The centerpiece of Susa—the administrative capital of the Achaemenid Persian Empire—was the palace named for Darius I (550–486 BCE). Constructed on an artificial mound 49 ft (15 m) high, the palace covered more than 250 acres (100 hectares).

Four inner courtyards led to a monumental hall supported by 36 columns carved in the Persian style, topped by double bull figures. The foundation inscription speaks of gold, lapis lazuli, and carnelian brought from central Asia, and silver and ebony from Egypt. The hall's roof was of great cedar beams imported from Lebanon. Glazed bricks adorned the inner walls, depicting lions,

griffins, and the Immortals, the Persian ruler's bodyguards. The palace was completed by Darius's son Xerxes I (c. 519–465 BCE), who added a monumental gateway.

PARTHENON

Athens, Greece, *see pp. 38–39*

TEMPLE OF CONCORDIA

Agrigento, Sicily, Italy, c. 430 BCE

Of all the buildings in the Valle dei Templi (Valley of Temples) erected by the ancient Greek city-state of Akragas, the Temple of Concordia is the best preserved. Built of limestone, it has columns on all sides, arranged 6 by 13. Originally the columns were red, and their proportions were carefully tweaked to produce "optical correction" to make them appear balanced, such as varying the column widths and the distances between columns, leaning or tapering the columns, and adding slight bulges two-thirds of the way up.

It is not known to whom the temple was dedicated—its name comes erroneously from a Roman inscription nearby. During the 6th century, the temple was converted into a Greek Orthodox church.

PETRA

Petra, Jordan, 4th century BCE

The Nabataean rulers of the trading city of Petra grew rich on extracting tolls from merchant caravans passing through the desert between Mesopotamia and Syria. They used this wealth to carve elaborate structures in the red sandstone rock faces of their capital. The most elaborate is Al-Khazneh (the Treasury), possibly built as a mausoleum for King Aretas IV (8 BCE–40 CE).

Its 128-ft- (39-m-) high facade is decorated with Hellenistic-style columns. Six on the lower level are flanked by statues of the Greek heroes Castor and Pollux, while the second level is crowned by an enormous trophy. In contrast, the chambers cut into the interior are plain and unadorned.

TEMPLE OF ISIS AT PHILAE

Aswan, Egypt, c. 280 BCE

Built for the Pharaoh Ptolemy II (308–246 BCE), the Temple of Isis is part of a complex whose origins lie in the 7th century BCE. On an island in the Nile—long sacred to the goddess Isis—the temple has two granite colonnades with 32 columns leading to a monumental pylon (gateway), flanked by huge lion statues and originally by two obelisks. The first pylon, which is decorated with friezes of Ptolemy XII

(112–51 BCE) smiting his enemies, leads to an outer courtyard containing the *mammisi*—the house commemorating Isis giving birth to Horus.

A second pylon, 40 ft (12 m) high, leads to an inner courtyard with the most sacred sanctuary. Before the whole area was flooded in 1970 after the building of the Aswan High Dam, the 50,000 stones of the temple were moved and rebuilt on a nearby island.

DAMBULLA CAVE TEMPLES

Dambulla, Sri Lanka, 3rd century BCE

Consisting of five cave temples set into a 525-ft (160-m) rock face, Dambulla is the best preserved cave-temple complex in Sri Lanka. It contains some 22,600 sq ft (2,100 sq m) of Buddhist wall paintings, created between the 2nd century BCE and the 18th century CE, and showing scenes from the life of the Buddha.

The first cave, the Devarajlena Vihara (Cave of the Divine King) contains a 46-ft (14-m) statue of the sleeping Buddha. It is just one of more than 150 statues of the Buddha and his disciples, as well as several of Sri Lankan kings and the Hindu deities Vishnu and Ganesh. Dambulla still operates as a Buddhist monastery, as it has done for more than 2,000 years.

TEMPLE OF JUPITER

Baalbek, Lebanon, 16 BCE–3rd century CE

Part of a shrine complex, the Temple of Jupiter was the largest in the Roman world. The podium on which it sits is composed of 800-ton stones. Its propylaea (exterior entrance way) led to a main court surrounded by 84 columns of granite from Aswan in Egypt. The principal sanctuary measured 288 ft (88 m) by 157 ft (48 m) and was fronted by 54 huge columns in the Corinthian style, each one 65 ft (20 m) tall and 8 ft (2.5 m) wide—the largest in Classical antiquity.

After lightning damaged the building in 524, most of it was dismantled on the orders of the Byzantine Emperor Justinian (483–565 CE), and the stones were used in buildings in Constantinople. Today, only six columns and their entablature still stand.

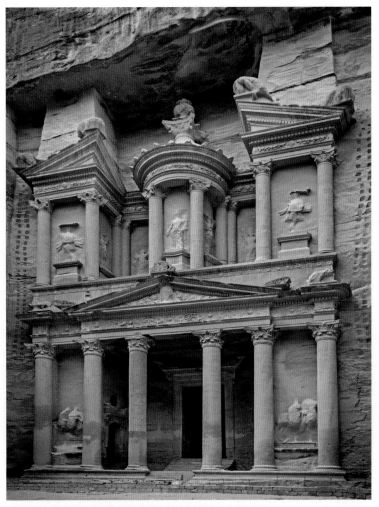

▲ **The entrance to Petra's Treasury**, flanked by statues of the twins Castor and Pollux from Greek and Roman mythology

▲ **The Philae temple complex** on its island in the reservoir of the Aswan Low Dam

▲ **The Ruwanweliseya Dagoba** was one of the tallest monuments of its time.

GREAT STUPA

Sanchi, India, *see p.63*

RUWANWELISEYA

Anuradhapura, Sri Lanka, c. 140 BCE

Also known as the Great Stupa, the Ruwanweliseya is a dagoba (a domed shrine for sacred relics) commissioned by King Dutugemunu (161–137 BCE) in the Anuradhapura kingdom to house relics of the Buddha. Its design reflects key elements of the Buddha's teaching: the large hemispherical dome represents the totality of his doctrine; the four sides of the square on the dome are for the Four Noble Truths; the dome's eight concentric rings are for the Noble Eightfold Path; and the enormous crystal on top is for the goal of enlightenment.

The 338-ft- (103-m-) tall dagoba is decorated with a frieze of 344 elephants. Although renovated under successive Sri Lankan kings, it fell into ruins by the 19th century and was restored after a fund-raising effort by Buddhist monks.

ROYAL MAUSOLEUM OF MAURETANIA

Tipasa, Algeria, 3 BCE

The Numidian king Juba II (50 BCE–24 CE) ordered the construction of the Royal Mausoleum of Mauretania for his wife, Cleopatra Selene II (the daughter of Mark Antony and Cleopatra VII of Egypt). It was constructed to reflect both traditional Numidian style and the mausoleum of the Roman Emperor Augustus (63 BCE–14 CE).

A pyramid on a circular base, it is around 197 ft (60 m) in diameter and was originally 131 ft (40 m) high. It was adorned with a circle of 60 Ionic columns, and the interior had two vaulted rooms, possibly burial chambers, though they were robbed long ago.

Known locally as the "tomb of the Christian Woman" because of a cross-like carving, it was partly destroyed by an Ottoman admiral in the 16th century, before its restoration in the 1860s.

PYRAMID OF THE SUN

Teotihuacan, Mexico, *see p.69*

SEGOVIA AQUEDUCT

Segovia, Spain, c. 50–100 CE

The Roman aqueduct that spans a gorge in Spain carried water 10 miles (16 km) from the Río Frío to the city of Segovia. Some 2,667 ft (813 m) in length, its 211 pillars support 167 arches (in a double layer in the center where the terrain dips), and the structure stands up to 94 ft (28.5 m) above the valley floor. It was built with 24,000 granite blocks without mortar. It is not known exactly

when the aqueduct was built, but it was probably during the reign of one of the Roman Emperors Domitian (51–96 CE), Nerva (30–96 CE), or Trajan (53–117 CE). It is the only aqueduct from Roman Spain still intact, but it was partially destroyed in 1072 before being reconstructed 400 years later. The original dedication plaque and statue of Hercules, once in a niche on the structure's side, are missing.

COLOSSEUM

Rome, Italy, *see pp.54–55*

PALACE OF THE JAGUARS

Teotihuacan, Mexico, 2nd century CE

The Palacio de los Jaguares (Palace of the Jaguars) is the Spanish name for part of the Aztec complex of ruins at Quetzalpapálotl, which is located close to the monumental Pyramid of the Moon in the ancient central Mexican city of Teotihuacan (see pp.68–69). The temple is named for the murals of jaguars on its walls. Many are depicted wearing headdresses with plumes of quetzal feathers and blowing on conch shells dripping with blood.

The walls also bear the carved image of a goggle-eyed god, most probably Tlaloc, the Aztec rain deity, who may also be depicted in the form of a five-pointed starfish on the main murals. Other parts of the complex have murals showing feathered snails, owls, green parrots, and butterflies. Along with the city of Teotihuacan as a whole, the temple was abandoned for unknown reasons around 750 CE.

▲ **A mural in the Palace of the Jaguars** shows two jaguars wearing headdresses. Each has a shell, or possibly a heart, in its mouth.

AMPHITHEATER OF EL JEM

El Jem, Tunisia, c. 238 CE

The architectural centerpiece of the Roman city of Thysdrus, the El Jem amphitheater could hold 35,000 spectators and was the largest of its type in North Africa (and the third-largest in the Roman Empire). Construction probably began around 238 CE under the Emperor Gordian II, whose family came from the area.

It measured 486 ft (148 m) in length and 400 ft (122 m) in width, and its oval-shaped walls consisted of three levels of Corinthian arcades, with multiple portals through which the crowd entered. Parts of the tiered stone interior seating survive. In the 6th century, after the gladiatorial spectacles and beast hunts that had been held there ended, the

▲ **The entrance to the Mogao Caves**—a treasure trove of Buddhist art that includes thousands of paintings and sculptures

amphitheater served as a citadel. Over the centuries, it has suffered damage in battle and looting to build El Jem.

TAQ-I KISRA

Salman Pak, Iraq, *see p.49*

MOGAO CAVES

Dunhuang, China, c. 366 onward

Located in a series of 492 caves southeast of the ancient oasis trading town of Dunhuang, the Mogao complex is one of the finest examples of Buddhist cave grottoes. Also known as the Caves of the Thousand Buddhas, they contain 485,000 sq ft (45,000 sq m) of painted murals and more than 2,000 Buddhist sculptures. Their creation began around 366 CE and continued for a millennium.

The earliest caves show Indian influence and contain a central stupa around which devotees circled in prayer. At their height during the Tang dynasty (618–907 CE), the caves housed 18 monasteries. This was also the period in which 230 caves were

carved as well as a 117-ft- (35.5-m-) high statue of the Buddha, one of the largest in the world.

TAQ-E BOSTAN

Kermanshah, Iran, 4th century CE

Tāq-e Bostān (or Tāq-i-Bustān) means the "Arch of the Garden" and is a site with some of the best-preserved monumental rock reliefs from the Sasanian Persian Empire (224–651 CE). It is located in the Zagros Mountains beside a sacred spring whose waters were collected in a basin beneath it.

One relief shows the investitures of the Persian rulers Shāpūr II (309–379 CE) and Shāpūr III (d. 388 CE). Another, set in an artificial cave, is in the form of an iwan—a four-sided hall open on one side which became typical of Persian architecture. The Shāpūr II relief shows the ruler receiving a ring and diadem from the supreme Persian deity, Ahura Mazdā. Shāpūr II is also trampling underfoot a bearded man who represents the Roman emperor Julian (c. 331–363), who was defeated by the Persians in 363 CE.

XUANKONG TEMPLE

near Datong, China, c. 500 CE

The 40 halls of the Xuankong Monastery perch precariously on the side of Mount Hengshan, 264 ft (75 m) above the ground, giving the complex its nickname, the "Hanging Temple." The builders—legend says it was a single monk Liao Ran—hammered holes in the cliff and inserted huge oak beams which have borne the building's weight for more than 1,500 years.

The monastery is reached by internal stone staircases dug out of the rock. The temple is dedicated to three Chinese religious traditions—Confucianism, Daoism, and Buddhism—and one hall has statues of the founders of all three. The monastery's position, under an outcrop of rock in the cliff-face shelters it from sunlight and rain, which may explain its excellent state of preservation.

TIWANAKU

Tiwanaku, Bolivia, c. 500–900 CE

Before the Inca, Tiwanaku was a flourishing empire in Bolivia. Its capital city, Tiwanaku, reached a population of 20,000. Nestled in an Andean valley near Lake Titicaca, the site has monumental structures and megalithic building blocks, with elaborate carvings, many of large human and puma heads. One of many such structures, Akapana is a terraced 54-ft- (16.5-m-) high earthwork on an east-west axis, dug from the surrounding moat and faced with stonelike andesite. Monumental gateways stand on platforms, mounds, or sunken levels, and large, free-standing carvings also survive. The Tiwanaku's architecture, urban planning, and raised-field farming influenced the later Inca Empire.

SONGYUE PAGODA

Henan province, China, *see p.107*

CHURCH OF HAGIA SOPHIA

Istanbul, Turkey, *see p.85*

EUPHRASIAN BASILICA

Poreč, Croatia, 543–554 CE

One of the finest examples of Byzantine ecclesiastical architecture, the Euphrasian Basilica, dedicated to the Virgin

▲ **The ruins of a temple complex at Tiwanaku.** At its center stands a monumental stone statue known as the Ponce Monolith.

▲ **Xuankong Temple**, built on a precipice, is a center for the three Chinese philosophies of Buddhism, Taoism, and Confucianism.

Mary, includes the octagonal baptistery of an even earlier building. Commissioned by Bishop Euphrasius, it is the first church in the Byzantine Empire's western provinces to have three aisles closed by three apses.

The arcade of slender gray marble columns decorated with birds and intertwining branches gives the interior a spacious feel. The walls are lavishly decorated with mosaics, one of the Virgin with the Christ Child being the most prominent, although the bishop also had himself portrayed (and his monogram stamped on all the pillars' capitals). A 115-ft (35-m) bell tower was added in 1522.

JOYA DE CERÉN

La Libertad, El Salvador, c.550–c.650 CE

Around 1,400 years ago, the Loma Caldera volcano in El Salvador erupted, preserving the Mayan farming village of Joya de Cerén under 33 ft (10 m) of ash. Unlike when Mount Vesuvius buried the Roman city of Pompeii in 79 CE, it seems that the inhabitants of

Joya de Cerén had time to flee. Larger Mayan sites such as Chichén Itzá (see pp.74–77) are dramatic, but Joya de Cerén gives valuable insight into everyday life in a small Mayan village.

Excavations have revealed an area of 7,900 acres (3,200 hectares), with public, religious, residential, and storage buildings. They were constructed with rammed earth, adobe, or earthquake-resistant wattle-and-daub, and they often had thatch or grass-covered roofs. A sweat house has a rare domed roof with a hole for ventilation in its center.

HORYUJI TEMPLE COMPLEX

Ikaruga, Japan, see p.113

ZENKŌJI TEMPLE

Nagano, Japan, 642 CE

Dating from the very dawn of Buddhism in Japan, the Zenkōji temple complex contains the first Buddha statue to have been brought to Japan. The original statue was brought by the nobleman Honda Yoshimitsu. It is only allowed to be seen by the chief priest, but a new replica is unveiled every six years.

Notable features of Zenkōji are the 18th-century Sanmon gate, which houses statues of the four heavenly kings; the huge Niomon gate, with its pair of Nio—fierce warrior guardians; and the statues of the 16 bodhisattvas, who gave up the possibility of their own enlightenment in order to show the path of salvation to others.

Zenkōji's 98-ft- (30-m-) high main hall is one of the largest wooden buildings in Japan.

TEMPLE OF THE INSCRIPTIONS

Palenque, Mexico, see p.75

UMAYYAD MOSQUE

Damascus, Syria, see pp.94–95

▲ **The three-story pagoda** of Hokki-ji Temple is a rare example of architecture from Japan's Asuka period (593–710 CE).

THE THREE-STORY PAGODA OF HOKKI-JI TEMPLE

Ikaruga, Japan, 706 CE

The 80-ft- (24-m-) high pagoda at the center of the Hokki monastery may be the oldest surviving wooden pagoda in the world. Built around a central pillar with elongated brackets, it has 12 exterior pillar supports and a complex arrangement of beams and rafters. The precise alignment of the temple complex's main hall and its pagoda on an east-west axis was the precursor of the

Hokki-ji style of similar temple arrangements. The complex, which may have been a nunnery, was built to honor Avalokiteśvara, the bodhisattva of compassion, and it contains an 11-ft- (3.5-m-) high wooden statue of him. The monastery was traditionally said to have been founded by the regent Taishi Shōtoku (574–622 CE) and was built on the site of one of his former palaces.

BULGUKSA TEMPLE

Gyeongju, South Korea, see p.111

KAILASA TEMPLE

Ellora, India, 756–773 CE

The largest of the 34 rock-cut Hindu and Jain temples at Ellora in the Sahyadri Hills, Kailasa was built on the orders of the Rashtrakuta king Krishna I (r. 756–773). The temple, 107 ft (32.5 m) high, was carved, from top to bottom, out of the hillside without the use of scaffolding. At 276 ft (84 m) long and 174 ft (53 m) wide, it is the world's largest monolithic rock structure.

The temple's architecture shows influence from the Chalukya and Pallava styles of southern India. It may have acquired its name from the enormous sculpture of the deity Ravana (an aspect of Shiva) shaking Mount Kailasa. The courtyards and interiors contain monumental friezes and sculptures, including gods, elephants, and 45-ft- (15-m-) high victory pillars.

PALATINE CHAPEL

Aachen, Germany, 793–813 CE

The sole remaining portion of the palace of the Frankish ruler Charlemagne (c. 747–814 CE), the Palatine Chapel, was consecrated shortly after his death, and it was later extended to become Aachen Cathedral. Built on an octagonal pattern that was common in early Romanesque churches, the domed church was originally flanked by two smaller basilicas. An elaborate atrium in the west gave access to the tribune gallery with Charlemagne's throne.

The architect, Odo of Metz (742–814 CE), used a double shell to bear the weight of the dome and imported marble from Ravenna and Rome to decorate the inside of the church and create mosaics, replaced in the 16th century with stucco. Charlemagne was buried in the choir of the chapel, and his remains were later placed in an elaborate gold shrine.

▲ The octagonal **Palatine Chapel** now forms the central part of Aachen Cathedral.

PUEBLO BONITO

Chaco Canyon, NM, *see p.79*

BOROBUDUR GREAT STUPA

Java, Indonesia, *see p.119*

MOSQUE OF IBN TŪLŪN

Cairo, Egypt, 879 CE

The oldest mosque in Egypt to still exist in its original form, the Mosque of Ibn Tūlūn was founded by Ahmad ibn Tūlūn, a governor of the Abbasid Caliphate. The complex formed part of his new suburb of al-Qata'i, which is now part of Cairo.

Instead of columns, the mosque has plaster-covered brick piers to carry the weight of its roof, which encloses four arcaded halls. This, along with the spiral-like minaret being opposite the mihrab, are features derived from Samarra in Iraq. Around 530 ft (162 m) long, it is one of the largest mosques in Cairo. The 128 interior windows on the upper level have pointed arches, which were unusual at the time, and are elaborately stuccoed.

The mosque has been restored several times over the centuries, including after a fire in 980 CE, which destroyed the fountain that had been the main feature of one of the courtyards, as well as further restorations in 1296 and 2004.

CAHOKIA

Cahokia, Illinois, c. 900–1350

The 3,200-acre (1,300-hectare) site of Cahokia in southwest Illinois originally had 120 mounds used as platforms for buildings by the Middle Mississippian culture, which flourished there from c. 900 CE.

Cahokia, whose wealthy population reached up to 20,000, had a grand central plaza with a large pyramid-shaped earthwork with flat terraces, that was later named Monk's Mound. Almost 99 ft (30 m) high and 950 ft (290 m) long, it took around 22 million cubic ft (600,000 cubic m) of clay, gravel, and rock to build. A wooden structure on the mound's summit, 105 ft (32 m) by 50 ft (15 m), may have been a temple or a residence for Cahokia's rulers.

By the mid 14th century, Cahokia had declined, possibly due to environmental stresses, and the site was abandoned.

MAINZ CATHEDRAL

Mainz, Germany, *see p.101*

AL-AQSA MOSQUE / DOME OF THE ROCK

Jerusalem, Israel, 11th century

Temple Mount in Jerusalem is a sacred place to Muslims, Jews, and Christians. At the spot where Islamic tradition tells that the Prophet Muhammad ended his miraculous night journey from Mecca, the Al-Aqsa Mosque was built on the orders of the Umayyad caliph 'Abd al-Malik (c. 646–705 CE) to replace an earlier small prayer house.

Due to earthquakes, the current structure largely dates from the 11th century, but the internal decoration of gilded copper panels and marble friezes is original. It has seven aisles running from north to south and colonnades supported by large piers. Saladin (r. 1169–1193) had the mosque renovated in 1187, after it

▲ **The aluminum-covered dome** of the Al-Aqsa Mosque, in the Old City of Jerusalem, glows in the light of dawn.

had been converted to a church by crusaders, adding an elaborate *minbar* (pulpit) of wood and ivory.

CLAY PALACE OF GHARDAÏA

Ghardaïa, Algeria, 11th century

Algeria's remote M'zab Valley on the northern edge of the Sahara houses five *ksour* (fortified villages) built by the M'zabite people— Berber followers of the Ibāḍī branch of Islam. One of the *ksours*, Ghardaïa, is built largely of clay and gypsum which keep the interiors cool. Terraces of houses, roofed with palm wood, rise toward a plaza and a pyramid-shaped mosque. Narrow streets are arranged in concentric circles and wind toward the village's outer walls, reflecting a sense of community. Each house is set on the hillside so that every room receives sunlight. The jewel of Ghardaïa is a large palace. Built from thick walls of stone and clay with clean, neat subtractive decoration, it is a place of worship, governance, community events, and education.

▲ **The Mosque of Ibn Ṭūlūn**, with its spiral minaret, brick piers, and central ablution fountain, was built in the 9th century.

▲ **Chartres Cathedral**, with its vast nave, flying buttresses, and magnificent stained-glass windows, marks the high point of French Gothic architecture.

KANDARIYA MAHADEVA TEMPLE

Khajuraho, India, *see p.123*

PEYREPERTUSE

Pyrenees, France, *see p.175*

ABBAYE AUX HOMMES

Caen, France, c.1063

Established by William I of Normandy (c.1028–1087) in his ducal capital of Caen, the Abbey of Saint-Étienne is also known as the Abbaye aux Hommes (Men's Abbey) as it was originally for Benedictine monks. Construction of the Romanesque masterpiece in white Caen stone was overseen by the monk Lanfranc (c.1005–1089). The original nave and transept remain, supplemented by a 13th-century Gothic choir.

The ribbed vault was added in 1120 and is an early example of what became a mainstay of Gothic churches and cathedrals.

William I was buried in the abbey, though his remains were lost during the 16th-century French Wars of Religion. A sister foundation, the Abbaye aux Dames (Ladies' Abbey) is nearby, and William I's wife, Matilda, was buried there in 1083.

BASILICA OF ST-DENIS

Paris, France, 1135

The reconstruction of the 7th-century basilica at St-Denis was begun in 1135 and it created the first truly Gothic church. Abbot Suger (see p.412) supervised the work and redesigned the western facade, adding huge buttresses and three doorways to create clearly defined zones. Combining slender interior columns, rib vaults, and a pointed-arch design, Suger was able to incorporate large stained-glass windows, allowing light to bathe the interior.

Suger only finished the facade and the apse. The nave was built under Abbot Eudes Clément, who saw it completed in 1281. St-Denis became the necropolis of the French royal house, with more than 70 fine statues dating from the 12th to the 16th centuries. 43 kings were buried there, but the royal tombs are now empty as the remains were removed after the French Revolution of 1789.

KOUTOUBIA MOSQUE

Marrakech, Morocco, *see p.145*

ANGKOR WAT

Siem Reap, Cambodia, *see p.129*

NOTRE-DAME DE PARIS

Paris, France, 1163–c.1350

Standing on Paris's Île de la Cité, on the site of two earlier churches, the cathedral of Notre-Dame de Paris took more than 200 years to complete, the nave only being finished around 1250. The huge interior 427 ft (130 m) by 157 ft (48 m) and its exterior decoration make it one of the greatest medieval Gothic cathedrals. Flying buttresses added in the 1180s added support. The splendid western facade is flanked by two huge Gothic towers and features the Gallery of Kings (carvings of Old Testament rulers), a rose window dedicated to the Virgin Mary, and a set of richly carved doorways. The building was badly damaged by a fire in 2019, but donations from around the world raised funds for its restoration.

BAB OUDAYA

Rabat, Morocco, c.1195

Bab Oudaya, or Bab al-Kabir, is the monumental gateway to the kasbah (or citadel) of Rabat constructed about 50 years earlier. Built for the Almohad caliph Abū Yūsuf Ya'qūb al-Mansūr (c.1160–1199), it is around 43 ft (13 m) high and 52 ft (16 m) wide. The gateway has an outer facade with a large horseshoe arch decorated with interlaced geometric patterns and a carved Qur'anic inscription in Kufic script.

The interior of the gateway has three chambers, making it hard for intruders to storm the gate. Plans for an enlarged, grander kasbah and a new mosque were intended to complete the building, but they were never finished, leaving the Bab Oudaya (which was named for a tribe who settled there in the 19th century) as a monument to al-Mansūr's ambition.

CHARTRES CATHEDRAL

Chartres, France, c.1200

One of the best examples of Gothic architecture, the cathedral of Notre-Dame de Chartres was built after fire destroyed its predecessor in 1194. The limestone church was consecrated in 1260. Its tall arcades and especially heavy clerestory meant that innovative flying buttresses were needed to support their weight.

▲ **The walls of Chan Chan** were adobe brick finished with mud. Many, such as these at the Tschudi palace, were carved with animal designs.

The sculptures of the Royal Portal, carved in the mid 12th century, reveal a new interest in naturalistic portrayal. The cathedral is famous for its 176 stained-glass windows, some using a vibrant color that became known as "Chartres blue." The west facade has two asymmetrical towers: one in the Romanesque style and a Gothic-style one added in 1513.

BETE GIYORGIS

Lalibela, Ethiopia, *see p.83*

CHAN CHAN

Trujillo, Peru, c. 1100–1470

The capital of the Chimú culture, which flourished on the north coast of Peru from around 950 CE, Chan Chan covered an area of around 14 miles² (36 km²). Some of its mud-brick buildings have survived because of the area's low rainfall. The core of the city was a series of adobe brick palaces, today called *ciudadelas*, each of which was built by a ruler and then abandoned when a successor erected a new one.

A *ciudadela* had an *audiencia* (assembly space), sunken gardens, and storerooms. The walls were decorated with friezes of animals such as crabs, turtles, and fish. Most of the population lived in more modest mud-brick houses on the edge of the royal zone. Chan Chan was abandoned after the Incas conquered it in 1470.

▲ **The monumental Bab Oudaya,** with its horseshoe arch surrounded by Qur'anic inscriptions, was built in the late 12th century.

CHURCH OF ST. MARY MAGDALENE

Vézelay, France, 1150–1190

The Benedictine abbey at Vézelay, first founded in the 9th century, was largely built during the 12th century. It became a major pilgrimage center as the reputed burial site of the remains of Mary Magdalene. The church was later remodeled around 1840 by Eugène Viollet-le-Duc (see pp.416–17).

Its 205-ft (62.5-m) nave offered ample scope for an architect whose specialty was restoring medieval buildings. Viollet-le-Duc modified the facade and doors, remodeled the horseshoe-shaped arches with colored stone and relief-carved capitals for the pillars, and added flying buttresses. He gave new life to a church that is one of the masterpieces of the Burgundian Romanesque.

SHŌRENIN TEMPLE

Kyoto, Japan, late 12th century

A monastery of the Tendai Sect of Japanese Buddhism, Shōrenin was built as one of the five Monzeki Temples whose head priests were always members of the imperial family. Shōrenin was endowed by Emperor Go-Toba (1180–1239) as a place where his seventh son—who eventually

▲ **Standing on the impregnable rock of Doms**, the lavishly ornamented Palais des Papes is one of the largest medieval Gothic buildings in Europe.

became its abbot—could study. In a picturesque setting at the foot of the Higashiyama (eastern mountains), Shōrenin has winding gardens and a collection of buildings. Shijokodo Hall contains objects of worship, including a mandala showing a plan of the Buddhist universe, while several ancient camphor trees grow in the gardens.

The site was used as an imperial residence after a fire destroyed the imperial palace in 1788, retaining the connection between the temple and the imperial family.

SPRUCE TREE HOUSE

Mesa Verde, Colorado, 1200s

With 114 rooms, Spruce Tree House was the third-largest cliff dwelling in the Ancestral Pueblo complex at Mesa Verde in Colorado (see p.79). On the northeast edge of Spruce Tree Canyon, it was built when the Ancestral Pueblo were moving from the mesa tops to the greater safety of the cliffs.

The house took around 80 years to construct, and each of the 100 or so families had their own room and joint share of eight kivas, deeply excavated ceremonial chambers. The division of the building into two sections with a central tower suggests that there was some form of social distinction. Spruce Tree House was abandoned in the late 1200s, soon after it was completed, as changes in weather patterns forced the Ancestral Pueblo to migrate.

AMIENS CATHEDRAL

Amiens, France, *see pp.164–165*

ALHAMBRA

Granada, Spain, *see pp.148–149*

BURGHAUSEN CASTLE

Burghausen, Germany, 1255

Said to be the longest castle in the world, Burghausen was built by Henry XIII, Duke of Lower Bavaria (1235–1290), on the site of an earlier fortification. Successive expansions gave the castle complex an overall length of just over 3,280 ft (1,000 m). By the late 15th century, when it was completed under Duke Georg der Reiche (1455–1503), the castle lay far closer to the frontiers of the Ottoman Empire, so it had become a fortification of some strategic importance.

Largely Gothic in style, the castle has five main courtyards with moats, portcullises, and drawbridges. It incorporates the 13th-century Chapel of St. Elizabeth and a large arsenal building constructed in 1420 to house the fort's growing collection of gunpowder weaponry.

PALAIS DES PAPES

Avignon, France, mid 14th century

The largest medieval Gothic building in Europe and the largest Gothic palace in the world, the

▲ **Spruce Tree House**, sheltered under a sandstone arch, is one of the best-preserved cliff dwellings in Colorado.

▲ **The courtyard of the Al-Attarine Madrasa** is decorated with carved stucco ornamentation and intricate tile work.

Palais des Papes (Palace of the Popes) was home to nine Popes during the period when the papacy moved from Rome to Avignon in France (1309–1377). Begun on the orders of Pope Benedict XII (d. 1342) at the site of a previous Romanesque palace, the first phase, the Palais Vieux (Old Palace), was built around a trapeze-shaped court with a banqueting hall, chapel, and papal apartments. The complex was expanded under Pope Clement VI (1291–1352) to create the Palais Neuf (New Palace), designed by Jean de Louvres with a lavish 170-ft (52-m) Grand Chapel. Each papacy left its architectural mark on the castle.

The interior frescoes were created by the Sienese artists Simone Martini (c. 1284–1344) and Matteo Giovanetti (c. 1300–1368). After the Papacy returned to Rome in 1377, the building lost its purpose and deteriorated until its restoration in the 20th century.

AL-ATTARINE MADRASA

Fez, Morocco, 1323

Built by the Marīnid sultan Abu Sa'id Uthman II (c. 1276–1331) as one of several such religious schools in the old city of Fez, Al-Attarine Madrasa (Medersa El Attarine) takes its name from the nearby perfume market, Souk al-Attarine. With space for 50 to 60 students and their teachers, the madrasa is a two-story structure entered via an archway leading to an angled passageway and then on into a galleried courtyard with a marble fountain.

The east and west facades each have five arches resting on slender marble columns or on tiled square pillars with kufic inscriptions. The interior walls are covered in highly decorated sculpted plaster, with arches and colorful mosaic paneling, while the cedarwood doors are covered with bronze plates etched with intricately interlocking patterns.

▲ **The Tower of Pisa**, famously leaning, was built from white marble and designed in the Romanesque style.

GREAT MOSQUE OF DJENNÉ

Djenné, Mali, *see p.151*

ALCÁZAR DE LOS REYES CRISTIANOS

Cordoba, Spain, 1327

Built on the site of an earlier Muslim fortress, the Alcázar de los Reyes Cristianos (Fortress of the Christian Kings) was both a stronghold and a palace. Most of it was built during the reign of Alfonso XI of Castille (1311–1350). Broadly rectangular, the site is surrounded by outer walls of ashlar which had four (now three) corner towers named for Lions, Tribute, the Inquisition, and, previously, the Dove.

The austere exterior hides an unexpectedly splendid interior with courtyards and gardens (see p.146) in the Western Islamic style with flowers, herbs, trees, fountains, and a royal bath house. The Hall of Mosaics is decorated with Roman mosaics repurposed from a former hippodrome. Later, the building was the headquarters for the Spanish Inquisition and in the 19th century it became a prison.

THE TOWER OF PISA

Pisa, Italy, 1173–1350

The eight-story cylindrical campanile (bell tower) of Pisa's cathedral, received its nickname "the Leaning Tower of Pisa" due to a marked tilt caused by the unstable clay, sand, and shells on which it was built. Work ceased in 1178, when only three of its striking layers of marble columns had been built because the tilt was already evident.

Construction began again in 1272 with stronger materials, and the stories were shortened on one side, but the tilt continued to get worse. In 1838, a trench was dug around the base, but this caused a flood, making the tower tilt even more. Restoration work completed in 2001 removed soil from the foundations, which stopped further deterioration, but the tower is still 3 ft (1m) higher on one side than it is on the other.

GOLDEN PAVILION

Kyoto, Japan, *see p.139*

MOSQUE OF BIBI KHANUM

Samarkand, Uzbekistan, *see p.143*

GUR-I AMIR

Samarkand, Uzbekistan, 1404

The burial place of the Turkic conqueror and ruler Timur (1336–1405), the Gur-i Amir was originally conceived as a resting place for Timur's grandson and intended heir, Muhammad Sultan, who died prematurely in 1403.

Using a technique common in Iran at the time, a double dome with an inner shell was used to support the weight of the large dome. Melon-shaped, it is ribbed with aquamarine tiles and encircled by Qur'anic inscriptions. The square interior, adorned with onyx marble, alabaster, stucco, and inscriptions in gilt, transitions to the dome with a series of vertical flanges and pendentives.

An underground chamber in the mausoleum was also used for the burials of Timur's son Shāh Rokh (1377–1447) and his grandson Ulūgh Beg (1394–1449), who was the founder of Samarkand's famous observatory.

THE FORBIDDEN CITY

Beijing, China, 1406–1420

The world's largest imperial palace complex, the Forbidden City was built on the orders of Emperor Yongle (1360–1424) of the Ming dynasty. Construction began in 1406 and took a million workers. It was home to 24 emperors until the last, Puyi (1906–1967), was forced to leave in 1924 after the Chinese Revolution. The site covers around 180 acres (72 hectares) inside imposing defensive walls. Access is via the Meridian Gate, whose central entrance only the emperor could use. This leads to the Outer Court, which is used for public ceremonies.

The largest structure, the Hall of Supreme Harmony, is supported by 72 pillars (including 6 of gold) and is where emperors would sit on the Dragon throne. The Inner Court held the imperial family's private chambers: the Palace of Heavenly Purity for the emperor and the Hall of Terrestrial Tranquility for the empress.

HOSPITAL OF THE INNOCENTS

Florence, Italy, 1419–1439

Commissioned by Florence's guild of silk merchants, the Ospedale degli Innocenti is considered to be the first orphanage in Europe. Designed by Filippo Brunelleschi (see p.412), who was a member of the guild, the building represented a new direction, away from Gothic and toward a more Classical style of architecture.

Gray stone and white stucco create a plain, harmonious style, with freestanding columns supporting an arcade of nine semicircular arches. The heights of the columns match the width of the arcade, making each section a perfect cube. Over each column, a ceramic roundel sculpted by Andrea della Robbia (1435–1525) contains a baby on a blue wheel, representing the place where mothers could leave their babies.

Brunelleschi only worked on the lower level; the upper story with the children's rooms was finished in 1439 without the Corinthian pilasters that he had planned.

THE HALL OF PRAYER

Beijing, China, *see p.133*

MACHU PICCHU

Peru, *see p.157*

▲ **The colorful Forbidden City** in the heart of China's capital

▲ **The Hospital of the Innocents**, with its arcade designed by Filippo Brunelleschi

▲ **The church of Santa Maria Novella**, in Florence, has a facade that blends the Romanesque and Renaissance styles.

CA' D'ORO

Venice, Italy, 1436

A palace whose name means "Golden House," Ca' D'oro was built for the Venetian merchant Marino Contarini alongside the city's Grand Canal. Its design blended Byzantine architecture with elements of Venetian Gothic. Along with multicolored marble, this created a facade that is both flamboyant and elegant.

A recessed colonnade on the ground floor leads directly into the building's interior. The floors above feature Moorish-style enclosed balconies and rows of columns supporting quatrefoil tracery windows, mirroring a similar design to the Doge's Palace, also in Venice (see p.170). The fortunes of the palace rose and fell with those of the Venetian state and by the 1840s it was partially ruined. The architect Giovanni Battista Meduna (1800–1880) undertook a significant renovation, and in 1927 the building became a museum.

SANTA MARIA NOVELLA

Florence, Italy, 1456–1470 (facade)

The Gothic-style Dominican church of Santa Maria Novella was begun in 1278, but it was nearly two centuries before its facade, and crowning glory, was completed. The lower part, in Romanesque style, was the work of the Dominican architect Fra Jacopo Talenti da Nipozzano (c. 1330–1362). A century later, Leon

▲ **The Ca' d'Oro** is one of the best surviving Venetian Gothic palazzos. Its facade is based on that of the Doge's Palace.

Battista Alberti (see p.413) made it a masterpiece of the Florentine Renaissance. For the first time, he designed on strictly mathematical and humanist lines, with repeated squares and square ratios. He incorporated a square-studded frieze, a grand pediment with the Dominican emblem of the Sun, and green Prato marble to contrast with the white marble. This was also the first of many churches to feature his innovative "S"-shaped volutes on the roof.

CAPPELLA COLLEONI

Bergamo, Italy, 1470–1476

Bequeathed by Bartolomeo Colleoni (1400–1475), the captain of a mercenary band, as a mausoleum for his daughter Medea, the Cappella Colleoni chapel was built on the former sacristy of the Basilica of Santa Maria Maggiore.

Designed by Giovanni Antonio Amadeo (c. 1447–1522), the chapel's square shape with a central hall and octagonal dome merges with the basilica next door. Its facade is decorated with polychrome marble lozenges, and the main door is surmounted by a rose window flanked by medallions of two great Roman warriors, Julius Caesar and Trajan, reflecting the benefactor's martial prowess. The facade also has bas-reliefs of the labors of Heracles and statues of the Virtues. Inside, the marble tomb of Colleoni features an equestrian statue in gilded wood and a triumphal arch.

ST. MICHAEL ARCHANGEL

Dębno, Poland, c.1490

Built to replace a 13th-century structure, the late-15th century St. Michael Archangel church combines Gothic and traditional folk art in a unique manner. Made from larch and fir wood, it was built with wooden pegs rather than with nails. The steep shingled roof has an extended gable and a low tower with a pyramid cap.

The relatively plain exterior hides a magnificent polychrome interior with sculptures by the local artist Jozef Janos. The comparative poverty of the region and neglect of the church paradoxically saved it from the overlaying of later styles such as the Baroque, and so it remains in pristine condition.

GINKAKU-JI COMPLEX

Kyoto, Japan, 1482–1490

The Ginkaku-ji was built for the shogun Ashikaga Yoshimasa (1436–1490) for his retirement and was later converted to a Zen temple. Known as the Silver Pavilion, its designer originally intended it to be coated in the metal. The temple contains an important statue of the bodhisattva Kannon, and it became a focus for traditional Japanese culture, such as Noh theater and garden design.

On the same site is The Togudo Hall, originally designed as Yoshimasa's personal shrine (he became a monk in 1485). It includes a room for the Japanese tea ceremony, which was developing at this time, in part through Yoshimasa's encouragement. In 1550, the whole complex, apart from the Silver Pavilion and Togudo Hall, was destroyed in a fire.

ST. PETER'S BASILICA

Rome, Italy, *see pp.216–217*

CHÂTEAU CHAMBORD

Chambord, France, *see p.207*

PAVILION OF MYRIAD SPRINGS

Beijing, China, 1535

Located in the Imperial Gardens of the Forbidden City, the Pavilion of Myriad Springs is a square pavilion with a circular tower and verandas on four sides. A later addition to the Forbidden City, it was built under the Ming emperor Jiajing (1507–c. 1567).

The position of the cross-shaped pavilion in the east symbolizes the direction of spring. A tour de force of Chinese woodcarving, the highly ornate roof has overhanging decorative eaves. The building's structure and its position mirror the Pavilion of Myriad Autumns which lies on the west side of the gardens. The Pavilion of Myriad Springs was extensively restored during the Qing dynasty (1644–1912).

▲ **The Pavilion of Myriad Springs** is one of the four pavilions that stand in the corners of the Imperial Gardens in the Forbidden City. Each symbolizes a season of the year.

▲ **Made of local granite**, the fortress-like El Escorial was built to commemorate the Spanish victory over the French at the Battle of St. Quentin in 1557.

HEILBRONN TOWN HALL

Heilbronn, Germany, 1535

Heilbronn's 13th-century Rathaus (Town Hall) was remodeled in 1535 with an exterior punctuated by two rows of rectangular windows and, above, three stories of dormer windows in the steeply pitched roof. The decoration is plain except for an angel bearing the city's coat of arms and a famous astronomical clock.

The clock was originally made in 1580 by Isaac Habrecht, with three large dials indicting the solar time, the phases of the moon, and the procession of the Zodiac. On the dial for time, two angels rotate each hour; one blows a trumpet and the other turns an hourglass. Although the building was destroyed during World War II, its replacement retained the look of the original facade and the clock.

ST. BASIL'S CATHEDRAL

Moscow, Russia, *see p.181*

SÜLEYMANIYE MOSQUE

Istanbul, Turkey, *see p.183*

PALAZZO FARNESE

Caprarola, Italy, *see pp.198–199*

RÜSTEM PASHA MOSQUE

Istanbul, Turkey, 1563

Located on a raised terrace close to the city's spice market, the Rüstem Pasha Mosque was built on the orders of Princess Mihrimah (1522–1578), daughter of the Ottoman sultan Süleyman I (1494–1566) in memory of her husband, the grand vizier Rustem Pasha (d. 1561).

Its design, by the Ottoman master-architect Mimar Sinan (1491–1588), is fairly conventional: a rectangular base and an octagonal structure with a single minaret and central dome on four half-domes. However, the mosque is notable for its interior, which has one of the greatest collections of 16th-century Iznik tiles of Ottoman ceramic. Their hues of cobalt blue, turquoise, and scarlet and depictions of peonies, lotuses, rose buds, intertwining tendrils, and arabesques create a virtual garden of its walls (see p.185). The creation is all the more striking as Sinan was known for his sparing use of ornamental tiles.

EL ESCORIAL

San Lorenzo del Escorial, Spain, 1563–1584

Constructed by Juan Bautista de Toledo (c.1515–1567) and Juan de Herrera (c. 1530–1597), El Escorial was initially the burial site for the Holy Roman Emperor Charles V (1500–1558), but it later became the main residence for King Philip II of Spain (1527–1598). The largest Renaissance building in the world, it covers 8 acres (3.3 hectares).

Based around a monastery, initially for the Hieronymite Order, but since 1885 for the Augustinian Order, the complex consists of a tripartite rectangle, with the main church in the center. The site has five cloisters to the south where the royal palace and offices were located. The interior of the huge church, based on a Greek cross within a square and decorated only by Doric pilasters, is an austerely Spanish response to the extravagances of the Renaissance elsewhere at the time.

BEN YOUSSEF MADRASA

Marrakech, Morocco, 1564–1565

One of the largest Islamic schools in the Maghreb, the Ben Youssef Madrasa housed up to 800 religious students until it closed

in 1960 and is now a museum. It was built under the Saadian sultan Abdallah al-Ghalib (1517–1574) on the site of an earlier 12th-century Almoravid mosque.

At 141 ft (43 m) by 131 ft (40 m), the building is almost a square accessed by a single corridor with marble basins. Its main courtyard, centered around a large marble pool, is festooned with intricate cedarwood coving, tiling, and stucco, with the mihrab (a niche showing the direction of Mecca) of the prayer hall to the southeast similarly decorated and framed within a horseshoe-shaped arch. Students were accommodated in small rooms above the arcades which run around seven smaller courtyards leading off from the central courtyard.

THE RED FORT

Agra, India, 1565–1573

Not far from the Taj Mahal, on the right bank of the Yamuna River, stands the Red Fort. Its 1½-mile- (2.5-km-) long walls enclose the main palaces and audience halls of the Mughal emperors. Although commissioned by the emperor Akbar (1542–1605), the fort's interior was largely developed under Shah Jahan (see pp.192–193). Notable buildings include Jahāngīr's Palace, the Pearl Mosque built from white marble, the Hall of Private Audience, and the tall Octagonal Tower. After his deposition by his son Aurangzeb (1618–1707), Shah Jahan was imprisoned in the Muthamman Burj tower, from where he could see the Taj Mahal, his other great commission (see p.193).

FATEHPUR SIKRI

Fatehpur Sikri, India, 1571

Founded by the Mughal emperor Akbar (1542–1605) as his capital— a role it served for just 15 years— Fatehpur Sikri is a city of red sandstone that blends Islamic and Hindu architecture (see p.194) in a synthesis which mirrored the emperors' own religious views.

The Jodha Bai Mahal, the house of Akbar's favorite wife, contains a Hindu temple, in accordance with her religion, while the Jami Masjid contains a tomb to the local Sufi Saint Shaikh Salim Chishti (1478–1572). A series of walled courtyards contain pavilions, notably the Diwan-i-Am (Hall of Audience) and the Diwan-i-Khas, with a circular platform on a central column, where Akbar held private meetings. In 1585, Akbar moved the capital to Lahore, and then, in 1599, to Agra.

▲ **The main courtyard** of the Ben Youssef Madrasa, with its pool and mosaic tile work

NIJO CASTLE

Kyoto, Japan, 1603

Constructed in the imperial capital Kyoto for Tokugawa Ieyasu (1543–1616), the first shogun of a united Japan, Nijo Castle consists of two huge concentric rings of fortifications. The site includes extensive gardens and the Chinese-style Karamon Gate, with curved gables and intricate wood-carvings, which leads to the castle's most splendid edifice—the Ninomaru Palace.

Its five buildings are constructed largely of Japanese cypress, and its interiors are all furnished with tatami mats. How far a visitor could enter depended on their rank—the *kuroshoin* or black study was permitted only to the Tokugawa clan. Its floorboards were equipped with a special mechanism so that if an intruder stepped on them, they would rub against nails beneath, making them squeak.

SHEIKH LOTFOLLAH MOSQUE

Isfahan, Iran, 1603–1618

Standing on the eastern side of Isfahan's Naqsh-e Jahan Square, the Sheikh Lotfollah Mosque is a masterpiece of Safavid architecture. Built as a private chapel for the Persian Shah Abbas I (1571–1629), it does not have a courtyard like most mosques, and the dome is sand-colored and decorated with turquoise blossoms, diverging from the normal Safavid choice of sky blue. A dark passage, in part intended to help orient the mosque toward the *qibla* (the direction of prayer), leads into a central square space, where eight arches carry the dome, each lined in *haft-rangi* (seven-colored) tiles with Qur'anic inscriptions.

To avoid public attention, the Imperial family entered the mosque via an underground passage from the Ali Qapu Palace on the other side of the square.

▲ **One of four highly decorated, towering outer gopuras** through which visitors enter the Meenakshi Temple. A further ten towers of varying heights stand in the inner sanctuary.

THE BLUE MOSQUE

Istanbul, Turkey, 1609–1617

Also known as the Sultan Ahmed Mosque, the Blue Mosque contains the tomb of the Ottoman ruler Ahmed I (1590–1617), who endowed it. One of the last classical Ottoman mosques, it also contained a madrasa, hostel, and school. Designed by the architect Sedefkar Mehmed Aga, a pupil of the master Mimar Sinan, it has five principal domes and, controversially at the time, six minarets. Back then, only the Prophet's Mosque in Mecca had six minarets—so the sultan paid for a seventh in Mecca.

The stunning blue of the main dome's tiles lends the mosque its nickname, but the interior also has more than 20,000 hand-painted tiles, with extravagant flower and fruit designs, as well as 200 stained-glass windows. The mihrab, with a stalactite niche of white marble, is particularly fine.

MASJID-I-SHAH

Isfahan, Iran, *see p.189*

MEENAKSHI TEMPLE

Madurai, India, 14th–17th centuries

Also known as the Minakshi-Sundareshwara Temple, the Meenakshi Temple has a twin dedication to Meenakshi, the city of Madurai's guardian goddess, and to Sundareshwara, an avatar

▲ **The sandstone-clad Lahori Gate** on the western wall of Delhi's Red Fort

of Lord Shiva. Truly monumental, the temple has outer walls that measure 780 ft (238 m) by 833 ft (254 m) with 14 gopuras (tower-gateways) soaring 164 ft (50 m), through which worshippers must pass on their way to the inner sanctuary.

The original 12th-century buildings were destroyed, so the current buildings date from the 14th century and have been expanded and reconstructed steadily over three centuries. Key features of the complex include the Thousand-Pillar Hall which is adorned with sacred

sculptures, the Golden Lotus Pond for pilgrims to bathe in, and more than 30,000 sculptures.

THE QUEEN'S HOUSE

Greenwich, UK, 1616–1635

Designed by Inigo Jones (see p.413) as a residence for Anne of Denmark (1574–1619), the wife of James I, the Queen's House was the first fully Classical villa built in England. Work stopped when Anne died in 1619 and was not completed until 1635, for Charles I's wife Henrietta Maria (1609–1669).

The house is the fruit of a visit Jones had made to Italy several years before, and its white cube-like structure and six-columned loggia were inspired by the architecture of Andrea Palladio (see p.234), but with Jones's own features such as a balustraded parapet on the roof. The interior of the building is notable for the Tulip Stairs, the earliest self-supporting spiral staircase in Britain, which was named for the flower pattern of its brilliant blue, wrought-ironwork, curving handrail.

TAJ MAHAL

Agra, India, *see p.193*

THE RED FORT

Delhi, India, 1639–1648

The octagonal fort Lal Qila is better known as the Red Fort due to its red sandstone ramparts. It was founded by the emperor Shah Jahan (1592–1666) when he transferred the Mughal capital to Delhi. The site covers 255 acres (103 hectares) and includes the Diwan-i-Aam, where the emperor received the public; the Diwan-i-Khas, where the emperor received courtiers and royals; imperial apartments; the three-domed Moti Masjid (Pearl Mosque); and the Hayat-Bakhsh Bagh or "life-bestowing" park. Jahan's new buildings were constructed near Salimgarh, an existing fort built in 1546, and together they form the Red Fort Complex.

SANTI LUCA E MARTINA

Rome, Italy, *see p.211*

▲ **The Queens House** introduced the Palladian style to the UK.

▲ **The black-and-white-tiled Marble Courtyard** of the Palace of Versailles

PALACE OF VERSAILLES

Versailles, France, 1661–1670

The chateau of Versailles, 12 miles (19 km) west of Paris, began life as a hunting lodge for Louis XIII (1601–1643), but in 1661, it was transformed into an elaborate palace under his son Louis XIV (1638–1715), who moved the French court there in 1682.

The Baroque architect Louis Le Vau (1612–1670) enveloped the original building on three sides, beginning with the hugely elaborate gardens on the west side. His successor, Jules Hardouin-Mansart (see p.415), added the Grand Gallery and the Hall of Mirrors, in which the treaty ending World War I was signed in 1919. His last additions were huge wings for the royal courtiers (1688) and an ornate chapel with Corinthian columns (1689–1708). The palace acquired an opera house in 1763–1770, and ceased to be a royal residence after the French Revolution of 1789.

CHURCH OF SAN LORENZO

Turin, Italy, 1668–1680

The Church of San Lorenzo was designed by Guarino Guarini (1624–1683)—a Baroque architect, mathematician, and Catholic cleric of the Theatine Order. The site's confined space necessitated a complex structure, whose octagonal shape on a Greek cross with eight side chapels is crowned by a magnificent dome, and its ornate interior is one of the masterpieces of the Baroque.

The eight chapel walls curve inward toward the cupola, with the dome held up by a complex intersecting rib structure which forms an eight-pointed star and culminates in a lantern that lets

▲ **Sunlight streams through the lantern** of the octagonal Church of San Lorenzo.

light into the interior. Guarini's plan for an elaborate facade was never built, but the stucco work, gilding, and polychrome marble pillars and altars more than make up for its absence.

HASHT BEHESHT PALACE

Isfahan, Iran, 1669

Meaning "Eight Paradises," Hasht Behesht Palace is a building where the number eight recurs throughout the architectural design. It was built on the orders of the Safavid Shah Sulayman I (1648–1694) as a private palace in Isfahan's Bulbul Garden.

A refinement of a typical Safavid pavilion construction, the palace's 98 ft (30 m) by 87 ft (26.5 m) rectangular shape is cut at the corners to form an octagon. Resting on a 6-ft- (2-m-) high platform, the building consists of four large iwan halls that open out to the gardens, while in the middle a two-story octagonal hall, decorated with murals and polychrome tile work, has eight

▲ **One of the many imperial villas** at the Chengde Mountain Resort

rooms. A silver-lined fountain at the center, creates an elegant and harmonious sense of space.

SCHÖNBRUNN PALACE

Vienna, Austria, 1696–1700 with later alterations

Johann Bernhard Fischer von Erlach (1656–1723), the greatest Austrian architect of his time, designed the Schönbrunn Palace for the Holy Roman Emperor Leopold I (1640–1705). It was subsequently used by Hapsburg rulers until the dynasty came to an end in 1918. Although it is vast by any normal standards, Fischer originally made plans for a much bigger palace, but they were rejected as unrealistic.

Many changes have been made to the original building, notably in the 1740s by Nikolaus Pacassi (1716–1790). He made fussy alterations to the main facade and redesigned the interiors in a rich Rococo style. The most notable later change, in 1817, was that the

exterior was changed from blue to the ocher shade that is now known as "Schönbrunn yellow."

MELK ABBEY

Melk, Austria, 1702–1738

The Benedictine Abbey in Melk, set high on a ledge above the Danube River, was founded in 1089 but remodeled in the 18th century to create a landmark of the Baroque. The elongated facade, some 1,050 ft (320 m) with twin towers and domes, uses red-brown marble to create a striking effect very different from the usual white stucco of Baroque ecclesiastical architecture. Giant pilasters in the interior and bulging balconies create a strangely curved sense of space.

The interior features are the Imperial Staircase leading to apartments reserved for the royal family, the huge Marble Hall dining room, and the library with a ceiling fresco by Paul Troger (1731). A fire in 1974 led to a major restoration.

CHENGDE MOUNTAIN RESORT

Chengde, China, 1703–1792

The complex of palaces, gardens, and temples at Chengde begun by the Qing Emperor Kangxi (1654–1722) took nearly 90 years to complete. Around 140 miles (225 km) northeast of Beijing, the imperial summer retreat was popular with Qing emperors, and its palace zone was fashioned as a miniature version of Beijing's Forbidden City. The private imperial apartments were in the Yanbozhishuang Hall, where two Qing emperors died.

Chengde became famous for its 72 scenic locations designed to mirror famous beauty spots in China: the Tower of Mist and Rain is the twin of a tower in Zhejiang province. The Puning (Universal Peace) monastery has a 120-ft (36.75-m) pagoda containing the world's tallest wooden statue of the bodhisattva Avalokiteshvara. It has 1,000 arms and weighs more than 132 tons.

BLENHEIM PALACE

Woodstock, UK, 1705–1725

Huge and dramatic, Blenheim Palace was created as a national gift of thanksgiving for the first Duke of Marlborough (1650–1722) after his momentous victory over the French at the Battle of Blenheim in 1704. Marlborough chose as his architect Sir John Vanbrugh (1664–1726), who was assisted by Nicholas Hawksmoor (1661–1736), who was professionally trained in architecture. Blenheim Palace is the most famous building from the brief period when a full-blooded Baroque style was popular in England.

It had a difficult gestation; escalating costs caused delays in paying the workforce. Vanbrugh also quarreled with the Duchess of Marlborough, who wanted a comfortable home rather than a grandiose monument, leading to his resignation in 1716.

CHURCH OF THE TRANSFIGURATION

Kizhi, Russia, 1714

The Church of the Transfiguration is one of two remarkable 18th-century wooden churches in the settlement of Kizhi on a small island of the same name in Lake Onega in northern Russia. The second, the Church of the Intercession, is considerably smaller and was used in winter when the other was too large to heat.

The Church of the Transfiguration is one of the masterpieces of Russian architecture. With its breathtaking array of 22 domes, it has been described as the wooden equivalent of Moscow's St. Basil's Cathedral. The carpentry skills are extraordinary, the logs were cut so precisely that they fit together without nails. Other historical wooden buildings have been moved to the island, which is now a national open-air museum.

AMALIENBURG HUNTING LODGE

Munich, Germany, *see p.219*

SANSSOUCI PALACE

Potsdam, Germany, 1745–1747

Frederick the Great of Prussia (1712–1786), who commissioned the Sanssouci Palace, was deeply interested in the arts and made sketches to guide his architect, Georg Wenzeslaus von Knobelsdorff (1699–1753). By the standard of royal palaces, it is small, with only a single story, and was intended as a quiet refuge for escaping the troubles and formality of court life: its name comes from the French *sans souci*, meaning "without a care."

Appropriately, the building is in a light and elegant Rococo style. It stands at the top of a series of vineyard terraces and is surrounded by a large park adorned with fountains, statues, and garden buildings, including the delightful and quirky Chinese House (see p.221).

CATHERINE PALACE

Tsarskoye Selo, Russia, 1748–1756

Named after the second wife of Peter the Great, the Catherine Palace was her summer residence. However, the building was given its present external form under her daughter, the Empress Elizabeth (1709–1762). She had Catherine's comparatively modest residence expanded into a palace that was intended to rival Versailles in both size and magnificence.

The architect was Bartolomeo Francesco Rastrelli (1700–1771) whose style combines elements of Baroque and Rococo: the bulk and sense of grandiloquence are Baroque, but the light colors and frothy details are Rococo. Under succeeding rulers, the interior of the palace was substantially modified. For Catherine the Great (1729–1796), the Scottish architect

▲ **The Church of the Transfiguration** has a cascade of 22 dazzling bulbous domes covered with aspen, while the roof is made with planks of spruce.

▲ **The Rococo Catherine Palace** has dazzling white pillars, gilded stucco, and sky-blue walls.

Charles Cameron (c. 1745–1812) created apartments in a refined Neoclassical style. The last major addition was the main staircase in the 1860s by the architect Ippolito Monighetti (1819–1878).

WINTER PALACE

St. Petersburg, Russia, 1754–1762

This gigantic building was the main residence of the Imperial Russian family from the 18th century up until the Revolution of 1917. During the summer, the royal family preferred to live in the countryside at the Catherine Palace (see left), returning to St. Petersburg and the Winter Palace for the rest of the year. This is the fourth palace to be built on the site, with each one larger and more magnificent than its predecessor.

Empress Elizabeth (1709–1762), the daughter of Peter the Great, commissioned the current building, but she did not live to see it completed. The architect was Bartolomeo Francesco Rastrelli (1700–1771) who was an Italian who settled in Russia. In spite of its colossal size, the building has an exuberant, cheerful quality, though the original interiors were destroyed by fire in 1837.

The building now forms part of the enormous State Hermitage Museum of art and culture.

▲ **The single-story Sanssouci Palace** stands on a hill that Frederick the Great transformed into a series of terraced vineyards. Steps lead down from the house to an ornamental Baroque garden.

CHURCH OF SANTA PRISCA AND SAN SEBASTIAN

Taxco, Mexico, *see p.223*

THE PANTHÉON

Paris, France, *see pp.232–233*

BRANDENBURG GATE

Berlin, Germany, 1789–1791

The ceremonial Brandenburg Gate was commissioned by Friedrich Wilhelm II of Prussia (1744–1797), as part of his plans to make Berlin a great cultural center. The architect, Carl Gotthard Langhans (1732–1808), based it on the Propylaea, the gateway to the Acropolis in Athens, but its proportions are slimmer than in ancient Greek architecture. The four-horse chariot with a figure of Victory by German sculptor Johann Gottfried Schadow on top of the Gate was copied after being damaged in World War II. The Gate has acquired changing symbolic connotations: as an emblem of Prussian and later German nationalism, of the Nazi party, of a divided Berlin during the Cold War, and finally of freedom after the reunification of Germany.

BASILICA OF SANT'ANDREA

Mantua, Italy, 1472–1700s

Leon Battista Alberti (see p.413), one of the giants of Italian Renaissance architecture,

▲ **The 15th-century Basilica of Sant'Andrea** had its spectacular dome added by Filippo Juvarra in the 1730s.

▲ **The Neoclassical White House** has been renovated many times. Its south portico was added in 1824.

designed the Basilica of Sant'Andrea for Ludovico Gonzaga, Marquis of Mantua. Alberti died in 1472, before construction began, but his plans were faithfully followed by Luca Fancelli (1430–1494). The nave and the west front, the most striking features of Alberti's design, were completed by the early 1490s. The west front recalls a Roman triumphal arch, and the majestic barrel-vaulted nave also evokes the grand solemnity of the architecture of Classical antiquity. Here, Alberti created the most imposing Renaissance church interior of the 15th century.

Work on the rest of the church continued for a long time: the dome, by Filippo Juvarra (1678–1736), was not begun until 1732.

WHITE HOUSE

Washington, D.C., 1792–1800 with later additions

Every US President since John Adams (1797-1801) has used this handsome Palladian building as their official residence and workplace. The name "White House" was formally adopted by President Theodore Roosevelt in 1901, but it had long been used informally, due to the light stonework contrasting with the red bricks of nearby buildings. Irish-born architect James Hoban (1762–1831) was the original designer of the building, and he also supervised its reconstruction after it was badly damaged by British forces in the War of 1812.

Subsequently there have been many additions and alterations, including two major extensions in the 20th century: the West Wing, which contains the presidential Oval Office, and the East Wing.

ST. ISAAC'S CATHEDRAL

St. Petersburg, Russia, 1818–1858

The huge Neoclassical St. Isaac's cathedral was one of several buildings in St. Petersburg that expressed a spirit of triumphalism following Russia's defeat of Napoleon. Czar Alexander I (1777–1825) surprisingly awarded the commission to a young, inexperienced architect, Auguste de Montferrand (1786–1858), who had only recently arrived from France. His proposals were criticized by established Russian architects, and in response he evolved a new design. Externally the building is bold, with a portico and enormous columns of red granite on all four sides, and a dome with a novel iron framework.

Internally, the building has extremely sumptuous decoration. It was converted into a museum in 1931, but religious services are sometimes held there.

ST. PANCRAS STATION

London, UK, *see pp.244–245*

PALACE OF WESTMINSTER

London, UK, *see p.253*

PALAIS GARNIER

Paris, France, *see p.257*

NEUSCHWANSTEIN CASTLE

Bavaria, Germany, *see p.265*

TEMPIO MAGGIORE

Florence, Italy, 1874–1882

In 1848, Jews living in Florence were granted full civic rights, and the impressive Tempio Maggiore, or Great Synagogue, was built in recognition of this. The architects Mariano Falcini, Vincenzo Micheli, and Marco Treves created the building in a hybrid style, mingling elements from various traditions.

The central dome, for example, recalls that of the Byzantine Hagia Sophia in Istanbul (see p.85). Likewise, the horseshoe arches in the entrance and elsewhere are typical of the architecture of the Islamic West. Internal decoration is also in the Western Islamic style. The building was damaged during World War II and again by the flooding of the Arno River in 1966, but it has been carefully restored.

SAGRADA FAMILIA

Barcelona, Spain, *see pp.274–275*

▲ **The exterior of the Tempio Maggiore** is an eclectic mix of Islamic, Byzantine, and Greco-Roman styles.

▲ **The Subotica Synagogue** is a unique blend of Jewish and Hungarian influences. Its designers were inspired by the work of Ödön Lechner, who championed Art Nouveau architecture.

HÔTEL TASSEL

Brussels, Belgium, *see p.271*

GRAND PALAIS

Paris, France, 1897–1900

The enormous Grand Palais was created as the main exhibition hall for the Exposition Universelle held in Paris in 1900. The World's Fair was one of a series of international fairs that had begun with the Great Exhibition in London in 1851. They showcased the artistic, industrial, and technological achievements of the nations participating.

Charles Girault (1851–1933) headed the team of architects who designed the Grand Palais. The barrel-vaulted glass roof (inspired by Paxton's Crystal Palace, see p.238) is the most conspicuous feature of the building, but it is also notable for its Beaux-Arts stone facade and a wealth of Art Nouveau ironwork. Since the 1900 exhibition, the building has been put to various uses, including hosting sporting events.

SUBOTICA SYNAGOGUE

Subotica, Serbia, 1901–1902

Vibrant, colorful, and richly decorated, the Subotica Synagogue is one of the most impressive and distinctive religious buildings of its era. It was designed by the Hungarian architects Marcell Komor and Dezső Jakab, who formed a partnership in 1897.

The central dome shows the influence of Byzantine architecture, but there are also elements of Art Nouveau and Hungarian folk art in the fluent style. After World War II, the small Jewish community that survived in Subotica was unable to maintain the synagogue and in 1979 it was presented to the city on condition that it was restored and used for cultural purposes. After many delays, the fully restored building finally opened in 2018 as a tourist attraction and concert venue.

THEATRO MUNICIPAL

Rio de Janeiro, Brazil, 1905–1909

The Theatro Municipal is the most imposing building from a period when Rio de Janeiro (then the capital of Brazil) was being transformed into a modern city, with slums cleared, sanitation improved, and streets widened, paved, and lit. A competition to design the theater was won by Francisco de Oliveira Passos (1878–1958), who was a young engineer and the son of the city's mayor. This aroused accusations of favoritism, but Passos, who later became a politician, nevertheless remained in charge of the project. He was assisted by the French architect Albert Guilbert (1866–1949). The theater is in an eclectic style, with a strong Beaux-Arts influence, and it consciously recalls Paris's Palais Garnier (see p.257). Internally, the rich decoration includes mosaics and stained glass. An annex was added to the building in the 1990s.

PALAIS STOCLET

Brussels, Belgium, 1905–1911

In 1904, Adolphe Stoclet (1871-1949), a young Belgian industrialist and art collector, used the fortune he inherited from his father to create one of the most original private homes of the period. Stoclet had become a friend of the Austrian architect Josef Hoffmann (1870–1956), who designed the Palais Stoclet in a bold, angular style that eschews all historical references.

Although the external forms are severe, the materials are luxurious and the details refined. Hoffmann was a member of the Wiener Werkstätte (Viennese Workshop), a cooperative studio of artists and craftsmen, and he enlisted his colleagues to contribute to the sumptuous interior decoration.

Among them was Gustav Klimt, the great Austrian painter of the day, who designed superb mosaics for the dining room.

FAGUS FACTORY

Alfeld, Germany, *see p.285*

EINSTEIN TOWER

Potsdam, Germany, *see p.295*

VICEROY'S HOUSE

New Delhi, India, *see p.281*

VILLA TUGENDHAT

Brno, Czech Republic, 1929

Designed by Mies van der Rohe (see p.419), Villa Tugendhat is built into a southwest facing slope overlooking a generous garden. Arranged over three stories, it is entered from the street at the top level, where the bedrooms are. A staircase then winds down to the ground floor with open-plan living spaces. Large plate glass windows retract into the floor, opening the interior to the lawn, and cruciform chrome steel columns support the structure's

concrete slabs. A curved screen of ebony semi-encloses the dining area, and a wall of Moroccan onyx forms the backdrop to the seating area. The house is serviced by a warm air system in the basement, which also provides air conditioning in summer.

CHRYSLER BUILDING

New York City, NY, *see p.309*

VILLA SAVOYE

Poissy, France, *see pp.306–307*

▲ **The sumptuous Beaux-Arts interior** of Rio de Janeiro's Theatro Municipal

▲ **Fallingwater** stands astride the Bear Run tributary of the Youghiogheny River in Fayette County, Pennsylvania.

EMPIRE STATE BUILDING

New York City, NY, 1931

For almost 40 years the Empire State Building was the tallest building in the world, and although it has now been overtaken in height by dozens of other skyscrapers, it remains a much-loved symbol of New York City. It was designed by the firm of Shreve, Lamb, & Harmon and was built with astonishing speed, beginning in March 1930 and officially opened on May 1, 1931.

The architects worked in close partnership with the building contractors to ensure maximum efficiency in all aspects of construction. The building has a steel skeleton faced with brick and limestone. Although the design is bold, powerful, and rational, there are Art Deco flourishes in the details. The building's name comes from New York State's nickname—the "Empire State."

FALLINGWATER

Mill Run, Pennsylvania, 1937

Fallingwater was reputedly drawn in the space of one morning while Frank Lloyd Wright (see p.418) waited for his client, Edgar Kaufmann, to arrive at his home-office in Wisconsin. Kaufmann expected a house with a view of the eponymous waterfall, so was surprised to see that Wright had designed his house to cantilever over the waterfall instead. Construction began in 1936, and nervous engineers second-guessed Wright's design by adding extra support and reinforcement to the concrete. The intersecting internal volumes of the house flow into the dappled light of the forest through horizontal windows and waxed stone floors. The hearth is built onto a ledge of rock jutting through the floor, and the sound of the river permeates the interior of the house.

VILLA MAIREA

Noormarkku, Finland, *see pp.300–301*

PALAZZO DELLA CIVILTÀ ITALIANA

Rome, Italy, *see p.315*

GLASS HOUSE

New Canaan, Connecticut, 1949

The architect Philip Johnson (see p.420) built this house as his own weekend retreat. He was one of the leading figures of 20th-century American architecture, and in its sleek Minimalism, the house exemplifies some of the key ideas in his Modernist outlook. These include a transparent wall of glass all around the building to create a feeling of continuity of space between the inside and the outside, the use of industrial materials in a domestic setting, and an open plan that dispensed with traditional rooms.

A brick cylinder contains the bathroom, but otherwise the internal space is divided only by low cabinets. Johnson was a great admirer of architect Mies van der Rohe (see p.419), who designed some of the furniture used in the house.

EAMES HOUSE

Santa Monica, CA, *see p.319*

EDITH FARNSWORTH HOUSE

Plano, Illinois, 1951

The Edith Farnsworth House (formerly the Farnsworth House) was designed by Mies van der

Rohe as a weekend retreat in Illinois for his client, Edith Farnsworth. Mies took the key architectural features of his earlier work and stripped away all the ancillary spaces to design a house as a glass box, uninterrupted except for a service core with bathrooms and a kitchen.

The house opens to an upper terrace in the west, which in turn steps down to a larger terrace to the south. Intriguingly for such an uncompromisingly modern design, Mies included an impractically small fireplace—the idea of the hearth seemingly more important than its potential to create heat. Mies also refused to employ double-glazed glass, as it would appear less transparent.

GUGGENHEIM

New York City, NY, 1959

At the age of 76, Frank Lloyd Wright (see p.418) was commissioned for a building to house the art collection of Solomon R. Guggenheim. It was to be his last building, completed six months after his death at the

age of 91. Wright envisaged the experience of the gallery as a leisurely walk down a spiral ramp, descending from a top-lit atrium, to which visitors would first ascend via an elevator.

Construction began in 1956, but Wright and the Museum Director James Sweeney fell out irrevocably over the design. Sweeney wanted flat rather than sloping walls, and he objected to the light from the clerestory windows, which were promptly covered when the museum opened. Nonetheless, the gallery was a success, acting as the precursor of a generation of "starchitect" museums all around the world.

BETH SHOLOM CONGREGATION

Elkins Park, Pennsylvania, 1959

The Beth Sholom Congregation was one of the final works of the illustrious American architect, Frank Lloyd Wright (see p.418). The synagogue officially opened a few months after his death in

▲ **The Beth Sholom Congregation** in Pennsylvania is Frank Lloyd Wright's modern take on an ancient temple.

1959. When discussing the building's unusual shape, he explained that he tried to evoke an image of cupped hands, as if the congregation were "resting in the very hands of God." Externally, because of its steeply inclined walls, the building has also been

likened to a Mayan pyramid. The roof is translucent, and by day the spacious interior of the synagogue (which has no internal supports) is suffused with natural light. At night, when lit from within, it has been described as glowing like a beacon.

▲ **The Edith Farnsworth House** has floor-to-ceiling glass that opens the dwelling onto its natural surroundings.

INDEPENDENCE ARCH

Accra, Ghana, 1961

The unusually shaped monument of Independence Arch is part of Independence Square. The plaza was created in Accra, Ghana's capital, to mark the country's independence from British colonial rule in 1957. After independence, Ghana became part of the British Commonwealth and the arch was completed in time for Queen Elizabeth II's visit in 1961.

The monument features three parallel arches with two horizontal platforms, from which spectators can observe the ceremonies and events held in the square. Facing the other way, windows on the upper lever look out to the Gulf of Guinea. Across the square, perpendicular to the Independence Arch is the more Classical-inspired Black Star Gate, prominently topped with a five-pointed black star—the national symbol of Ghana

CHURCH OF SANTO ANTÓNIO DA POLANA

Maputo, Mozambique, 1962

The architect of the striking Church of Santo António da Polana was Nuno Craveiro Lopes (1921–1972), the son of a former President of Portugal. He moved

▲ **Popularly known as the "lemon squeezer,"** the Modernist Church of Santo António da Polana has a concrete dome and sparkling, colored-glass windows.

to Mozambique (a Portuguese colony until 1975) to escape political problems in his home country. The church is in the suburb of Polana in the capital Maputo. It exemplifies the era's international trend for Modernist churches built on a roughly circular plan. (Liverpool Metropolitan Cathedral in the UK is another example). Nuno Craveiro Lopes has said that the unusual shape, with its deep folds of concrete,

suggests an inverted flower, and others have likened it to a giant lemon juicer.

BERLIN PHILHARMONIE

Berlin, Germany, 1963

Home to the Berlin Philharmonic Orchestra, the work of Hans Scharoun (1893–1972) pioneered the vineyard-style of stepped terraces that went on to influence concert halls around the world.

His concept was to create a more intimate relationship between music and audience. This was reinforced by the acoustic design: the concave forms of the roof reflect sound evenly around the space, which in turn gathers the audience closer around the stage on all sides. The acoustic shape is also expressed externally, where a gold aluminum skin aids the allusion of a large draping stage curtain or tent.

BOA NOVA TEAHOUSE

Porto, Portugal, see p.323

SYDNEY OPERA HOUSE

Sydney, Australia, see p.333

NATIONAL THEATRE

London, UK, see p.327

NAKAGIN CAPSULE TOWER

Tokyo, Japan, see p.337

CASA GILARDI

Mexico City, Mexico, see p.341

POMPIDOU CENTRE

Paris, France, see p.343

NEUE STAATSGALERIE

Stuttgart, Germany, see p.347

HALLGRÍMSKIRKJA

Reykjavik, Iceland, 1945–1986

The soaring tower of the largest church in Iceland, Hallgrímskirkja, is the most spectacular landmark of the capital Reykjavik, and it is visible from all parts of the city.

▲ **Independence Arch** was built to celebrate Ghana's independence from British colonial rule.

The building is named in honor of Hallgrímur Pétursson, a 17th-century Icelandic clergyman and poet. It was designed by the state architect Guðjón Samúelsson as a symbol of national Icelandic identity, and its features have been likened to aspects of Icelandic culture, history, and landscape.

The Modernist stepped concrete facade, for example, evokes the "organ pipe" appearance of basalt rock formations (see p.334), and the dome of the cylindrical sanctuary recalls the shape of Viking helmets. Internally, the building is austere with almost no decorative elements, as befits an Evangelical-Lutheran church.

VITRA FIRE STATION

Weil Am Rhein, Germany,
see p.357

THE DANCING HOUSE

Prague, Czech Republic, 1996

"Dancing House" is the popular nickname of Prague's Nationale-Nederlanden Building because its two towerlike structures resemble a pair of embracing dancers. More informally, it is known as "Fred and Ginger," in reference to Fred Astaire and Ginger Rogers, the celebrated dancing couple of Hollywood movies. The building's formal name comes from the Dutch company for whom it was built: Nationale-Nederlanden.

The office block was designed by the Canadian-American architect Frank Gehry (see p.422) in association with the Czech architect Vlado Milunić (1941–2022). The building is a leading example of Deconstructivist architecture, in which traditional ideas of stability and harmony are undermined by the fracturing of forms or the warping of surfaces. Although the building has many admirers, some critics feel it is inappropriate for its setting amongst the historic buildings of Prague.

▲ **With its twisted shape and unaligned windows**, the Deconstructivist "Dancing House" swirls amid the traditional architecture of Prague.

GUGGENHEIM MUSEUM BILBAO

Bilbao, Spain, *see pp.354–355*

JIN MAO TOWER

Shanghai, China, 1999

When the 1,380-ft (420.5-m) Jin Mao Tower was completed in 1999, it was the tallest building in China and the third-tallest in the world. The skyscraper, whose name translates as "Golden Prosperity Building," was designed by Skidmore, Owings, & Merrill.

The lower part of the tower is mainly occupied by offices, and above is a luxury hotel. There are also entertainment, exhibition, and shopping facilities in an adjacent "podium" structure at the base of the building. The tower slightly tapers in stages as it rises, evoking traditional Chinese pagodas. In another nod to tradition, there are frequent references to the Chinese lucky number eight throughout the architecture—there are 88 stories, for example.

THE LIBESKIND BUILDING AT THE JEWISH MUSEUM BERLIN

Berlin, Germany, 1999

In 1989 the Polish-American architect Daniel Libeskind (1946–) won an open competition to create a new building for the Jewish Museum in Berlin. The project had special resonance for Libeskind, as many of his relatives had been killed in the Holocaust. He said he wanted to create "a building that tells a story, not just an abstract set of walls and windows." The structure, built of concrete with titanium cladding, has a bold zigzagging plan, forming a shape that has been likened to a broken Star of David. Inside the building, sharp, slanting surfaces and unusually shaped and placed openings create an unsettling atmosphere. Libeskind himself has used the words "disorientating" and "foreboding."

The project established his reputation, launching him on a high-profile international career.

MODE GAKUEN COCOON TOWER

Tokyo, Japan, 2008

Mode Gakuen is Japan's leading fashion college, with branches in Nagoya and Osaka as well as Tokyo, and an international student body. In 2005 it organized a competition for a new building to house a medical college and an IT college as well as a fashion school, all run by Mode Gakuen.

The competition was won by Tange Associates. The curved blue glass exterior of the building is covered with a latticework of white aluminum strips, evoking an insect's cocoon. This was meant

to symbolize the nurturing of the students inside. In 2008 it won a Skyscraper of the Year award with one jury member describing it as "an incubation chamber of ideas and talent that will burst out into dazzling butterflies of creativity."

THE BIRD'S NEST

Beijing, China, 2008

The National Stadium built for the 2008 Beijing Summer Olympics is more widely known as the "Bird's Nest" because its interwoven steelwork resembles the twigs of a nest. The stadium was also used

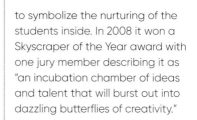

▲ **The Jewish Museum in Berlin** was designed to express both the cultural importance of the city's Jewish population and the horrors that the Jews suffered under Nazi rule.

▲ **The gigantic Bird's Nest** in Beijing is based on the design of traditional Chinese ceramics.

for the 2022 Winter Olympics. The design used 42,000 tons of steel and represented a high-water mark of material extravagance in the design of sports infrastructure.

The elliptical stadium has an internal concrete structure and an external steel frame that are separate from each other for earthquake resistance. The crosshatched latticework frame, made of uncoated steel, was inspired by the patterns of Chinese pottery and is coated with a waterproof polymer membrane. Computer software was used to calculate its complex geometry.

MAPUNGUBWE INTERPRETATION CENTER

Mapungubwe, South Africa, 2009

South African architect Peter Rich (1945–) sought a low-tech approach for the Mapungubwe Interpretation Center, built to tell the history of the Mapungubwe area on the border of South Africa and Botswana. The structural solution for the visitor center created jobs for local laborers and utilized materials sourced close to the site. The timbrel vault domes are made from 200,000 compressed tiles of soil and cement, built up in layers by hand,

with minimal framework, and then finished with local sandstone. The design and materials offer protection from the heat of the sun and provide warmth in cool weather, while retaining a strong connection to the spectacular and remote landscape.

BURJ KHALIFA

Dubai, United Arab Emirates, 2010

Famous as the tallest building in the world, Burj Khalifa is more than 2,716.5 ft (828 m) high and has more than 160 stories. The most powerful symbol of Dubai's boom

as a commercial and financial center, the building was designed by Adrian Smith of the firm of Skidmore, Owings, & Merrill. During construction it was known as Burj Dubai (Dubai Tower), but on completion it was named Burj Khalifa in honor of Sheikh Khalifa bin Zayed Al Nahyan, the President of the United Arab Emirates at the time.

The skyscraper has an unusual "Y"-shaped, 3-armed plan with a hexagonal core. As the building soars upward, it is irregularly stepped back in profile. This creates an elegant, spiraling form and helps to combat wind impact.

MARINA BAY SANDS

Singapore, 2011

A luxury resort complex centered around a hotel, Marina Bay Sands is made up of three 495-ft (191-m) towers capped by a curved linking "SkyPark" terrace with the world's largest rooftop infinity pool. Each tower has a concave facade and is angled at 26 degrees in an arrangement inspired by playing cards propped against each other. The extensive leisure, entertainment, and shopping facilities reflect Singapore's status as a major international tourist attraction.

The resort was designed by the Israeli-born, American-based architect Moshe Safdie (1938–). Singapore is sometimes called the "Garden City" because of its parks and tree-lined streets, and the most original feature of Marina Bay Sands is the SkyPark Observation Deck crowning the hotel towers—a garden in the sky.

YUSUHARA WOODEN BRIDGE MUSEUM

Yusuhara, Japan, 2011

The dramatic and unusual Yusuhara Wooden Bridge Museum links a hotel and a spa on opposite sides of a road in hilly country in Japan. It was designed by Kengo Kuma & Associates, with the architect Junpei Matsushima in charge of construction. Both sides of the central skywalk have small workshops and exhibition spaces. Wood has played a central part in the history of Japanese architecture, and Junpei Matsushima describes the Bridge Museum as "a modern construction inspired by traditional techniques". The main material is locally produced *sugi* (red cedar) in small laminated *hanegi* (corbels). Rather than using long timbers, these *hanegi* are overlapped from a central column to create the cantilever structure. This style is reminiscent

▲ **Evoking traditional Japanese architecture**, the Yusuhara Wooden Bridge Museum is made primarily of local red cedar.

▲ **The design of Lideta Market** blends modern and traditional Ethiopian elements to create a cool, spacious interior.

of the traditional Japanese construction method of *To-Kyo* (square framing).

SHANGHAI TOWER

Shanghai, China, 2016

At 2,074 ft (632 m) high, the Shanghai Tower is the tallest building in China. The skyscraper was designed by Gensler, and the architect Jun Xia, who worked for Gensler, has been credited with the main design. It has been described as a symbol of Shanghai's aspiration to be a leading financial center.

The tower has nine zones, one above the other, each with its own atrium. The building's striking twisting shape is intended to counter the effect of wind at high altitudes, especially typhoons, to which Shanghai is susceptible.

LIDETA MARKET

Addis Ababa, Ethiopia, 2016

In 2017, the Lideta Market won the prestigious Prix Versailles and was described as "the world's best shopping center." The Spanish architect Xavier Vilalta (1980–) combined modern ideas with local cultural traditions. He avoided the glass and steel typically used in malls in favor of a lightweight concrete facade, which transmits less heat into the interior.

The patterning of the building's external skin, with perforated fractals, recalls fabric designs of traditional Ethiopian clothing while also aiding ventilation and lighting. Internally, a spacious atrium connects all the floors, each of which has a varied layout of small shops, as in an age-old market, rather than a parade of large retailers. Photovoltaic umbrellas on the roof give shade and solar energy, and a drainage system collects rainwater.

ICONIC TOWER

New Administrative Capital, Egypt, 2023

Africa's tallest building, the Iconic Tower is the centerpiece of Egypt's New Administrative Capital (NEC)— a city being built from scratch in the desert between Cairo and Suez. As yet unnamed, the city is expected to replace overcrowded Cairo as Egypt's administrative and financial capital and to have a population of six million. The tower was designed by Dar Al-Handasah Consultants, with China State Construction Engineering Corporation its main building contractor. To stop the 1,290-ft- (393-m-) tall skyscraper sinking into the desert ground, it sits on 7.3 sq miles (19 sq km) of reinforced concrete, which was poured in record time with an extra-fast pumping system designed specially for the project.

THE ARC GYMNASIUM

Bali, Indonesia, see p.367

▲ **A carving of Imhotep** in Deir el-Medina—a settlement that housed the workers who built the tombs in the Valley of the Kings

DIRECTORY OF ARCHITECTS

The role of architect is relatively recent. This list reflects this reality, with its preponderance of 19th- and 20th-century western architects. As this book shows, wonderful architecture has been produced wherever humans have made their home around the world, whatever they have called their designers and engineers. The world of architecture is currently working to escape the gravitational pull of a "western" tradition that has dominated it for decades.

IMHOTEP

Egyptian, c. 2660 BCE

Little is known about Imhotep, though he is thought by many to have been the architect of the Step Pyramid of Djoser at Saqqara in Egypt (see p.26), the earliest colossal stone pyramid and funerary monument in the country.

Given Imhotep's important role in the royal court, he probably oversaw the pyramid's construction. In the pyramid complex, there is an inscription on the statue of Djoser (the first pharaoh of the 3rd Dynasty,) that bears Imhotep's name and describes him as "royal chancellor ... and overseer of mansions and painters."

Imhotep has also been credited as the author of several works of didactic literature—none of which has survived. In 525 BCE he was deified by the ancient Egyptians as a god of wisdom and medicine, and possibly also of architecture.

HIPPODAMUS OF MILETUS

Greek, c. 5th century BCE

Widely regarded as the father of European city planning, Hippodamus was born in western Anatolia. According to Aristotle, he was the first man to think rationally about the layout of a city, making him a pioneer of urban planning. Hippodamus believed that the ideal city should consist of around 10,000 free, male citizens, with an overall population of 50,000, including women, children, and slaves. He divided male citizens into groups and the land into sacred, public, and private spheres. His design for Piraeus, the port of Athens, had wide streets radiating out in a grid pattern from a central agora (public square)—a plan that he copied for the ancient city of Thurium in southern Italy.

Such grid patterns were later adopted in other cities, notably in Alexandria and Antioch. Because of this, Hippodamus gave his name to the "Hippodamian Plan," a city laid out using a grid pattern, with a main street and public square.

DINOCRATES

Greek, d. 278 BCE

In 322 BCE, Alexander the Great appointed Dinocrates as Director of Surveying and Urban Planning for the new city of Alexandria on the Mediterranean coast of Egypt. Dinocrates laid the city out according to a Hippodamian grid pattern and worked with Crates of Olynthus, a hydraulic engineer who designed the city's water and sewer systems to accommodate the low-lying site. He was also involved in rebuilding the Temple of Artemis at Ephesus in present-day Turkey, one of the original Seven Wonders of the World, after it was destroyed by fire in 356 BCE.

He designed the funerary monument in Babylon to Hephaestion, Alexander's main general, and an unfinished monument to Alexander's father. His other works include temples and city plans in Delphi, and a vast Hellenic tomb that was found in 2012 in Greek Macedonia.

VITRUVIUS

Roman, c. 75–15 BCE

In his ten-volume treatise *De architectura*, Vitruvius wrote about the history of architecture and engineering and also drew on his personal experience to offer advice. It includes his philosophy that all buildings should have "*firmitas, utilitas, et venustas*" (strength, utility, and beauty). These three principles were widely adopted in Roman architecture and later revived during the European Renaissance of the 15th century. As the only work of this kind to survive from antiquity, *De architectura* is regarded as the first written theory of architecture.

Little is known about Vitruvius's life, and even the first and last parts of his full name—Marcus Vitruvius Pollio—are uncertain. He probably served as a senior officer in the artillery in charge of operations, and as an engineer he specialized in the construction of the *ballista* (a war machine that launched either bolts or stones) and siege engines.

APOLLODORUS OF DAMASCUS

Greek, c. 100 CE

As the favored architect and engineer of the Roman emperor Trajan (r. 98–117 CE), Apollodorus was responsible for Trajan's Column, the stadium of Domitian, and many markets and temples in the Forum, all in Rome. He also built bridges across the Danube and the Tagus in Spain and designed triumphal arches for Trajan in Ancona and Benevento in Italy.

An ethnic Greek born in Damascus in present-day Syria, Apollodorus worked as a military engineer before Trajan summoned him to Rome, where he became consul in 91 CE. His designs were practical and sturdy, and he is credited with introducing several eastern innovations to Roman architecture, notably the dome.

At some point, Apollodorus fell foul of Trajan's successor, Hadrian (76–138 CE), and he was executed around 130 CE. Apollodorus is one of the few Classical architects whose name is still known today.

▲ **Dinocrates proposed** a colossal statue of Alexander the Great on Mount Athos. It was to sit amid a town, though it was never realized.

ABBOT SUGER

French, c. 1081–1151CE

An adviser to the French kings Louis VI (1081–1137) and Louis VII (1120–1180), Abbot Suger commissioned the rebuilding of the Basilica of St-Denis (see p.382) in the new Gothic style. This made the burial church of the French monarchs the first Gothic building in Europe. Its old west front was redesigned to echo the Roman Arch of Constantine, and the rose window was the earliest example of its kind. Other features, such as the ribbed vault, the light-filled chancel, and flying buttresses to support high walls containing large windows, were also developments on the earlier Romanesque style.

Suger's origins are unknown, but he became abbot of St-Denis in 1122. As adviser to the king, he served as regent in from 1147 to 1149 while Louis VII went on the Second Crusade. He recorded the improvements made to St-Denis in *Liber de rebus in administratione sua gestis* and wrote histories of the French kings.

WILLIAM OF SENS

French, d. 1180

Although little is known about William of Sens, it is recorded that he learned his craft while working on Sens Cathedral—the first complete Gothic cathedral in France. He also knew of other early Gothic cathedrals, notably Notre-Dame de Paris and Rheims. The monk and chronicler Gervase of Canterbury (c. 1141–c. 1210) wrote that when the choir of Canterbury Cathedral burned down in 1174, William's ideas based on his work in Sens, were chosen to rebuild the choir. His innovations included a six-part rib vaulting that spread the load of the roof down to flying buttresses and the use of a pale Caen limestone to contrast with the dark pillars of Purbeck marble. He also designed the Corona—an extension to the cathedral for the shrine of Thomas Becket who was slain there in 1170. With these changes, William of Sens created the first important example of the Early Gothic style in England.

FILIPPO BRUNELLESCHI

Italian, 1377–1446

Known as the founding father of Renaissance architecture, Filippo Brunelleschi designed the large brick dome of the cathedral of Santa Maria del Fiore (the Duomo) in Florence. Such an engineering

▲ **Kuai Xiang and the Forbidden City** that he designed are depicted in this painted artwork from the Ming dynasty (1368–1644).

▲ **Abbot Suger's innovations** enabled the high ribbed vaults and tall glass windows of the remodeled Basilica of Saint-Denis.

feat had not been accomplished since Classical times. Initially a master goldsmith and sculptor of cast bronze, Brunelleschi went on to design the Hospital of the Innocents (orphans) in Florence (see p.387), as well as redesign the Basilica di San Lorenzo and many churches and chapels. He also developed the mathematical technique of linear perspective, which opened the way for naturalistic representation in Renaissance art. In 1421, after inventing a new river transport ship, he was granted western Europe's first patent. Brunelleschi was born and died in Florence, the home of all his major buildings.

KUAI XIANG

Chinese, 1377–1451

At the heart of China's capital of Beijing, lies the Forbidden City (see pp.386-387). The vast palace complex was designed by the architect and engineer Kuai Xiang when the Yongle Emperor (1360–1424) moved the imperial capital from Nanjing to Beijing in 1421

Kuai Xiang was barely 30 when he received this commission, so he used the Imperial Palace in Nanjing as a model, including features of earlier Tang and Song dynasty palaces in his design. He also drew on Confucian and Taoist traditions, as well as traditional astronomical beliefs.

Kuai Xiang was born in Xukuo (Xiangshan) in eastern China and probably trained as a carpenter. When he moved to Beijing, he took his fellow carpenters with him as designers. The "Xiangshan Carpenters" is a group of artisans who remain active today.

FILARETE

Italian, c.1400–c.1469

Antonio di Pietro Averlino, better known as Filarete, wrote *Libro architettonico* as a fictional narrative. In the 25-volume work,

▲ Leon Battista **Alberti's design** for Sant'Andrea of Mantua in Italy has the largest barrel vault built since ancient Rome. Three chapels with barrel vaults branch off it, all with painted coffers.

he gave a detailed account of the technical aspects of architecture, such as site selection, construction methods, and choice of materials. He raged against the Gothic style popular at the time, calling it a "barbarous modern style" and argued for the use of Classical Roman styles. Famously, the book included the plan for an ideal city named Sforzinda after Francesco Sforza, Duke of Milan. The city was planned to be set out as an eight-pointed star, surrounded by a moat, although it was never built.

At its center were three squares and a ten-story tower of Virtue and Vice with an observatory and a brothel. Born in Florence, Filarete trained as a craftsman, possibly under the painter and architect Lorenzo Ghiberti (c.1378–1455), who named him Filarete—"lover of virtue". He later became an engineer and worked on architectural projects in Milan and Rome, where he died.

LEON BATTISTA ALBERTI

Italian, 1404–1472

A Renaissance humanist and polymath, Leon Battista Alberti was a founder of modern architecture. In three ground-breaking works, *De pictura* (1435), *De re aedificatoria* (1452), and *De statua* (1464), he laid out the scientific and mathematical rules of balance on which the Florentine Renaissance was built.

Alberti was born in Genoa, studied law, took holy orders, and served in the papal court. His first major commission was the facade of the Rucellai Palace in Florence. Later projects included turning the Gothic church of San Francesco into a chapel, the upper facade of the Santa Maria Novella church (see p.388), and two churches in Mantua. Because he was more concerned with the social impact of a building than its practicalities, few of his works were realized.

INIGO JONES

English, 1573–1652

The first significant modern English architect, Inigo Jones introduced Roman Classical architecture and the Italian Renaissance to England. He designed the Queen's House in Greenwich (see p.393)—the first English building in the new Classical style—and the Banqueting House in Whitehall. He was also responsible for London's first planned square, Covent Garden.

Inigo Jones was born in London, possibly of Welsh background, and a rich patron sent him to study in Italy. He then went to Denmark, where he worked on two palaces for Christian IV (1577–1648). Back in London, in 1613, he became Surveyor of the King's Works, and his royal position resulted in his involvement in the design of up to 1,000 new buildings, although his exact role on them is unclear.

▲ **Francesco Borromini's first** independent commission was the church of San Carlo alle Quattro Fontane in Rome.

USTAD AHMAD LAHORI

Persian, 1580–1649

According to the court histories of Emperor Shah Jahan (1592–1666), Ustad Ahmad Lahori designed some of the Mughal Empire's most famous buildings, including the Taj Mahal in Agra (see p.193) and the Red Fort in Delhi.

Little is known about Lahori, but his name suggests that he was originally from Lahore, in present-day Pakistan. After working on the Taj Mahal, he was commissioned in 1638 to help plan the emperor's new capital, Shahjahanabad (Old Delhi). The Red Fort, a fortified palace at the heart of the walled city, blends Persian, Islamic, and Hindu traditions, and is an example of Mughal architecture at its finest. Lahori is also credited with designing the city's Jama Masjid (Friday Mosque), but he died before construction began.

PIETRO DA CORTONA

Italian, 1596–1669

A key figure in Roman Baroque architecture, Pietro da Cortona trained in painting in Florence. His most outstanding architectural project is the church of Santi Luca e Martina in Rome (see p.211). Da Cortona transformed the ancient church, shaping it into a Greek cross and adding a central dome. He also designed the Villa del Pigneto in Rome and produced designs for the restoration of the Pitti Palace in Florence and the Louvre in Paris.

FRANCESCO BORROMINI

Italian, 1599–1667

A devotee of Michelangelo's architectural work, Francesco Borromini studied the ruins of antiquity and developed his own form of Baroque architecture. He manipulated Classical forms and introduced symbolic meanings into his buildings.

Born Francesco Castelli in Ticino, part of the Swiss Confederacy, he initially followed in his stonemason father's footsteps. In 1619, he moved to Rome and changed his name to Borromini. He designed the church of San Carlo alle Quattro Fontane on Rome's Quirinal Hill in 1643, and later worked on the Oratorio dei Filippini and the church of Sant'Ivo alla Sapienza.

▲ **An 1873 statue of Christopher Wren** is one of eight statues at Burlington House in London, home to the Royal Academy of Arts.

ROBERT ADAM

Scottish, 1728–1792

With his father, William Adam (1689–1748) and his brothers John (1721–1792) and James (1732–1794) all architects, it is not surprising that Robert became an architect, too. His four-year stay in Rome from 1754 led him to develop the "Adam style"—a Neoclassical integration of architecture and interior design that linked walls, furniture, carpets, fixtures, and fittings together in a single, uniform scheme.

The Adam style incorporated Classical Roman design with Greek, Byzantine, and Baroque styles, while rejecting the popular Palladian style. Its success made Robert Adam one of the most fashionable architects of the day. Much of his work was remodeling existing houses, notably Kedleston Hall in Derbyshire, but the covered Pulteney Bridge in Bath was his own design. He also contributed much to Edinburgh's New Town and designed pseudo-medieval country houses in Scotland.

CHRISTOPHER WREN

English, 1632–1723

Originally a scientist, Christopher Wren came to architecture later in life. In 1664, he was asked to design the Sheldonian Theatre in Oxford and a chapel for Pembroke College in Cambridge. A visit to Paris in 1665 exposed him to Baroque architecture. The following year, the Great Fire destroyed two-thirds of London. Wren submitted plans for its rebuilding, which were never adopted, but as Surveyor of Works to Charles II (1630–1685), he oversaw the design and rebuilding of 51 city churches.

He designed the new St. Paul's Cathedral, the Royal Hospital in Chelsea, and the Old Royal Naval College in Greenwich, as well as the remodeled south front of Hampton Court Palace.

JULES HARDOUIN-MANSART

French, 1646–1708

Throughout his life, Jules Hardouin-Mansart worked to glorify his master, Louis XIV of France (1638–1715), designing buildings and laying out public squares in what is known as the Louis XIV style. Among his works are the domed chapel of Les Invalides, the Place Vendôme in Paris, the Grande Trianon chateau at Versailles, and the expansion of the Palace of Versailles.

Born Jules Hardouin, he studied under his uncle François Mansart (1598–1666), an initiator of the Classical tradition in France. Hardouin inherited his uncle's plans and drawings, and later added Mansart's name to his own. He first worked as a building developer, but in 1672 devoted himself entirely to architecture.

MATTHÄUS DANIEL PÖPPELMANN

German, 1662–1736

The son of a shopkeeper in Westphalia, Matthäus Daniel Pöppelmann spent most of his life as an architect in Dresden in Saxony. In 1705, he became state architect to the court of Augustus II (1670–1733) and senior state architect in 1718. In this role, he drew up plans to rebuild the royal palace in Dresden, though only the Zwinger Palace was realized—a series of one- and two-story buildings around a square court intended for pageants, festivals, and other royal entertainments. Pöppelmann also enlarged the Dutch palace and the Pillnitz Palace in Dresden, drew up plans to redesign Warsaw, and designed many fortifications and other buildings throughout Saxony, of which the most impressive was the Augustus Bridge over the Elbe.

▲ **Matthäus Daniel Pöppelmann's** Zwinger Palace is a masterpiece of the late Baroque.

▲ **John Nash's** graceful sweeping terrace on Regent's Crescent, London, has been restored with its Regency facade and colonnade.

JOHN NASH

English, 1752–1835

One of the most prominent architects of Georgian England, John Nash created many Neoclassical buildings. His projects were often sponsored and financed by the Prince Regent, later George IV (1762–1830) and the developer James Burton and his son Decimus. Born the son of a millwright in London, Nash trained with the architect Sir Robert Taylor. He moved to Wales in 1784, where he designed medium-size country houses, returning to London in 1797. After meeting the Prince Regent,

he was selected to create the master plan for the Regent Street area and to design Regent's Park. He also remodeled St. James's Park, Buckingham Palace, and the ceremonial Marble Arch. Outside London, he created the Royal Pavilion in Brighton (see p.265) and a number of fine country houses.

AUGUSTUS PUGIN

English, 1812–1852

The revival of Gothic architecture in 19th-century Victorian Britain owes much to Augustus Pugin. The numerous churches he designed and built, and above all his interior

design of the newly rebuilt Palace of Westminster in London (see p.253) and the exterior design of its clock tower popularized this revival style of architecture.

Pugin was the son of a French draftsman who emigrated to England during the French revolution and created a series of Gothic architectural drawings that greatly influenced his son. Pugin worked with his father before setting up on his own, designing a number of revival houses and other buildings. In 1834, he converted to Roman Catholicism, and his Catholicism later brought him commissions to design St. Chad's Cathedral in

Birmingham and St. Aidan's Cathedral in Enniscorthy in Ireland, among other prestigious projects.

EUGÈNE VIOLLET-LE-DUC

French, 1814–1879

Eugène Viollet-le-Duc's writings on the relationship of form and function and on decoration had a profound impact on a generation of modern architects, particularly of the Art Nouveau school. Yet he made his name not in designing new buildings but in restoring medieval structures, notably Notre-Dame de Paris (see p.382) and the Sainte-Chapelle royal

▲ **A.W.N. Pugin** is known for being an author and theorist as well as a leading architect of the Gothic revival.

chapel in Paris, Mont Saint-Michel in Normandy, and the walls of the medieval city of Carcassonne.

Viollet-le-Duc was born in Paris. His grandfather was an architect, and his father the overseer of the residences of Louis XVIII. He was appointed to the new Commission of Historic Monuments of France, at the age of just 24 and was made professor at the École des Beaux-Arts in 1863. While working on the Paris Exposition Universelle of 1878, he proposed the main building be a museum—a proposal that led to the opening of the National Museum of French Monuments in 1882, after his death.

ANTONI GAUDÍ

Catalan, 1852–1926

A proud Catalan, Antonio Gaudí was the greatest exponent of *Modernisme,* also called Catalan Art Nouveau, the movement that sought to enhance and promote Catalan identity at the turn of the century. Gaudí's buildings, almost all in Barcelona, combined his passion for architecture, nature, and religion. He attended to every

detail of his creations, rarely working from drawings but using three-dimensional scale models and creating each part as he conceived it. Gaudí gained recognition for his first important commission, the Casà Vicens, and then worked for the industrialist Eusebi Güell, designing the Güell Palace and Park.

In 1883, he was put in charge of the Sagrada Familia basilica (see pp.274–275). Gaudí completely changed the initial design and devoted himself to the project for nine years until his death. The Sagrada Familia is unfinished, but Gaudí's idiosyncratic and imaginative designs together still define the city he so loved.

VICTOR PIERRE HORTA

Belgian, 1861–1947

Victor Horta was one of the founders of the Art Nouveau movement, the decorative, dynamic art movement that swept Europe in the late 19th century. His Hôtel Tassel in Brussels (see p.271) is often considered to be the first-ever Art Nouveau

house. The son of a shoemaker, Horta was born in Ghent, where he studied music and art. He worked for an architect in Paris, and then, in 1880, he studied architecture at the Royal Academy of Fine Arts in Brussels. The Hôtel Tassel made his name and was followed by a number of Art Nouveau buildings, notably the Hôtel Van Eetvelde and the Hôtel Aubecq. His later work moved away from Art Nouveau, becoming more Classical in style.

HECTOR GUIMARD

French, 1867–1942

The Art Nouveau glass-and-iron canopies that cover the entrances to the Paris metro (see p.273) are one of the endearing symbols of the city. They were designed by Victor Guimard, whose 50 or so

buildings established Art Nouveau in the public mind. Guimard was born in Lyon and, in 1882, enrolled at the School of Decorative Arts in Paris. Once qualified, he began to study architecture at the École des Beaux-Arts. In the summer of 1895, he met the Belgian architect Victor Horta and admired the floral lines of his Hôtel Tassel.

By now, devoted to Art Nouveau, he began to design a number of buildings in Paris, notably the Castel Béranger apartment building. Its success led to commissions for other projects such as the Hôtel Guimard. As Art Deco emerged after World War I, Guimard adapted to the new style while retaining some elements of his previously decorative style. Fearing for his Jewish wife's safety in Nazi-dominated Europe, he and his wife moved to New York in 1938, where he died in 1942.

▲ **The lobby of Hector Guimard's** Castel Béranger has glazed sandstone and Art Nouveau shapes in iron and stained glass.

FRANK LLOYD WRIGHT

American, 1867–1959

Perhaps the most famous domestic architect of the 20th century, Frank Lloyd Wright built houses that became the basis of residential design in the US. He designed in harmony with the environment—a philosophy he called "organic architecture," best exemplified by the Fallingwater house (see p.402).

Frank Wright was born in Wisconsin in 1867 and adopted half his mother's maiden name as his middle name. In 1886, he decided to become an architect and entered the University of Wisconsin-Madison but left without a degree. In 1893, he opened his own practice in Chicago and went on to design

around 1,000 buildings, many in the Prairie style: a design with a one-story projection, an open-plan layout, a low-pitched roof with overhanging eaves, and strong horizontal lines. His most famous building is the inverted bowl-shaped Guggenheim Museum in New York, which he did not live to see open.

ALBERT KAHN

American, 1869–1942

Detroit is one of the main centers of American industry, and Albert Kahn was its designer. Among his many projects were skyscrapers, office buildings, mansions in the suburbs, and the Ford River Rouge automobile complex—when completed in 1928, it was

the largest integrated factory in the world. In 1937, Kahn was responsible for 19 percent of all architect-designed industrial plants in the US.

Kahn was born into a Jewish family in Prussia and emigrated with his family to Detroit in 1881. He quickly learned English and in 1883 got a job in an architecture firm. In 1902 he formed a partnership with his brother Julius (1874–1942), developing the Kahn system of reinforcing concrete with steel in order to construct large, open interiors in factories. So successful was Kahn that in 1929 he set up a design and trading office in Moscow to train Soviet architects.

WALTER GROPIUS

German-American, 1883–1969

Widely regarded as one of the masters of Modernist architecture, Walter Gropius was also the renowned founder of the Bauhaus art school, home to many of the leading lights in interwar European art and design.

Born in Berlin, Gropius studied architecture in Munich and Berlin before setting up a partnership with Adolf Meyer (1881–1929) in 1910. They designed a number of Modernist buildings, notably the Fagus factory (see p.285). In 1919, Gropius was appointed master of the Bauhaus and he designed its new school building in Dessau in 1925. He left Nazi Germany in 1934, settling first in London and then in the US in 1937, where he designed Modernist buildings, notably his own house in Lincoln, Massachusetts, which is credited with bringing the Modernist style of simplicity, economy, and aesthetic beauty to the US.

GUNNAR ASPLUND

Swedish, 1885–1940

The main architect behind Nordic Classicism was Gunnar Asplund. The style, which combined

vernacular architecture and Neoclassicism, flourished in Scandinavia between 1910 and 1933. Asplund was educated at the Academy of Fine Arts in Stockholm, but an exposure to Classical architecture on a trip to Greece and Italy early on made a strong impression.

Among his significant works was the Woodland Chapel in the Stockholm South Cemetery, the extension to Gothenburg's city hall, and the Stockholm City Library. As professor of architecture at the Royal Institute of Technology from 1931, his work in the last decade of his life became increasingly Modernist in style. Considered to be one of the most important Modernist architects in Sweden, Asplund had a major influence on a later generation of Nordic architects.

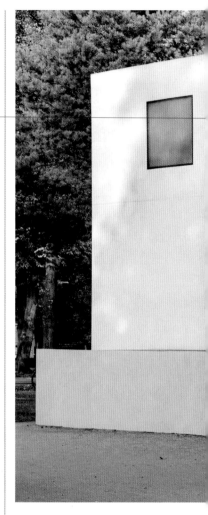

▲ **Frank Lloyd Wright** with a model of his planned Price Tower in 1953. It was completed in Oklahoma in 1956.

▲ **Interlocking cuboids** are characteristic of Walter Gropius's "Director's House" on the Bauhaus complex in Dessau, Germany.

LUDWIG MIES VAN DER ROHE

German-American, 1886–1969

A pioneer of Modernist architecture, Ludwig Mies van der Rohe built some of the most iconic modern buildings in the US. He represented the modern age, creating simplicity with steel and plate glass. As he famously said, "Less is more."

Mies was born in Aachen, Germany, where he worked in his father's stone-carving shop before moving to Berlin. In 1908, he began as an architecture apprentice. He built the Villa Wolf in 1926 and then the German Pavilion of the 1929 Barcelona International Exhibition and the Villa Tugendhat in the Czech Republic (see p.401). As the final director of the Bauhaus art school, he was boycotted by the Nazis for his Modernist tastes and emigrated to the US in 1937, where he became head of architecture at the Illinois Institute of Technology. Among his many works are the 330 North Wabash skyscraper in Chicago, the Seagram Building (see p.304), and the weekend retreat Edith Farnsworth House (see p.402).

LE CORBUSIER

Swiss-French, 1887–1965

The architect Charles-Édouard Jeanneret-Gris adopted the pseudonym of Le Corbusier in 1920, taken from an altered form of his maternal grandfather's name. Dedicated to better living conditions for urban residents, Le Corbusier produced city plans, notably, the master plan for the new city of Chandigarh in India.

Born in the Jura Mountains in Switzerland, he attended the local art school. Largely self-taught as an architect, in 1912 Le Corbusier designed a house for his parents, and became interested in the use of reinforced concrete. In 1917, he moved to Paris and started an architectural practice with his cousin, Pierre Jeanneret (1896–1967). In a series of articles for *L'Esprit Nouveau* in 1922–23, Le Corbusier famously declared, "a house is a machine to live in."

A series of commissions followed, such as the Villa Savoye (see pp.306–307). After the war, he created the Unité d'Habitation apartment block (see p.303) and the United Nations headquarters in New York (see p.321). Although an atheist, Le Corbusier designed many fine religious buildings.

RICHARD NEUTRA

Austrian-American, 1892–1970

Renowned for his elegant houses in California, Richard Neutra devoted considerable attention to the real needs of his clients rather than imposing his own artistic vision on them. His blending of art, landscape, and practical comfort can be seen in the Miller House and the Kaufmann Desert House (see p.321).

Neutra was born in Vienna in the Austro-Hungarian Empire and served in the Austrian army during World War I. He studied at the Vienna School of Technology and the private architecture school of Adolf Loos. In 1923, he emigrated to the US. There he briefly worked with Frank Lloyd Wright and designed many well-regarded buildings in the International Style.

▲ In 1961, **Philip Johnson** presents his plan for the New York State Theater at the Lincoln Center (later the David H. Koch Theater).

RICHARD BUCKMINSTER FULLER

American, 1895–1983

Richard Buckminster Fuller was an inventor and theorist of systems as well as an architect. Among the many terms that he coined were "Spaceship Earth," a worldview encouraging global cooperation.

Most notably, he popularized the geodesic dome—a lightweight, transparent globular structure of rigid triangular elements—the most famous of which was on display at the Expo 67 World's Fair in Montreal, Canada.

Fuller was born in Milton, Massachusetts. Twice expelled from Harvard University, he suffered with his health and, reexamining his life in 1927, he embarked on a career to benefit humanity. A series of inventions and ideas followed.

ALVAR AALTO

Finnish, 1898–1976

Alvar Aalto's buildings were total works of art, in which he and his wife Aino designed not just the building, but its interior and contents as well. As the inventor of bent plywood furniture, Aalto had a huge impact on design.

His buildings range from the Nordic Classicism of his earlier works to International Style Modernism in the 1930s and a more organic Modernist style in the 1940s. In total, Aalto designed more than 500 buildings, mostly in Finland.

LOUIS KAHN

Estonian-American, 1901–1974

Louis Kahn developed a style that was both monolithic and monumental. His buildings did not hide their weight or materials, as demonstrated by the solid blocks of the Salk Institute for Biological Studies in La Jolla, California (1965), and the Brutalist Jatiya Sangsad Bhaban parliament (see p.303) in Dhaka, Bangladesh (1982).

Born into a Jewish family in Estonia, Kahn emigrated to the US at age five and later studied architecture at the University of Pennsylvania School of Fine Arts. He set up private practice in 1935 and in 1947 became a design critic and professor of architecture at Yale University. It was only in the 1950s that he developed his famous Modernist style. In 1957, he became a professor in the School of Design at the University of Pennsylvania.

PHILIP JOHNSON

American, 1906–2005

Working in the Modernist and Postmodernist styles, Philip Johnson designed some of the most iconic modern buildings in the US, most notably the pink granite-clad tower at 550 Madison Avenue, New York (see p.349).

Johnson was born in Cleveland, Ohio, the son of a lawyer. He studied philosophy at Harvard University and made trips to Europe, where he met Ludwig Mies van der Rohe (see p.419), starting a lifelong collaboration.

Johnson used his fortune on the new architecture department at the Museum of Modern Art in New York. After a brief foray into politics, he enrolled in the Harvard Graduate School of Design in 1941. He set up practice in 1946 and worked on Modernist and then Postmodernist buildings, such as the Glass House (see p.303), the David H. Koch Theatre in New York, and the Crystal Cathedral in California.

OSCAR NIEMEYER

Brazilian, 1907–2012

The designer of Brazil's modern capital of Brasília, Oscar Niemeyer was a key figure in modern architecture. Eschewing hard, inflexible angles and straight lines, he was attracted to "free-flowing, sensual curves." His innovative use of reinforced concrete became highly influential.

Niemeyer was born in Rio de Janeiro and studied architecture there. His first major work was a tower in Rio for the Ministry of Education. The project was overseen by Le Corbusier, but Niemeyer assumed control in 1939.

In 1956, Niemeyer began designing buildings for Brasília. The cathedral (see p.324), the two semi-spheres of the National Congress building (see p.305), and the colonnaded Itamaraty Palace dominate the skyline. Among his other fine works is the Niterói Contemporary Art Museum in Rio.

EERO SAARINEN

Finnish-American, 1910–1961

Architect and industrial designer Eero Saarinen designed several popular public buildings and monuments, notably the main terminal at Dulles International Airport in Washington, D.C., (see p.320), the TWA flight center at New York's JFK airport (see p.334), and the majestic Gateway Arch in St. Louis, Missouri (see p.321).

Saarinen was born in Finland and emigrated with his family to the US at the age of 13. He studied architecture at Yale University and in 1936, began work in his father's practice. He created a series of Modernist chairs, most of which were produced by Knoll, and in 1948 he won a competition to design the Gateway Arch in St. Louis.

His success with the General Motors Technical Center in Warren, Michigan, led to a series of highly regarded corporate and academic buildings.

▲ **Designed by Eero Saarinen**, Yale University's David S. Ingalls hockey rink is nicknamed "The Whale". Its arched concrete backbone extends to the front with raised lighting.

LINA BO BARDI

Italian-Brazilian, 1914–1992

Architect, designer, journalist, and activist Lina Bo Bardi's varied buildings combine Modernist influences with Brazilian artistic and cultural traditions.

Born in Italy, Bo Bardi studied architecture at the University of Rome, but moved to Brazil in 1946. In 1951, after launching *Habitat* magazine, she designed her home in São Paulo, the Glass House, a Modernist masterpiece with a glazed facade raised on metallic pillars. She went on to design São Paulo's new Museum of Art building, whose vast reinforced concrete body seems to hover over the shaded space beneath.

Her many other public projects included theaters and community centers. Bo Bardi also designed furniture, including a cowhide folding chair, and theater sets. In 2021, at the Venice Architecture Biennale, she was posthumously awarded the Special Golden Lion for Lifetime Achievement.

I. M. PEI

Chinese-American, 1917–2019

The ethereal glass and metal pyramid floating above the entrance to Paris's Louvre Museum (see p.239) is I. M. Pei's most controversial and admired work.

Pei is celebrated for infusing the clean lines and monumentality of Modernism with a cultural sensibility. His major works include the East Building of the National Gallery of Art in Washington, D.C., and the Bank of China Tower in Hong Kong. In 2009, his intensive Islamic studies informed the blocks and arches of his Museum of Islamic Art in Doha.

Ieoh Ming Pei grew up in China and Hong Kong before studying at the Massachusetts Institute of Technology. Further study at Harvard University under Walter Gropius led to his lifelong commitment to Modernism. Pei's practice was renamed Pei Cobb Freed & Partners in 1989. His global awards and prizes include the 1983 Pritzker Architecture Prize.

▲ **I. M. Pei's design** for the Museum of Islamic Art in Doha blends traditional Islamic architecture with modern technology.

MINNETTE DE SILVA

Sri Lankan, 1918–1998

A pioneer of Modern Regionalism (later called Critical Regionalism), Minnette de Silva brought Modernist architecture to Asian settings, traditions, and crafts.

The daughter of activists in Kandy, Sri Lanka, de Silva made an impact at the RIBA in postwar London. Back in Kandy, her first project, Karunaratne House (1947–1951), was an experimental melding of Modernist materials with artisanal woven panels, murals, and clay tiles. The new housing scheme was designed in consultation with potential householders. The curving, whitewashed structure of the Senanayake apartments in Colombo is considered her most Corbusian structure. Previously overlooked, de Silva was finally awarded the Sri Lanka Institute of Architects gold medal in 1996.

GEOFFREY BAWA

Sri Lankan, 1919–2003

One of the most influential Asian architects of his generation, Geoffrey Bawa created a distinctive style of architecture that blended Modernism with traditional Sri Lankan themes and building materials.

Educated in Colombo and Cambridge, UK, Bawa initially practiced law but then retrained as an architect. The da Silva house in Colombo was the first of his buildings to meld traditional Sri Lankan architecture with open planning, and his own house was created around a series of open courtyards and verandas, set in a tropical garden.

Bawa's most notable buildings include the Sri Lankan Parliament Building at Kotte (1979–1982), Ruhuna University, Matara (1980–1986) and the Minimalist Jayawardene House (1999–2002).

JAMES STIRLING

British, 1926–1992

An unorthodox innovator in postwar architecture, Glasgow-born James Stirling was an early adopter of the exposed raw steel and brick of Brutalism.

After studying at the University of Liverpool, he worked with James Gowan (1923–2015). Their ground-breaking projects in the 1950s and '60s included low-rise garden apartments at Ham Common, London, and the red brick and tile towers of the Engineering Building, University of Leicester (see p.304).

For traditionalists, Stirling was everything undesirable about the "new architecture"; his Cambridge University History Building (1967) was seen as an exemplar of malfunctioning design. Working solo, Stirling's design evolved into colorful, geometric Postmodern forms, as in the Neue Staatsgalerie in Germany (see p.347). In the UK, RIBA's Stirling Prize for excellence was founded in his name in 1996.

BALKRISHNA DOSHI

Indian, 1927–2010

Balkrishna Doshi fused Modernism with Indian traditions. Born in Pune, he studied architecture in Mumbai and was influenced by Le Corbusier with whom he worked in France, Chandigarh, and Ahmadabad.

Doshi designed numerous housing complexes, such as the low-cost ATIRA complex in Ahmedabad (1959), a series of vaulted units with rear courts. Other noteworthy designs include his own studio, Sangath (1981), near Ahmedabad, which is half buried in the ground under insulated concrete vaults covered in white ceramic surfaces that protect it from heat and dust.

▲ **The Ray and Maria Stata Center**, on the MIT campus, has Frank Gehry's trademark tilting sections and colliding shapes.

▲ **Kisho Kurokawa's** National Art Center in Minato-ku, Tokyo, has a wavelike glass facade with two inverted cones.

Other works include the Gandhi Labour Institute in Ahmedabad (1980–1984) and the National Institute of Fashion Technology in New Delhi (1991–1995).

ALISON AND PETER SMITHSON

British, 1928–1993 and 1923–2003

A couple who argued for a new British Brutalism, Alison and Peter Smithson rose to prominence when they won a competition to design Hunstanton Secondary Modern School in Norfolk in 1950. The school took three years to build because of postwar steel rationing, but in spite of functional flaws, it heralded a new era for modernizers. In 1956, the Smithsons designed a prescient "House of the Future" at the *Daily Mail* Ideal Home Exhibition. It featured a courtyard garden and open-plan living space.

Prolific in their avant-garde writing and teaching, the Smithsons broke down barriers between high and low culture and advocated for buildings founded on pragmatism and the demands of location. Robin Hood Gardens, a mid-rise housing complex in Poplar, east London (1966–1972) exemplified their neighborhoods conceived as "streets in the air."

FRANK GEHRY

Canadian-American, 1929–

Gehry's Deconstructivist style creates dynamic structures that conjure fluidity from solid stone, glass, and metal.

Born in Toronto, Gehry studied architecture at the University of Southern California and city planning at Harvard University before forming his own company in 1962. He won the Pritzker Prize in 1989. His Guggenheim Museum Bilbao (see pp.354–355) fired a worldwide enthusiasm for museum design. Celebrated elements of his projects include the hodgepodge roof panels at Biomuseo in Panama City, the glass sails of the Fondation Louis Vuitton in Paris, and the "Fred and Ginger" towers of the Prague Nationale-Nederlanden (see p.405).

KISHO KUROKAWA

Japanese, 1934–2007

The Metabolist philosophy that informed the early work of leading architect Kisho Kurokawa centered on impermanence in architecture: a notion apt for a nation that had reconstructed cities after World War II. In architectural practice, this translated into prefabricated modular elements that could be added or removed over time. The prime example was Kurokawa's Nakagin Capsule Tower in Tokyo (see p.337), composed of ready-made pods plugged into a central core of facilities.

Later, Kurokawa favored history and context over Futurism. His design for the Hiroshima City Museum of Contemporary Art has an empty circular space at its heart to represent the dropping of the atomic bomb.

NORMAN FOSTER

British, 1935–

The name of Norman Foster has become a byword for sleek Modernism applied creatively to

▲ **Norman Foster's diagrid extension** to the Hearst Tower in New York sits on top of the original 1928 stone-clad building.

buildings ranging from art galleries to airports. His most noteworthy works are reinventions using glass: the covered quadrangle at London's British Museum (see p.342) and the glass cupola rising from the Reichstag in Berlin.

Born in Manchester, UK, Foster studied architecture at the University of Manchester and then at Yale University. In 1967, he established Foster Associates (now Foster + Partners). His many buildings include "The Gherkin" (30 St. Mary Axe) in London, the triangular Hearst Tower in New York, and the Millau Viaduct in France. His circular spaceship design for Apple Park in Cupertino, California, features forestry and a huge central pond.

▲ **Zaha Hadid designed** London's Aquatic Centre for the 2012 Olympic Games with fluid, watery lines and a wave-inspired roof. The outer shell is made with steel, aluminum, and timber.

RENZO PIANO

Italian, 1937–

Renzo Piano first gained international recognition for the incongruous and playful Pompidou Centre in Paris (see p.343) in the 1970s.

Born into a family of builders in Genoa, Piano became a student and then a teacher at Milan Polytechnic. An early advocate of high-tech, his designs for public buildings and spaces include Kansai International Airport Terminal in Japan (1994), which was designed so successfully with sliding joints that it was unscathed by an earthquake a year later.

Ahead of the curve in sustainable architecture, Piano's California Academy of Sciences in San Francisco (2008) has exhibition and research spaces beneath the undulating domes of a living roof. In the UK, Piano is best known for The Shard in London (see p.239).

REM KOOLHAAS

Dutch, 1944–

A 21st century "starchitect" of Deconstructive style, Rem Koolhaas was described by the judges awarding him the Pritzker Prize in 2000 as "a visionary and implementer, philosopher and pragmatist." Raised in Rotterdam in the Netherlands and in Jakarta, Indonesia, Koolhaas abandoned an early career in journalism to study at London's Architectural Association. His Office for Metropolitan Architecture (OMA), cofounded in Rotterdam and London in 1975, is celebrated for its radical output.

In 1998, OMA won a competition to design the first new structure to sit among Mies van der Rohe's iconic buildings at the Illinois Institute of Technology. In Beijing in 2012, he built two towers bridged to form a distorted loop for the China Central Television (CCTV) headquarters (see p.277). Later designs include the Garage Museum of Contemporary Art in Moscow, Russia, and the Taipei Performing Arts Center, Taiwan. Koolhaas has also written the architectural books *Delirious New York* and *S, M, L, XL*.

KEN YEANG

Malaysian, 1948–

Writing his PhD on ecological design and planning in the 1970s, Ken Yeang revealed a prescient understanding of the need for the seamless integration of buildings and natural environments. Widely regarded as the inventor of the bioclimatic skyscraper, Yeang designs with natural ventilation and solar geometry and builds vertical gardens into tall buildings.

Born in Penang, Yeang studied at London's Architectural Association and Cambridge University. His company, T. R. Hamzah & Yeang, has offices in Malaysia, London, and Beijing. His key buildings include Chongqing Tower, China; India's first bioclimatic skyscraper, the Spire Edge World Trade Centre; and the Solaris in Singapore, in which a spiral ramp of trees and plants wraps the office building from basement to sky terrace.

ZAHA HADID

Iraqi-British, 1950–2016

Iraqi-born British architect Zaha Hadid is remembered as much for her abstract-inspired paintings of designs as for the sensuous, undulating buildings that earned her the title "Queen of the Curve."

Educated in Beirut and the UK, Hadid studied at London's Architectural Association before founding her own practice in 1979. Her London buildings include the Serpentine North Gallery and the Evelyn Grace Academy. An early adopter of parametric design software, Hadid created daring designs including the Bergisel Ski Jump in Innsbruck, Austria; the geometric structures of Rome's MAXXI museum in Italy (see p.358); and the dancing curves of Baku's Heydar Aliyev Center in Azerbaijan (see p.358).

In 2004, Hadid was the first woman to win the Pritzker Prize. Controversially, she is also remembered for designs that were never built because of their perceived extravagance and impracticality. Her design for Japan's National Stadium, for example, was reconceived entirely for the 2020 Olympics.

KENGO KUMA

Japanese, 1954–

While many architects begin with a grand concept, Kengo Kuma focuses first on the ambience of a space and the detailed choice of appropriate, often local,

▲ **Diébédo Francis Kéré** outside his striking creation for the 2017 temporary pavilion at the Serpentine Gallery in London.

DIÉBÉDO FRANCIS KÉRÉ

Burkinabé-German, 1965–

Born in Gando in Burkina Faso, Diébédo Francis Kéré left home at age seven for a stifling classroom crammed with 100 students in the town of Tenkodogo. Scholarships took him to Berlin to study carpentry and then to the city's Institute of Technology to study architecture. While still a student, he fulfilled a childhood vow to build a comfortable and functioning school in his home village, and he went on to form a nonprofit foundation.

Kéré is celebrated for innovative, economically viable buildings in remote African locations, constructed with sun-dried bricks of local clay and cement and canopy roofs. The first African to win the Pritzker Prize, Kéré has offices in Germany and Burkina Faso. Global projects include the Xylem pavilion built from reclaimed timber at the Tippet Rise Art Center in Montana and the 2017 Serpentine Pavilion in London.

DAVID ADJAYE

Ghanaian-British, 1966–

The cultural sensitivity in the designs of Ghanaian-born David Adjaye emerged from a childhood spent in several countries before his diplomat father settled the family in London.

Adjaye studied at South Bank University and the Royal College of Art in London. He began Adjaye Associates in 2000, and it has studios in Accra, London, and New York. For the Smithsonian National Museum of African American History and Culture in Washington, D.C., Adjaye designed pyramid tiers that echo Yoruba culture and metalwork scrims that reflect the historic iron grilles on African American buildings in New Orleans.

His other projects include the Nobel Peace Center in Oslo and the Moscow School of Management. *Adjaye Africa Architecture: A Photographic Survey of Metropolitan Architecture* is compiled from his ten years of research in 54 African cities.

materials. He aims for structures that disappear into their environs. His philosophy is applied equally to a restroom on a hiking trail, with umbrella-shaped roofs mirroring the surrounding peaks, to the oval National Stadium for Tokyo's 2020 Olympics, fringed with greenery and wooden eaves. The small zigzagging roofs of his Folk Art Museum in Hangzhou in China blend into the slopes of a former tea plantation, and the cliff-like structures of the V&A Dundee stretch along Scotland's Tay River.

The son of an architect, Kuma studied at the University of Tokyo and at Columbia University in New York. His company, Kengo Kuma & Associates, has offices in Japan, China, and Paris and carries out projects in more than 30 countries.

▲ **David Adjaye's** Smithsonian Museum of African American History and Culture has a bronze-colored latticed covering.

GLOSSARY

ACANTHUS A plant used as a model for ornamentation on Corinthian capitals.

ACROPOLIS The citadel of an ancient Greek city, containing temples and public buildings.

ADOBE A sun-dried mud brick, used mainly in Africa, South America, and Central Asia.

ALABASTER A light-colored, translucent, soft stone favored by sculptors.

AMBULATORY A covered passageway used for processions.

APSE A semicircular, usually vaulted, area at the east end of a church, which originally contained the altar.

AQUEDUCT A structure in the form of a channel or bridge, that the Romans used to transport water.

ARABESQUE Decorative ornament using intertwined, flowing, symmetrical shapes based on leaves, tendrils, and plants.

ARCADE A series of arches on columns or pillars, which are either free-standing or attached to a wall.

ARCHITRAVE The lowest part of an entablature in Classical architecture; more generally, a molded strip around a doorway or window.

ART DECO A style of architecture and decoration popular in the 1920s and '30s in Europe and North America. It combined bright colors and geometrical ornament with motifs drawn from ancient Egyptian art.

ART NOUVEAU A late 19th-century decorative style that drew on nature as the primary inspiration for its curved forms.

ASHLAR Stone that has been cut and smoothed into regular-shaped blocks and laid in a brick-like fashion.

ATRIUM An inner court open to the sky but surrounded by a roof.

BALUSTRADE A series of vertical shafts topped by a railing; used as a decorative enclosure for a balcony or staircase.

BAPTISTERY A building or room used for Christian baptisms; baptisteries are often circular or polygonal in shape, with the font placed in the center.

BAROQUE A style of architecture popular during the 17th and early 18th centuries, noted for its sweeping theatricality.

BARREL VAULT A structure that acts like a series of arches placed one after another to make a semi-cylindrical ceiling.

BAS-RELIEF See Relief carving.

BASILICA A rectangular building with a long nave that was used in ancient Rome for public administration. The form was later adopted for early Christian churches.

BATTER The inclined face of a wall.

BEAM A horizontal structure spanning an opening and carrying a load, such as a floor or wall. Traditionally made of wood, beams are now usually concrete or steel.

BEAUX-ARTS An ornate form of Classical architecture, fashionable in France in the late 19th century and imitated elsewhere in Europe and the US. Named after the École des Beaux-Arts in Paris.

BLIND ARCADE An arcade in which the arches are attached to a wall.

BOSS An ornamental knob placed at the intersection of ribs in a vault or ceiling.

BRACKET A small projecting member used to support a weight.

BREEZE BLOCK A large brick made from cement and ashes.

BRISE-SOLEIL A permanent sun shield covering the windows of a building.

BRUTALISM An architectural style of the 1950s and '60s that used monolithic blocklike forms and exposed concrete.

BUTTRESS A mass of masonry built against a wall to provide additional strength. See also Flying buttress.

BYZANTINE The architecture of the 4th-century Byzantine Empire, often associated with religious buildings, such as basilicas.

CAMPANILE A bell tower, usually detached from the building to which it belongs.

CANTILEVER A horizontal projection from a wall (a beam or a balcony), that is supported at one end only by downward force.

CAPITAL The structure that crowns a column.

CAPSTONE A stone laid on top of a wall, a dolmen, or another structure.

CARYATID A sculpted female figure used as a column or support.

CASEMATE A vaulted room that forms part of a fortification.

CAST IRON Iron that has been cast in a mold. Used widely for railings, gates, street furniture, and decoration.

CELLA The principal inner room of a Greek temple containing the statue of the deity.

CEMENT The substance used to bind together the materials in concrete or mortar, to make them harden into a solid.

CHANCEL The eastern part of a church reserved for the choir and clergy.

CHHATRI A dome-shaped pavilion on the roof of a building, commonly associated with Indian architecture.

CHINOISERIE A style of architecture and decoration popular in 18th-century Europe, inspired by pagodas and Chinese art.

CHURRIGUERESQUE An extravagant form of late Baroque architecture, named after the Churriguera family and most commonly found in Spain and Mexico.

CLASSICAL Relating to the architecture of ancient Greece and Rome.

CLERESTORY A row of windows above an arcade, often in the nave of a church.

COFFER A decorative sunken panel in a vault or ceiling.

COLONNADE A row of columns that supports an entablature or arches.

COLUMN A cylindrical upright support, consisting of a base, shaft, and capital.

COMPUTER-AIDED DESIGN (CAD) Computer software packages used by architects when designing buildings and other structures. First introduced in the 1960s, and widely used from the 1990s.

CONCRETE A composite material made from cement, water, and an aggregate such as sand or gravel.

CORBEL A projecting block used to support part of a structure, such as a roof beam or a vault

CORNICE A projecting horizontal molding running along the top of a building; specifically, the upper part of the entablature in Classical architecture.

COURSED MASONRY A layer of bricks or stones, running horizontally in a wall in a regular fashion.

COVING A plain, concave molding used to conceal the joint between a wall and a ceiling.

CRENELLATED Describes a building with battlements, particularly the high and low points on the top of a parapet.

CRUCIFORM Describes a structure in the shape of a cross, such as a Christian church.

CUPOLA A small dome that roofs a tower.

DAGOBA See Stupa.

DECONSTRUCTIVISM A late 20th-century architectural movement influenced by Postmodernism; it disrupted traditional shapes to create radical forms.

DORMER A vertical window placed in a sloping roof, with its own roof and gable.

DRESSED STONE Quarried stone that has been shaped and sized.

DRUM A cylindrical shell that supports a dome or a cupola.

EAVES The edges of a roof that overhang the walls of a building.

ELEVATION The external face of a building; an architectural drawing showing more than one external facade.

ENTABLATURE The upper part of a classical order: a horizontal band running above the columns and made up of three strips—the architrave at the bottom, the frieze above, and the cornice at the top.

EXPRESSIONISM A 20th-century art movement that led architects to try and create more expressive buildings and experiment with new materials.

FACADE The front or face of a building.

FINIAL The ornamental feature at the top of a pinnacle or gable.

FLYING BUTTRESS A buttress in the form of an arch that carries the lateral thrust of a roof or vault toward a support on the outside of a building. It is a key component of Gothic cathedrals.

FORMWORK A frame for molding mud or concrete. Traditionally made from wood, but now often made of steel.

FRESCO A wall painting in which the pigment is applied when the plaster is wet.

FRIEZE The part of a Classical entablature between the architrave and the cornice.

FUTURISM An early 20th-century art movement, originating in Italy, that celebrated technology and dynamism.

GABLE The upper part of the end wall of a building with a pitched roof, usually triangular in shape.

GALLERY In churches, an upper level built over the aisle and which opens out onto the nave; in large houses, a long room on an upper floor for recreation.

GOTHIC The main style of architecture in Europe during the Middle Ages, featuring tall stone vaults, flying buttresses, pointed arches, and large stained-glass windows.

GREEN BUILDING Construction that is environmentally responsible.

GROIN VAULT A vault made up of two barrel vaults that intersect at right angles.

HIPPED ROOF A roof in which all sides slope downward to the walls and there are no gables.

HISTORICISM A preference for reviving historical architectural styles and motifs.

HYPOSTYLE A large space over which the roof is supported by massed rows of columns. The term is applied to the forestlike halls of Egyptian temples.

INDUSTRIAL ARCHITECTURE Buildings serving the needs of industry, such as factories, mills, and warehouses. Such buildings became particularly important during the Industrial Revolution.

IWAN A portal consisting of an arch recessed in a wall, often facing the central courtyard in Islamic mosques and madrasas.

JALI An ornamental pierced screen used in Islamic and Indian architecture.

JAMB The side-post or lining of a doorway or other aperture.

JOIST A load-bearing structural component spanning short distances between walls to support a floor or ceiling; a form of beam typically made of timber.

KEYSTONE The central wedge-shaped stone at the top of an arch or vault rib.

KIOSK An open pavilion or summerhouse supported by pillars; most frequently found in Turkey and Iran.

KIVA A ceremonial structure in pueblos that is usually round and partially or entirely underground.

LANCET WINDOW A tall, narrow window with a pointed top, used in Gothic buildings.

LANTERN A small circular or polygonal structure, often with windows, on top of a roof or dome.

LINTEL A supporting horizontal beam that spans an opening in a wall or between columns.

LOGGIA A gallery or room, sometimes pillared, that is open on one side.

LONGHOUSE A long, narrow dwelling, usually wooden-framed, used by many ancient peoples and some contemporary indigenous cultures.

MASTABA An Egyptian tomb, built above ground, with sloping sides and a flat roof.

METOPE A square panel, either carved or plain, in a Classical frieze, set between two triglyphs (grooved blocks).

MEZZANINE An intermediate floor in a building that does not extend over the whole space of the floor below.

MIHRAB A niche in the prayer hall of a mosque that is positioned to indicate the direction of Mecca, and is often elaborately decorated with tiles.

MINARET In Islamic architecture, a tall tower, usually forming part of a mosque, from which the call to prayer is given.

MINIMALISM A 20th-century movement in art and architecture that focused on simplicity in design, removing ornament in favor of clean lines and empty space.

MOCARABE A form of ornament used in Islamic architecture, in which miniature arches and stalactite forms adorn ceilings and vaults.

MODERNISM An early 20th-century movement concerned with adapting architecture to social needs. Modernist architects believed that the form that a building takes should be dictated by its function. They built with steel, concrete, and glass and largely rejected ornament.

MORTISE–AND–TENON JOINT The joining of two pieces of wood at right angles, with the tenon as peg and the mortise as slot.

MOSQUE A Muslim place of worship, used for prayer and oriented toward Mecca. A mosque may incorporate a madrasa (school) as well as a prayer hall.

MULLION An upright post that divides an opening, often a window, into sections.

NARTHEX The open porch of a church, or a vestibule at the entrance of a church.

NAVE The central portion of a church used by the congregation.

NEOCLASSICAL Refers to the revival of simple forms associated with Classical architecture

NICHE A recess set into a wall to hold a statue or decorative object.

OCULUS A window, or opening, at the apex of a dome.

OGEE A double curved shape, made up of a convex and concave curve, applied to a molding or an arch.

ORDER A Classical column arrangement, including the base, shaft, and capital, which supports the entablature. There are three main orders. Corinthian columns have ornate capitals featuring acanthus leaves. Doric columns are typified by plain capitals and no base to the column. Ionic columns are characterized by scroll-shaped volutes on the capitals.

PAGODA A tiered Chinese or Japanese tower, frequently related to Buddhism.

PALLADIAN A term referring to the Neoclassical style of Andrea Palladio.

PARAPET A low wall around the edge of a roof, terrace, or balcony.

PAVILION A subsidiary building positioned either separately or as an attachment to a main building, usually associated with pleasure.

PEDIMENT The triangular gabled end of a temple roof above the entablature.

PENDENTIVE A concave structure that forms the link between two straight walls and the curved lower edge of a dome.

PERISTYLE In Classical architecture, a colonnaded walkway around an inner courtyard.

PIER A solid masonry support for a structure such as an arch.

PILASTER A projecting vertical band of masonry designed like a column to conform to one of the Classical orders.

PILOTIS Narrow columns used to support buildings and raise them above the ground in Modernist architecture. They were used most famously by Le Corbusier.

PINNACLE A spherical upright structure crowning a spire or buttress.

PLINTH A slab beneath the base of a column, or the projecting base of any other structure.

PORTAL A doorway or entrance, especially an imposing one.

PORTICO A covered entrance porch to a Classical temple or other building, fronted by columns, and usually forming the central feature of a facade.

POST AND LINTEL A simple construction method using a header (lintel) as the horizontal member, supported at its ends by two vertical columns or pillars (posts).

POSTMODERNISM A playful style of architecture in the second half of the 20th century, created partly in reaction to the strictures of Modernism.

PRANG A tall, towerlike spire, often richly carved, common in the Khmer Empire.

PUEBLO The architecture of the Indigenous people of the southwestern US.

PYLON A masonry tower with a central opening that forms the entrance to an ancient Egyptian temple.

RAMMED EARTH A method of mud building in which the mud is packed into a formwork. *See* formwork.

REINFORCED CONCRETE A type of concrete with a high tensile strength, achieved by embedding steel bars.

RELIEF CARVING A carving that projects from a flat background. A bas-relief stands out only slightly from its background.

RENAISSANCE A cultural movement in Europe in the 14th–16th centuries that challenged the authority of the Catholic Church, returned to Classical ideals, and asserted individual expression.

RIB A projecting structural member used to carry the infilled panels of a vault.

ROCAILLE An 18th-century ornamentation using elaborately stylized pebble- and shell-like motifs. An aspect of Rococo.

ROCOCO A decorative style that evolved from the Baroque, using a variety of materials to create a playful effect.

ROMANESQUE A style that developed in the 6th century from an interest in Roman culture. It is characterized by the round arch and the basilica.

ROTUNDA A building or a room with a circular floor plan covered by a dome.

RUSTICATION Roughened, textured masonry arranged in large blocks with deep joints between them.

SHINGLES Flat, rectangular pieces of asphalt or other roofing material.

SPANDREL The triangular space between the curves of adjacent arches.

SPROCKET A short timber placed on the back and at the foot of a rafter to form projecting eaves.

SQUINCH A small arch across an internal corner of a tower, used to support a dome or spire above.

STAVE A vertical wooden post or plank.

STELA A tall stone or wooden slab, generally with text or ornamentation on it, used as a monument, boundary marker, or official notice.

STOA A detached portico, used as a meeting place in ancient Greece.

STRAPWORK A form of ornament consisting of interlaced bands.

STUCCO A durable, slow-setting plaster made up of gypsum, lime, and sand.

STUPA An early Buddhist shrine, in the shape of a hemispherical dome. Also known as a dagoba.

SUPERSTRUCTURE The parts of a building above the foundations.

THERMAE Roman public baths.

TORII A gateway at the entrance to the precincts of a Japanese shrine.

TRACERY A system of ornamental glazing bars, usually made of stone, dividing the top of a window into small compartments. Widely used in Gothic architecture.

TRANSEPT The part of a cruciform church that is at right angles to the main part of the building.

TRANSVERSE An arch separating one section of a vault from the next.

TRUSS A flat structural framework of beams, joists, and posts. The simplest truss is a single triangle, but trusses usually consist of a combination of triangles.

TYMPANUM The area between the horizontal lintel of a doorway and the arch above it, often containing a stone panel carved in relief.

VAULT An arched ceiling built of stone, brick, or concrete.

VOLUTE A spiral scroll used as part of the decoration on an Ionic or Corinthian capital. *See also* Order.

VOUSSOIR A wedge-shaped stone used to form an arch or vault.

WHARENUI A Māori meeting house

ZIGGURAT A mud-brick stepped pyramid in Mesopotamian sacred architecture.

INDEX

ACKNOWLEDGMENTS

The publisher would like to thank the following for their help with this book: Simon Adams and Esther Ripley for additional text; Timothy Topper and Philip Wilkinson for editorial assistance; Scarlett O'Hara for proofreading; Helen Peters for the index; Peter Bull Art Studio for CGI artwork on pages, 26-27, 38-39, 54-55, 94-95, 164-165, 198-199, 232-233, 244-245, 274 and 300-301; Kate Hockenhull for the directory picture research; Vikram Singh and Nand Kishor Acharya for technical assistance.

Millie Latack, Smithsonian Architectural History & Historic Preservation Specialist Carly Bond, Smithsonian Architectural History & Historic Preservation Specialist Avery Naughton, Licensing Coordinator, Licensed Publishing; Paige Towler, Editorial Lead, Licensed Publishing; Jill Corcoran, Senior Director, Licensed Publishing; Brigid Ferraro, Vice President, Business Development and Licensing; Carol LeBlanc, President Special thanks to Kealy Gordon.

The name of the Smithsonian Institution and the sunburst logo are registered trademarks of the Smithsonian Institution. For more information, please visit www.si.edu

The publisher would like to thank the following for their kind permission to reproduce their photographs:

(Key: a-above; b-below/bottom; c-center; f-far; l-left; r-right; t-top)

2-3 Alamy Stock Photo: Peter Mocsonoky. **4-5 Dreamstime.com:** Zoroasto Felix dos Santos. **7 4Corners:** Massimo Borchi. **8-9 Getty Images / iStock:** borchee. **10-11 Shutterstock.com:** Merydolla. **12 Alamy Stock Photo:** Sailingstone Travel (t). **Getty Images:** CM Dixon / Print Collector (b). **13 Alamy Stock Photo:** Ryan Watkins (b, tc, tl). **14 Alamy Stock Photo:** funkyfood London - Paul Williams (tr). **Dreamstime.com:** Juliane Jacobs (bl). **Getty Images:** John Elk (br); Min Geolshik (bc). **Getty Images / iStock:** Diana Sahina (cr); sneska (tl). **15 Alamy Stock Photo:** Martin Juhasz (t). **Dreamstime.com:** GoranJakus (c). **16 Dreamstime.com:** Javarman (bc). **16-17 Getty Images / iStock:** Starcevic (t). **17 AWL Images:** ImageBROKER (bc). **Getty Images:** DEA / S. Vannini (br). **James Wang:** (bl). **18 Alamy Stock Photo:** Album (b). **Dreamstime.com:** Frui (t). **19 Dreamstime.com:** Sergey Mayorov (b); Rasool Ali (tl). **Getty Images / iStock:** Simon1luk (tc). **20 Alamy Stock Photo:** BE&W agencja fotograficzna Sp. z o.o. (tl); IanDagnall Computing (cb); Granger - Historical Picture Archive (bc). **Archaeology Illustrated:** (tr). **Bridgeman Images:** Zev Radovan (bl). **21 Alamy Stock Photo:** Barry Iverson (cr); robertharding (bc). **Shutterstock.com:** Poliorketes (t). **22 AWL Images:** Catherina Unger (bc). **22-23 Dreamstime.com:** Venemama (t). **23 Alamy Stock Photo:** Michael Kemp (bl); Meeyoung Son (bc). **24 Alamy Stock Photo:** Design Pics (bc). **24-25 Getty Images / iStock:** Anton Aleksenko. **26 Getty Images:** Moment / Kitti Boonnitrod (cla). **Getty Images / iStock:** xavigm (bl). **28 Dreamstime.com:** Boonsom (br). **Getty Images:** Corbis Historical / Paul Almasy (cl). **Getty Images / iStock:** holgs (cr). **Shutterstock.com:** AlexAnton (bc). **29 123RF.com:** Marcin Ciesielski (cla). **Alamy Stock Photo:** Wirestock, Inc. (bl). **Dreamstime.com:** Magedmichel (tr). **Getty Images:** DEA / G. Dagli Orti (br). **30-31 Alamy Stock Photo:** robertharding (tc). **30 Alamy Stock Photo:** Graham, David (c); Alfredo Garcia Saz (bl); Juergen Ritterbach (br). **31 Dreamstime.com:** Dave Primov (t). **Getty Images / iStock:** Goddard_Photography (br). **Getty Images:** Moment / Nick Brundle Photography (bl). **32 akg-images:** Florent Pey (c). **Alamy Stock Photo:** Emily Marie Wilson (r). **32-33 Dreamstime.com:** Marcin Ciesielski / Sylwia Cisek (c). **33 Alamy Stock Photo:** Album (cl); Ivan Sebborn (cr); robertharding (br). **AWL Images:** Danita Delimont Stock (tl). **Shutterstock.com:** Bist (tr). **34 Alamy Stock Photo:** Paul Brown (br). **Dreamstime.com:** Annachizhova (t); Jose Ramon Pizarro Garcia (b). **35 Alamy Stock Photo:** LatitudeStock (bc); Paul Maguire (bl). **36 Dreamstime.com:** Scorp37. **37 Getty Images / iStock:** scaliger. **38 Alamy Stock Photo:** Robert Wallwork (bl). **© The Trustees of the British Museum. All rights reserved:** (cl). **Dreamstime.com:** Anyaivanova (tl); Sergio Bertino / Serjedi (bc). **39 Alamy Stock Photo:** Adam Eastland (tr). **40 Alamy Stock Photo:** Vikas Aggarwal (tl). **Dreamstime.com:** Lambroskazan (r). **41 Alamy Stock Photo:** Erin Babnik (cb); Brigida Soriano (tl); Prisma Archivo (b). **Getty Images / iStock:** duncan1890 (tr). **Shutterstock.com:** Gianni Dagli Orti (crb). **42 Alamy Stock Photo:** Stefano Paterna (tl). **Dreamstime.com:** Dudlajzov (bl); Scaliger (br). **Shutterstock.com:** Nejdet Duzen (tr). **43 Alamy Stock Photo:** Boerescu Flaviu (t); Alexey Morozov (bl); Sklifas Steven (br). **44 Alamy Stock Photo:** Science History Images (b). **Getty Images:** Jean-Philippe Tournut (t). **45 Alamy Stock Photo:** Dario Bajurin (cr). **Dreamstime.com:** Brasilnut (tr); Borna Mirahmadian (b). **Getty Images:** Izzet Keribar (cl). **46 Alamy Stock Photo:** World History Archive (bc). **Bridgeman Images:** Ali Meyer (bl). **Dreamstime.com:** Borna Mirahmadian (br). **Getty Images:** DEA / Archivio J. Lange (tr). **Getty Images / iStock:** tunart (tl). **47 Dreamstime.com:** Frenta (bl). **Getty Images / iStock:** BornaMir (cr); Pe3check (t). **48 Alamy Stock Photo:** robertharding / Nico Tondini (l). **49 Getty Images / iStock:** mtcurado (bl); Mohammad Nouri (br). **The Metropolitan Museum of Art:** Rogers Fund, 1932 (tr). **Shutterstock.com:** AP / Karim Kadim (c). **50-51 Alamy Stock Photo:** StevanZZ (t). **50 Getty Images / iStock:** Azulillo (b). **51 Alamy Stock Photo:** Album (bc); elroce (bl). **52 Getty Images:** joe daniel price. **53 Dreamstime.com:** Richard Semik. **54 Getty Images:** Kino Alyse (tr). **Getty Images / iStock:** D. Lentz (bl); Sean Pavone (br). **Roger B. Ulrich:** (cl). **56 Dreamstime.com:** Anna Yordanova (r). **Carole Raddato:** (cl). **57 Alamy Stock Photo:** Don Despain (t); Noppasin Wongchum (cr). **Bridgeman Images:** NPL - DeA Picture Library (br). **Getty Images:** Elizabeth Beard (bl). **58 123RF.com:** tichr (tl). **Alamy Stock Photo:** Ionut David (bl). **Dreamstime.com:** Axel2001 (br); Andrei Vasilev (cl); Davidzean (tr). **59 Getty Images / iStock:** Alexlukin (t). **Getty Images:** Eduardo Estllez (br). **60-61 Dreamstime.com:** Nicolaforenza. **60 Alamy Stock Photo:** Michael Harris (br); Mo Peerbacus (cr). **Depositphotos Inc:** 3D-Agentur (c). **61 AWL Images:** Danita Delimont Stock (cr); Stefano Politi Markovina (bl). **Dreamstime.com:** Stefano Valeri (tr). **Getty Images:** E+ / minemero (br). **62 Getty Images / iStock:** ePhotocorp (r); ksumano (l). **63 Dreamstime.com:** ePhotocorp (tr). **Getty Images / iStock:** ePhotocorp (tl); mathess (b). **64 Alamy Stock Photo:** Anil Dave (bl); NiKreative (bc). **Getty Images:** Mukul Banerjee Photography (br); Chris Caldicott / Design Pics (tr). **Shutterstock.com:** rajenmakharia (tl). **65 Alamy Stock Photo:** Architecture2000 (b). **Getty Images / iStock:** saiko3p (tr); Balaji Srinivasan (tl). **66 Alamy Stock Photo:** Sebastien Lecocq (t). **Dreamstime.com:** Aroas (b). **67 akg-images:** Nicholas Saunders (bl). **Dreamstime.com:** Marktucan (tr); Jeremy Richards (br). **Getty Images:** Janine Costa / AFP (bc). **Paul Hessell:** (tl). **68 Dreamstime.com:** Carolina Jaramillo (t). **69 Bridgeman Images:** Archivio J. Lange / NPL - DeA Picture Library (tc). **Getty Images / iStock:** Dreamframer (b). **Shutterstock.com:** Chameleons Eye (tr). **70 Alamy Stock Photo:** Granger - Historical Picture Archive (tr); Suzuki Kaku (bc). **AWL Images:** imageBROKER (bl). **Getty Images / iStock:** Byelikova_Oksana (br); Jui-Chi Chan (tl). **71 Dreamstime.com:** Rafa Cichawa (c); Diego Grandi (t). **Getty Images / iStock:** diegograndi (b). **72-73 AWL Images:** Tim Mannakee. **74 AWL Images:** Matteo Colombo (t). **Dreamstime.com:** Diego Grandi (b). **75 Alamy Stock Photo:** Speshilov Sergey (tc); Peter M. Wilson (tr). **Bridgeman Images:** Archivio J. Lange / NPL - DeA Picture Library (cr). **Getty Images:** CostinT (b). **76 Alamy Stock Photo:** Keren Su / China Span (tr); Witold Skrypczak (bc). **Dr. Diane Davies:** (bl). **Dreamstime.com:** Stefano Ember (br). **Getty Images / iStock:** OlegAlbinsky (tc). **Science Photo Library:** Sergi Reboredo / VWPICS (tl). **77 Alamy Stock Photo:** agefotostock (tl). **Getty Images / iStock:** cinoby (b); Robert_Ford (tr). **78 Getty Images / iStock:** SergeYatunin (l). **79 Alamy Stock Photo:** Norman Barrett (bc); Spring Images (tr); Reid Dalland (br). **Getty Images / iStock:** miralex (cr). **Getty Images:** Sumiko Scott (bl). **Jim Shoemaker:** (cl). **80 Alamy Stock Photo:** Suzuki Kaku (t). **Getty Images:** Jekesai Njikizana / AFP (b). **81 akg-images:** Werner Forman (cr). **Alamy Stock Photo:** Hemis (tr); Christopher Scott (tl, bl); Suzuki Kaku (br). **Getty Images:** arkland_swe (bc). **82 AWL Images:** Nigel Pavitt (t). **Getty Images:** Carl Court (b). **83 Alamy Stock Photo:** Ivan Batinic (tl); Eric Lafforgue (tr). **AWL Images:** Amar Grover (cr); Nigel Pavitt (bc, br, bl). **84 AWL Images:** Tim Mannakee (t). **Dreamstime.com:** Dmitriy Moroz (b). **85 Dreamstime.com:** Ahmet Ariturk (tc); Alvaro German Vilela (tr). **Getty Images:** Emad aljumah (b). **86 Alamy Stock Photo:** jozef sedmak (cl). **Shutterstock.com:** D-VISIONS (cr). **87 Alamy Stock Photo:** funkyfood London - Paul Williams (tl); RealyEasyStar / Claudio Pagliarani (bl). **Dreamstime.com:** Ninlawan Donlakkham (tr); Evren Kalinbacak (br). **Photo Scala, Florence:** Fondo Edifici di Culto - Min. dell'Interno (bc). **88 Dreamstime.com:** Valeria Cantone (br); Costas1962 (t); Laimdota Grivane (c); Jasmina (bl). **89 AWL Images:** Jon Arnold (bl). **Dreamstime.com:** Boris Breytman (br). **Getty Images / iStock:** KavalenkavaVolha (t). **90-91 Getty Images / iStock:** fotosuper (t). **90 Getty Images:** Moment / Marco Bottigelli (bc). **91 Dreamstime.com:** Roland Nagy (bl). **Getty Images:** Stockbyte / Perry Mastrovito (bc). **92-93 Dreamstime.com:** Brian Maudsley (t). **92 Dreamstime.com:** Aidar Ayazbayev (b). **94 Getty Images / iStock:** tenzinsherab (cb). **Shutterstock.com:** Fly_and_Dive (tl). **95 Dreamstime.com:** Farhadi (tl). **Getty Images / iStock:** mtcurado (tr). **96 Alamy Stock Photo:** CPA Media Pte Ltd (br); robertharding (tl). **Getty Images / iStock:** Siempreverde22 (tr). **Getty Images:** sola deo gloria (bl). **97 Dreamstime.com:** Jonathan Wilson (br). **Getty Images:** DEA / C. Sappa (cb); Universal History Archive (bl). **Shutterstock.com:** akturer (tl); Tarek-Mahmoud (tr). **98 Depositphotos Inc:** Jukov (bl). **Dreamstime.com:** Evgeniy Fesenko (tr, br). **Getty Images:** Nico Tondini / robertharding (tl). **99 Getty Images:** Roger Wood / Corbis / VCG (br). **Shutterstock.com:** Mistervlad (bl); nurdem atay (t). **100 Alamy Stock Photo:** NJphoto (b); Michal Sikorski (t). **101 Alamy Stock Photo:** Bildarchiv Monheim GmbH (cr); Romas_ph (l). **AWL Images:** Hans Georg Eiben (br). **102 Alamy Stock Photo:** imageBROKER (br). **AWL Images:** ImageBROKER (tl); Jason Langley (tr). **103 Alamy Stock Photo:** agefotostock (bl). **AWL Images:** Mark Sykes (tl, tr). **Getty Images:** Angelo Hornak (bl). **104 Alamy Stock Photo:** Godong (bl). **Getty Images:** Stefan Cristian Cioata (tr). **Getty Images / iStock:** enviromantic (tl). **104-105 Alamy Stock Photo:** travellinglight (cb). **105 AWL Images:** Hans Georg Eiben (br); Hemis (tc). **Getty Images:** Graham Lucas Commons (tr). **106 Alamy Stock Photo:** Chinaim (b). Di Luo: (t). **107 Alamy Stock Photo:** Tuul and Bruno Morandi (c). **Shutterstock.com:** Adrian8 (br); beibaoke (l, tr). **108 Alamy Stock Photo:** Travel Pictures (br); Jonathan Wilson (bl). **Dreamstime.com:** Jackchen (cb); Outcast85 (tr). **Getty Images / iStock:** jaturunp (tl). **109 Alamy Stock Photo:** Ivan Vdovin (c). **Dreamstime.com:** Wan Xiaoxu (br). **Getty Images:** Zhang Peng / LightRocket (t). **Shutterstock.com:** Skreidzeleu (bl). **110 Getty Images / iStock:** Iseo Yang (l). **111 Alamy Stock Photo:** JIPEN (bl); Jorge Tutor (tr). **Dreamstime.com:** Frenta (bc). **Shutterstock.com:** ALNET (br); Stock for you (c). **112 Dreamstime.com:** Jlabouyrie (t). **Getty Images / iStock:** Iseo Yang (b). **113 Alamy Stock Photo:** CulturalEyes - AusGS2 (b); Ivan Vdovin (t). **Getty Images:** Sankei (tc). **114 Alamy Stock Photo:** Jarmo Piironen (bc). **Dreamstime.com:** Sanga Park (tl). **Getty Images:** Pictures From History / Universal Images Group (br). **Shutterstock.com:** mTaira (bl); Richie Chan (tr). **115 Dreamstime.com:** Ziggymars (br). **Shutterstock.com:** beibaoke (bl); cowardlion (t). **116-117 Dreamstime.com:** Snehitdesign (t). **116 Getty Images / iStock:** pejft (bl). **117 Alamy Stock Photo:** Viktor Onyshchenko (bc); Zoonar GmbH (bl). **118 The Metropolitan Museum of Art:** Purchase, Mrs. W. Murray Crane Gift Fund, 1971 (r). **Shutterstock.com:** nicepix (l). **119 Dreamstime.com:** Julie Mayfeng (tc); Vicnt (tl). **Getty Images:** Oyi Kresnamurti / EyeEm (b). **120 Alamy Stock Photo:** Abdul Momin (br). **Dreamstime.com:** Ishnchat (tl); Vit Baisa (bc). **Getty Images:** Saha Entertainment (bl). **Shutterstock.com:** Sean Pavone (tr). **121 Alamy Stock Photo:** Tuul and Bruno Morandi (bc). **Dreamstime.com:** Sean Pavone (t). **Getty Images / iStock:** Alois Radler Woess (cr). **122 Alamy Stock Photo:** imageBROKER (t). **Dreamstime.com:** Kunal Khurana (b). **123 Getty Images:** Dinodia Photo (b). **Getty Images / iStock:** JeremyRichards (tl). **Shutterstock.com:** Kevin Standage (tc). **124 Alamy Stock Photo:** kaushal jangid (bc); robertharding (tr, bl). **Getty Images:** Ankur Dauneria (tl). **Getty Images / iStock:** ePhotocorp (br). **125 Dreamstime.com:** Klodien (tr). **Getty Images / iStock:** mchen007 (tl); williamhc (b). **126-127 Getty Images:** Kevin Roxby. **128 AWL Images:** Michele Falzone (br). **Getty Images:** Moment / Amir Ghasemi www.focalfantasy.com (l). **129 Alamy Stock Photo:** Ccelia (ca). **AWL Images:** Michele Falzone (b); Nigel Pavitt (cla). **Dreamstime.com:** Dejjf82 (cra). **130 Alamy Stock Photo:** Charles O. Cecil (tl); John Michaels (cr); Hemis (br). **Getty Images / iStock:** f9photos (bc). Getty Images: Michael Nolan (bl). **131 Alamy Stock Photo:** Nora Sahinun (t). AWL Images: Jason Langley (cr); Jason Langley (bc). **132 Shutterstock.com:** SMC Photo (t). 133 Alamy Stock Photo: View Stock (tr); Mark Williamson Stock Photography (br). **AWL Images:** Christian Kober (l). **Dreamstime.com:** Steveheap (cr). **134 Alamy Stock Photo:** Qin Ningzhen (br); Xinhua (bl). **Dreamstime.com:** Sofiaworld (tl). **Getty Images:** Weiming Chen (tr). **135 Alamy Stock Photo:** Imaginechina Limited (tl). **AWL Images:** David Bank (bl); Maurizio Rellini (br). **Getty Images:** DuKai photographer (tr); Colin Marshall (bc). **136 Alamy Stock Photo:** View Stock (br); Robert Wyatt (tl). **Getty Images / iStock:** redtea (bl). **Shutterstock.com:** beibaoke (tr). **137 Dreamstime.com:** Zjm7100 (br). **Shutterstock.com:** NG-Spacetime (bl); Richie Chan (tr). **138 Alamy Stock Photo:** Arcaid Images (b). **Shutterstock.com:** Tanwa Kankang (t). **139 Bridgeman Images:** Michel Guillemot (cra). **Getty Images / iStock:** Wirestock (l). **San Diego Museum of Art:** (tr). **Shutterstock.com:** yoko_ken_chan (cr). **140 Alamy Stock Photo:** Inaki Arbulo (br). **Getty Images:** B.S.P.I. (tl). **Shutterstock.com:** Julian52000 (bl); Lee Yiu Tung (tr). **141 Dreamstime.com:** Sean Pavone (t); Sean Pavone (br, bl). **142 Alamy Stock Photo:** Tibor Bognar (r). **Shutterstock.com:** Nicola Messana Photos (l). **143 Dreamstime.com:** Demerzel21 (br). **Shutterstock.com:** Nicola Messana Photos (c); saiko3p (bl); YMZK-Photo (tr); monticello (bc). **144 Getty Images:** Philippe Lissac (r). **Shutterstock.com:** josepmarti (l). **145 Alamy Stock Photo:** Abdellah Azizi (cr). **Dorling Kindersley:** Alan Keohane (tc). **Shutterstock.com:** PavelJiranek (b). **146 Peter Cook:** (bc). **Dreamstime.com:** Gillesr7 (bl). **Getty Images / iStock:** JavierGil1000 (tl); saffiresblue (br). **Getty Images:** miralex (tr). **147 Alamy Stock Photo:** Kumar Sriskandan (br). **Getty Images:** Danny Lehman (bl); Tanatat pongphibool ,thailand (t). **148 Alamy Stock Photo:** Peter Noyce ESP (cr). **AWL Images:** Alan Copson (tr); J.Banks (br). **Bridgeman Images:** Future Publishing Ltd (cl). **149 Alamy Stock Photo:** Martin Florin Emmanuel (tr); Michael Harris (cr). **Shutterstock.com:** kavalenkau (br); Cezary Wojtkowski (tl). **150 Alamy Stock Photo:** Yadid Levy (bc). **Getty Images:** imageBROKER / Michael Runkel (t). **151 Alamy Stock Photo:** Eye Ubiquitous (cra); Susan Liebold (ca); Michal Sikorski (bc). **Getty Images / iStock:** Donhype (cla). **152 Alamy Stock Photo:** Design Pics Inc (bl); Marco Destefanis (bc). **AWL Images:** Mark Hannaford (br); Nigel Pavitt (cr). **Getty Images:** Universal Images Group / Arterra (cl). **153 Alamy Stock Photo:** Elena Bobrova (br); John Elk III (cr). **Getty Images:** Moment / manogamo (cl). **154 Dreamstime.com:** Antwon Mcmullen (t). **155 Alamy Stock Photo:** Heritage Image Partnership Ltd (cr); Suzuki Kaku (bl); Brian Overcast (br). **Getty Images:** DEA / Archivio J. Lange (bc); Simon McGill (tr). **Shutterstock.com:** ikarusmedia (tl). **156 Alamy Stock Photo:** Rubens Alarcon (t). **AWL Images:** Jan Miracky (b). **157 Alamy Stock Photo:** Alvaro Bueno (tr); Gabbro (cra). **AWL Images:** Jan Miracky (b). **Dreamstime.com:** Luca Roggero (cla). **Getty Images / iStock:** SL_Photography (tl). **158 Alamy Stock Photo:** Sue Bishop (br); Alvaro Bueno (tc). **AWL Images:** Karol Kozlowski (tl). **Getty Images / iStock:** saiko3p (tr); SL_Photography (clb). **Getty Images:** traveler1116 (bl). **159 AWL Images:** Karol Kozlowski (t). **Getty Images / iStock:** saiko3p (b). **Shutterstock.com:** Carlos Sala Fotografia (br). **160 AWL Images:** Danita Delimont Stock (br). **Dreamstime.com:** Petr Svec (l). **161 Alamy Stock Photo:** Design Pics Inc (cl); Brad Mitchell (tl). **Dreamstime.com:** Phoenixlabs (bc). **Getty Images:** LightRocket / Wolfgang Kaehler (c). **SuperStock:** Alaska Stock - Design Pics / Sunny K Awazahura R (bl); All Canada Photos / Michael Wheatley (br). **162 Alamy Stock Photo:** Andrew Wood. **163 Getty Images:** Angel Villalba. **164 Alamy Stock Photo:** Hemis (tl). **Dreamstime.com:** Natalia Bratslavsky (tr). **Shutterstock.com:** high fliers (tc). **165 Dreamstime.com:** Photogolfer (tr). **166 Getty Images:** Loop Images / Universal Images Group (c). **167 Dreamstime.com:** Claudio Giovanni Colombo (tr); Chris Dorney (bl); Emotionart (cb); Pierre Jean Durieu (br). **Getty Images:** joe daniel price (tl). **168 Alamy Stock Photo:** Roger Fletcher (br). **Getty Images:** Anna Kurzaeva (bl); narvikk (tl). **Shutterstock.com:** Viliam.M (tr). **169 Dreamstime.com:** Luciano Morpurgo (br). **Getty Images:** joe daniel price (t); Travelpix Ltd (bl). **170 Alamy Stock Photo:** Album (br); Penny Atkinson (tr). **Getty Images:** Ketkarn sakultap (tl). **Getty Images / iStock:** Vladislav Zolotov (bl). **171 Alamy Stock Photo:** Nathaniel Noir (bl). **Getty Images:** Gunter Grafenhain (t); Angel Villalba (br). **172 AWL Images:** Robert Birkby (t). **Getty Images:** ullstein bild / Hohlfeld (bc). **173 Alamy Stock Photo:** eye35 (tr); tim gartside travel (br); Dave Stamboulis (bl). **AWL Images:** Christian Mueringer (bc). **Bridgeman Images:** National Trust Photographic Library / Andreas von Einsiedel (cl). **Dreamstime.com:** Eatonphotography2019 (tl). **174 123RF.com:** Valery Egorov / valeryegorov (r). **Alamy Stock Photo:** ian badley (l). **175 Alamy Stock Photo:** Santi Rodriguez (b); Sites & Photos / Shmuel Magal (tc). **Shutterstock.com:** Gareth Kirkland (tl). **176 Alamy Stock Photo:** The National Trust Photolibrary (tl). **Dreamstime.com:** Bossaperdue (bc); Kmiragaya (bl); Debu55y (br). **Shutterstock.com:** bimserd (tr); Phil Trott (tc). **177 Dreamstime.com:** Peter De Jong (cr); Sorin Colac (t). **Getty Images:** Tim White (bl). **178-179 Getty Images:** Allan Baxter. **180 Alamy Stock Photo:** Svetlana Day (l). **AWL Images:** Ivan Vdovin (br). **181 AirPano images:** (cl). **Alamy Stock Photo:** Vyacheslav Lopatin (bl). **Depositphotos Inc:** Sergiev Posad (bc). **Dreamstime.com:** Boris Breytman (br); Vladimir Sazonov (cr). **182 Bridgeman Images:** Archives Charmet (b). **Getty Images:** Izzet Keribar (t). **183 Alamy Stock Photo:** MDart (tr). Shutterstock.com: aydngvn (tc); RuslanKphoto (b). **Turul Yazar:** (tl). **184 Getty Images:** Salvator Barki (tr). **Getty Images / iStock:** greta6 (tl). **Shutterstock.com:** LizCoughlan (b). **185 Alamy Stock Photo:** Ayhan Altun (c); Sener Dagasan (tl); B.O'Kane (tr). **Dorling Kindersley:** Angela Coppola / University of Pennsylvania Museum of Archaeology and Anthropolog (bl). **Dreamstime.com:** Ihsan Gercelman (bc, br). **186 Dreamstime.com:** Bojan Jeremic (br); Jasmina (tr). **Shutterstock.com:** Nejdet Duzen (tl); Shevchenko Andrey (bl). **187 Getty Images / iStock:** Viteevatiy (tr). **Shutterstock.com:** Nejdet Duzen (br); Official (bl). **188 Alamy Stock Photo:** CPA Media Pte Ltd (r). **Getty Images:** Kelly Cheng Travel Photography. **189 Alamy Stock Photo:** Alexandre Rotenberg (tr). **Dreamstime.com:** Lukas Bischoff (tl, b). **Getty Images:** Richard Ross (tc). **190 akg-images:** New Picture Library srl (tr). **Getty Images:** Jason Edwards (bc); Jean-Philippe Tournut (br); Feng Wei Photography (br). **Getty Images / iStock:** Selcuk Oner (cr). **Shutterstock.com:** Matyas Rehak (tl). **191 Dreamstime.com:** Frenta (t); Cinar Yilancioglu (b). **Getty Images:** Ekkachai Pholrojpanya (c). **192 Alamy Stock Photo:** incamerastock (b). **Shutterstock.com:** saisnaps (t). **193 Alamy Stock Photo:** Dinodia Photos (tl). **Getty Images / iStock:** marcmh (tc). **194 Alamy Stock Photo:** DB Pictures (tl). **Dreamstime.com:** Meinzahn (br). **Getty Images:** photosindia (bl). **195 Dreamstime.com:** Dmitry Rukhlenko (bl). **Getty Images:** Amir Mukhtar (cr). **Shutterstock.com:** Amit kg (t). **196 Photo Scala, Florence:** bpk, Bildagentur fuer Kunst, Kultur und Geschichte, Berlin (bc). **197 Bridgeman Images:** Andrea Jemolo. **198 Alamy Stock Photo:** colaimages (bl). **Depositphotos Inc:** massimosanti (cb). **Dreamstime.com:** Gennaro Leonardi (bc); Massimo Santi (br). **Getty Images:** DEA / G. Berengo Gardin (cla). **200 Dreamstime.com:** Diegomartincoppola (br). **Getty Images / iStock:** OscarCatt (c); rabbit75_ist (cl). **Photo Scala, Florence:** Andrea Jemolo (b). **201 Alamy Stock Photo:** agefotostock (crb); robertharding (tr); Hemis (bl). **Getty Images:** Moment / Piero M. Bianchi (br). **202 Alamy Stock Photo:** Stefano Politi Markovina (cl). **Dreamstime.com:** Stefano Valeri (bl). **Getty Images:** Corbis Historical / Angelo Hornak (cr). **202-203 Bridgeman Images:** Andrea Jemolo (bc). **203 Alamy Stock Photo:** Ian G Dagnall (br). **Dreamstime.com:** Massimo Santi (cl). **Shutterstock.com:** RudiErnst (tr). **204-205 Alamy Stock Photo:** Album (t). **204 Getty Images:** DEA Picture Library (bc). **205 Alamy Stock Photo:** Azoor Photo (bc). **Getty Images:** DEA / G. Dagli Orti (bl). **Wikimedia:** Lars Aronson / Public Domain (br). **206 Alamy Stock Photo:** Magite Historic (br). **AWL Images:** Chris Mouyiaris (l). **207 Alamy**

Stock Photo: Herv Lenain (cl); robertharding (fcl); fabio lotti (c). AWL Images: Hemis (bc). 208 Alamy Stock Photo: Edifice (ca); Steve Taylor ARPS (cla); The Picture Art Collection (cr). Dreamstime.com: Sergii Korshun (br). Getty Images: Christophel Fine Art (bl). 209 Alamy Stock Photo: William Barton (bl). AWL Images: Hemis (br). Wikimedia: Ingo Mehling / CC BY-SA 4.0 (t). 210 Getty Images: DeAgostini (t); Heritage Images / Fine Art Images (bc). 211 Bridgeman Images: Andrea Jemolo (cr, br). Dreamstime.com: Antony Mcaulay (l); Stefano Valeri (tr). 212 Alamy Stock Photo: Giulio Ercolani (cl); mauritius images GmbH (cr). Dreamstime.com: Scaliger (c). Getty Images / iStock: corradomallia (bc). 213 Alamy Stock Photo: Arcaid Images (cl). AWL Images: Hemis (bl). Bridgeman Images: Alamy (tr). 214 akg-images: Erich Lessing (br). Alamy Stock Photo: Alvaro Bueno (bl). Getty Images / iStock: diegograndi (tl). Shutterstock.com: Wead (tr). 215 Alamy Stock Photo: martin thompson (tr). AWL Images: Hemis (bl). Bridgeman Images: Andrea Jemolo (br). 216 Bridgeman Images: Future Publishing Ltd (l); Luisa Ricciarini (br). Photo Scala, Florence: (cr). 217 123RF.com: natalia volkova (br). Alamy Stock Photo: MB_Photo (bl). AWL Images: Cahir Davitt (tr). Getty Images: Steve Christo / Corbis (cl); Electa / Mondadori Portfolio (cr). Getty Images / iStock: PytyCzech (tl). 218 Alamy Stock Photo: Directphoto Collection (t). Bridgeman Images: (b). 219 Alamy Stock Photo: Jim Monk (b). Getty Images: Eye Ubiquitous (tl). 220 Alamy Stock Photo: Bildarchiv Monheim GmbH (cr); Tibor Bognar (tl); isogood (tr). Dreamstime.com: Antonio Ribeiro (bl). 221 Alamy Stock Photo: Hemis (bl); imageBROKER (br). Shutterstock.com: Mistervlad (t). 222 Alamy Stock Photo: Album (r); Have Camera Will Travel | Central & South America (l). 223 AWL Images: Hemis (tl). Dreamstime.com: Oksana Byelikova (tr). Getty Images: Tim Graham (bl). Getty Images / iStock: kiev4 (br); sedmak (bc). 224 Alamy Stock Photo: agefotostock (t). Library and Archives Canada: Arthur H. Tweedle (bc). 225 Alamy Stock Photo: Arterra Picture Library (bl); Realimage (br). Dreamstime.com: Sophia Granchinho (c); Volodymyr Shevchuk (bc). Getty Images: White Fox / AGF / Universal Images (tr). 226 Alamy Stock Photo: Michael Dwyer (t). Ken Zirkel: (b). 227 Alamy Stock Photo: Erin Paul Donovan (tr). Dreamstime.com: Wilsilver77 (tl). Library of Congress, Washington, D.C.: (bl); Carol M Highsmith (bc). Shutterstock.com: achiaos (br). 228-229 Getty Images: Ratnakorn Piyasirisorost. 230 Dreamstime.com: Christian Offenberg. 231 Getty Images: btrenkel. 232 Alamy Stock Photo: CNP Collection (tc); pocholo (tr). Dreamstime.com: Wieslaw Jarek (tl). Getty Images / iStock: Vladislav Zolotov (bl). 233 Alamy Stock Photo: Martin Bache (tr). Dreamstime.com: Zeytun Images (tc). 234 123RF.com: claudiodivizia (r). Alamy Stock Photo: tony french (bl). Getty Images: drnadig (tl). 235 Alamy Stock Photo: frederic araujo (tr). Dreamstime.com: William Perry (tl); UlyssePixel (bc). Getty Images: Mitch Diamond (cb); LordRunar (bl). 236 Alamy Stock Photo: Fadi Al-barghouthy (tl). Dreamstime.com: Demerzel21 (tr). Getty Images: Jeremy Walker (bl). 236-237 Shutterstock.com: Vlas Telino studio (cb). 237 Alamy Stock Photo: Ian Dagnall (tr); Sean Pavone (br). Getty Images: David Briard (tl). 238 Alamy Stock Photo: KGPA Ltd (t); Alfredo Garcia Saz (b). 239 Alamy Stock Photo: Nattee Chalermtiragool (bl); Peter Cripps (br). AWL Images: Alan Copson (bc). 240 AWL Images: Nadia Isakova (t). 241 Alamy Stock Photo: Jack Cousin (br); Im_photography (tl); Glen Foster (bl); imageBROKER (bc). Bridgeman Images: Historic England (tr). 242-243 Dreamstime.com: Vichaya Kiatyingangsulee (t). 242 Bridgeman Images: National Museums & Galleries of Wales (b). 244 Alamy Stock Photo: John Gaffen 2 (bc); Infrequent_ Flyer (tl); Justin Kase zsixz (br). Mary Evans Picture Library: Historic England (bl). 245 Getty Images: SSPL (tl). Shutterstock.com: PhotoLondonUK (tr). 246 Alamy Stock Photo: Mark Waugh (br). Dreamstime.com: Elroce (bc); Matt Turner (t). Getty Images / iStock: SueBurtonPhotography (bl). 247 Alamy Stock Photo: Nick Maslen (tr); Chris North (t). Dreamstime.com: Julia Sahin (br). Getty Images: Francois Guillot / AFP (cb). Shutterstock.com: Hamed Yeganeh (bl). 248 Alamy Stock Photo: Phil Metcalfe (br). Dreamstime.com: Ac Manley (tl). Shutterstock.com: Catarina Belova (bl); Sion Hannuna (tr). 249 Alamy Stock Photo: Hemis (tc). Dreamstime.com: Eddie Cloud (br). Getty Images: Pedro Gomes (tr). 250 Shutterstock.com: logoraf. 251 Alamy Stock Photo: Heritage Image Partnership Ltd (bc). Dreamstime.com: Jenkins Jenkins (br); Leungphotography (bl). Getty Images: The Print Collector (cr). 252 Alamy Stock Photo: Kilian O'Sullivan-VIEW (b). Dreamstime.com: Andrew Howson (t). 253 Dreamstime.com: Tomas1111 (b). Getty Images / iStock: Rossella De Berti (cr). Getty Images: Eric Van Den Brulle (cl). RIBA Collections. 254 Alamy Stock Photo: Tim Gainey (br); Scenics & Science (bl); Kilian O'Sullivan-VIEW (bc). Getty Images: Rudy Sulgan (tr). Shutterstock.com: Snehal Jeevan Pailkar (tl). 255 Alamy Stock Photo: picturelibrary (tr); Edward Westmacott (bl). Dreamstime.com: Klodien (tl). Library of Congress, Washington, D.C.: Carol M. Highsmith (cr). 256 123RF.com: Wieslaw Jarek (t). Stephane Mahot: (b). 257 Alamy Stock Photo: Avalon.red (tc); Stockbym (tl). Shutterstock.com: Andrew Chisholm (tr); givaga (b). 258 Dreamstime.com: Edichenphoto (cl); Alfredo Garcia Saz (b). Getty Images: Jos Rodrigues (tr). 259 Alamy Stock Photo: GL Archive (br); Eric Nathan (tc); Hemis (bl). AWL Images: Hemis (bc). Dreamstime.com: Steven Cukrov (tl). Getty Images / iStock: BrendanHunter (tr). 260 Alamy Stock Photo: Serhii Chrucky (bl). Dreamstime.com: Marcos Souza (tl); Vadim Startsev (tr). Getty Images: Matteo Colombo (br). 261 Alamy Stock Photo: Ian Dagnall (br); Francois Roux (tr). Getty Images / iStock: nycshooter (bc). 262 Alamy Stock Photo: Charles O. Cecil (l). Getty Images: Werner Forman / Universal Images Group (r). 263 Alamy Stock Photo: Charles O. Cecil (tl, cr); robertharding (tl); John Steele (bl). Alexander Turnbull Library, National Library Of New Zealand, Te Puna Matauranga o Aotearoa: (br). 264 Getty Images: John W Banagan (l); imageBROKER / Norbert Neetz (r). 265 Alamy Stock Photo: Andrey Shevchenko (bl); Joe Wainwright (bc). Dreamstime.com: Naumoid (br). Getty Images: Atlantide Phototravel (tl). Getty Images / iStock: bluejayphoto (tr). 266 Alamy Stock Photo: craft images (l). Getty Images: Fine Art Images / Heritage Images (br). 267 Alamy Stock Photo: The National Trust Photolibrary (tr, b). Bridgeman Images: National Trust Photographic Library / Andreas von Einsiedel (cr); The Stapleton Collection (cl). 268 Alamy Stock Photo: Arcaid Images (bl); The National Trust Photolibrary (tl, tc); John Morrison (tr). John Miller: (br). 269 Alamy Stock Photo: John Peter Photography (cr); The National Trust Photolibrary (t); Hazel McAllister (bl). Dreamstime.com: imagoDens (br). 270 AWL Images: Hemis (t). Getty Images: Popperfoto (b). 271 Alamy Stock Photo: agefotostock (tr, cr); Heritage Image Partnership Ltd (br). 272 akg-images: Herv Champollion (cr). Alamy Stock Photo: Azoor Photo Collection (br); robertharding (tr). Dreamstime.com: Marcorubino (tl). Getty Images / iStock: fotojanis (bl). 273 Alamy Stock Photo: Aitan (c); Have Camera Will Travel | Central & South America (t); Hackenberg-Photo-Cologne (br). Dreamstime.com: Laurent Ruamps (bc). 274 Alamy Stock Photo: charistoone-images (cr). AWL Images: Stefano Politi Markovina (br). Dreamstime.com: Marcorubino (t). 275 Alamy Stock Photo: EyeEm (tr). AWL Images: Alan Copson (bl); Steve Vidler (tl). Dreamstime.com: Rhombur (br). 276 Shutterstock.com: claus+mutschler. 277 Depositphotos Inc: marcociannarel (bc). Dreamstime.com: Prasit Rodphan (br). Getty Images / iStock: Eloi_Omella (bl). 278-279 Unsplash: John Ko. 280 Alamy Stock Photo: ephotocorp (r); Sipa US (l). 281 Alamy Stock Photo: ImageDB (tl, tc). Getty Images: image by WMay (b). Getty Images / iStock: ImageDB (tr). 282 Alamy Stock Photo: B.O'Kane (bl). Dreamstime.com: Peng Ge (tr). Getty Images: Massimo Borchi / Atlantide Phototravel (br). Getty Images / iStock: VitalyEdush (tl). 283 Dreamstime.com: Alexandre Fagundes De Fagundes (c); Filedimage (br). Shutterstock.com: Ankor Light (bl); Richie Chan (t). 284 Alamy Stock Photo: Hemis / © DACS 2023 (t); LMA / AW (b). 285 Alamy Stock Photo: Bildarchiv Monheim GmbH (tr); Image Professionals GmbH (tl); mauritius images GmbH / © DACS 2023 (tr). Shutterstock.com: Inspired By Maps (b). 286 Alamy Stock Photo: Todd Bannor / Stockimo (tr). Dreamstime.com: Jjfarq (br); Camille Tsang (tl). Getty Images: Hulton Archive (bl). 287 Alamy Stock Photo: EU / BT (cl); FP Collection / © DACS 2023 (bc). Getty Images: Hedrich Blessing Collection / Chicago History Museum (br); ullstein bild (tl). 288 Alamy Stock Photo: Bildarchiv Monheim GmbH (tl); Hemis / © DACS 2023 (tr); imageBROKER (b). 289 Dreamstime.com: Sirio Carnevalino (b). Shutterstock.com: EQRoy (t). 290 Alamy Stock Photo: Chronicle (r). Museo della Grafica di Pisa: (l). 291 Alamy Stock Photo: Lois GoBe (bc). Bridgeman Images: NPL - DeA Picture Library (tl). Getty Images: C. Balossini / De Agostini Picture Library (bl); DeAgostini (tr). Postales Inventadas: (br). 292 Alamy Stock Photo: Tatiana Korchemikina (l). Getty Images: Sovfoto / Universal Images Group (r). 293 akg-images: Andrea Jemolo (tr, bl). Alamy Stock Photo: Andrii Chagovets (bc). Denis Esakov: (tl). Shutterstock.com: Evgeniy Vasilev (br). 294 Alamy Stock Photo: Antony McAulay (l). Photo Scala, Florence: bpk, Bildagentur fuer Kunst, Kultur und Geschichte, Berlin (r). 295 Alamy Stock Photo: imageBROKER (tl); Petr Svarc (bc). Getty Images: ullstein bild (bl). Shutterstock.com: Diego Grandi (br). 296 Alamy Stock Photo: Digital-Fotofusion Gallery (l). Bridgeman Images: © DACS 2023 (br). 297 akg-images: Florian Monheim / Bildarchiv Monheim GmbH (bc). Alamy Stock Photo: Bildarchiv Monheim GmbH (br). Dreamstime.com: Place-to-be (bl). Centraal Museum, Utrecht: Rietveld Schrderhuis, Photo Stijn Poelstra (t). 298 Fondation Le Corbusier: © F.L.C. / ADAGP, Paris and DACS, London 2023 (l). 299 Alamy Stock Photo: imageBROKER. 300 Alamy Stock Photo: Image Professionals GmbH (tr). Lindman Photography: (cl). 301 Lindman Photography. 302 Alamy Stock Photo: Peter Forsberg (tl). Getty Images: Maremagnum (b); The Image Bank Unreleased / Barry Winiker / © ARS, NY and DACS, London 2023 / (tr). 303 Alamy Stock Photo: Serhii Chrucky (c); Randy Duchaine (t); Chris Hellier / © F.L.C. / ADAGP, Paris and DACS, London 2023 / (bc). Getty Images: Eye Ubiquitous / Universal Images Group (bl); Freddie Reed / Mirrorpix (br). 304 Alamy Stock Photo: Jarmo Piironen (tr). Getty Images: Quim Llenas / Cover (tl). Ken Ohyama: (bl). Wikipedia: NotFromUtrecht / CC BY-SA 3.0 (br). 305 Alamy Stock Photo: Arcaid Images (br); François-Olivier Dommergues (tr); Diego Grandi (bl). 306 Alamy Stock Photo: Javier Martnez Morn / © F.L.C. / ADAGP, Paris and DACS, London 2023 (br); Geoffrey Taunton / © F.L.C. / ADAGP, Paris and DACS, London 2023 (tr). Dorling Kindersley: © F.L.C. / ADAGP, Paris and DACS, London 2023 (cl). Richard Powers: © F.L.C. / ADAGP, Paris and DACS, London 2023 (cr). 307 Alamy Stock Photo: Bildarchiv Monheim GmbH / © F.L.C. / ADAGP, Paris and DACS, London 2023 (tr); Geoffrey Taunton / © F.L.C. / ADAGP, Paris and DACS, London 2023 (tl); Bildarchiv Monheim GmbH / © F.L.C. / ADAGP, Paris and DACS, London 2023 (b); Universal Images Group North America LLC / DeAgostini / © F.L.C. / ADAGP, Paris and DACS, London 2023 (tl). 308 Alamy Stock Photo: Nick Brooks (r); NiKreative (l). 309 Alamy Stock Photo: mcx images (r). Dreamstime.com: Ramblingman (c); Drew Stewart (tc). Adam Kane Macchia: (l). 310 Alamy Stock Photo: Tom Hanslien Photography (tr); Ivo de Rooij (tl); LatitudeStock (b). 311 Alamy Stock Photo: Chris Hellier (r); Edmund Sumner (tl); Don Smetzer (fbl); Eric Nathan (bl); mauritius images GmbH (br); Kevin Ma (fbr). 312-313 Getty Images: Alexander Spatari (tc). 312 Alamy Stock Photo: Kenneth Grant (bl); Eric Lafforgue (tl); Michael Ventura (br). 313 Alamy Stock Photo: Igor Prahin (bl/phnom penh). Dreamstime.com: Michael Williams (br). Getty Images: Ricardo DeAratanha / Los Angeles Times (tr). 314 Alamy Stock Photo: IanDagnall Computing (b). Getty Images: Musa Kayrak (t). 315 Alamy Stock Photo: Panther Media GmbH (tc). Dreamstime.com: Maurizio Paolo Grassi (cr). Shutterstock.com: eugenialibera (tr); Kiev.Victor (b). 316 Alamy Stock Photo: Ian Nellist (br). Dreamstime.com: Bernard Bialorucki (bc); Steveheap (tl); Claudiodivizia (tr); Makasanaphoto (bl). 317 Getty Images / iStock: Djapeman (t); godrick (br). Shutterstock.com: Tupungato (cr). 318 akg-images: arkivi (r). OTTO: Connie Zhou (l). 319 Alamy Stock Photo: mauritius images GmbH (c). Getty Images: Carol M. Highsmith / Buyenlarge (tl). Richard Powers: (tc). 320 OTTO: Darren Bradley (bl); Francis Dzikowski (cl). Shutterstock.com: EQRoy (br). Joachim Wichmann: (cr). 321 Alamy Stock Photo: Paul Brady (cb). Getty Images / iStock: mshch (br). OTTO: Joe Fletcher (t); Tim Street-Porter (bl). 322 Alamy Stock Photo: Anna Dave (l). Shutterstock.com: omtatsat graphic (r). 323 Alamy Stock Photo: Arcaid Images (bc); Konrad Zelazowski (tl); B.O'Kane (br). Shutterstock.com: Lina Balciunaite (tr); N_FUJITA (bl). 324 Alamy Stock Photo: Robert Proctor (t). Dreamstime.com: Rodrigolab (b). 325 Alamy Stock Photo: Dinodia Photos (bc). Dreamstime.com: Radub85 (bl). Shutterstock.com: Greg Baker / AP (br). 326 Alamy Stock Photo: Chris Hellier / © F.L.C. / ADAGP, Paris and DACS, London 2023 (r). RIBA Collections: Architectural Press Archives (b). 327 Alamy Stock Photo: Wil T Batista (tr). Dreamstime.com: James Williams (tc). RIBA Collections: Lasdun Archive (tl). Shutterstock.com: T-McD Photography (b). 328 Alamy Stock Photo: Arcaid Images (cl); mauritius images GmbH (c). Dreamstime.com: Marketa Novakova (tr). Arieh Sharon Digital Archive, The Yael Aloni Collection, ariehsharon.org: (bl). University of Toronto Scarborough Library: Archives & Special Collections, UTSC Photographic Services fonds, Aerial View of Scarborough College, 001C-2-5-50. (br). 329 Alamy Stock Photo: Everett Collection Historical (br). Library of Congress, Washington, D.C.: (bl). RIBA Collections: John Maltby (t). 330 Getty Images / iStock: wsfurlan (tr). Science Photo Library: Peter Menzel / © ADAGP, Paris and DACS, London 2023 (bl). Shutterstock.com: Dan J Brown (tl). 331 Alamy Stock Photo: Rawdon Wyatt (bl). Dreamstime.com: Glenn Nagel (tr); Gansham Ramchandani (br). 332 Dreamstime.com: Stephan Dost (t). Shutterstock.com: DavidGraham86 (b). 333 Alamy Stock Photo: Oneworld Picture (tc). Dreamstime.com: Marco Brivio (tr); Pressfoto (b). Shutterstock.com: Alizada Studios (tl). 334 Alamy Stock Photo: Bailey-Cooper Photography (cr); Stockbym (tl); Steve Speller (bc). Dreamstime.com: Berk Ozdemir (bl); Pavel Svoboda (tc). Getty Images / iStock: deymos (br); littleny (tr). 335 AWL Images: Walter Bibikow (tl). Dreamstime.com: Dudlajzov (tr). Science Photo Library: Martyn F. Chillmaid / © DACS 2023 (b). 338-339 Getty Images: Atlantide Phototravel. 340 Bridgeman Images: (r). Getty Images: View Pictures / Universal Images Group (l). 341 Alamy Stock Photo: A. Astes (bl); Yueqi Li / © Barragan Foundation / DACS 2023 (tr); Fernando Guerra-VIEW (bc). Dreamstime.com: Kam Lung Kong (br). Shutterstock.com: Mathilde Marest (tl). 342 Getty Images: Jean-Francois Cardella / Construction Photography / Avalon (t). Getty Images / iStock: Circle Creative Studio / Richard Rogers Partnership (b). 343 Alamy Stock Photo: Iain Masterton / Piano + Rogers (tr). Dorling Kindersley: Piano + Rogers (ftr). Shutterstock.com: Kiev.Victor / Piano + Rogers (tc); lapas77 / Piano + Rogers (tl); Charles Leonard / Piano + Rogers (b). 344 Alamy Stock Photo: Dennis Gilbert-VIEW (br); Richard Glover-VIEW (bl). Arcaid Images: Richard Bryant (tr). Getty Images / iStock: ez_thug / RSHP (tl). RIBA Collections: Gerald McLean / RSHP (tc). 345 Alamy Stock Photo: FP Collection (br). Arcaid Images: Richard Bryant (t). Dreamstime.com: Ac Manley (cr). Getty Images / iStock: _ultraforma_ / Richard Rogers Partnership (bl). 346 Getty Images: Bettmann (b). Shutterstock.com: cktravels.com (t). 347 Alamy Stock Photo: Arcaid Images (c); imageBROKER (b). Dreamstime.com: Claudiodivizia (tl, tr). 348 Alamy Stock Photo: Arcaid Images (b); Ted Hsu (tr). Dreamstime.com: Claudiodivizia (bl). Shutterstock.com: Claudio Divizia (tl); EQRoy (tc). 349 Alamy Stock Photo: Alpha Stock (bl); Arcaid Images (tr); Reuters (br). Dreamstime.com: Claudiodivizia (bc). Getty Images: Valentin Bontemps / AFP / Ricardo Bofill / Taller de Arquitectura (cl); Alan Schein Photography (cr). Shutterstock.com: William A. Morgan (tl). 350 Alamy Stock Photo: Stefano Politi Markovina (l); Sunshine Pics (br). Getty Images: Gerhard Wolfram / ullstein bild (tr). 351 Dreamstime.com: Wei Huang (tr); Ricardo Rocha (bl); Nichapa Srimai (br). 352 RIBA Collections/ Richard Rogers Partnership. 353 Courtesy of Zaha Hadid Architects: (br). Foster + Partners: (bc). Getty Images / iStock: Laurence Dutton (cr). MIT Museum: Lincoln Laboratory (bl). 354 Alamy Stock Photo: Jon Bower Spain (tc); Christian Kober 1 (cr); David Herraez (br). Depositphotos Inc: 3D-Agentur (l). 355 Alamy Stock Photo: Ian Dagnall / © ARS, NY and DACS, London 2023 (cl); Loop Images Ltd (tl). AWL Images: Marco Bottigelli (br). Getty Images: View Pictures / Universal Images Group / © ARS, NY and DACS, London 2023 (tr). 356 Courtesy of Zaha Hadid Architects: © Zaha Hadid Foundation (r). Getty Images: Prisma / Universal Images Group (l). 357 Alamy Stock Photo: Arcaid Images (tr); Im_ photography (tl); Danita Delimont (tc). Courtesy of Zaha Hadid Architects: © Zaha Hadid Foundation (cr). Shutterstock.com: Peeradontax (b). 358 AWL Images: Walter Bibikow (tl). Dreamstime.com: Hakan Can Yalcin (tr). Duccio Malagamba: COOP HIMMELB(L)AU (br). Shutterstock.com: Pit Stock (bl); Ken Wolter (bc). 359 Alamy Stock Photo: CNMages / Bernard Tschumi Architects (c); Peter Horree (br). Getty Images: Arterra / Universal Images Group (t). Shutterstock.com: Dimi Jeckov (bl). 360 Alamy Stock Photo: Hackenberg-Photo-Cologne (b). August Fischer: (t). 361 Alamy Stock Photo: Arcaid Images (bc). Aldo Amoretti: Atelier Peter Zumthor & Partner (bl). AWL Images: Mauricio Abreu (br). August Fischer: Atelier Peter Zumthor & Partner (tr); Atelier Peter Zumthor & Partner (cl); Atelier Peter Zumthor & Partner (cr). 362 Alamy Stock Photo: Stephen Dwyer (l). Getty Images: Matt Cardy (r). 363 Lacaton & Vassal Architects: (cra). Phillippe Ruault: (cla). 364 Amsterdam Archive / Stadsarchief: (cla). Seamus Payne: (br). Thomas Schlijper: (clb). 365 Getty Images / iStock: ProCreators (t). Andrew Lee: Collective Architecture (bc). Timothy Soar: (crb). 366 Iwan Baan Photography: (l). Getty Images: Peter Guttman (br). 367 Ibuku: (c). Tomasso Riva: (tr). 368 Iwan Baan Photography: (t). Heritage Foundation of Pakistan: (bl). Agnese Sanvito: (br). Shutterstock.com: ushi (bc). 369 Alamy Stock Photo: Reuters / George (bl). Atelier Architecture Perraudin: Photo © Damien Aspe (br). Heritage Foundation of Pakistan: (tr). 370-371 Dreamstime.com: Edwardstaines. 372 Shutterstock.com: Heracles Kritikos. 373 Dreamstime.com: Icon72. 374 Alamy Stock Photo: Peter Horree. 375 Getty Images: photography by Ulrich Hollmann (t). Shutterstock.com: Amr mahmoud Soliman (b). 376 Dreamstime.com: Jeewee (tl). 376-377 Alamy Stock Photo: robertharding (b). 377 Getty Images / iStock: rweisswald (t). 378 Alamy Stock Photo: Jonathan Wilson (b). Getty Images / iStock: yurybirukov (t). 379 Shutterstock.com: Wako Megumi (r). 380 Getty Images / iStock: StefanoZaccaria. 381 Shutterstock.com: Mr_Karesuando (b); Taha Raja (t). 382 Getty Images: Manfred Gottschalk. 383 Dreamstime.com: Saiko3p (b). Getty Images / iStock: Stefano Barzellotti (t). 384 Alamy Stock Photo: Emily Riddell (b). Getty Images / iStock: jacquesvandinteren (t). 385 Dreamstime.com: Wirestock. 386 Getty Images / iStock: QQ7. 387 Dreamstime.com: Victoria Ditkovsky (t). Getty Images: Atlantide Phototravel (b). 388 Dreamstime.com: Anton Aleksenko (b). Getty Images / iStock: SvetlanaSF (t). 389 Alamy Stock Photo: ZUMA Press, Inc. 390 Getty Images / iStock: MarquesPhotography (t). 391 Dreamstime.com: Anibal Trejo. 392 Getty Images / iStock: Rafal Cichawa. 393 Alamy Stock Photo: robertharding (b). Getty Images / iStock: Roop_Dey (t). 394 AWL Images: Tim Mannakee (t). Dreamstime.com: Perseomedusa (b). 395 Dreamstime.com: Bonandbon Dw. 396 Getty Images / iStock: arcticswede. 397 Getty Images / iStock: miralex (t). Shutterstock.com: Mike Mareen (b). 398 4Corners: Luigi Vaccarella (b). Shutterstock.com: dibrova (t). 399 Getty Images: Claudio Ciabochi / Education Images / Universal Images Group. 400 123RF.com: tupungato. 401 Dreamstime.com: Diego Grandi. 402 Shutterstock.com: Sean Pavone (t). 402-403 Alamy Stock Photo: Grant Smith-VIEW (b). 403 Beth Sholom Elkins Park: Beth Sholom Preservation Foundation (t). 404 Alamy Stock Photo: Ulrich Doering (b). Getty Images / iStock: derejeb (t). 405 Getty Images / iStock: Travel Faery. 406 Getty Images: Insights / Universal Images Group (l). 407 Shutterstock.com: cowardlion. 408 Kengo Kuma and Associates. 409 Vilalta Studio. 410 Alamy Stock Photo: Art Directors & TRIP. 411 Alamy Stock Photo: Chronicle. 412 Alamy Stock Photo: Album (r). Dreamstime.com: Jonathan Braid (b). 413 Dreamstime.com: Luca Ponti. 414-415 Dreamstime.com: Demerzel21 (t). 414 Alamy Stock Photo: Christopher Holt (b). 415 Getty Images / iStock: Nikada (b). 416 Getty Images / iStock: oversnap. 417 Alamy Stock Photo: B.O'Kane (b); Chronicle (t). 418 Getty Images: Bettmann (l). 419 Getty Images / iStock: ezypix. 420 Getty Images: Bettmann. 421 Alamy Stock Photo: B.O'Kane (t). AWL Images: Jon Arnold (b). 422 Alamy Stock Photo: Ken Wolter. 423 Alamy Stock Photo: Arcaid Images (r). 424 Alamy Stock Photo: marc zakian. 425 Alamy Stock Photo: Bettina Strenske (t); Michael Ventura (b)

All other images © Dorling Kindersley

DEFINITIVE CULTURAL GUIDES

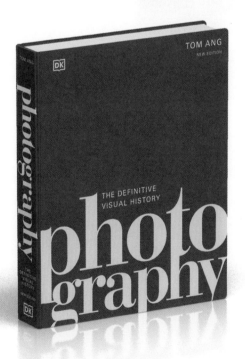

DK For the curious